Tupolev
BOMBERS

Tupolev BOMBERS

General Editor
David Donald

AIRtime Publishing Inc.

United States of America • United Kingdom

Published by AIRtime Publishing Inc.
USA: 120 East Avenue, Norwalk, CT 06851
Tel (203) 838-7979 • Fax (203) 838-7344
email: airpower@airtimepublishing.com
www.airtimepublishing.com
UK: CAB Intl. Centre, Nosworthy Way, Wallingford OX10 8DE
Tel +44 (0)1491 829230 • Fax +44 (0)1491 829334
email: airpower@btinternet.com

ISBN 1-880588-62-5

Editors
David Donald and Rob Hewson

Contributing Authors
Lt. Col. Anatoliy Artemyev, Soviet/Russian Navy retd. (Tu-142, Tu-16)
Piotr Butowski (Tu-95MS, Tu-160)
Steven J. Zaloga (Tu-22/22M)
Additional material by David Donald and Rob Hewson

Artists
Mike Badrocke, Piotr Butowski, Zaur Eylanbekov, Aleksey Mikheyev,
Mark Styling, John Weal, Andrey Zhirnov, Vasiliy Zolotov

Jacket Design
Zaur Eylanbekov

Controller
Linda Deangelis

Publisher
Mel Williams

Special thanks to Jon Lake, Vadim Yegorov and
the Swedish Air Force

PRINTED IN ITALY

To order more copies of this book or any of our other titles call toll free
within the United States 1 800 359-3003, or visit our
website at: *www.airtimepublishing.com*

Other books by AIRtime Publishing include:
United States Military Aviation Directory
Carrier Aviation Air Power Directory
Superfighters The Next Generation of Combat Aircraft
Phantom: Spirit in the Skies Updated and Expanded Edition
Russian Military Aviation Directory (Spring 2003)

Retail distribution via:

Direct from Publisher
AIRtime Publishing Inc.
PO Box 5074, Westport, CT 06881, USA
Tel (203) 838-7979 • Fax (203) 838-7344
Toll-free 1 800 359-3003

USA & Canada
Specialty Press Inc.
39966 Grand Avenue, North Branch
MN 55056
Tel (651) 277-1400 • Fax (651) 277-1203
Toll-free 1 800 895-4585

UK & Europe
Midland Counties Publications
4 Watling Drive
Hinckley LE10 3EY
Tel 01455 233 747 • Fax 01455 233 737

INTRODUCTION

Although he was designing and building heavy aircraft even before World War II, in the West the name Andrey Tupolev will forever be synonymous with the Cold War and the unprecedented arms race that characterized that period. Those years saw the development and operational service of a number of fearsome soviet strategic bombers, built for the purpose of delivering a devastating nuclear strike against the United States and its allies. The bane of NATO planners during the fifties, sixties, seventies and eighties, these aircraft are best known by the names NATO assigned to them - 'Bear,' 'Badger,' 'Blinder,' 'Backfire' and 'Blackjack.' This book provides in-depth analysis of these impressive aircraft and many of their variants.

Tupolev BOMBERS

CONTENTS

Tupolev
Tu-95/142
Russia's Mighty 'Bear'

Above: Blessed with very long range and economic operation, the Tu-95 was a natural choice for a maritime patrol aircraft. Successful experience with the Tu-95RTs 'Bear-D' in the oceanic surveillance and targeting role led to the development of the Tu-142 'Bear-F', dedicated to hunting submarines. A series of new versions has attempted to keep the Tu-142 abreast of Western sub developments, and central to the AVMF's war plans.

Main picture: With four of the most powerful turboprops ever put into production driving 32 giant propeller blades, the Tu-95 remains an awe-inspiring spectacle a half-century after the type's first flight. Yet with a bellyful of missiles – plus others in clusters under its trademark swept wings – the Tu-95MS 'Bear-H' is also still a formidable weapon. In the 21st century it is belatedly following its B-52 counterpart into the conventional missile arena.

Comparisons between the 'Bear' and the B-52 are inevitable: both were conceived as their respective nations' principal vehicles of strategic nuclear deterrence in the pre-missile era and, despite the development of more survivable aircraft for the penetration mission, both were to regain a major strategic role as the natural platforms for the air-launching of cruise missiles. Whereas the B-52 retained and expanded its conventional bombing capabilities, the 'Bear' branched out into the reconnaissance arena, in turn spawning an important family of anti-submarine warfare platforms. In both missile platform and ASW roles, the Tu-95/142 remains an essential fixture in today's Russian air forces.

Tu-95 – missile-carriers

At the beginning of the 1970s there were five large air bases within Soviet strategic aviation: Uzin, Semipalatinsk, Mozdok, Engels and Ukrainka. Myasishchev M-4 and 3M 'Bison' bombers were stationed at Engels and Ukrainka, whereas the three remaining bases accommodated Tu-95 'Bears'. Two regiments – the 409th TBAP (Tyazhelobombardirovochnyi Aviatsionnyi Polk, Heavy Bomber Air Regiment) and the 1006th TBAP – were stationed at Uzin, Ukraine, and two more were stationed at Semipalatinsk, Kazakhstan: the 1223rd TBAP and the 1226th TBAP. The fifth Tu-95 unit – the 182nd TBAP – was stationed at Mozdok in Northern Ossetia. The main targets for Soviet strategic bombers were in the USA and, for the air division stationed at Ukrainka, China. The location of fixed air bases for heavy bombers in the southern part of the Soviet Union should not be misleading: strategic aviation uses forward 'jump' airfields at Anadyr, Tiksi, Magadan and Vorkuta, which are located much closer to the US.

Apart from special versions such as the Tu-95RTs maritime reconnaissance aircraft and Tu-142 anti-submarine warfare aircraft, production of the original 'Bear' came to an end in 1965. Powered by temporary 2TV-2 engines, the Tu-95 (or *izdeliye* V) prototype undertook its maiden flight on 12 November 1952 with Alexey Perelyot at the controls. It crashed on 11 May 1953, killing the crew. The

prototype of the final version, powered by four powerful Kuznetsov NK-12 turboprops, took-off only two years later on 16 February 1955, piloted by Mikhail A. Nyukhtikov. In October 1955, production plant No. 18 at Kuibyshev (formerly, till 1935, and presently, since 1991, the town's name is Samara) built the first two series aircraft. From 1955 to 1965 the factory made 49 'Bear-A' bombers (30 Tu-95s and 19 Tu-95Ms) and 71 missile-carriers (48 Tu-95K 'Bear-Bs' and 23 Tu-95KM 'Bear-Cs'). Several other variants which saw service were only small modifications of the above-mentioned versions: the Tu-95A and Tu-95MA were adapted for dropping nuclear bombs, the Tu-95KD received an inflight refuelling system, and the Tu-95MR 'Bear-E' had additional reconnaissance equipment. The Tu-95U and KU were trainer conversions.

Since the basic airframe has remained unchanged for many years, the history of the Tu-95 is, in essence, the history of its armament. The heavy Kh-20 missile carried under the fuselage of the Tu-95K (or Kh-20M of the Tu-95KM) became obsolete after only a few years: it was too slow to avoid anti-aircraft defences, and its seeker needed the target to be illuminated by the aircraft's radar, so the aircraft had to approach dangerously close to the target. The Kh-20M (AS-3 'Kangaroo') missile weighed 12000 kg (26,455 lb) and carried a 3-MT nuclear warhead over a distance of 450-650 km (280-405 miles) at a speed of 2120 km/h (1,317 mph). The 'simple' Tu-95 and Tu-95M were proven to be even less useful – they had no missile armament so that they had to directly overfly the target to drop their bombs.

Second-generation missiles

Dramatic changes in aircraft armament came about at the beginning of the 1970s. It was decided then to transfer on to the Tu-95 the much more modern missile systems developed for the Tu-22M 'Backfire' and Tu-16 'Badger' bombers. According to a government resolution of 13 February 1973, modernisation was planned in two separate programmes. Fifty recently made Tu-95KMs (from series production of 1961-1965) and Tu-95Ks (from production of 1958-1962) were to be equipped with the recent and most powerful K-22 missile system, which employed the Kh-22 missiles developed for the Tu-22M. The less advanced (but cheaper) K-95-26 missile system, with KSR-5 missiles from the Tu-16K-26 'Badger-G' bomber, was to be provided for 33 older Tu-95s and Tu-95Ms.

This K-95-26 air-missile complex was to include the Tu-95M-5 aircraft (*izdeliye* VM-5), two KSR-5 missiles, and Volga missile initialisation and launching system. The KSR-5 (AS-6 'Kingfish') missile, developed by the OKB-2-155 design bureau (now MKB Raduga) at Dubna near Moscow, was in series production from 1966. This was a simplified version of the Kh-22 (see below) designed for the modernisation of Tu-16s. The KSR-5 (*izdeliye* D-5) was equipped with an active radar seeker and was intended for attacking targets offering a high radar contrast, such as ships, bridges and power stations. The missile weighed 3900 kg (8,598 lb), including a 700-kg (1,543-lb) warhead. Dimensions were: length 10.52 m (34 ft 6 in), diameter 0.90 m (2 ft 11 in) and wing span 2.61 m (8 ft 7 in). The KSR-5 flew at up to 3200 km/h (1,988 mph) speed and its range was 240 km (149 miles).

KSR-5s were carried by the Tu-95M-5 on two beams under the wing root, freeing the fuselage bomb bay for other armament. The Rubin-1KV radar was identical to that fitted in the Tu-16K-26. A Tu-95M-5 prototype was converted from series Tu-95M No. 601 from the 409th TBAP at Uzin. The conversion process was protracted: the aircraft arrived at the Kuibyshev factory in January 1973 and the upgrade was not completed until October 1976, when the Tu-95M-5 performed its first flight. On 21 May 1977, after 32 test flights, development of the Tu-95M-5 was halted. Work on the Tu-95M-5 had progressed at a snail's pace because it was obvious from the start that the more advanced upgrade of the Tu-95K/KM into the Tu-95K-22 was more promising. Moreover, a new age of Soviet strategic aviation development began in the summer of 1976 when work started on the Kh-55 strategic cruise missile.

A converted Tu-95KM, No. 2608, became the prototype for the Tu-95K-22 (*izdeliye* VK-22) 'Bear-G'. Rework of this aircraft began at Kuibyshev in May 1974 and the modernised aircraft made its maiden flight on 30 October 1975. The air-missile complex K-95-22 included – as well as the aircraft – Kh-22M missiles, PNA-B (NATO 'Down Beat') radar, as well as the Kama missile initialisation and launch system. Two missiles were carried under the wing roots on BD-45 pylons (which, like the missiles, radar and other equipment, was borrowed from the Tu-22M); a third missile was suspended under the fuselage on the former BD-206 pylon, equipped with an adapter. In spite of three available pylons, the aircraft only carried a maximum of two missiles. Other equipment was also improved, including the large Rezeda active jammer in the aircraft's tail and the smaller Siren jammer in the nose.

At 3600 km/h (2,237 mph), Raduga's Kh-22M (AS-4 'Kitchen') missile is 50 per cent faster than the Kh-20M, while it is half the weight at 5800 kg (12,786 lb). There are two variants: one with an active radar seeker and a 900-kg (1,984-lb) conventional warhead, and one with a Doppler-inertial navigation system and 150-kT nuclear warhead (the standard variant was the nuclear weapon). The range of the first variant is 310 km (193 miles), being limited by the seeker's capability, while the nuclear missile can reach 510 km (317 miles). Length of the Kh-22M is 11.65 m (38 ft 3 in), diameter 0.92 m (3 ft) and wing span is 3.0 m (9 ft 10 in).

Tests of the Tu-95K-22 continued for a very long time. The official commissioning was no earlier than 1987, which was after the commissioning of the Tu-95MS with cruise missiles. However, some Tu-95K/KMs from front-line units were converted into Tu-95K-22s long before the official commissioning, so that the first Kh-22M missiles were launched from a military Tu-95K-22 as early as 1981.

Another development was the adaptation of the Tu-95 for the tactical task of destroying enemy airfields. The importance of such missions was fully realised after the 1967-1973 Middle East wars. On the initiative of the Long-Range Aviation command, some Tu-95K-22s were modified to carry containers, each with 15 250-kg (551-lb) bombs. Two containers could be suspended on a double beam under the fuselage, or a container on each of the three missile-carrying pylons. A single-pass salvo of 30-45 bombs was intended to completely destroy the airstrip.

Rebirth

In August 1976 came a message which brought about a revolution in Soviet strategic aviation: under development in the US was the new AGM-86 Air-Launched Cruise Missile. The ALCM was equipped with a terrain-reference navigation system which correlated the nature of the ground over which it was flying with a map stored in the missile computer memory. The Russians were also working on such a system, but as they were not overly optimistic as to its eventual success, they intended to abandon the programme. The information from the United States triggered off a storm.

The final incarnation of the first-generation 'Bear' was the Tu-95K-22 'Bear-G', modified from the earlier Tu-95K 'Bear-B' and KM 'Bear-C'. The most obvious new feature was the adoption of Rezeda jamming equipment in an extended tailcone in place of the tail turret (also fitted to some Tu-95RTs 'Bear-Ds'), while a Siren jammer was mounted in a nose 'pimple'. Additional equipment (such as the Kurs missile datalink) was housed in fuselage pods, while the wings, as here, often mounted air sampling pods for monitoring nuclear particles in the atmosphere. Tu-95K-22s were concentrated at Ukrainka with the 1223rd and 1226th TBAP, but have since been replaced by the Tu-95MS.

The Tu-95MS began operations in early 1983. Training sorties often involved pairs or groups of aircraft flying long-range missile launch profiles.

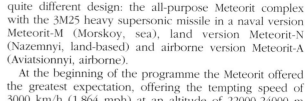

Above: The massive Obzor-MS ('Clam Pipe') nav/bomb radar takes up much of the space in the nose, suspended on a rotating pedestal mounted on the roof of the radar bay. Above it is a much smaller scanning antenna, either side of which are the mountings for EW antennas. The yellow pipe takes fuel from the nose-mounted probe and feeds it along the starboard side of the fuselage to the main tanks. The strut-mounted antenna is noteworthy, a feature possibly associated with the Tu-95MSM upgrade.

Right: Close-up of the nose shows the hemispherical multi-faceted Mak-UT infra-red detection/missile warning system and, alongside, an antenna for the active jamming system.

Using 'jump' airfields in the Russian Far East, Tu-95MSs have sporadically tested US air defences around Alaska. This intercept was undertaken in 1985 by F-15s of the 21st TFW.

quite different design: the all-purpose Meteorit complex with the 3M25 heavy supersonic missile in a naval version Meteorit-M (Morskoy, sea), land version Meteorit-N (Nazemnyi, land-based) and airborne version Meteorit-A (Aviatsionnyi, airborne).

At the beginning of the programme the Meteorit offered the greatest expectation, offering the tempting speed of 3000 km/h (1,864 mph) at an altitude of 22000-24000 m (72,178-78,740 ft) over a promised range of 5000 km (3,107 miles). The Meteorit-A was 12.8 m (42 ft) long and weighed 6380 kg (14,065 lb) at launch. The missile had folding swept wings and folding tailplanes, as well as small canards; it was powered by a ram-jet cruise engine with ventral air intake. Unfortunately, only one poor-quality photograph of this missile is known and only scant information is available.

Meteorit was tested for a very long time with poor results. The first one was launched on 20 May 1980 from a land-based launcher at the Kapustin Yar exercise ground; the test was a failure. Only the fifth launch, on 16 December 1981, was considered a success, although the missile flew only 50 km (31 miles). The airborne Meteorit-A (AS-X-19 'Koala') was launched for the first time from the experimental aircraft Tu-95MA on 11 January 1984 – and again without success. The second launch on 24 May also failed. The Tu-95MA (converted from the fourth series Tu-95MS) carried two Meteorits suspended under the wing roots, and had the option for two more missiles carried between the engines. Since at the time the Tu-95MS with Kh-55 missiles was entering service in military units, work on the Meteorit-A airborne missile was halted at the end of 1984. Until the late 1980s the Russians still hoped to bring the Meteorit into service, continuing tests of the seaborne version, but eventually the whole programme was terminated at the end of 1989 after more than 30, mostly abortive, tests.

In December 1983, the Raduga Kh-55 (AS-15 'Kent') missile was commissioned into service in the air forces, while in April 1984, the Novator Granat (SS-N-21 'Sampson') system for submarines was commissioned into service in the navy. The ground forces were attempting to introduce the RK-55 (SSC-X-4 'Slingshot') into service, but all 84 ready missiles were scrapped at the test stage in accordance with the Soviet-US treaty of December 1987 covering the liquidation of medium-range missiles.

Cruise missile tests

Tests with the Kh-55 missile were much more successful than those of the Meteorit. The Tu-95M-55, or *izdeliye* VM-021, test bed aircraft intended for testing Kh-55 missiles took off for the first time on 31 July 1978 (it was the aircraft formerly used for testing the KSR-5 missile, i.e. Tu-95M-5). Conversion for its new role was undertaken from July 1977 to June 1978. Former equipment and some fuel tanks were replaced by the APP-95 Dub (Oak) missile preparation system (APP = Aparatura Podgotovki i Puska, initialisation and launch equipment), and by DISS-7 and MIS-45 navigation systems. Initially, a single launcher was planned inside the Tu-95M-55's bomb bay, but later a six-round MKU-6-5 rotating launcher was installed, as planned for the series production aircraft. Between 1978 and 1982 the aircraft made 107 experimental flights and launched 10 Kh-55s. On 28 January 1982, the Tu-95M-55 crashed during take-off from Zhukovskiy airfield, killing all 10 on board.

In 1978, the DMZ (Dubnenskiy Mashinostroitelnyi Zavod) factory in Dubna built a small batch of Kh-55 missiles intended for tests, and soon afterwards series production began in a factory at Kharkiv (Ukraine). On 14 December 1980 the factory delivered the first series missile to the armed forces. This weapon was ceremonially launched on the Day of the Soviet Army – 23 February 1981 – at Semipalatinsk (the identity of the launching aircraft remains unknown: at that time only two aircraft were adapted for this task, the experimental Tu-95M-55 and the Tu-142MS prototype).

Over the course of several months, the design team of the Ramenskoye PKB (Priborostroitelnoye Konstruktorskoye Byuro, instrument design bureau) received enormous financial aid for continuation of its work on 'correlation-extreme' navigation. On 9 December 1976, the government took an important resolution in ordering from three design teams new missiles in airborne, sea-launched (from surface ships and submarines) and land-based versions. The Raduga missile design bureau at Dubna submitted a project for the Kh-55 – a small, subsonic airborne missile similar to the AGM-86 (early proposals included also sea- and land-based versions). The Novator design bureau at Sverdlovsk (now Yekaterinburg) proposed the similar naval complex 3K10 Granat, with the 3M10 missile and a land-based version. Lastly, NPO (Nauchno-Proizvodstvennoye Obyedineniye, Scientific-Manufacturing Corporation) Mashinostroyeniya at Reutov near Moscow suggested a

Production of Kh-55s was accorded the highest priority. In 1981, the Kharkiv factory produced 40 missiles, and in the ensuing years the production rate increased dramatically. In September 1982 the department manufacturing the Kh-55 in Kharkiv adopted 24-hour shiftwork. At the same time, the factory in Smolensk started production of the new Kh-55SM version. In December 1986, production of Kh-55s at Kharkiv was stopped, although in the first quarter of 1987 the factory built 16 missiles with additional fuel tanks for tests with the Tu-160, carried out by the Tupolev design bureau. From that time Kh-55 missiles were only built at Smolensk. In total, about 1,500 missiles had been manufactured by the early 1990s.

The strategic cruise missile Kh-55 (*izdeliye* 120) is used against targets of known co-ordinates. The Osina (Aspen) missile initialisation and launch system prepares the missile launch, which consists among other things in bringing the inertial navigation axes of the missile exactly into line with those of the aircraft, and in transferring a digital map of the terrain from the aircraft's onboard computer into the

missile's memory. The Kh-55 missile is guided to the target by its inertial navigation system. In some sections of the route the correction system is switched on which, by means of Doppler navigation radar and radio altimeter, sees the terrain over which it is flying and compares it with the three-dimensional map stored in the computer memory

For a period in the early 1990s, the 'Bear-H' became more visible with select airshow appearances, during which it impressed onlookers with its sheer size and brutish power, as demonstrated above at the 1993 Zhukovskiy show. Following the appearance of a single aircraft in 1993, the 1994 IAT show at RAF Fairford drew two 'Bears', a VVS Tu-95MS being accompanied by a Tu-142MK from the AVMF. The 'Bear-H' (left) was from the 182nd TBAP at Mozdok. Below a Tu-95MS practises for an airshow appearance with the MiG-29s of the 'Swifts' team.

Above: *Tu-95MS bombers sporadically probed and prodded at US defences, approaching from various directions. In July 1988 this bomber was one of two intercepted off the Canadian coast by F-15s from the Massachusetts ANG, which had been on alert at Loring AFB, Maine.*

Above: *The Tu-95MS16 introduced uprated armament with two twin-barrelled GSh-23 cannon replacing the single-barrelled AM-23s. The gun-aiming radar remained the PRS-4 Krypton unit, known to NATO as 'Box Tail'. The four-gun tail was derived from that fitted to the Tu-22M2, and was also applied to the Tu-142MZ.*

Right: *At Tushino in 1995 the flypast included this Tu-95MS simulating refuelling from an Il-78, flanked by a pair of Su-27s from the 'Russian Knights' team.*

(in the West such a system is called Tercom, Terrain Contour Matching). If necessary, a course correction is made. Thanks to this system, the missile accuracy can be below 100 m (328 ft), which is more than sufficient for a missile with a nuclear warhead. The BSU-55 (Bortovaya Sistema Upravleniya, Board Control System) missile auto-pilot allows for obstacle avoidance at low altitude and horizontal manoeuvring for avoiding interception.

Of conventional aerodynamic configuration, the Kh-55 missile has unswept folded wings and folding control planes. The wing and control planes are unfolded after launch, and the Soyuz R95-300 cruise turbofan engine is lowered from the bottom of the missile's aft end. Flight to the target is typically between Mach 0.48 and Mach 0.77 at low altitude. To extend its range, the missile can be fitted with two conformal fuel tanks scabbed on to the side. The missile is used only with a 200-kT nuclear warhead.

Two-type missile force

As in the US, which adapted the new B-1B and older B-52 to carry ALCMs, the Russians prepared two platforms for the Kh-55. The Tu-160 'Blackjack' supersonic bomber was then in the early stages of development and eventually achieved initial operational capability (IOC) in 1987. The 'Bear' was a cheaper and readily available carrier for the new missiles. This time, however, the Russians did not confine themselves to a mid-life upgrade of existing aircraft, but resumed production of the Tu-95, expecting future development of the weapons. Since the most modern variant of the 'Bear' was then the Tu-142M anti-submarine warfare aircraft made by the factory at Taganrog, its airframe was chosen as the platform for the new armament. In July 1977, Tupolev was ordered to redesign the Tu-142M into a Kh-55 missile-carrier, designated Tu-142MS.

According to the initial design, the aircraft was to carry 12 Kh-55 missiles, six on each of two tandem MKU-6-5 revolving launchers. However, proper fore-and-aft balanc-

ing of the aircraft with two launchers turned out to be impossible, and one of the armament chambers had to be dispensed with. Thus, the basic version of the aircraft carries six Kh-55 missiles on a single drum inside the fuse-lage. An overloaded variant, with shorter range and slower speed, can carry 10 more missiles under the aircraft's wings (each wing carries one cluster with two missiles between the fuselage and inner engine, and one cluster with three missiles between inner and outer engines).

At Taganrog, the conversion of Tu-142MK airframe No. 42105 into the first Tu-142MS began in the second quarter of 1978 and was completed in September 1979. In the same month the aircraft made its maiden flight. When compared with the Tu-142MK the aircraft has a shorter front fuselage with a new, wider cockpit and Leninets Obzor-MS radar in the nose. The bomb bay is located on the aircraft's centre of gravity. New electronic warfare and communication systems were fitted, as were modernised NK-12MP turboprop engine offering longer service life. A new electric system was equipped with a more powerful generator.

Into production and service

When series production began in 1981, the aircraft was redesignated as the Tu-95MS (*izdeliye* VP-021) 'Bear-H'. On 3 September 1981, the first series aircraft Tu-95MS, No. 01, performed the first successful launch of a Kh-55 missile. On 26 March 1982, Tu-95MS No. 2 flew to Akhtubinsk to begin state acceptance tests. On 31 December 1983, upon introduction of adjustments resulting from the state acceptance tests, the Tu-95MS aircraft with Kh-55 missiles was officially commissioned into service. The factory at Taganrog also built the Tu-142 and converted Il-76MDs into A-50 'Mainstay' early warning aircraft, and the planned Tu-95MS production run unquestionably exceeded its capacity. Accordingly, at the beginning of 1983, Tu-95MS production was moved to Kuibyshev.

On 17 December 1982, the first two aircraft (Nos 01 and 02) were delivered to the 1023rd TBAP at Semipalatinsk. A month later, the next Tu-95MS arrived at Semipalatinsk, and in February 1983 pilots from the 1023rd TBAP launched Kh-55 missiles for the first time during exercises. In 1984 the next unit – the 1126th TBAP stationed on the same airfield at Semipalatinsk began receiving its new aircraft. In 1985 the 1006th TBAP at Uzin acquired its first Tu-95MS, and in 1987 the 182nd TBAP at Mozdok began to convert to the 'Bear-H'. Older Tu-95K-22 aircraft from these air bases were moved to Ukrainka, to replace Myasishchev M-4 and 3M bombers. The displaced 'Bisons' were either converted into tankers or withdrawn.

There are two production versions of Tu-95MS. The difference between these two versions is commonly related to the number of missiles carried: older aircraft designated conventionally as Tu-95MS6 carry six missiles inside the weapon bay, whereas the newer machines (Tu-95MS16) carry 10 additional missiles under the wings. However, the difference between the two is much more significant.

In June 1983, just as series production of the Tu-95MS and its Kh-55 missiles was beginning, a government resolution was issued concerning their modernisation. Both the Tu-95MS16 and Kh-55SM missile arose from this programme. The most important alteration was replacing the Osina missile launch system with the much more modern Sprut (Octopus) system, as used in the Tu-160, enabling the simultaneous launch of 12 or more missiles. The aircraft's self-defence and communications systems were also improved: two double-barrelled GSh-23s cannon in the rear turret replaced the original AM-23 single-barrelled guns. The missile's onboard sensors were improved by increasing their resistance to jamming. In 1986, the modernised Tu-95MS16 aircraft and Kh-55SM (*izdeliye* 125) missile entered production, and were officially commissioned into service with the Soviet air forces. During START negotiations, Russia presented the Kh-55

and Kh-55SM missiles with the 'official' designations RKV-500A and RKV-500B, corresponding to their Western designations AS-15A and AS-15B.

According to official data submitted on 31 July 1991 during signature of the START I treaty, in September 1990 the Soviet Union had 84 Tu-95MS aircraft with 672 'RKV-500' missiles, as well as 63 older combat versions (Tu-95K-22, K and M), and 11 Tu-95U training aircraft at the Ryazan-Dyagilevo training centre. Several aircraft built in the next year were delivered to Uzin, Ukraine. In February 1992 Russia's President Boris Yeltsin announced the decision to cease Tu-95MS production, at a total of 88.

Tu-95 in Soviet air forces, September 1990, by variant

Air Base	MS16	MS6	K-22	K	M	U	Total
Uzin-Shepelovka	21	-	-	1	1	-	23
Mozdok	22	-	-	-	-	-	22
Semipalatinsk	13	27	-	-	-	-	40
Ukrainka	-	-	46	15	-	-	61
Ryazan-Dyagilevo	-	-	-	-	-	11	11
Total	**56***	**27**	**46**	**16**	**1**	**11**	**157**

* One Tu-95MS16 was awaiting delivery at the Kuibyshev factory, thus the total number of aircraft according to the START treaty was greater by one than the number given in the table. Additionally, several aircraft of various versions were assigned to the LII flight-test centre at Zhukovskiy.

Above and left: The art of mid-air refuelling is never easy, but the central position of the probe and the Tu-95's stability make the process straightforward. When refuelling from Il-78s 'Bears' use the UPAZ pod mounted on the rear fuselage rather than the wing-mounted pods.

Bottom: Eight Tu-95MSs line up on the Engels ramp, with Tu-160 'Blackjacks' in the distance. The 'Bears' were previously assigned to the 182nd TBAP at Mozdok, but have been withdrawn from their previous base, close to Chechnya, and now serve with the 184th GvTBAP.

Below: 184th GvTBAP aircraft are adopting the names of cities. This Tu-95MS is named Kaluga.

After the disintegration of the USSR most of the Tu-95MS aircraft remained beyond the borders of the Russian Federation. Kazakhstan inherited 40 bombers at Semipalatinsk, whereas the Ukraine had 25 bombers at Uzin. Russia quickly reached agreement with Kazakhstan and all 40 aircraft flew to Ukrainka air base in Russia's Far East (the last four bombers departed for Russia on 19 February 1994). In exchange for the bombers, Kazakhstan obtained tactical aircraft. The agreement with Ukraine turned out to be much more difficult. After several years of negotiations, concerning mainly the Tu-160s of the 184th GvTBAP at Priluki, in November-December 1999 Ukraine sold to Russia only three Tu-95MS 'Bears', the remaining aircraft being scrapped. In 1998, the aircraft from Mozdok air base, located dangerously close to the Chechnya trouble spot, were transferred to Engels.

At present (according to official data for July 2001) Russia has 63 Tu-95MS aircraft with 504 Kh-55 missiles, as well as two Tu-95s of older versions. These aircraft are distributed between three air regiments: the 184th Guards TBAP at Engels, and the 1223rd and 1226th TBAPs at Ukrainka. About 60 per cent of these aircraft are recent versions with the Sprut system; the remainder being from the first series with the Osina system. From 1999 on, Tu-95MS bombers have been named after towns, examples being *Saratov, Smolensk, Blagoveshchensk, Kaluga* and *Ryazan*.

Like all Russian military aviation, Tu-95s do very little flying. Average flying time of a pilot in the 37th Air Army (long-range air forces) amounted in 2001 to a mere 20 hours (10 hours in 2000). Nevertheless, for the first time in several years, Russian strategic aircraft began venturing out

on long-range flights. During the Zapad-99 exercise in June 1999 a pair of Tu-95MSs made a 15-hour flight from Engels to the Iceland region. On the way back one of the aircraft launched a Kh-55 missile on an exercise ground near the Caspian Sea. In September 1999, two pairs of Tu-95MSs took off from Anadyr and Tiksi airfields in Chukotka, Russian Far East, and approached the Canadian coast. In November and December 2000 two Tu-95MSs were temporarily ferried to Anadyr airfield, three to Tiksi and two to Vorkuta. In 2001 Russia planned another series of long-distance sorties, including a flight to Cam Ranh Bay in Vietnam, but these missions were not carried out. In late April 2002, two 'Bear-Hs' again ventured out into the Pacific during a Far East military exercise, and were intercepted by USAF F-15Cs from Alaska.

Current modernisation programme

As already noted, the history of the Tu-95 mirrors the history of Russian airborne strategic missiles, and this continues today. The basic function of the Tu-95 until 1990 was nuclear deterrence (the only weapon of the Tu-95MS – the Kh-55 cruise missile – exists only with a 200-kT nuclear warhead). However, as early as the late 1980s Russia began considering the transformation of the Tu-95MS into a dual-purpose weapon for both nuclear and conventional missions. This marked a significant change from the military-political point of view. Previously, Russian strategic aviation armed only with nuclear missiles could be used only as a deterrent in times of peace or as the ultimate weapon in a global conflict. By adopting non-nuclear weapons, strategic aviation could also be used in smaller conflicts of varying scale, beginning, for instance, with the use of single missiles against terrorist training camps at the other end of the world. This trend was abruptly amplified in the early 1990s when the Cold War was over, and the US demonstrated the great capability of strategic aviation armed with smart conventional weapons in Desert Storm.

In 1992 design work began on the Tu-95MSM aircraft with a new Sigma missile launch system and new Kh-101 conventional strategic missiles (and later also with the modernised Kh-555, new medium-range Kh-SD and strategic nuclear Kh-102 missiles, all derived from Kh-101 technologies). From autumn 1999 conversion of air force

Demonstrating a spirited take-off during the Zhukovskiy show, this Tu-95MS is assigned to the LII test centre for various trials, hence the calibration markings on the rear fuselage. As the massive mainwheels go through their somersaulting manoeuvre during retraction, drag increases markedly. Another peculiarity during gear retraction is the nose-up pitch change resulting from so much weight being moved aft, and its consequent effect on the aircraft's centre of gravity.

Inside the Tu-95MS

Above: In the rear of the forward crew compartment, facing aft, is the first navigator's position, dominated by a large screen for the Obzor-MS radar.

Right: The flight deck of the initial production Tu-95MS differed only in detail from earlier 'Bears'. Later aircraft featured a more modern flight deck with central console mounting the throttles.

Below: The engineer's position is also only subtly different from earlier aircraft. Again, in Tu-95MS16s the station was considerably revised.

Below: The second navigator's station is on the port side, next to the first navigator. Defensive electronic warfare equipment is also controlled from here, although the necessary equipment has been removed in this case. It normally occupies the space below the screen.

Above: The communications station, opposite that of the flight engineer, has the cryptographic terminal installed, albeit hidden from prying eyes.

Missiles carried by Tu-95MS/MSM

	Kh-55	Kh-55SM	Kh-101	Kh-SD	Kh-65SE
Launch weight	1210 kg	1500 kg	2200-2400 kg	1600 kg	1250 kg
Warhead	nuclear 200 kT	nuclear 200 kT	conventional 400 kg	conventional 400 kg	conventional 410 kg
Length	6.04 m	6.04 m	7.45 m	6.04 m	
Body diameter	514 mm	770 mm			514 mm
Wing span	3.1 m	3.1 m			3.1 m
Minimum flight alt.			30-70 m	30-70 m	40-110 m
Ceiling			6000 m	6000 m	
Cruise speed			190-200 m/s	190-200 m/s	160 m/s
Maximum speed	260 m/s	250 m/s	250-260 m/s	260-270 m/s	260 m/s
Accuracy	100 m	100 m	12-20 m	12-20 m	
Maximum range	1500 km	2000 km	5000 km		250-280 km

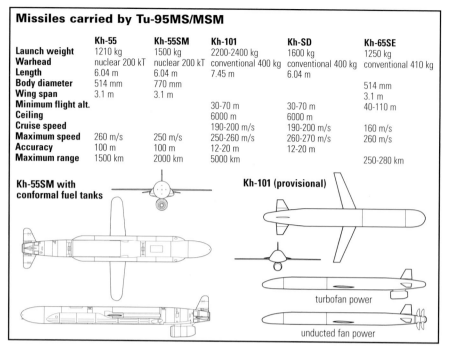

Kh-55SM with conformal fuel tanks

Kh-101 (provisional)

turbofan power

unducted fan power

aircraft was carried out by the Air Force's 360th ARZ (Aviaremontnyi Zavod, repair plant) at Ryazan. The aircraft are upgraded on the occasion of major overhauls, which also prolong service life to 30 years. The Tu-95MSM should remain in service until around 2020 (unless further modernisation and service life extension is undertaken in the future). All 35 or so Tu-95MS aircraft with the Sprut system are being upgraded, the last due in 2005; older aircraft with the Osina system will not be modernised.

There is little information about tests of new armament for the Tu-95MSM. The Kh-101 missile, the most important item of the whole programme, is now being introduced into series production. According to unconfirmed information, the air force's Tu-95s fired Kh-101 missiles for the first time during exercises on 6-8 October 1998. In January 2002, the then commander-in-chief of the Russian Air Force, Anatoliy Kornukov, informed about his decision on starting series production of "new accurate missiles for the strategic aviation" (Kornukov did not mention which type of missile, but it may be guessed from the description that it was the Kh-101). According to Kornukov, the missile will be supplied to military units in 2003.

Work on the Kh-101 (*izdeliye* 111) strategic missile began as early as the late 1980s as a replacement for the Kh-55. The fundamental innovation was installing a much more accurate homing system, enabling the use of a conven-

tional warhead instead of a nuclear one. The Kh-101 missile has a classic configuration with slightly swept fixed wings, and fixed control fins. The propulsion system of the Kh-101 remains unknown. According to one report, the missile is propelled by a turboprop engine, with pusher airscrews installed in the rear part of the fuselage, but another propulsion system with a turbofan engine, similar to that of Kh-55, is also possible.

Guidance to the target is by inertial navigation system with electro-optical correction system. Television terminal guidance system is activated in the direct vicinity of the target. This system compares the image seen by the camera against the target picture stored in the missile's memory. Probably, although this has not been confirmed, the Kh-101 is also equipped with a GPS receiver for accurate positioning. The missile warhead contains a penetrating charge with combined high explosive and incendiary effects. The Kh-102 missile with nuclear warhead (and with simpler homing system) will be developed from the Kh-101 in the future. The Tu-95MSM is capable of carrying up to eight Kh-101 missiles in four clusters, two under each wing, while six additional missiles of another type (Kh-55, Kh-555 or Kh-SD) can be carried in the bomb bay.

Cruise missile conversion

In 2001, the overhaul of Kh-55 missiles and their upgrade to Kh-555 standard were ordered from the DMZ factory at Dubna (according to unconfirmed information, the Kh-555 missile was launched on 12 January 2000 for the first time). The most important alteration is installing the terminal guidance system of the Kh-101, as well as a conventional, instead of nuclear, warhead. It is very probable that the Kh-555 missile will be fitted with a new engine. The R-95-300 turbofan of the Kh-55 is almost 20 years old and was manufactured in series at Zaporozhye, Ukraine. Russia will certainly prefer a Russian-made engine. There are several new engines of similar class, which can be taken into consideration. The most likely option is a new engine developed by the Lyulka-Saturn company in Moscow, designated *izdeliye* 36MT, which is now undergoing static tests (this engine was installed in the new version of the Kh-59MK tactical missile, which was formerly also powered by the R-95-300). Other engines that may be considered are the TRDD-50 designed by OMKB at Omsk, and Moscow Soyuz's modernised RDKF1-300 or new R-125-300.

In the long run, Russia plans to use equipment prepared for the Kh-101 (Sigma missile launch system, inertial navigation system with electro-optical correction, as well as TV terminal seeker) in the new medium-range missile Kh-SD (Sredney Dalnosti, medium-range). There are two types of Kh-SD warhead: penetrating (e.g. against deep fortifications, command posts) or cassette (e.g. against airfields and other surface targets). No information is available on the appearance, construction and propulsion system of the missile. The Tu-95MSM will carry six Kh-SD missiles inside the bomb bay plus – optionally – eight missiles under the wings.

Information about Kh-SD partly tallies with data for the Kh-65 missile, already known from summer 1992 when, during Mosaeroshow at Zhukovskiy, a small brochure about it was issued. Next year, a full-size mock-up of its anti-ship version, designated Kh-65SE, was shown (in Abu Dhabi in February 1993 and then in September at Zhukovskiy and at Nizhnyi Novgorod). Some parameters of the Kh-65 are identical or very close to those of the Kh-SD, including length, flight speed and warhead weight. The Kh-65's weight is smaller (which may be a result of additional fuel tanks in the Kh-SD) and the guidance system is different. The external appearance of the Kh-65 is very similar to that of the Kh-55, the only conspicuous difference being the wide, flat forward fuselage. The missile is powered by a TRDD-50 turbofan engine installed under the rear part of fuselage.

According to the initial information from 1992, the Kh-65 was intended for attacks against stationary targets of known coordinates and its homing system was to be similar to that of the Kh-101 (inertial-Doppler navigation with electro-optical position correction), but without a terminal homing system. The range of Kh-65 was quoted at 580-600 km (360-373 miles). The Kh-65SE anti-ship version is intended for attacks against big radar-contrasting targets with radar cross section exceeding 300 m², particularly naval ships in a strong jamming environment. The missile has an active radar seeker for terminal guidance. The range of this version of the missile is 250-280 km (155-174 miles). The Kh-65 has been displayed as part of the armament of some tactical aircraft, such as the Su-35 and Su-27IB. It is possible that the Kh-65 missile is one of the variants of the Kh-SD programme. The general designation Kh-SD would suggest a development programme for a new family of medium-range air-to-surface missiles, rather than of a specific type.

Piotr Butowski

Having been developed to launch just one type of weapon (the nuclear Kh-55), the 'Bear-H' is entering the conventional arena and is in the process of acquiring the ability to carry several types of weapon, both nuclear and conventional. Blessed with a capacious bomb bay, it is possible that the Tu-95MS might also be used for free-fall bombing in benign threat environments – as is the case with the B-52 – turning the story of the 'Bear' full-circle.

Right: With production of the Tu-160 proceeding with occasional single aircraft and development of a new bomber hampered by funding difficulties, the Tu-95MS/MSM will remain the backbone of Russia's strategic bomber fleet for some years. Young airframes, capable systems and the current vogue for stand-off cruise missiles ensure a bright future for the 'Bear'.

Left: Engels is the focal point of Russian strategic aviation, housing a regiment of 'Bear-Hs' and one of 'Blackjacks'. On the banks of the Volga in central Russia, Saratov is the closest major city to the base, and the 184th GvTBAP's lead aircraft was named in its honour. The 'Blackjacks' are assigned to the 121st GvTBAP, which absorbed the aircraft returned from Priluki, Ukraine, where the 184th GvTBAP was formerly based.

Tupolev Tu-95MS 'Bear-H'

184th Gvardeyskiy Tyazhelo-Bombardirovochnyi Aviatsionnyi Polk 37th Air Army, Engels air base

This 'Bear-H' is the commander's aircraft of the 184th GvTBAP, and wears the name of the city (Saratov) local to Engels air base. It is adorned with the blue fin leading edge traditionally applied to the aircraft assigned to unit commanders. In company with another Tu-95MS, this aircraft made one of the type's rare long-range flights – to the North Pole – on 11 September 2001, the date of the Al Qaeda terrorist attack on New York and Washington.

Mission system
Housed in the massive radome is the antenna for the Leninets/St Petersburg Obzor-MS navigation/attack radar (NATO: 'Clam Pipe'), above which is a small radome for a weather radar. The K-016 Sprut missile initialisation and launch system (older Osina system for early aircraft) is installed to provide accurate navigational data to the inertial systems of the missiles before launch.

Weapons
The normal load of the Tu-95MS16 consists of six Kh-55SM (AS-15B 'Kent') lo[n]g range nuclear cruise missile[s] on an MKU-6-5 rotary launch[er] inside the fuselage bomb ba[y]. Additionally, 10 more Kh-55SMs can be suspende[d] under the wings in four clusters (two on each inner pylon and three on each pyl[on] between the engines), altho[ugh] these pylons were remove[d] under the START treaty. Ear[ly] Tu-95MS6 aircraft carry the older Kh-55 (AS-15A 'Kent') missiles in the fuselage bay only.

Crew
The Tu-95MS is operated by a crew of seven, comprising two pilots, navigator (with access to the astrodome), navigation/offensive weapons operator, defence systems operator, and flight engineer in the forward pressurised compartment. The tail gunner has a separate cabin. All crew (except tail gunner) enter the cockpit via the nosewheel bay.

Tu-95MS 'Bear-H' specification

Dimensions: length 49.13 m (161 ft 2 in); wing span 50.04 m (164 ft 2 in); wing area 289.9 m² (3,120 sq ft); height 13.30 m (43 ft 7.5 in); maximum fuselage diameter 2.90 m (9 ft 6 in)
Undercarriage: retractable, with steerable twin nose wheels. Four wheel bogies on each main unit, retracting into large fairings on the wing trailing edges, in line with the inner engines. Main wheel tyre size 1450 x 450 mm (57 x 17.7 in); nose wheel tyre size 1140 x 350 mm (44.9 x 13.8 in); wheel base 14.83 m (48 ft 8 in); wheel track 12.55 m (41 ft 2 in)
Weights: empty 94400 kg (208,113 lb); maximum take-off 185000 kg (407,848 lb); maximum in flight, after in-flight refuelling 187000 kg (412,257 lb); fuel 81670 kg (180,048 lb); maximum landing 135000 kg (297,619 lb)
Performance: maximum speed 830 km/h (516 mph); maximum speed at sea level 550 km/h (342 mph); cruise speed 735 km/h (457 mph); take-off distance at MTOW 2540 m (8,333 ft); g-limit +2; ceiling 10500 m (34,450 ft); range with nominal combat load (6 x Kh-55) 10520 km (6,537 miles); range with maximum combat load (16 x Kh-55) 8500 km (5,282 miles); endurance without inflight refuelling 14 hours; range with single inflight refuelling 14100 km (8,762 miles)
Powerplant: four Trud/Samara NK-12MP turboprops, each rated at 11190 ekW (15,000 ehp). Each eight-bladed AV-60K propeller unit comprises two four-bladed co-axial contra-rotating reversible-pitch propellers. Flight refuelling probe ahead of the cockpit, on the nose.

Airframe and control surfaces
The wings are constructed from four-spar inner panels (35° quarter-chord sweep) and three-spar outer panels (33.5° quarter-chord sweep), with 2.5° anhedral. Each wing has two-section double-slotted trailing-edge flaps and three-section ailerons (with tabs). Spoilers and three wing fences are mounted on each upper wing surface. Conventional tail control surfaces include variable-incidence tailplanes, adjustable in-flight according to the fuel used (between 1° down and 3° up); elevators and rudder are all tabbed. The semi-monocoque, circular-section fuselage has a bomb bay in the centre about 8.1 m (26 ft 7 in) long. Flight control is mechanical, hydraulically boosted and controlled by the SAU-3-021 autopilot.

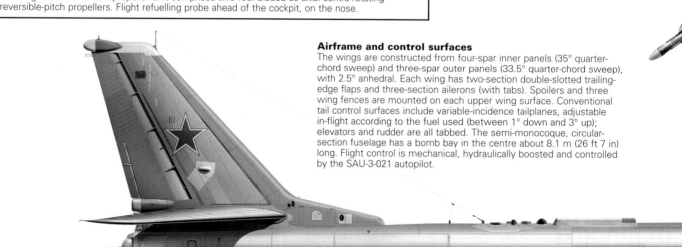

Zaur Eylanbekov

Navigation and ILS
The NPK-VP-021 flight navigation system consists of astro- and radio-navigation sub-systems. The latter includes inertial navigation, Doppler radar, long-range and short-range radio navigation devices. The instrument landing system enables the aircraft to take-off in 400-m (1,312-ft) visibility and 30-m (100-ft) cloud base, and land in 1000-m (3,280-ft) visibility and 100-m (328-ft) cloud base.

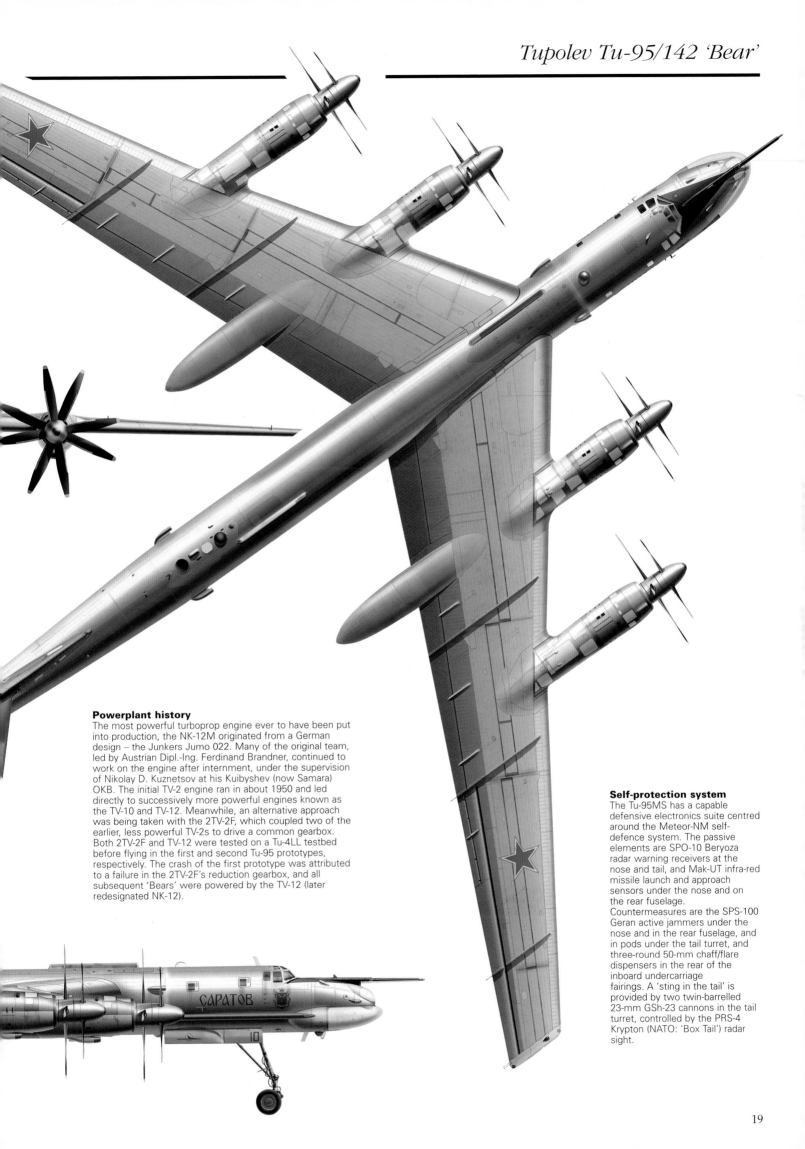

Powerplant history

The most powerful turboprop engine ever to have been put into production, the NK-12M originated from a German design – the Junkers Jumo 022. Many of the original team, led by Austrian Dipl.-Ing. Ferdinand Brandner, continued to work on the engine after internment, under the supervision of Nikolay D. Kuznetsov at his Kuibyshev (now Samara) OKB. The initial TV-2 engine ran in about 1950 and led directly to successively more powerful engines known as the TV-10 and TV-12. Meanwhile, an alternative approach was being taken with the 2TV-2F, which coupled two of the earlier, less powerful TV-2s to drive a common gearbox. Both 2TV-2F and TV-12 were tested on a Tu-4LL testbed before flying in the first and second Tu-95 prototypes, respectively. The crash of the first prototype was attributed to a failure in the 2TV-2F's reduction gearbox, and all subsequent 'Bears' were powered by the TV-12 (later redesignated NK-12).

Self-protection system

The Tu-95MS has a capable defensive electronics suite centred around the Meteor-NM self-defence system. The passive elements are SPO-10 Beryoza radar warning receivers at the nose and tail, and Mak-UT infra-red missile launch and approach sensors under the nose and on the rear fuselage.
Countermeasures are the SPS-100 Geran active jammers under the nose and in the rear fuselage, and in pods under the tail turret, and three-round 50-mm chaff/flare dispensers in the rear of the inboard undercarriage fairings. A 'sting in the tail' is provided by two twin-barrelled 23-mm GSh-23 cannons in the tail turret, controlled by the PRS-4 Krypton (NATO: 'Box Tail') radar sight.

At first glance the Tu-142 looked very similar to the Tu-95RTs upon which it was based, especially if fitted with the undernose fairing for sensor tests. However, there were some notable changes, the most obvious being the 12-wheel main undercarriage. More importantly, the wing was of revised section and slightly enlarged, with a new flap arrangement. The earlier bag tanks were abandoned in favour of integral tanks in the wing box. The second Tu-142 introduced an extended forward fuselage, a modification required to house the large mission crew and its equipment.

Production of the Tu-95RTs 'Bear-D' reached 52, plus one converted Tu-95M, and it became the most visible version on 'snooping' missions around NATO nations and their navies. The variant was the first with a dedicated maritime mission, and naturally provided the basis for development of the Tu-142 'Bear-F'. With its primary mission of over-the-horizon targeting no longer relevant, the Tu-95RTs was retired from service in the mid-1990s. Here an example is escorted by a Tornado F.Mk 3 from the RAF's No. 5 Squadron.

Tu-142 – sub-hunting 'Bear'

In the early 1960s the Soviet navy (Voyenno-morskoy flot – VMF) perceived a need for a long-range anti-submarine aircraft, in order to counter the threat posed by the West's growing fleet of nuclear strike-capable submarines. Initial requirements stood at 160 aircraft to equip two navy fleets, although this was later revised to 114, and finally to 100.

On 28 February 1963 the Soviet government released a requirement covering the improvement of ASW forces and of the means of detecting and destroying high-speed submarines. One of the items on the list was the creation of an anti-submarine aircraft based on the Tu-95 bomber. Known as the Tu-95PLO (*protivolodochnaya oborona*, anti-submarine warfare), the aircraft was to be presented for joint tests in 1964. A prototype of the Berkut-95 system was prepared for tests in the Il-38 'May', and this was expected to be installed in the Tu-95PLO. The Berkut system relied on a mix of human and automated control. Decision-making in navigational and tactical matters was largely left to the crew, in accordance with the conditions, while the very primitive computer software could be used when deemed useful.

In September/October 1963 the outline plan for what had been redesignated Tu-142 was submitted. In answer to a VVS stipulation, the Tu-142 should be able to operate from unpaved strips able to support 6 kg/cm² (85.34 lb/sq in). In November of the same year it was revealed to a model committee that the ASW variant would be based on the Tu-95RTs 'Bear-D' maritime reconnaissance and target-illuminating version.

To meet the unpaved field requirements, the designers developed a complex and heavy landing gear. Twelve aircraft from the first series had each of their main legs equipped with 12 low-pressure wheels mounted in pairs on three axles. The nose leg had two wheels with a turn angle of 45° and the tail section had a two-wheel retractable bumper. Retraction and extension of the main undercarriage and tail support was electro-mechanical, while the forward leg was hydraulically activated. Emergency release of the landing gear was provided. In order to accommodate a main gear of this kind, it was necessary to increase the size of the aft portion of the inboard engine nacelles, which housed the gear. This in turn led to a reduction in flap area.

Progress on Tu-142 development was delayed more than once. On 17 January 1968, under pressure from the Soviet navy and air forces, the Military-Industrial Commission (VPK) noted that "the prototype, constructed in 1967, and first production aircraft are still not ready for factory tests. The Berkut equipment is in a stage of setup and adjustment…" "The second production example is being modified with a lengthened cockpit, and the static tests of the airframe has not begun." The VPK decided that the Tu-142 had to be presented for production tests in 1968 (prototype in March, first production aircraft in May and the second production aircraft, with the lengthened forward section, in July). The Tu-142 fitted with the Berkut PPS (*poiskovo-pritselnaya sistema*, search and targeting system) was to be presented for joint state tests in the second quarter of 1968.

First flight

The first Tu-142 aircraft were under construction at plant No. 18 at Kuibyshev, where main production of the type was planned. The first flight of the prototype (No. 4200), took place on 18 June 1968 from Kuibyshev's airfield, flown by a crew led by test pilot I. K. Vedernikov. The second aircraft from the factory (No. 4201), with a cockpit lengthened by 1.7 m (5 ft 7 in), took to the air on 3 September. The third aircraft (No. 4203), with the lengthened cockpit and a complete set of equipment, flew on 31 October. These aircraft carried out most of the tests required by the programme. Subsequently aircraft No. 4200 (and later No. 4243, the first Tu-142MK 'Bear-F Mod 3' which had been seen at Zhukovskiy for years) were used as flying laboratories and testbeds for the engines intended for the Tu-22M3 'Backfire-C' bomber and Tu-144 'Charger' supersonic airliner.

Above: A Tu-142MK sweeps over Kuznetsov in a display of Russian naval power. The MK serves in slightly greater numbers than the later Tu-142MZ, and remains an important asset, despite having less capable ASW systems although it was upgraded in the early 1990s. Much of the 'Bear-F' fleet is mothballed, and flying is severely restricted compared with Cold War times.

By government resolution dated 14 December 1972, the Tu-142 fitted with the Berkut-95 PPS was accepted into service with the Soviet navy. Basic performance characteristics were:

- 12300-km (7,643-mile) range at 182-tonne (179.1-ton) take-off weight with a 5500-kg (12,125-lb) combat load and 5 per cent reserves
- 4-hour 30-minute time on station at 4000 km (2,485 miles) from base
- 830 km/h (516-mph) maximum speed
- 11000-m (36,090-ft) ceiling
- 2350-m (7,710-ft) take-off run at 182 tonnes
- 1200-m (3,937-ft) landing run at 106 tonnes

By early 1973 18 Tu-142s had been completed at Kuibyshev (two in 1968, five each year in 1969, 1970 and 1971, and one in 1972). This number included 12 aircraft with the larger main undercarriage.

In the early 1970s, the Ministry of Aviation Industry (Ministerstvo Aviatsionnoy Promyshlennosti – MAP) decided to transfer Tu-142 manufacture to plant No. 86 at Taganrog. According to some documents the Taganrog plant could build six/seven Tu-142Ms per year in 1976-1980, and in subsequent years up to 15. A new runway had to be constructed at the plant's airfield. The manufacturing documentation was transferred to Taganrog along with a sample aircraft (No. 4242). Due to the time required to upgrade the airfield in 1975-1976, the plant rolled out 10 aircraft (Nos 4232 through 4241). All of them were made according to the sample aircraft, and featured the forward cabin lengthened by 2 m (6 ft 7 in), and main landing gear with four-wheel bogies.

ASW equipment

When an aircraft was equipped with the PPS, it became known as a 'complex', or weapon system. The ingredients of a complex included the aircraft, the PPS, ground resources and control facilities. The offensive loads were not officially part of the complex.

By September of 1970 factory tests were completed. These revealed that the aircraft did not meet its set specifications, particularly in range. At a 182-tonne (179.1-ton) take-off weight the range was 9860 km (6,127 miles). Early aircraft had 5.8-m (19-ft) diameter AV-60P series 01 propellers. In order to improve range, they were replaced by 5.6-m (18-ft 4-in) diameter AV-60K series 01 propellers, which were more efficient in cruising mode.

Tu-142 No. 4231 was chosen to go through a new series of tests in order to prove that the aircraft could meet the requirements. It was stripped of various items such as the Gagara infra-red monitor, active countermeasures and radio-intelligence equipment. This reduced weight by 3685 kg (8,124 lb) and allowed the Tu-142 to meet the required numbers. General Designer Andrey Nikolayevich Tupolev appealed to the minister of defence with a letter, in which he expressed a disagreement with VVS requirements regarding the necessity to operate the heavy aircraft from unpaved runways. In his reply dated 6 October 1970, the minister recognised Tupolev's point. As a result, the triple-axle landing gear was replaced by a lighter, double-axle unit, taken from the Tu-114 'Cleat' airliner. Accordingly, the size of the main gear fairings and flaps were restored to those of the Tu-95RTs.

Far left: For years a routine feature of any 'Bear' crew member's life was the constant attention from NATO aircraft when operating over international waters. US Navy carrier battle groups naturally drew the attentions of maritime patrol 'Bears', which in turn led to regular intercepts by US Navy aircraft. As well as fighters, supporting tankers regularly got in close for a look at the giant patrollers, as demonstrated by this KA-6D from Forrestal's VA-85 'Black Falcons'.

Known to NATO has 'Bear-F' (sometimes with the retrospective Mod 0 suffix), initial Tu-142 production (12 aircraft) featured massive fairings for the enlarged 12-wheel rough-field undercarriage. This is one of two aircraft which were used for various tests, including the fitment of various sensors in an undernose fairing.

In standard form the Tu-142 lacked the undernose radome. The result was the 'cleanest' of the maritime 'Bears', its lines spoilt only by the Berkut-95 radar and the bulge for the enlarged nosewheels. This is a very early aircraft, built with the much extended nacelles for the rough-field landing gear. Operations with the new aircraft got under way in 1970, and the type soon came into contact with NATO interceptors over the North Sea and north Atlantic.

For the Tu-142 the anti-submarine equipment initially comprised the Berkut-95 PPS and equipment for the carriage and release of submarine detection/destruction equipment. Onboard search equipment included the 15-GHz pitch-roll-stabilised radar (RLS); radar scope (SPIU); a TsVM-263 computer with communications coupling unit; geographical coordinates panel; and other devices.

The SPIU used 40 channels (38 used, two in reserve) to receive and distribute data sent by sonobuoys to the onboard computer. An ARK-UB compass unit was used in conjunction with the radar scope for homing the aircraft to the buoy. During flight in automatic mode, the TsVM-263 processed flight data and communicates heading corrections to the autopilot. When in a search mode, the computer – using data received from sonobuoys – calculated the position of the submarine and direction in which it was moving. Based on these results, the TsVM automatically adjusted the flight profile and tracked the target. On the basis of available data, the computer estimated the probability of a successful attack, and sent out signals for opening of the bomb bay and release of weapons.

Sonobuoys were the only source of the information about underwater conditions. There were three types of sonobuoys: RGB-1, RGB-2 and RGB-3. Each of them contained a hydroacoustic channel, data transmitter, beacon, parachute box and power supplies.

■ **RGB-1 – passive, non-directional:** the acoustic system descended to 35 or 70 m (115 or 230 ft) and received noise in the 6.25-7.75 kHz range. Basic modes of operation were a 'duty mode' with an automatic start-up, which activated the data transmitter if received signals exceeded a preset level, and a 'marker' mode, in which the buoy's beacon was constantly on, the acoustic channel being left in 'duty' mode. In 'duty' mode the buoy worked for up to three hours. During tests in the Black Sea, the range of detection of a diesel-powered submarine moving at 11-15 km/h (6-8 kt) was 1500-2100 m (1,640-2,297 yards). Range of communication between the aircraft and buoys was at least 40 km (25 miles). Each buoy was 1.2 m (3 ft

11 in) long, 150 mm (5.9 in) in diameter and weighed 14.2 kg (31.3 lb). A complete set contained 24 buoys.

■ **RGB-2 – passive, directional:** these were intended to measure and transmit magnetic bearing data on 'noisy' contacts. After entering water the RGB-2's transmitter worked continuously. The acoustic system descended to 20 m (66 ft) and rotated at 8 rpm, for an endurance of 45 minutes. Magnetic bearing definition was accurate to 3°. The RGB-2 measured 1.85 m (6 ft 1 in) in length, 230 mm (9 in) in diameter and 45 kg (99 lb) in weight. A complete set contained 10 buoys.

■ **RGB-3 – active:** after entering the water the RGB-3 worked in a 'noise-bearing finder' mode, but was switched to an 'echo-bearing finder' mode by command from the aircraft. Reflected acoustic signals from a submarine were transformed into electrical fluctuations received by the aircraft. In 'radiating' mode the RGB-3 worked for five minutes. Range of submarine detection was not less than 1500-2000 m (1,640-2,187 yards). Length of the RGB-3 was 2.84 m (9 ft 4 in), diameter was 392 mm (15.5 in) and weight was 185 kg (408 lb). A complete set contained four buoys.

Although never used in service, in search-only configuration the aircraft could carry a maximum of 440 RGB-1 sonobuoys. The optimal loadout – search and destroy – comprised 176 RGB-1s, 13 RGB-2s, four RGB-3s, three torpedoes (or APR-1 Condor anti-submarine missiles), 14 PLAB-250-120s (*protivolodochnaya avia bomba*, anti-submarine bomb – the first number means that the weapon has the dimensions of the FAB-250 high-explosive bomb, the second indicates the weight) and 14 marker bombs. These represented the weapons in use by Soviet naval aviation at the time of the Tu-142's development.

Underwater weapons

Torpedoes were considered to be the main weapon against enemy subs. The acoustic torpedo AT-1 became operational in 1962. The range of its automatic homing system was estimated at 300 m (328 yards), speed was 52 km/h (28 kt), depth of operation was up to 200 m (656 ft), weight was 560 kg (1,234 lb) and range was 4000 m (4,374 yards). With these specifications the torpedo did not satisfy the requirements for the Tu-142. Nevertheless, initially it was included in some mission loading configurations of the aircraft.

A more advanced weapon, the AT-2, entered service in 1973. After descending to its initial depth it started a programmed search, entering a left-hand cylindrical spiral 140 m (460 ft) in diameter, travelling at 43 km/h (23 kt). The programmed trajectory began at a depth of 40-45 m (130-148 ft). A change of spiral pitch on the first section of the trajectory occurred due to the automatic change in the trim of a torpedo from 11° to level. The homing system worked in an active/passive mode in cycles. For 35 per cent of the time it worked in active mode but for the remainder was passive.

This method of search provided observation across a range of depths. If the level of noise emitted by a potential target exceeded the reflected signal, the active-passive cycle was broken and the homing was controlled by the passive channel. In the case where the target was identified through a reflected signal, all further actions were based on commands from the active channel. If the target was lost, the equipment was switched back to the active/passive mode. Depth of operation for the AT-2 was 20-400 m (66-1,312 ft), diameter was 533 mm (21 in), weight was 1000 kg (2,205 lb) and speed was up to 74 km/h (40 kt).

Subsequently, the AT-2 was modernised to become the AT-2M. The pneumatic systems were replaced by hydraulic ones, the explosive warhead was increased in weight by 20 kg (44 lb) and the silver-zinc accumulators were replaced by new batteries. Production ended in 1978 after 975 torpedoes had been produced.

On 29 June 1971, by order of the defence minister, the APR-1 Condor anti-submarine missile became operational. The Condor's trajectory was established before launch: search in a straight line at a speed of 20 kt (37 km/h). On detection of the target the thrust of the engine was increased for six to seven seconds, boosting speed to 60 kt (111 km/h). The missile then performed a 900-m (984-yard) dash while homing on the target. The APR-1 was effective against targets submerged by up to 400 m (1,312 ft). By the time production ended in 1977, 263 missiles had been manufactured.

Taking into account the shortcomings of Berkut PPS, revealed in operations of the Il-38, the Tu-142 was equipped with the ANP-3V-1K automatic navigational device. It had two systems of coordinates: rectangular and polar. These two systems were essential for en route navigation and for manoeuvring in the target area. Among other things, the system allowed 'Bear-F' to fly a circular path of constant radius. Developers of the Berkut had divided the tasks to be handled by the system into three stages: flight in a given area, action in the tactical area and return to base.

Flight in a given area was carried out on one of several connecting great circles (lines of shortest distance between two points on a sphere). Navigational calculations were handled by the TsVM computer. When the aircraft deviated off course the computer issued a turn command, which was then passed to the autopilot, which then corrected the heading. At a distance of 90-130 km (56-81 miles) to the next waypoint on a route, the new data was entered.

On arrival in the search area, RGB-1 buoys were deployed. Buoys were sown either as a barrier or a field (to uniformly cover the area of search in calculated intervals and distances). In order to set a barrier, the TsVM was given the coordinates of its beginning and end, as well as desired interval between buoys. After that, the computer issued control commands for the aircraft, and calculated the points for opening the bay doors and dropping the buoys. Setting of a field could be also made in automatic mode.

After all the buoys had been deployed, the TsVM was tasked to supervise the buoys by flying the aircraft along and across the barrier. The TsVM issued appropriate commands to the aircraft to make the next turn. The navigator and the SPIU operator watched the display of the first channel to catch the moment a buoy indicated a response (the moment was also entered into the TsVM's memory) and to classify the contact. If the contact appeared authentic, the aircraft was directed to the active buoy under the directions of the ARK-UB radio compass.

After the decoder of the buoy's transmitter beacon was activated, the position of the buoy in relation to the aircraft was shown on the radar display. The crew then had an opportunity to choose one of several actions: to drop a 'confirming' RGB-2 to check the data, sow a barrier of buoys perpendicular to the probable heading of the target, or to drop an RGB-3 active buoy for accurate detection. In the case when the sub's heading was unknown, the crew commanded a 'Scope', in which RGB-1s were dropped encircling the area of detection, followed by the 'Flight around target' command which allowed subsequent supervision of the circular buoy pattern.

With an RGB-2 buoy in the water directional data could be received, from the SPIU to the TsVM. By overlapping the bearing marks with a mark of the target, the coordinates of the submarine and its speed could be calculated. If necessary, a 'confirming' RGB-3 was released. After processing of all data, the choice of weapons and the task of their preparation was done by the radar operator. According to test data, the time spent by a crew from initial detection of the submarine to weapon release ranged from 19 to 27 minutes.

Radar-tracking searches for surface targets were not complicated. Search of the area was performed using alternating port and starboard tacks. Surface attacks were made with the help of the radar, without taking into account the speed of the target's movement. The major shortcoming of the Berkut-95 was its inability to perform the task of tracking in an automatic mode.

Tu-142 in service

In May 1970, the first two Tu-142s were shipped from the manufacturer to the Northern Fleet's air branch, where the 76th Independent Long-Range Anti-submarine Warfare Air Regiment (Otdelniy Protivolodochniy Aviatsioniy Polk Dalnego Deystviya – OPLAP DD) had been undergoing

A revised flight deck layout with a raised roof was the main external feature of the 'Bear-F Mod 2'. The changes gave the pilots a much improved look forward. Confusingly, the Tupolev OKB and Taganrog plant referred to these aircraft as the Tu-142M. However, in service they retained the Tu-142 designation, as they were still fitted with the original Berkut-95 system. The fairings on the end of the tailplanes initially contained antennas for the Arfa and Kristall systems, but in later Tu-142s served the Lira long-range navigation system.

The 'Mod 2' became the standard for the first-generation Berkut-equipped aircraft. Delivery of newer Tu-142Ms to the Kipelovo unit in the early 1980s allowed the transfer of Tu-142s to the Pacific Fleet's 310th OPLAP DD, which had been established in 1978. As well as operations from its home base at Kamennyi Ruchei (near Vladivostok), the Pacific unit flew sorties from Cam Ranh Bay and Da Nang in Vietnam from 1979. From 1982 to the early 1990s this became a permanent detachment, with four aircraft assigned.

Berkut-equipped Tu-142s remained in service into the 1990s, although the fleet dwindled from 1988.

Below right: The stalky undercarriage and ample ground clearance under the Tu-95/142's fuselage made it a natural for use in the engine testbed role. Initially, the redundant second Tu-95 prototype was converted to Tu-95LL standard (illustrated), being used to test engines for the Tu-22, Tu-144 and Tu-22M. It was lost in an accident in 1973, and was replaced by the first Tu-142 prototype which, after conversion to Tu-142LL standard, went on to test engines for the Tu-22M3, Tu-144 and Tu-160. It was retired in the mid-1980s due to fatigue concerns.

Below and below far right: To replace the first Tu-142LL, a second testbed was converted from the prototype Tu-142MK. ASW equipment was removed and replaced by test equipment, while the refuelling probe and MAD boom were removed. In 1990 it set several time-to-height records for its weight class but has since fallen into disrepair at Zhukovskiy.

activation since June 1969 at Kipelovo naval air station. Special attention was paid to selecting aircrews. The positions of crew commanders were filled with pilots qualified as 'pilot 1st class' and experienced in flying heavy aircraft. Often, they were former air detachment commanders.

November 1971 saw the second squadron formed, with the regiment having received nine aircraft by then, and another one being delivered in 1972. Two others were operated by the Combat Training Centre, so by 1973 the AVMF had 12 Series I aircraft (Nos 4211 through 4222). When the third squadron formed, the regimental activation was complete.

Conversion training was easy enough since the fleets' air branches had seasoned instructors trained on the Tu-95, while difficulties – both objective and subjective – would normally crop up afterwards during the learning of the basics of combat. The conversion trainees were assisted by navigators and engineers from an Il-38 regiment garrisoned at the same naval air station, whose Il-38s were outfitted with Berkut systems.

Service Berkut-95 software programmes differed somewhat from those of the prototype. In particular, a conclusion was made that the kill probability against submarines in training torpedo releases could be enhanced by making the attack run perpendicular to the vessel's course. During their training, Tu-142 aircrews would use practice bombs against a land bombing range, with all data being entered into the surveillance and targeting system as if they were live ordnance. This allowed complicated anti-submarine

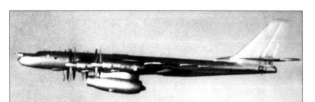

torpedo employment to be practised without using the precious weapons.

From time to time this led to amusing incidents. For instance, it occurred to a navigator that his aircraft was approaching the target from the wrong direction, so he 'corrected' the heading accordingly. The computer automatically acted on his initiative – and released the bombload on the barracks of the bombing range support team, completely shattering the armoury. Thankfully there were no casualties, as the buildings were empty. There were some problems with training aircrews since the number of buoys supplied for Naval Aviation's combat training was limited to 30-40 annually. The bulk of the buoys supplied would be used to resupply combat buoy kits.

Tracking submarines

Under the combat training schedule, special attention was paid to practising submarine-tracking techniques. In an hour-long tracking session around 35-65 RGB-1 buoys were expended, although seasoned aircrews would expend 30-40 buoys in an hour, achieved by a number of techniques. Thus, sometimes the surveillance and targeting systems were not used. Instead, a more speedy approach was at times resorted to. With a short time delay, buoys would be deployed as a triangle or a rectangle, dubbed '*semi-tavr*' and '*tavr*', to pinpoint the contact. The flight profile was maintained via the ANP-3V-1K. Following that, the ANP-3V-1K would be used to set linear or arch surveillance barriers. Radars proved to be ineffective in setting up surveillance barriers due to the wrong imagery scale on the radar scope.

On training missions and during actual tracking of unidentified submarines, tension would greatly increase between crew members, and the careful selection of the crew played an important role in their effectiveness. Everybody's nerves would be set on edge in expectation of

a contact on the next sonobuoy barrier. If a foreign submarine was being tracked, incompetent commanders would get in the way with their endless requests for minute reports of where buoys were deployed, and recommendations where they should be deployed. A key factor was the crew's ability to navigate accurately en route, especially when operating at the full combat radius.

The first sortie to the North Sea in search of foreign submarines was undertaken on 27 July 1970 by a pair of Tu-142s flown by regimental commanding officer V. I. Dubinskiy and squadron commander Lieutenant-Colonel V. A. Shimanskiy. To maximise the precision of their approach to the designated area, the crews approached the shoreline a few times and updated their positions through the use of known radar-contrast reference points. As experience was gained, the intensity of flight operations gradually grew. Tu-142 aircrews got excellent practical experience while tracking an unidentified submarine spotted by a Be-12 amphibian on 8 August 1974 in the Barents Sea. Occasional brief search missions in limited areas of the North Sea and the northern section of the Atlantic resulted in the detection of unidentified submarines, and subsequent tracking.

Northern Fleet Tu-142s would also fly in small tactical groups to the Pacific Fleet, via the so called Arctic Route, to take part in the Fleet's planned operations to monitor the submarine situation in the area. Also, they would operate on their own, flying a few sorties to the northern part of the Philippine Sea in 1977.

To augment the Pacific Fleet's anti-submarine warfare (ASW) capability, a decision was taken to reassign several

Tu-142 aircraft from the Northern Fleet. In 1976 saw a Tu-142 squadron activated at Khorol airfield. The air and ground crews completed their ground school in August 1977 and commenced their flight training. Following the completion of the conversion programme, the 310th OPLAP DD deployed in 1978 to its permanent base – Kamennyi Ruchei NAS. By then, the regiment had received 14 Tu-142 aircraft.

Pacific Fleet aircrews gradually extended beyond the Seas of Okhotsk and Japan, and in January 1979 launched routine operations from the air bases at Da Nang and Cam Ranh in Vietnam, flights to which were accomplished across the Korean Straits or around Japan. In the former case, a sortie's duration totalled nine hours, while in the latter it took another 90 minutes. The 'Bears' would typically carry 268 RGB-1 and 10 RGB-10 sonobuoys. Owing to Da Nang's limited field length, take-off weight was normally limited to 165 tonnes (162.4 tons), including 70000 kg (154,321 lb) of fuel for 10 hours aloft. Afterwards, four Tu-142s were assigned to the 169th Air Regiment (Composite), deployed on a temporary basis to Vietnam by agreement.

From the first combat sortie to 1993, Tu-142 aircrews detected 56 foreign submarines and tracked them for some time. After that time, the detection rate grew somewhat. Tu-142s began to be retired in 1988.

Tu-142P

A little-known version was the Tu-142P, equipped with the Atlantida searching and targeting system (PPS). Today it is almost forgotten as there was only one aircraft

A characteristic cloud of rubber smoke signifies the arrival of a 76th OPLAP DD Tu-142MK back at its Kipelovo base. The 'Bear-F Mod 3' entered service with the Northern Fleet in 1979, and the 76th OPLAP DD completed its conversion to the updated version in 1981.

The Kongelige Norske Luftforsvaret (Royal Norwegian air force) was in NATO's front line in terms of intercepting the 76th OPLAP DD's Tu-142s as they headed out on missions from Kipelovo. Here a Tu-142MK 'Bear-F Mod 3' is watched closely by an F-16A from Bodø-based 331 Skvadron. The 'Foxtrots' plied much of their trade in the north Atlantic, the scene of intense submarine activity during the Cold War. In the 1990s such missions, which had once been routine, rapidly became a rarity.

A Tu-142MK rests on a snowy Kipelovo. As with the first-generation of 'Foxtrots', there was some confusion surrounding its designation. To the design bureau the aircraft was the Tu-142MK (K = Korshun) but, initially, the navy referred to it as the Tu-142M, having not used this designation for the revised Berkut aircraft. Subsequently, the AVMF did adopt the MK suffix, to differentiate between the Korshun-equipped aircraft and the later Tu-142MZ with Zarechye system.

(No. 4362). Its avionics incorporated an ECCM (electronic counter-countermeasures) system, infra-red jammer and the Atlantida anti-submarine system, which was essentially the Berkut upgraded to employ new weapon systems such as the APR-2 and UMGT-1 torpedoes.

The aircraft underwent tests in 1976 and was not mass-produced. It featured several external differences by comparison with the Tu-142: its horizontal stabiliser did not mount the Arfa tip fairing, the aircraft was fitted with fairings for SPS-151, SPS-152 and SPS-153 radar jammers (mounted in place of the navigator's front canopy, between frames 13-14 on both sides, and in the rear). Aerials were moved from the forward canopy to the nose. A radio equipment fairing was located on the port side. The wing leading-edge flap featured recesses for attaching aerials, which were enclosed by dielectric panels, requiring the anti-icing system near the recesses to be switched off. One of the aerials of the Siren system was also situated on the tip of the tailfin.

Additional equipment increased the aircraft's weight by 1300 kg (2,866 lb). The fuel load was also increased. The single point refuelling system could admit 83640 kg (184,391 lb), while an additional 4000 kg (8,818 lb) could be filled by gravity. The aircraft's powerplant comprised four NK-12MV engines from the 04-65 series, with AV-60K propellers. The aircraft's cruising range was 11800 km

(7,332 miles) at a take-off weight of 182 tonnes (179.1 tons).

Tu-142M – 'systems from scratch'

By the early 1960s, foreign-made submarine search systems had become more reliant on low-frequency buoys and hydroacoustic explosive sound generators (ESG). Similar research was underway in the Soviet Union as well. By the mid-1960s, the conceptual design of the Udar system (a Soviet response to the US Navy's Julie system) had been completed, as well as a number of other efforts that laid the groundwork for the Korshun ASW surveillance and targeting system. A government resolution of 14 January 1969 ordered the derivation of the Korshun-equipped Tu-142M from the baseline Tu-142. The first prototype was to commence its joint trials in the third quarter of 1972, and the second in the fourth.

There were delays, of course. In May 1974, the Military Industrial Commission noted: "The Taganrog Mechanical Plant has failed to complete the two Korshun-equipped Tu-142M aircraft on schedule [then the fourth quarter of 1973], there have been slipped schedules on the technical records – which were completed a year behind schedule, the Ministries of Aircraft and Radioelectronic Industries have failed to supply VNPK-154s to the Taganrog plant, etc." It was not until 4 November 1975 that test pilot I. K. Vedernikov performed the first flight. The first-stage tests involved three aircraft (Nos 4243, 4244 and 4264) from first-flight date to 23 October 1977. Those trials resulted in recommendations by the navy and air force commanders-in-chief, and the aviation industry minister to launch construction of the Tu-142M. At the time, only seven of the 31 performance requirements had been met. The bulk of the second-stage trials were completed by November 1978.

In a governmental resolution, dated 19 November 1980, the Tu-142M long-range ASW aircraft was officially fielded with the Naval Aviation with the following performance characteristics:

- service range of 12000 km (7,457 miles) at a 185-tonne (182-ton) take-off weight and five per cent reserves

Flying the Tu-142

There were no significant differences between flying the Tu-95RTs and Tu-142, which made the conversion smooth, but not without some peculiarities.

Taxiing to the holding point is done with all engines running, but only the controls of the two inboard engines are used. Sharp turns are out of the question due to the considerable lateral load on the outer wheels and the landing gear's shock strut. At a speed of 5-10 km/h (3-6 mph) the turn radius is at least 15 m (50 ft), growing to at least 50 m (165 ft) as the speed increases. Having taxied to the standing start, the flaps are extended to the take-off position of 27°, with the stabiliser going into the 2° position. As soon as the flaps begin extending, the nosewheel is automatically restricted to a turning angle of 8°.

With a 130-tonne (128-ton) take-off weight, the take-off is performed with the engines in the normal

power level (NPL) mode. If the runway is less than 2500 m (8,200 ft) in length, or the aircraft weighs over 130 tonnes, the full-thrust take-off mode is resorted to.

During the first half of the run, direction is maintained by nose wheel steering and brakes, while the rudder is used when the aircraft picks up speed to 130-150 km/h (81-93 mph). In a 130-tonne take-off, when the speed is 10-15 km/h (6-9 mph) lower than the lift-off speed, the nose wheel lifts off at an angle of 5-6°, but at a heavier weight it rises to 6-8°. At some airfields with low-quality runway surfacing (for instance, Khorol naval air station in the Pacific Fleet region) crews often report rather hard jolts when crossing the joints of the concrete slabs of the runway.

When taking off with the maximum take-off weight, the pilot has to pull the yoke back all the way with a load of 3-4 kg (6.6-8.8 lb) – the aircraft then pulls up its nose at a speed of 290-300 km/h (180-186 mph), with the load on the yoke decreasing. With the normal take-off weight at 130 tonnes, lift-off speed is 270-275 km/h (168-171 mph). Heavier take-

offs require a lift-off speed of 300-310 km/h (186-193 mph). Critical decision speed during the run is 250 km/h (155 mph): if an engine fails and the runway is longer than 3500 m (11,483 ft), then the run should be continued. If the runway is shorter, the take-off should be aborted.

Taking off can be difficult in a crosswind owing to the large empennage and fuselage, which have a tendency to weathercock. Furthermore, the anhedral of the wing (which facilitates rolling manoeuvres), places an extra load on the undercarriage on the side the wind is coming from. This turns the aircraft towards the wind, too. Therefore, direction during the take-off run is maintained by using brake pedals and pre-emptive acceleration of the outer engine on the side the wind comes from. The aircraft also tends to turn during the lift-off, therefore the nose wheel is lifted off at high speed to minimise this effect.

At an altitude of 10-15 m (33-50 ft) the wheels are braked and landing gear is retracted to prevent vibration. During the retraction process the bogies somersault and drag grows considerably, which results in a reduction in forward and vertical speed. With the gear retracted, the centre of gravity shifts 2-3 per cent rearwards and a pitching moment appears, to compensate for which the stabiliser is moved from the take-off position into the flight one. The engines are switched to the normal thrust mode. Customarily, the landing gear remains extended for circuits. Flaps are retracted at an altitude of at least 100 m (328 ft) in two or three stages, with the retraction of the flaps on both wings being carefully

The 240th GvOSAP (Guards Independent Mixed Aviation Regiment) at Ostrov is the AVMF's training unit for shore-based patrol and attack aircraft, with several types on charge. Among the fleet are a handful of 'Bear-Fs', including this Tu-142MK seen at the base's open day in July 2001.

- 4-hour 10-minute loiter time 4000 km (2,485 miles) from base
- 855-km/h (531-mph) maximum speed
- 735-km/h (457-mph) cruising speed
- 2530-m (8,300-ft) take-off run
- 1830-m (6,004-ft) landing roll at 130 tonnes (127.9 tons)

The aircraft had a wing span of 50 m (164 ft), was 53.1 m (174 ft 2 in) long and 13.6 m (44 ft 7 in) high, while its maximum take-off weight accounted for 185000 kg (407,848 lb), with fuel capacity equalling 86000 kg (189,594 lb) and payload totalling 4395 kg (9,689 lb). Maximum payload was 9000 kg (19,841 lb).

The 'complex' comprised the aircraft with its organic avionics (navigation aids, hydrologic reconnaissance equipment, Strela-142 communications suite, Sayany-M ECM system), the 2Kn-K Korshun-K ASW surveillance and targeting system (the 2Kn-K was mounted on aircraft No. 4293, while aircraft No. 4244's surveillance and targeting system was called Korshun, and those of aircraft Nos 4243, 4291 and 4292 was dubbed Kn-K), the MMS-106 Ladoga magnetometer and ground test equipment. Despite a higher degree of automation, the crew complement grew to total 11 personnel.

As compared to the 1971-vintage stretched-cockpit Tu-142, the Tu-142M's primary performance and dimensions remained relatively unchanged, with some minor alterations. Take-off weight rose and the forward cockpit was redesigned to house nine personnel, rather than the earlier eight. They were accommodated in seats with their backs inclined at 45°, while the pilots' seats were fitted with electric drives to move them fore and aft by 160-220 mm (6.3-8.7 in). Footboards and kneeboards were provided to reduce fatigue. The altered inclination of the instrument panel enhanced its visibility for the pilots. Two navigator/tactical action officers remained seated facing the tail, which proved to be inconvenient and increased fatigue. At the pilots' station the cockpit was widened by 180 mm (7 in) and an enlarged hatch provided some improvement in emergency escape. The view angle over the nose was increased by 1.5°, important for landing.

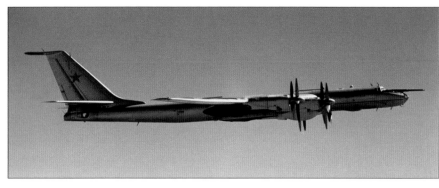

In the fuselage mid-section the surveillance and targeting system was fitted with a new fairing and the main cargo bay was drastically redesigned. The second cargo bay was merged with the technical compartment, and its lower part modified to serve as a bay for small-size bombs used as ESGs. The upper section of the bay accommodated components of the 2Kn-K, Kvadrat-2 ELINT system, communications suite, and other systems.

Revised controls

Controls differed only slightly from those of the Tu-142, for instance, the yoke travel was reduced and it was provided with a loading device generating an extra load on the yoke at high angle of attack, when fed relevant signals by the AUASP-142 sideslip and g-load automatic device. The Ka-142 was retained to enhance stability and controllability. To ensure sufficient power for the autopilot's actuators to operate the control surfaces, the elevators were equipped with extra flutter tabs and the trailing edges of the rudder and ailerons were modified. Control of flaps, stabilisers and primary systems was retained from the baseline variant.

A new NPK-142M flight navigation system was installed, comprising a main and back-up sub-systems. The main sub-system centred around an astro-inertial navigation system with an automatic correction device, the L14MA computer and TsVM-10TS-42 single-address 125,000-operations

Cruising at medium altitude, a Tu-142M/MK displays this version's most distinctive feature: the slightly upturned MMS-106 Ladoga MAD mounted at the top of the fin. Two Tu-142s had been used to test this equipment which, as fitted to the Tu-142M prototype (4243), was initially aligned with the top of the fin, rather than angled upwards. The Ladoga proved troublesome at first, requiring several systems to be switched off before it could be used, and was of limited tactical value.

---

synchronised. Resulting pitch changes are compensated by retrimming. To save fuel, the aircraft flies to its assigned zone in a continuous climb. Having reached 7100 m (23,294 ft), the aircraft continues its climb while maintaining Mach 0.63 – about 700 km/h (435 mph).

Some helicopters with a tail rotor are prone to what is called 'dynamic drift'. A similar phenomenon is featured by the Tu-142 as well, with the aircraft tending to deviate from its course to the right. This is due to the fact that the front propeller rotates to the right, while the rear one rotates in the opposite direction. The rear propeller both straightens the front propeller's vortex out and deflects it to the left. The offset vortex hits the vertical tail and turns the aircraft to the right. The trend can be corrected via the rudder's trim tab or ailerons.

Return from the patrol zone is performed at an altitude of 11000 m (36,090 ft). It is recommended that high-altitude flights in turbulent conditions be carried out at Mach 0.7, with the rudder and elevators to be operated smoothly. When entering a high temperature area (for example, when crossing the Atlantic), the aircraft can lose speed unless the engines' rpm is increased or altitude reduced. With the aircraft flying on three engines, its fuel consumption per kilometre rises by 3 per cent.

Unless there are restrictions, the commencement point and mode of descent are of special importance. In a powered descent from 11000 m (36,090 ft) to 500 m (1,640 ft), with the throttle controls moved to the trip catch (18°), the Tu-142 will cover 290 km

During the landing approach minor course corrections can be effected by rudder, without altering the wings-level attitude. The aircraft is prone to weather-cocking once on the runway, especially during the take-off run. At over 100 tons typical landing weight, touchdown is usually 'firm'.

(180 miles) in 26 minutes, burning 1550 kg (3,417 lb) of Avgas in the process. However, if the engines are throttled back completely for the descent, the aircraft will burn 400 kg (882 lb) of fuel to cover 150 km (93 miles) in 11 minutes. If this is followed by no further descent, the aircraft will cover another 230 km (143 miles) with 1150 kg (2,535 lb) of fuel used up, thus adding a distance of 90 km (56 miles) for the same amount of fuel.

Landing gear is deployed at 400 km/h (248 mph) or below, with the stabiliser being set at 2°. Between the downwind and base legs of the circuit (when descending after a circuit, the flaps deploy at 20°) the speed is set at 350-370 km/h (217-230 mph). After turning from base to final, the flaps are deflected to 27°, the speed drops down to 330-340 km/h (205-211 mph) and the speed of descent becomes 2-3 m (6.5-10 ft) per second with the outboard engines being set at the trip catch. Before flying past the outer marker, the flaps are extended to 35° while the stabiliser is set at 4°.

Owing to a low lateral stability reserve, directional errors made during the landing approach can be

remedied by 3-5° turns without rolling. The aircraft features low lateral stability, which makes the landing approach with a crosswind much easier to perform, and the drift can be rectified both by altering the course and by rolling. The latter does not cause the oscillations from one wing to the other ('Dutch roll'), for which the Tu-16 was notorious. The outer marker is overflown at an altitude of 200-220 m (656-722 ft) at a speed of 300-310 km/h (186-193 mph), which then decays to 270-280 km/h (168 mph-174 mph), with the vertical speed increasing to 3-4 m (10-13 ft) per second. The middle marker is overflown at an altitude of 70-80 m (230-262 ft).

Flare-out begins at an altitude of 10-15 m (33-50 ft), with the inboard engines being set at trip catches. At a typical weight of 106 tonnes (104.3 tons) touchdown occurs typically at 237 km/h (147 mph) at an angle of 8°. Following the nose wheel touching, the inboard engine controls are throttled back completely and the propellers are taken off the catch. The outboard engine controls are throttled back somewhere between 180-200 km/h (112-124 mph) to further decelerate the aircraft.

Above: As with the Tu-95RTs 'Bear-Ds' of the 392nd ODRAP before them, 76th OPLAP DD 'Bear-Fs' deployed from Kipelovo to San Antonio air base, near Havana, for operations in the west Atlantic. Here a Tu-142M is escorted along the eastern seaboard of the United States by an F-15A from the Langley-based 48th Fighter Interceptor Squadron.

Far right: This view highlights the prominent wing fences on the broad wings of the Tu-142MK. The conduit along the starboard side of the forward fuselage routes fuel from the probe to the main tanks.

Kipelovo air base, situated roughly halfway between Moscow and Archangelsk (the nearest major town is Vologda), is home to the 76th OPLAP DD, which has three squadrons assigned. Two fly the Tu-142MK/MZ and one operates the Tu-142MR. Thirty-two 'Bears' – almost the entire 76th OPLAP DD fleet – are visible in this line-up. In the middle of the line is a single Be-12, next to which is one of the Tu-142MR 'Bear-J' communications relay aircraft. Two more 'Bears' are visible on a dispersal in the woods, including another Tu-142MR.

per minute central computer. The back-up sub-system consisted of a VNPK-154 computer, DISS-7 Doppler system, Rumb-1B inertial heading and attitude reference system and a number of self-contained systems, for example, the long- and short-range radio navigation system, radar altimeters, automatic radio compasses and the on-board portion of the Os-1 landing system. Redundancy was believed to enhance the system's reliability.

According to calculations, the main subsystem was to maintain an accuracy in the region of 5-10 km (3-6 miles) per flight hour. The backup subsystem's expected accuracy was 1.5-2.5 per cent of the range. It took the NPK-142M at least an hour to be prepared for a mission. When switched on, the system fed the aircraft's initial position data to the surveillance and targeting system, and then complemented them with data on its speed, heading, altitude, roll and pitch.

The flight system included the Bort-42 flight director control system and AP-14PS autopilot, providing semi-automatic and automatic flight based on various input signals fed by the navigation system and 2Kn-K ASW surveillance and targeting system. The Strela-142M communications system was designed to provide interphone communications, land command post and ship communications, and also to record all incoming and outgoing voice and data traffic. The weapons suite was augmented with 16 multiple racks in the form of pods housing RGB-75 and RGB-15 buoy holders. Also, the weapons suite included another three types of multiple racks to mount RGB-25s, RGB-55As, bombs and torpedoes. The new second bay housed a container for various ESGs.

Elements of the 2Kn-K

Unlike the Berkut ASW system, the 2Kn-K system was supposed to detect submarines in both the acoustic and infrasonic wavebands. It comprises onboard equipment, radio-sonobuoys and MGAB small-size air bombs. Onboard equipment is built around four subsystems – radar (RLP), radiohydroacoustic (RGP), computer (BVP) and tactical data display (POTO). Also, it includes the A-081 automatic radio compass and a container housing the system's control panels. The MMS-106 Ladoga magnetometer and Nerchinsk sonic speed measurement system, as well as communica-

tions, release control and NPK-142M systems, operate in conjunction with the 2Kn-K.

The radar subsystem's transmitter emits sounding and coded signals, with variable frequency. The radar's output is 80 kW with a horizontal beam width of 1°, polarisation is both vertical and horizontal, and surveillance can be undertaken either in a specific sector to one side or across 360°. The radar can contact the beacons of sonobuoys at a range of 40-50 km (25-31 miles).

The Kayra-P (Kr-P) radiohydroacoustic subsystem provides the reception, visual and audio display and processing of data uplinked by sonobuoys and the Nerchinsk system, and feeds it to the POTO and BVP subsystems. It comprises units served by two radiohydro-acoustic subsystem (RGP) operators, each of which has two Kr-4 television displays. One of the screens displays data from four buoys, while the other can show data from the POTO or adjacent operator's workplace. Displayed imagery depends on the type of buoys and their operating modes – manual or automatic.

If the automatic mode fails to establish communications with the buoys, the Kr-4 displays 24 noise boxes. With a buoy transmitting its carrier frequency signal, a horizontal line appears in the relevant box, to be crossed by a vertical line following the arrival of the 'target' signal. The buoy's signal is fed to the processor, which operates in conjunction with the operative recorder for power processing or spectral analysis. Power processing allows an evaluation of the signal and a pass curve target blip on the display. Fed by the operative recorder, the Kr-4 displays show incoming signals processed in to the form of spectrograms of the noises detected, echograms indicating the submarine's position, and oscillograms showing the alteration of the level and heading of hydroacoustic signals.

Thus, the operators are presented with processed data from the buoys and can deduce whether a submarine has been detected or not, based on its typical signatures, and, if so, get a fix on it and gauge the nature of its operations.

Kayra-P also incorporates the 15A and 15AK modes for distinguishing the direct signal from an ESG explosion and an echo from the submarine. The 15A mode is designed for receiving signals from MGAB-OZ ESGs, when the depth in the designated area exceeds 5000 m (16,400 ft) and the range to the submarine is less than that. The 15AK mode is intended for processing data generated by detonating MGAB-LZ and MGAB-SZ ESGs. Communication with buoys is handled using 56 communications frequencies at a range of up to 80 km (50 miles) and at a flight altitude of 1500 m (4,920 ft).

Data fed by control panels and all 2Kn-K devices is processed by the BVP subsystem, which comprises an Argon-15 computer with a 208,000 short, addition-type operation capacity. The computer performs dead reckoning of the aircraft's position, buoy impact points and the target's movement, swaps data with other aircraft via the BSS datalink and issues aircraft control commands to the PNK autopilot. Control of the BVP is usually performed by the navigator, although sometimes the RGP operators and nav/TAOs work the system.

A tactical display is provided by the POTO subsystem, which also has an Argon-15 computer. The navigator's and pilot's displays, as well as those of the two RGP operators, show the aircraft's position, ground vector, buoy impact points, position of other assets, and possible submarine locations represented by two-digit signs, vectors and circles. The maximum area displayed by the POTO covers 200 km (124 miles) radius. Having compiled the tactical display, the POTO operates as a one-address computer,

swapping data with connected equipment with the exception of the BVP, which exchanges data with the POTO on cue from the BVP itself. An onboard command transmitter is used to prompt RGB-55A sonobuoys to transmit.

Water characteristics, notably the speed of sound through it, are determined using the Nerchinsk measuring system, which operates in conjunction with Kr-P receivers. It comprises an RTB-91 four-buoy bathythermograph device, with the buoys measuring water temperature 200 m (656 ft) down. The Strela-142M communications system, in conjunction with the 2Kn-K, provides tactical data exchange in the area between aircraft, and between aircraft and shore-based command posts.

The 2Kn-K system includes four types of buoys as search assets: RGB-75, RGB-15, RGB-25 and RGB-55A. The Berkut system's sonobuoys could be used as well.

■ **RGB-75 – passive non-directional:** designed for initial submarine search via the submarines' 2-60 GHz infrasonic waveband signatures. The kit comprises 24 RGB-75 sonobuoys whose transmitters operate continuously.

Below: Photographed from a NATO fighter, a 'Mod 3 Foxtrot' has its main stores bay open. In the 1970s and 1980s, when SLBMs formed the principal line of strategic deterrence, no game was more serious than underwater warfare, and chances like this for intelligence-gathering were eagerly taken. Fighter crews were ordered to get in close with hand-held cameras to try and get photos of what the 'Bear' held in its belly. During several tense intercepts, fighters were reportedly 'bombed' with sonobuoys as they passed underneath.

In 1976 the Indian Navy received five radar-equipped Lockheed Constellations from the Air Force to provide a long-range maritime patrol capability over the Arabian Sea and Indian Ocean. The 'Connies' soldiered on until 1984 when they could no longer operate effectively. Their withdrawal left a considerable gap in India's maritime surveillance effort, which needed to be filled with some urgency. In 1986 the Tu-142 was chosen to restore the lost capability, and from 30 March 1988 to October that year eight 'Bear-F Mod 3s' were delivered. The aircraft were essentially similar to the standard Tu-142MK, but had some sensitive items of equipment either deleted or downgraded for export. They were designated Tu-142ME, or Tu-142MK-E in some sources.

Indian Naval Air Squadron (INAS) 312 'Albatross' had operated the Constellations, and was chosen to fly the 'Bears'. The Tu-142MEs wear a depiction of the ocean-going bird on the nose, as displayed by this aircraft during a visit to Russia, probably for overhaul.

Approach to the marker is performed by the A-081 radio compass. The buoys mount no beacons, so their impact points are recorded by the BVP. Submarine acquisition range was supposed to equal 20-30 km (12.5-18.5 miles). Each buoy lasts four to five hours, weighs 9.5 kg (21 lb) and its hydrophone submerges to 150 m (492 ft).

■ **RGB-15 – passive non-directional:** designed to spot submarines by their acoustic signature in the infrasonic and sonic wavebands (2-5,000 Hz), as well as search and pinpoint submarines in conjunction with ESGs. The kit consists of 16 continuous-operation sonobuoys. The airborne operator sets the threshold level of data reception, based on the average noise level from all sonobuoys deployed. Again, the buoys have no beacons. Prompted by the radar, buoys perform negative modulation of the data transmitter's carrier frequency (a similar design was used by the US Navy's AN/SSQ-23 sonobuoys) and the radar scope displays a blip similar to that fed by the beacon. On board the aircraft the Kr-P equipment is used to analyse the spectrum of the signals in the 2-60 Hz waveband visually, and up to 5,000 Hz waveband by ear. When ESGs are used, RGB-15s receive direct signals and echoes from submarines, at a range of 5-10 km (3-6 miles). When operating without ESGs, the RGB-15's range is three to four times shorter. The RGB-15 weighs 9.5 kg (21 lb) and operates for 2 hours, with its hydrophone dropping down to 20, 150 or 400 m (66, 492 or 1,312 ft).

■ **RGB-25 – passive directional:** used to pinpoint a submarine and gauge its movement, the RGB-25 operates at 11 kHz. The buoy submerges down to 20 or 150 m (66 or 492 ft) where it is rotated at 6-12 rpm by an electro-mechanical drive to scan the area. Its bearing detection accuracy is 3°, endurance amounts to at least 40 minutes and weight is 45 kg (99 lb). The radio-frequency kit consists of 10 buoys fitted with self-contained beacons.

■ **RGB-55A – active non-directional:** designed to pinpoint low-noise submarines and gauge their operating

patterns before they attack, or to track them briefly. It is also effective in measuring the radial component of a submarine's speed. Following its splashdown, the buoy operates in the passive mode. Only after the aircraft issues a relevant command do the buoys begin 'pinging' with 150, 300 or 600-microsecond acoustic pulses. Echoes are relayed back to the aircraft. Data from two or three sonobuoys provide the fix on the submarine, and describe its pattern of movement. The kit includes 16 sonobuoys, split into four subkits. The 55-kg (121-lb) buoy lasts for up to an hour and deploys its acoustic system down to 20 or 200 m (66 or 656 ft).

When searching for submarines with RGB-15 buoys, three types of ESG can be used: the MGAB-OZ, MGAB-LZ and MGAB-SZ. The -OZ weighs 200 or 800 g (7 or 28 oz) and is used in deep-water areas to pinpoint submarines at ranges from the buoy equal to the distance to the bottom. It detonates at 25, 150 or 400 m (82, 492 or 1,312 ft). The -LZ is employed in areas of ocean with a flat bed and features a 2-m (6-ft 7-in) long, 100-g (3.5-oz) string charge. The charge is flushed out of the bomb casing by water pressure and is detonated at a predesignated depth. The MGAB-SZ bomb is designed for use in challenging hydrologic environments and houses a 200-g (7-oz) 40-coil spiral charge. When set off, the charge generates a series of 4,000-Hz pulses whose number depends on that of the coils. The detonation depth includes 20, 150 and 400 m (82, 492 or 1,312 ft). The aircraft carries 11 such charges.

Magnetic anomaly detection is undertaken by the MS-106 Ladoga system. The magnetometer is a ferrosound design consisting of a magnetic sensor in the upper vertical fin, an orienting system, a measuring device and other support devices. It differs from its predecessors in the two filters it utilises, one of which is used for search and the other for compensating for the aircraft's magnetic fields. The compensation system consists of three coils positioned along the aircraft's axes. The magnetometer's recorder receives signals for the previous 10 seconds, which facilitates their identification but causes a delay in their registration. The acquisition signal is displayed by the 'Signal Signature' panel, and by the magnetometer recorder's chart strip. The magnetometer acquisition range depends on a number of variable quantities but is roughly 600-700 m (656 to 765 yards). To operate the MS-106 in the early days, the crew had to switch off the generators of the first and fourth engines, the hydraulic pump, the autopilot and some other equipment. Later, the electric circuitry was improved.

Operational loadout

Tu-142Ms can operate in both the patrol, and seek-and-destroy configurations. For the latter they normally carry 66 RGB-75s, 44 RGB-15s, 10 RGB-25s, 15 RGB-55As, three AT-2M torpedoes and APR-1 or APR-2 ASW missiles. When RGB-15s are used for initial search with the use of ESGs, the K-142M container is loaded with up to 240 MGAB-LZ or MGAB-OZ charges, and 11 MGAB-SZs. Air-launched mines can be carried too.

The APR-2 anti-submarine torpedo boasts a sophisticated guidance package. After dropping it stabilises its roll and descends on a parachute with a vertical speed of 50 m (164 ft) per second. Following splashdown, the first-stage lock switches off, the command unit kicks in and the missile begins searching in a spiral manner with its engine off at an angular speed of 20° per second. The homer operates in the active/passive mode. With a target acquired, the engine starts and the missile homes in on its target. If no

Right: INAS 312 initially flew from INS Hansa at Goa-Dabolim, from where it was ideally placed to cover the seas to the west and south of India. This base ('DAB' tailcode) also housed the Il-38 'Mays' of INAS 315.

target is detected, the missile continues its search on a preset programme.

Naturally, the Tu-142M's ASW techniques underwent some radical enough modifications, which only added workload for the aircrew. Unlike the Tu-142, the Tu-142M employs the NPK-142M for flying to the designated zone. The 2Kn-K system in this case is not used. Entering a 1200 x 1200-km (745 x 745-mile) tactical zone, the BVP and POTO subsystems are switched on. The crew can use the BSS-142 to get situation updates received by the BVP and displayed by the POTO. Prior to that, the search area and its approaches are scanned with the radar for ships, whose noise would interfere with the sub hunt. In hunting for submarines in a designated area, sonobuoys are used, the magnetometer only employed on rare occasion.

'Swinging Tacks' and 'Converging (Diverging) Box' techniques are performed to deploy sonobuoys. Linear barriers are deployed by approaching a predesignated point from either a predetermined or spontaneous direction. To monitor the buoys, the 'Fixed Dimension Circuit Flight' technique is used, as with the Berkut system. If a submarine has to be pinpointed following its detection by RGB-75s and before tracking begins, RGB-15s or RGB-1As are dropped in a closed line via the 'Envelopment' technique. Further tracking is performed via the 'Semi-envelopment' or 'Linear Barrier' techniques, with the use of whatever buoys are available. To search and track stealthy submarines, RGB-15 sonobuoys were supposed to be used in concert with ESGs, or RGB-55As in the active mode. However, given the limited number of the latter, tracking with them was often not feasible.

At all stages of searching and tracking, RGP operators and the navigator process situational data through the use of the BVP and POTO, and perform visual and audio target evaluation and classification. Depending on the tactical situation, targets are engaged following their tracking or immediately after they have been detected and pinpointed. With the mission in the tactical area accomplished, the aircraft returns to base the way it does after a flight to a predesignated area. In combat, elements of the mission would have been accomplished in a different fashion.

Tu-142M/MK in service

In production at Taganrog from 1978, Tu-142Ms began entering the inventory of the 76th OPLAP DD of the Northern Fleet in 1979. The new system, with its numerous attendant 'bugs', slowed the conversion tempo. Snags were encountered by both air and ground crews. Trials had failed to reveal all the flaws of the surveillance and targeting system, which was justified officially by insufficient funds for testing. However, the real reasons were something else. It had become a general practice that even relatively unsophisticated systems would be fielded with loads of deficiencies.

When the Zarechye system development began, the Tu-142M with its Kn-K system was redesignated as the Tu-142MK, while the new variant with the Zarechye system was designated Tu-142MZ.

Above: The Indian 'Bear' population moved out of Dabolim to Arrakonam, resulting in a change of tailcode to 'ARK'. The fleet has been widely used in support of Indian Navy surface operations, especially during times of tension with Pakistan.

Above left: A Tu-142ME from INAS 312 is escorted by a pair of Sea Harriers from INAS 300, shore-based at INS Hansa. The 'Bear' squadron is thought to have lost one aircraft in an accident.

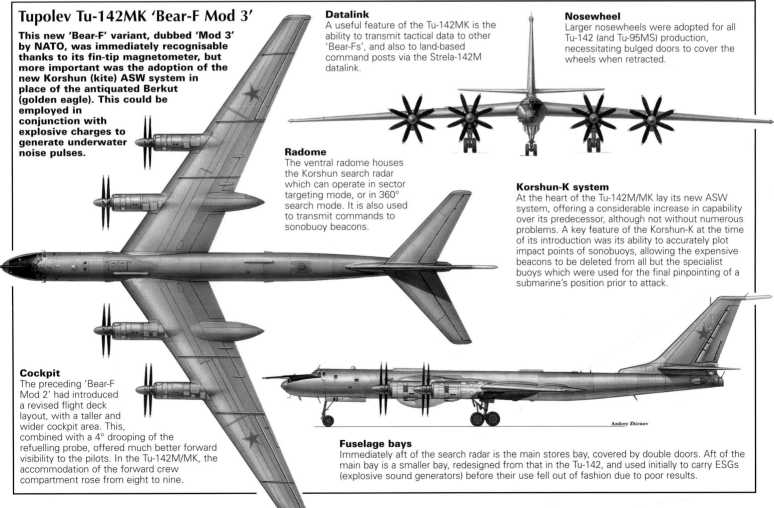

Tupolev Tu-142MK 'Bear-F Mod 3'

This new 'Bear-F' variant, dubbed 'Mod 3' by NATO, was immediately recognisable thanks to its fin-tip magnetometer, but more important was the adoption of the new Korshun (kite) ASW system in place of the antiquated Berkut (golden eagle) system. This could be employed in conjunction with explosive charges to generate underwater noise pulses.

Datalink
A useful feature of the Tu-142MK is the ability to transmit tactical data to other 'Bear-Fs', and also to land-based command posts via the Strela-142M datalink.

Nosewheel
Larger nosewheels were adopted for all Tu-142 (and Tu-95MS) production, necessitating bulged doors to cover the wheels when retracted.

Radome
The ventral radome houses the Korshun search radar which can operate in sector targeting mode, or in 360° search mode. It is also used to transmit commands to sonobuoy beacons.

Korshun-K system
At the heart of the Tu-142M/MK lay its new ASW system, offering a considerable increase in capability over its predecessor, although not without numerous problems. A key feature of the Korshun-K at the time of its introduction was its ability to accurately plot impact points of sonobuoys, allowing the expensive beacons to be deleted from all but the specialist buoys which were used for the final pinpointing of a submarine's position prior to attack.

Cockpit
The preceding 'Bear-F Mod 2' had introduced a revised flight deck layout, with a taller and wider cockpit area. This, combined with a 4° drooping of the refuelling probe, offered much better forward visibility to the pilots. In the Tu-142M/MK, the accommodation of the forward crew compartment rose from eight to nine.

Andrey Zhirnov

Fuselage bays
Immediately aft of the search radar is the main stores bay, covered by double doors. Aft of the main bay is a smaller bay, redesigned from that in the Tu-142, and used initially to carry ESGs (explosive sound generators) before their use fell out of fashion due to poor results.

With some experience in operating the Tu-142MK gained, it became possible to evaluate its capability. As was expected, submarine detection in medium and heavy shipping environments became much more difficult. At least 70 per cent of the submarines spotted by RGB-75 sonobuoys were acquired through spectral analysis of distinguishing signatures by means of discrete components. Problems emerged as far as automatic contact classification was concerned, with operators having to make drawings of noise spectra seen on displays, and then compare them with new displays during another cycle. A decision on a target's presence would be made on the basis of stable emergence of new spectral components from different buoys plotted against the earlier background. This technique was time-consuming and prone to errors. Operations revealed that in 20-30 per cent of contacts, signal processing by different Kr-P channels was not identical. The developer recommended the signals be controlled by means of a single RGB-75 and eliminate the channels providing different results. However, in such a case one or more channels would be precluded from data processing.

Since the RGB-75 range proved to be less than advertised, search techniques had to be revised: following an RGB-75 buoy kit deployment, the RGB-15 kit would be deployed to avoid data channel interference. In a couple of hours it had to be updated. This necessitated the expansion of the RGB-75's frequency channels at least twofold. When an RGB-15 sonobuoy contacted a submarine, its reaction time was 24 seconds: that of an RGB-75 was 400-600 seconds.

Other snags were hit during conversion to the RGB-15 and ESGs. To expand the areas being scanned, a buoy and an ESG had to be dropped at the same place, which reduced bottom interference but caused ESGs to splashdown and detonate before the buoys could kick in. Hence,

to deploy an ESG close to a buoy, the aircraft had to make another pass at least 4-6 minutes later. In shallows less than 1000 m (3,280 ft), ESGs were recommended to be detonated at 2-3 km (1.24-1.86 miles) away from the sonobuoy to produce an elliptical coverage area, whose focuses were the buoy and the ESG.

Echoes were normally received against a background of interference, therefore two to five ESGs had to dropped to the same point to get a reliable picture. For an operator to single out an echo via the audio channel, he had to be properly trained and have an ear for music. Low reliability, problems with echo selection, search signatures and other reasons led the air branches of the Fleets to virtually abandon ESG-equipped sonobuoys.

There were other problems. For instance, the RGB-55A's capabilities failed to be used to the fullest. Duration of an echo has to be at least 350-450 milliseconds for a human to be able to discern a difference in its tone. Such a period provides a chance to spot the Doppler effect. However, this duration was unavailable. Flying crews noted a considerable flaw by the developer – the navigator was deprived of a Kr-P display and was unable to participate in evaluating the hydroacoustic situation. The RLP subsystem got its share of flak for the size of the gate in the radar scope, which prevented efficient targeting when attacking pinpoint targets.

First operational forays

Tu-142Ms launched routine operations under combat duty plans in early 1979, with the first unidentified submarine being detected and tracked for 70 minutes as early as April the same year. In early 1981, search operations spanned 4200 km (2,610 miles) but the duration of flights had to be reduced owing to unpredictable weather in the north. The sorties were given thorough after-action reviews to gauge actual fuel consumption and train crews for transatlantic flights. In doing so, account was taken of the fact that the Tu-142M's fuel consumption per hour had grown by 500 kg (1,102 lb) from the Tu-142's 5500 kg (12,125 lb).

On 14 March 1983 a pair of Tu-142Ms made the type's first sortie to Cuba's capital city of Havana. Deployed to Cuban airfields, aircrews were searching for submarines in the Sargasso Sea and reported six submarines detected and tracked for a total of 11 hours 40 minutes. Sorties to Cuban airfields lasted till 1984, with variable frequency, and were terminated due to a decision made to have sonobuoys improved.

In 1984, several Tu-142s were outfitted with Uzor-5V 16-channel FM data recorders. Analysis of results provided the grounds to reproach the buoy developer over its product's poor information capability and efficiency. A 1985 exercise proved that crews were often unable to correctly evaluate the contact authenticity for reasons beyond their control. In the next year, a meeting held by the minister of aircraft industry took a decision to conduct additional trials.

These trials proved that the RGB-25 and RGB-75 were inefficient in sea states 3 to 5, and technical requirements had to be worked out for their replacement. The Tu-142M fleet was scheduled for improvement by 1989, following preliminary tests in 1988. At the same meeting a decision was made to replace the RGB-75 and RGB-15 with the common buoy RGB-16, operating in both continuous emission and autostart modes.

In other words, it was admitted that the 2Kn-K surveillance and targeting system failed to meet expectations. It, however, was a quantum leap compared with the Berkut, since it incorporated low-frequency and infrasonic buoys, and ESGs. The RGB-75 and RGB-15 designs had become cheaper and simpler by abandoning the beacon and autostart circuitry, there were more advanced data processing techniques, and the bulky RGB-3 had been replaced by the long-range RGB-55A. 2Kn-K gave the crews an opportunity to measure the speed of sound in water, while the tactical situation was shown on displays and could be datalinked automatically.

Of course, the main criticisms should have been taken by the research institutes and the customer organisations, which erroneously portrayed foreign-made submarines as very noisy (it is possible that it was done in coordination with the industry). Naturally, there was nobody to lay the blame for that on.

This was not the only problem. When long-range missions began, the air complex's deficiencies became obvious. Aircrews reported that the operation of the computer within the NPK-142M was below par seven or eight times out of 10. Navigators had to continuously enter corrections, set various measuring devices and correlate their readings. Over a brief period of operation, all three channels of the inertial attitude and reference system in the backup navigational loop failed together over two dozen times, leaving the pilots' and navigators' instrument unable to display the heading. This prompted numerous requests for a backup compass system. Crews asked for the ANP-3V, noting caustically enough that it would be a good replacement for the whole NPK-142M in terms of accuracy. Quite reasonable was the suggestion that the aircraft be outfitted with satellite navigation aids.

As the strategic scenario evolved, so the ASW aircraft fleet's task was modified. Along with developing new foreign submarine patrol areas, supporting the deployment and combat patrols of friendly 'boomers' and some other missions climbed high on the agenda.

The directive of the chief of naval operations, dated 30 October 1983, ordered the 35th ASW Long-Range Air Division activated before 31 December 1983 to comprise the 76th and 135th ASW Air Regiments. Its command was assumed by Colonel Akporisov, who later became the Naval Aviation's chief of staff as a lieutenant-general. There was no need at all to set up such a fancy unit, the reason for its activation was never revealed and the outfit itself was disbanded soon.

'Bears' for India

In 1988, eight Tu-142MKs, redesignated as Tu-142ME, were delivered to the Indian Navy as the only 'Bears' to be exported. They differed from the baseline variant in minor modifications to their avionics suites. They were delivered

Having served in a natural metal finish for most of its career, the naval 'Bear' fleet began to adopt an all-over anti-corrosion grey scheme in the late 1990s. Dielectric panels for antennas and the Ladoga MAD remained in white. A feature of all but the earliest Tu-142s is a white dome above the forward cabin, which houses a remotely controlled sextant for the astro-navigation system. In the Tu-95MS bomber this is replaced by a glazed dome.

Tu-142 'Bear-F' losses

The accident rate of the Tu-142 aircraft has turned out to be very low: for 100,000 hours of flying time, there would only be 3.5 accidents, including two crashes, as detailed below.

6 August 1976: occurred during a wide-approach traffic pattern training flight by Lieutenant Khazagerov, a first pilot candidate, and Major Morozov, a pilot instructor in the 76th independent long-range ASW air regiment of the Soviet Air Force. The report states that 15 minutes after take-off the crew detected a malfunction and started to go through the landing pattern sequence. The aircraft landed at a speed exceeding that required for the given flight weight by 30-40 km/h (19-25 mph). Having rolled straight for 740 m (2,428 ft), the aircraft turned right, rolled off the runway and drove into a deep ditch. The aircraft broke apart with three men dying on the spot.

20 April 1984: two aircraft from the 310th independent long-range ASW air regiment of the Pacific Fleet's air branch were flying in combat formation to their patrol area. The emergency occurred an hour and a quarter after take-off at an altitude of 7200 m (23,622 ft) and a speed of 730 km/h (454 mph). At that time, the aircraft were flying over the Sea of Okhotsk. According to the wingman, the aircraft of the leader, Colonel V.I. Zubkov, started to descend following a blast of black smoke and a white plume on the starboard wing. In about a minute, the aircraft caught fire and started spiralling downward, with a bank increasing up to 60-70°, and crashed in the water, without recovering from its dive. The cause was considered to have been the failure of the No. 3 engine (possibly of the propeller blade or of a turbine disc), which resulted in the severing of the aileron control wires and rupturing of the fuel system, hence causing a fire and putting the aircraft into a spiralling dive from which recovery was impossible.

Some eight years elapsed between the Tu-142MZ's first flight in 1985 and its formal acceptance by the AVMF in 1993. Aircraft were built from new at Taganrog, and a few were completed before production was halted in 1994. The variant entered service with the 76th OPLAP DD at Kipelovo, where this example is seen next to Tu-142MKs. Although studied, further Tu-142 upgrades have been put on hold as the Kn-N/ Zarechye system of the MZ remains capable, and the airframes are young.

Above: This Tu-142MZ was put on display at Zhukovskiy. The MZ inherited new defensive armament from the Tu-95MS, with a four-gun barbette in place of the earlier two-gun armament. At the same time, the lateral observation blisters were deleted.

Right: Close-up of the MZ's nose shows the undernose fairing which mounts a variety of antennas. The 'pimple' below the refuelling probe houses an antenna for the Geran active jamming system. Further Geran antennas are mounted either side of the forward fuselage, and in the tail. Radar warning is provided by the Sayany-RT system. The hemispherical antenna at the rear of the undernose fairing, protected by a cover, is the Mak (poppy) infra-red detection system. Note the landing light in the fuselage, which hinges down from its recess for use.

Below: Production Tu-142MZs benefitted from advances in turbine technology and were fitted with NK-12MP engines, offering much greater reliability.

to INAS 312 at INS Hansa at Goa-Dabolim, adding 'DAB' to the fin to signify their base. Today they remain in service, wearing 'ARK' on the fin since they moved to Arrakonam.

Tu-142MZ

On 4 January 1977, the government passed another decree to upgrade the navy's ASW systems. On 17 July 1979, it was followed by the defence industry's decision to develop the Zarechye system, designed to detect and pinpoint submarines using the RGB-1A/-2 mass production buoys of the Berkut system, the RGB-25/-55 sonobuoys of the Korshun system, and the RGB-16/-26 sonobuoys of the Nashatyr-Nefrit system. The Zarechye system prototype was developed by the Leninets Scientific Production Association, in cooperation with the Kiev-based Underwater Instruments Research and Development Institute. They started developing the system on 2 October 1977 to meet joint performance requirements of the air force and navy, which wanted the system to be fitted on the Nashatyr-Nefrit system with follow-on improvements.

The Zarechye sonar system and its next-generation RGB-16, RGB-26, and RGB-36 sonobuoys were designed to process and display hydroacoustic data, measure its parameters, and provide the Kn-N ASW system with data on

detected submarines. New computers, a greater number of data channels, introduction of a separate observation channel for all sonobuoys deployed, and more sophisticated data processing techniques considerably increased the system's efficiency.

Flight tests were to have started in the second quarter of 1982, however they failed to meet the timeframe and the tests had to be put off until the third quarter of 1984. A proposal was made to fit the aircraft with the Sayany ECM system to counter enemy air defence radar- and infrared-guided missiles, and the Kh-35 anti-ship missile. The Sayany system had been under development for several years, and many of its designers had left for their native country (Israel). Flight tests got under way in April 1985 without either Sayany system or the Kh-35.

Tu-142M No. 42172 was the Zarechye prototype. In order to get greater amounts of test information, the aircraft was equipped with various devices for controlling and recording its aerodynamics, electrical equipment, trajectory changes, and the new Kn-N ASW system. Flight tests were conducted over the Black, the Barents, the Norwegian and Okhotsk seas. They ended in November 1986 with 71 sorties flown. An effort to carry out official state tests of the aircraft in August 1987 ended in failure due to some shortfalls in the operation of the RGB-26 sonobuoys. The tests were decided to be conducted in two stages: the first stage was to be carried out without RGB-26 sonobuoys, while the second one was to test the whole set of the aircraft equipment. The second stage of the tests, begun on 13 November 1987, was completed on 30 November 1988. However, the decree on fielding the upgraded anti-submarine system was issued only in 1993. Test reports emphasised that the efficiency of the upgraded Kn-N ASW system was 2 to 2.5 times greater than that of the 2Kn-K, while its kill probability had been increased by 20 per cent due to increased accuracy of detecting a submarine's movements.

Crews who had tested the Tu-142MZ stressed that should the NPK-142 fail, it would be possible to control the aircraft with two operating engines. It seemed quite reasonable to fit the aircraft with auxiliary power plants in order to make do without airfield power sources when getting ready for take-off, as well as softer seats and biostimulants to reduce crew fatigue during long flights. Test navigators pointed out that it was necessary to change the layout of workstations, since the NPK-142M no longer featured the VNPK-154 standby system. They also emphasised poor reliability of the navigation system computer (its failure time totalled nine hours out of 22). During the tests 124 depth bombs of various types were dropped, 24 of which failed to operate.

Production halt

The first Tu-142MZ rolled off the assembly lines in 1993 (the Tu-142M was being simultaneously modernised in maintenance units). At the same time, mass production of the Tu-142 aircraft was stopped in 1994. The Kuibyshev and Taganrog plants had manufactured between them a total of 100 Tu-142s in various versions.

Series Tu-142MZ aircraft differed slightly from the prototype: the NK-12MK engines were replaced by the more reliable NK-12MP power plant, the aircraft incorporated some structural features inherited from the Tu-95MS missile-carrier, and featured an upgraded drop control system. AT-2M torpedoes could no longer be carried, while

Tupolev Tu-142MZ 'Bear-F Mod 4'

76th OPLAP DD
Kipelovo air base

An attempt to redress the shortcomings of the Tu-142MK, the MZ introduced a much better ASW system including a new family of sonobuoys. Buoys from the previous two generations could still be used. The prototype (42172) was a converted Tu-142MK.

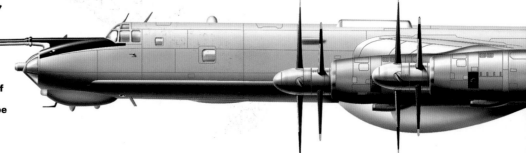

UMGT-1 torpedoes, APR-2 anti-submarine torpedoes, and UPLAB-50 training bombs could be carried externally. Naturally, the aircraft was equipped to carry the new RGB-16, RGB-2, and RGB-36 sonobuoys. In addition, the aircraft retained the ability to use the sonobuoys of the 2Kn-K ASW system. Most importantly, the Tu-142MZs were fitted with the modified Kn-N ASW system, in which the Zarechye sonar subsystem, which provides simultaneous processing and analysing of data, transmitted by sonobuoys in audio and subsonic frequencies, replaced the Kayra-P sonar.

Main differences between the Kn-N and the 2Kn-K ASW systems included the following: a TsIKL control mode, which allows the flight to be simulated on the ground; A-311 new radio-navigation system; improved ergonomics of the crew workstations; and the observation channel, which automatically decided whether a sub had been detected when working with the RGB-1, -16 and -26 buoys. In addition, the new system featured Trek (track) and Amplitudnyi Trek (amplitude track) modes, which made target detection considerably easier when processing

signals transmitted by the RGB-16 and the RGB-26 sonobuoys.

Other differences included: the frequency range of the RGB-16 sonobuoys was increased from 24 to 64, which lifted limitations on their joint deployment as their data transmitters operate continuously; mode 26 was introduced to carry out passive tracking with direction-finding, based on discrete components of noise signature of surface vessels and submarines; one of the data processing modes, transmitted by the RGB-36 sonobuoys, allowed the crew to simultaneously define the range rate, the range and the direction of a submarine in the active operation mode; the Kr-K system is capable of simultaneously processing data from eight RGB-16 sonobuoys in subsonic and low-sound frequencies, as well as passive detection; and measures were taken to increase the likelihood of detecting the signal against the background of ocean-floor noise with the help of depth bombs.

Kn-N employs three types of sonobuoys:

■ **RGB-16 – passive wide-range:** capable of receiving acoustic noise within a frequency range of 2 to 5,000 Hz with a submarine detection range of 12 to 15 km (7.5-9.3 miles). It weighs 9.5 kg (21 lb) and can operate for up to five hours (up to six hours with an automatic start). It boasts a more efficient underwater jamming-proof capability as compared to the RGB-75 and RGB-15, and a lower level of its own background noise within the low frequency range.

■ **RGB-26 – passive low-sound:** capable of tracking submarines in the passive mode with direction-finding of their noise signatures by discrete components. Operation time is 1.2 hours, while its weight is 13.9 kg (30.6 lb).

Overall, the ASW complex of the Tu-142MZ is known as Nashatyr-Nefrit (ammonia-jade). While this introduced a new and much improved sonar system in the form of the Zarechye suite, with a far greater degree of automation compared with the preceding 2Kn-K system, much of the avionics equipment was retained from the Tu-142MK, including the Korshun radar and the oft-criticised NPK-142M navigation system. Comprehensive electronic defences were added, resulting in a plethora of new antennas, while auxiliary power units were installed to allow autonomous operations from austere locations. Internally, many of the crew work-stations were improved with new layouts.

Left: Despite the addition of much new equipment, the navigator in the Tu-142MZ retains a station in the nose section, with a swivelling seat to allow the occupant to look forward through the glazed nose, or to the main instrument console to starboard. The navigator's domain is accessed via a crawlway between the instrument panels for the pilot and co-pilot.

Zaur Eylanbekov

Above: In its initial form (this is the prototype at Taganrog) the Tu-142MR was based on the Tu-142MK and featured a standard glazed nose, underneath which was a large radome housing the Groza-134VR radar. The aircraft lacked the port-side waveguide fairing of later production aircraft. The drogue for the VLF trailing wire antenna is clearly visible.

Right: Existence of the 'Bear-J' was publicly acknowledged in the West in 1986, although the exact nature of its role was not clear at the time. This view highlights the additional communications antennas on the lower rear fuselage sides.

Tu-142MRs entered full service in 1982 and were occasionally encountered by NATO interceptors. They were occasionally seen operating with 'Bear-Fs', as in this 1989 intercept by USAF F-15s of a Tu-142MR and Tu-142MK. When communicating with submarines by VLF, the Tu-142MR deploys its wire aerial to full length and flies a circle to keep the aerial as vertical as possible. At high weights this entails the aircraft operating very close to the stall, placing great strain on the pilots.

■ **RGB-36 passive-active directional:** capable of detecting a submarine's range rate, range and direction in the active operation mode. It weighs 58 kg (128 lb).

Tu-142MR relay aircraft

With the development of the Soviet submarine fleet came the need to maintain steady communication with submarines while submerged in remote areas of the ocean. As a result, a *retranslyator* (relay aircraft) version – the Tu-142MR 'Bear-J' – was created, based on the Tu-142M 'Bear-F Mod 3.' The governmental decree on the development of the Tu-142MR was issued on 3 October 1972. It was designed to carry out semi-automatic and automatic relay of messages, transmitted by coastal command posts in HF (high-frequency) and VLF (very low-frequency) ranges, and to relay messages transmitted by submarines, surface vessels, and naval command posts, to submerged subs in VLF frequencies.

In order to facilitate operation of the communications and relay system, the aircraft was equipped with the following autonomous systems: AC power supply system with turbo generators; hydraulic system for aerial extension device actuators; and a cooling system for the automatic waveguide tuner of the VLF transmitter. The structure of the

tailfin and the leading edge was also slightly changed to incorporate antennas.

In addition to the pilot and the co-pilot, the crew incorporates the navigator, flight engineer, four communications system operators and the gunner (in the tail cockpit). The nose section houses the Groza-134VR radar and the aircraft instrumentation system (if the aircraft is not fitted with the Sayany-RT system, the radome is situated under the fuselage). The canopy is VLF-proof – the forward silicate canopy and windowpanes boast translucent coating, bonded to the airframe. The Plexiglas of the pilot's and the navigator's windows are provided with detachable frames with a 1-mm thick steel (tinned) wire mesh. Pilots noted that the protective mesh impairs visibility and increases eye fatigue during long flights. The navigator's window mounts four tinned brass wire meshes. The radio operator's cabin is also protected by steel netting. The exterior surfaces are coated with colourless varnish and special backing enamel.

The aerial extension device, equipment and distribution devices of the power supply system, Etyud relay equipment, and transmitter and receiver units are all housed in the cargo bay of the aircraft. The forward part of the extending aerial external unit consists of an air intake, heat exchanger, two turning sections, front flap panel and locking device system. There is a fairing on the spine. A steel zinc-coated 7.5-mm (0.295-in) thick wire represents the aerial. It was determined that, following a certain number of cycles, the cable was likely to become jammed due to accumulation of twists and back-spin.

Maximum extension speed of the aerial is 5 m (16.4 ft) per second, while it retracts at up to 4 m (13.12 ft) per second. It takes 37 minutes to extend it to its full length of 7680 m (25,197 ft) and 48 minutes to reel back in. Flight altitude with a fully extended aerial is between 8000 and 10000 m (26,247 and 32,808 ft). The extending aerial external unit and the air intake increased drag considerably. With the aerial extended at an average flight weight of

138 tonnes (135.8 tons) and speed of Mach 0.66, fuel consumption rises to 5.3 kg/km (18.8 lb/mile).

When the weight exceeds 160 tonnes (157.5 tons), flight is conducted at angles of attack which are close to critical, and calls for close attention, and may even be dangerous in turbulent air. Under such conditions, it is almost impossible to engage the autopilot as it constantly switches off. The aircraft communications system was developed and manufactured by the Gorkiy-based Radio Communications Research and Development Institute. The system comprises two HF radios, two VHF and UHF radios, a VLF radio transmitter, two sets of VLF receivers, seven HF receivers, relay equipment, alphanumeric communications equipment and a scrambler. Control panels and interface units provide the equipment with a capability of simultaneous operation in VLF and HF frequencies.

Tu-142MRs are fitted with the Groza-134VR pulse radar to detect radar activity areas and carry out surface surveillance. The radar features a horizontally-searching aerial and an indicator of the azimuth-to-range type. All radar units, except for the antenna, are located in the pressurised compartment. The radar's detection range against large targets like industrial sites is 250 km (155 miles), while in storm clouds it is reduced to 140 km (87 miles).

Tu-142MR first-stage flight tests, totalling 45 sorties, lasted from 23 March until 20 October 1978. The second stage began on 3 April 1979 and finished on 5 May 1980. These flights were conducted from Kirovskoye airfield, Crimea, and Kulbakino airfield, Nikolayev. In 1982 the Tu-142MR aircraft entered the inventory of the Russian Armed Forces. The aircraft's cruising range is 12315 km (7,652 miles), its cruising speed is 735 km/h (457 mph), and its flight ceiling is 10700 m (35,105 ft). Take-off run is 2300 m (7,546 ft) and landing roll is 1800 m (5,905 ft).

Conclusion

The Tu-142's fate was similar to that of the Tu-95RTs, which were also constantly upgraded. There is no doubt that the wings of fast heavy aircraft are not designed for low-altitude flights, and from March 1985 a regular series of groundings has affected the fleet. In 1986 operation of the Tu-142M, built in 1978-86, was temporarily suspended due to cracks in the landing gear fairing, and it was only in April 1989 that the joint decision by the Ministry for Aircraft Industry, the air force, and the navy on rectifying the problems was adopted. Three times the navy has appealed to the defence industry and 12 times to the Ministry for Aircraft Industry over the issue of poor reliability of its long-range aircraft, Tu-142 included.

As noted above, aside from some minor airframe/aircraft system improvements, the modernisation of the Tu-142 followed a series of modifications to the mission equipment, as summarised below:

■ **Berkut-95:** with audio frequency sonobuoys. Apart from the extra range, the Tu-142 was no better than the Il-38, although the latter did not pose the same levels of maintenance problems as the 'Bear'. The Berkut-95 featured a number of shortfalls: high operation costs due to the necessity of massive employment of expensive sonobuoys, which had a limited submarine detection range; poor reliability of computers; lack of visual picture; and low automation level of processing raw data from

transmitters. Almost all Tu-142s, fitted with the Berkut-95, had left the AVMF inventory by 1992.

■ **Korshun (2Kn-K):** replaced Berkut-95 in 1980, including the RGB-75 and the RGB-15 low-frequency sonobuoys, which improved initial submarine detection capability. It also incorporated more sophisticated data processing systems, as well as depth bombs. Another important feature of the Korshun system was that its sonobuoys were much cheaper, thanks to the removal of transmitting beacons and automatic starts, and a shift from the bulky RGB-3s to range-finding sonobuoys. The tactical display had its own computer and was capable of displaying and transmitting tactical data from one aircraft to another and from the aircraft to the command post. Navigation and tactical functions were divided. Efficiency of the MMS-106 magnetometers, mounted on the aircraft, turned out to depend on many systems, and it was only in the 1990s that flight crews noted some increase in their efficiency. One of the shortfalls of the Korshun system was the low automation level of initial processing of data, and a great rate of false alarms. The navigation system also had some shortfalls. The aircraft crew received another member.

■ **Zarechye (Kn-N):** the shortcomings of sonobuoys of the 2Kn-K led to a replacement of the hydroacoustic subsystem, including a new family of buoys. New weapon systems were developed simultaneously with detection systems.

By mid-1996 the air branches of the two fleets operated 15 Tu-142s, 20 Tu-142MKs and 12 Tu-142MZs, more than half of which were in reserve storage. The Tupolev OKB offered to upgrade the Tu-142Ms, replacing their avionics, fitting them with new anti-submarine torpedoes, improving the airframe, and equipping them with the Morskoy Zmey (Sea Dragon) avionics. However, for a number of reasons, including financial restraints, no positive decision has yet been taken.

Lt Col Anatoliy Artemyev (Soviet/Russian navy, Retd); translation by Zaur Eylanbekov

Most, if not all, production Tu-142MRs were much closer to the Tu-142MZ in antenna configuration than the prototype. They had the Sayany-RT warning system installed in an undernose fairing and under the tail, linked by waveguide fairing on the port side, while the tail section incorporated the MZ's four-gun turret and lacked observation blisters. Addition of the Sayany-RT nose fairing in turn required the relocation of the Groza-134VR radar to a large thimble radome on the extreme nose in place of the glazed section.

Production of the Tu-142MR is thought to have numbered around 10 aircraft, with operational aircraft probably divided between Northern and Pacific Fleets. This view of a 76th OPLAP DD 'Bear-J' on the Kipelovo flightline shows details of the Groza installation, as well as the three most obvious external communications features: underbelly fairing for VLF trailing wire antenna, fin-tip probe antenna for HF communications, and spine bulge for an undisclosed, but probably satellite, communications system.

Fuselage

The monocoque fuselage is skinned in smooth aluminium sheets which vary in thickness from 1 to 4 mm. The fuselage is broken down into five major sections: nose glazing; a forward pressurised cabin; a central cylindrical section with diameter of 2.9 m (9 ft 6 in); a conical tail section; and a rear pressurised cabin with a defensive gun installation.

The forward cabin accommodates the crew (there are nine seats with standard seat belts) and various equipment. In case of emergency the crew leaves the aircraft via the nose wheel well. The entrance hatch is opened by compressed air and the nosewheel leg is extended. Three hydraulic actuators start hydraulic motors which move a mobile floor which runs between the crew stations to the exit hatch for a duration of 100 seconds.

The fuselage centre-section is 16 m (52 ft) long. Aft of the cockpit is a compartment containing a PSN-6A life raft. Behind the wing centre section is a cargo bay with two pairs of doors. Aft of this bay is one of the fuel tanks. The tail section has a compartment for two crew members, with windows and blisters. The fairing for the Krypton rear-facing radar is mounted above the rear turret. In case of an emergency, two crew members bale out through the entrance hatch. The cover of the hatch acts as a shield to protect the crew from the slipstream.

This view shows the radome for the Korshun radar, refuelling conduit, cooling air intake and main stores bay. Aft of the main bay is another set of doors for an auxiliary bay.

Wings

The wings of the 'Bear' are swept 35° at the quarter-chord. Swept wings were adopted as air compression begins to have an adverse effect on the aerodynamic characteristics in the Mach 0.715-0.74 (770-820 km/h/478-509 mph) speed regime, which could lead to boundary layer separation and a large drag rise. For the same reasons the wing is of rather thin section.

Compared to earlier Tu-95s, the Tu-142 has a new wing, modified to improve aerodynamic efficiency by 4-5 per cent. The leading edge was extended forward and then angled downward. Along the top surface of the wing there are three pairs of aerodynamic fences, each 190 mm (7.5 in) in height. The aircraft's wing is set at 2.5° anhedral, which improves controllability in the rolling plane.

With the exception of the centre section, almost the whole wing is an integral fuel tank, with eight compartments within the torsion box formed by spars, panels and ribs. As a swept wing generates less lift than an unswept one, it was necessary to install powerful double-slotted flaps with electromechanical control.

The outer wing panel consists of a central torsion box, detachable leading edge, trailing edge and aileron (suspended on nine hinges). The starboard aileron is equipped with a trim tab, and the port aileron has a balance tab.

Tail

By comparison with the Tu-95RTs, the Tu-142's tail unit was also modified. The stabilisers have been made adjustable for trim, while rudder and elevator areas were increased, as was their maximum deflection angles. The stabiliser tips of Tu-142s from the first series were used to mount the Arfa system and Kristall transmitter in streamlined fairings. The fairings had a metal container and dielectric panels. Starting with aircraft No. 4232, the Lira synchronisation device became standard. Leading edges of both fin and stabilisers were equipped with electrical anti-icing, as were those of the wings.

Differences in tail configuration were significant between the Tu-142MK (above) and Tu-142MZ (below). Quite apart from all the additional antennas and lack of glazed blisters, the MZ has a new turret with four, rather than two, 23-mm guns.

Control system

Flight control is effected through the two control columns and two pairs of pedals, which are connected with the control surfaces by rigid rods. GU-54A hydraulic actuators (boosters) are installed in the control system for rudders and ailerons. An artificial feel system is also installed for imitation of loads on rudders and ailerons. Spring loading devices and trimming mechanisms are installed, and with the help of cables they are connected to the AP-15RZ autopilot. A reversionary mode, with unassisted flight control, is also possible. Stability and controllability were enhanced by the Ka-142 unit.

In order to reduce the aircraft's asymmetric tendencies in the event of an outer engine failure, the MP-AF mechanism in the rudder control system will automatically deflect the rudder 11° to oppose the yawing effect. The mechanism works on a signal from the propeller auto-feathering system when the engine's throttle position indicator is at an angle greater than 85°.

Powerplant and fuel

The Tu-142's powerplant consists of four NK-12MP or NK-12MV turboprops with axial-flow compressors, annular combustion chambers, and a gas turbine of a jet type (the expansion of gas occurs in the exhaust nozzle). The engines are installed in nacelles at -1° to the wing chord.

Two four-bladed, variable-pitch AV-60K propellers are mounted co-axially on each engine. The pitch angle of the forward propeller varies between 5° and 91°, while the rear propeller moves between 7° and 92°. In flight the pitch angles change according to mode of flight, while the rotational speed remains constant at 735 rpm.

The forward propeller generates 54 per cent of the power and the rear one contributes 46 per cent. Failure of an engine in flight can lead to an enormous rise in drag, especially as the propeller changes to fine pitch as the engine spools down. If unchecked, this can lead to a loss of control. Consequently, propellers are equipped with systems for automatic and manual feathering (to

This is the original 12-wheel rough-field undercarriage fitted to the first 12 Tu-142s. These aircraft inevitably became known as 'centipedes' compared with later aircraft with standard four-wheel bogies.

maximum pitch angles of 91°/92°). Another mechanism also prevents the blades from changing to fine pitch and windmilling.

Transition of the blades to fine pitch after landing (achieved by unlatching the stop to permit the blades to move below the inflight fine-pitch stop with the engine decelerated below flight idle power) creates considerable drag, which provides an essential reduction of the landing run.

Fuel (kerosene -1, -2, TC-1) is distributed in eight integral tanks in the wing, and in three soft tanks in the wing centre section and rear section of the fuselage. Four independent fuel systems feed the engines (one system per engine). Emergency fuel dump is provided and takes 25-30 minutes. Refuelling on the ground is normally undertaken through four central points and two overwing fillers on each wing. Refuelling through 10 overwing fillers increases the quantity of fuel by 4000 kg (8,818 lb). The aircraft is capable of inflight refuelling using the Konus system.

Engines are controlled by throttles (RUD – Rychag Upravleniya Dvigatelem) and fuel shut-off valves located among pilots' and flight engineer's controls.

Aircraft systems

The aircraft has two hydraulic systems. One 150-kg/cm² (2,133 lb/sq in) system is used for basic and emergency wheel braking, release and retraction of the nosewheel leg, front wheel steering, operation of the emergency mobile floor, and the windshield wipers. A 75-kg/cm² (1,067-lb/sq in) system provides power to hydraulic actuators.

Electric circuits comprise a 27-V DC system, single-phase 400-Hz AC systems of 115-V and 200-V, and a three-phase 400-Hz circuit of 36 V. For high-altitude flights there are five KPZh-30 containers with liquid oxygen.

Defences

Defensive armament of the aircraft consists of a DK-12 tail turret with two 23-mm GSh-23 cannon, each with 600 rounds. The PS-253K sight and PRS-4 Krypton radar are used to aim the cannon. For detection of fighter radars the aircraft has an SPO-10 passive receiver, and SPS-100 ECM equipment is fitted.

In the rear of the undercarriage fairing are numerous three-round launchers for IR decoy flares.

This Tu-142MK is displayed with five pre-packed sonobuoy cassettes and standard PLAB-250 depth charges.

Weapons

Tu-142s have carried a wide range of maritime stores, usually depth charges (conventional or nuclear) and torpedoes. Mines are also available.

Right: The UMGT-1M Orlan torpedo is an option for the Tu-142MZ, along with the older APR-2. From nose to tail, the UMGT-1's section comprise: homing head, auxiliary equipment section, warhead, battery section, electric motor, steering section, propulsion unit and the braking unit.

MDM-3 air-dropped mine

MDM-5 air-dropped mine

KAB-250PL (S3V) guided depth charge

Sonobuoys

The Berkut generation of sonobuoys for the Tu-142 was based on the RGB-1 (below left), RGB-2 and RGB-3. An example of the latter is seen in the water (left) – like all buoys, the hydrophone submerges beneath the floating transmitter portion. With the Tu-142K/Korshun came new buoys in the form of the passive non-directional RGB-15 (below, painted yellow) and RGB-75 (below, silver), the passive directional RGB-25 (above) and active RGB-55A (above right). For loading into the stores bay the buoys are carried in cassettes (right), these being RGB-75s.

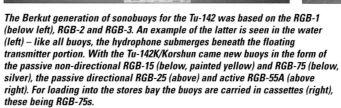

Right: The Tu-142's cockpit is relatively sparse, with basic flight instruments provided and a forest of warning lights above the console. The pilot has a tactical display screen to the right of the main instruments for flight direction. In the centre is a crawlway through to the navigator's position, above which is the control for the autopilot. This is mounted on a pull-out arm and can be swung to left or right for operation by either pilot. With access needed to the nose, there is no central console. Each pilot has throttle controls at his side, aft of the large trim wheel. This cockpit has been 'zapped' by the Swedish air force's SK 60-equipped 'Team 60' display team.

Far left: The flight engineer sits behind the pilot on the port side with engine control the main task. As well as comprehensive instruments, throttles are provided.

Left: Opposite the engineer is the radio operator. The empty space in the console is normally occupied by the sensitive cryptographic terminal.

Tu-142MZ 'Bear-F Mod 4'

1 Inflight refuelling probe
2 Geran active electronic jammer antenna
3 Arrow-shaped antenna for short-range radio navigation system
4 Glass nose of navigator's cockpit
5 Navigator's position
6 Inflight refuelling probe illumination lights
7 Antennas for electronic warfare and communication systems
8 Nose landing gear leg with twin KN2-4 wheels
9 Nose landing gear bay door
10 Cockpit entry ladder
11 Pilots' cockpit windshield
12 Pilot (port position)/copilot (starboard position)
13 Flight engineer (port position)/communications operator (starboard position)
14 Emergency exit
15 Bubble window for remote astro-compass
16 Zarechye sonobuoy system operator's position
17 Korshun search/attack radar operator's position
18 Navigator's position
19 Pressure bulkhead
20 ECM system waveguide cover
21 Geran active electronic jammer antenna
22 Korshun radar

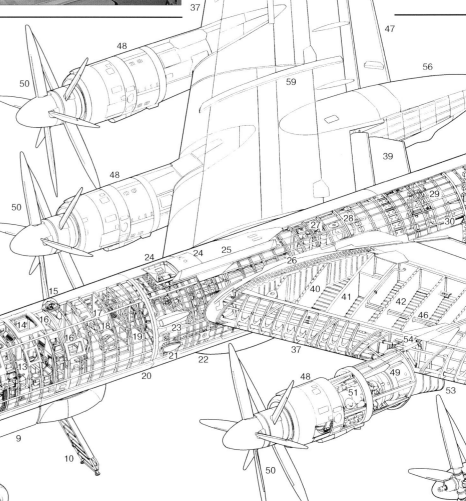

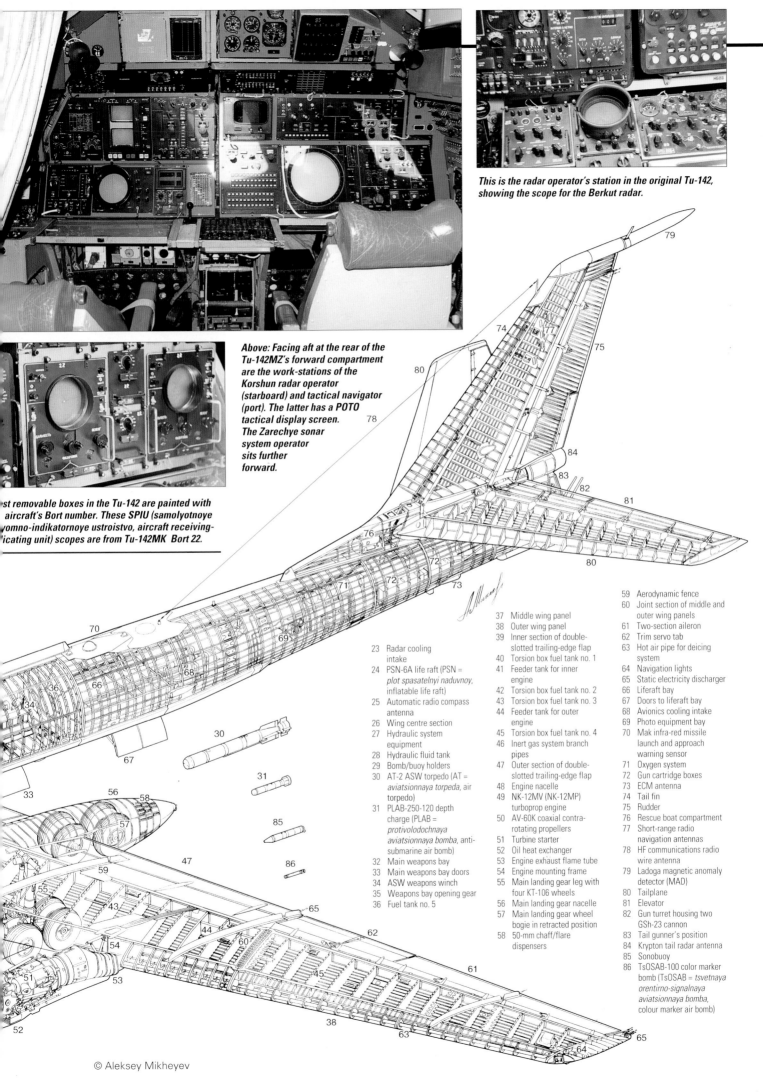

This is the radar operator's station in the original Tu-142, showing the scope for the Berkut radar.

Above: *Facing aft at the rear of the Tu-142MZ's forward compartment are the work-stations of the Korshun radar operator (starboard) and tactical navigator (port). The latter has a POTO tactical display screen. The Zarechye sonar system operator sits further forward.*

...st removable boxes in the Tu-142 are painted with ...aircraft's Bort number. These SPIU (samolyotnoye ...omno-indikatornoye ustroistvo, aircraft receiving-...icating unit) scopes are from Tu-142MK Bort 22.

23 Radar cooling intake
24 PSN-6A life raft (PSN = plot spasatelnyi naduvnoy, inflatable life raft)
25 Automatic radio compass antenna
26 Wing centre section
27 Hydraulic system equipment
28 Hydraulic fluid tank
29 Bomb/buoy holders
30 AT-2 ASW torpedo (AT = aviatsionnaya torpeda, air torpedo)
31 PLAB-250-120 depth charge (PLAB = protivolodochnaya aviatsionnaya bomba, anti-submarine air bomb)
32 Main weapons bay
33 Main weapons bay doors
34 ASW weapons winch
35 Weapons bay opening gear
36 Fuel tank no. 5
37 Middle wing panel
38 Outer wing panel
39 Inner section of double-slotted trailing-edge flap
40 Torsion box fuel tank no. 1
41 Feeder tank for inner engine
42 Torsion box fuel tank no. 2
43 Torsion box fuel tank no. 3
44 Feeder tank for outer engine
45 Torsion box fuel tank no. 4
46 Inert gas system branch pipes
47 Outer section of double-slotted trailing-edge flap
48 Engine nacelle
49 NK-12MV (NK-12MP) turboprop engine
50 AV-60K coaxial contra-rotating propellers
51 Turbine starter
52 Oil heat exchanger
53 Engine exhaust flame tube
54 Engine mounting frame
55 Main landing gear leg with four KT-106 wheels
56 Main landing gear nacelle
57 Main landing gear wheel bogie in retracted position
58 50-mm chaff/flare dispensers
59 Aerodynamic fence
60 Joint section of middle and outer wing panels
61 Two-section aileron
62 Trim servo tab
63 Hot air pipe for deicing system
64 Navigation lights
65 Static electricity discharger
66 Liferaft bay
67 Doors to liferaft bay
68 Avionics cooling intake
69 Photo equipment bay
70 Mak infra-red missile launch and approach warning sensor
71 Oxygen system
72 Gun cartridge boxes
73 ECM antenna
74 Tail fin
75 Rudder
76 Rescue boat compartment
77 Short-range radio navigation antennas
78 HF communications radio wire antenna
79 Ladoga magnetic anomaly detector (MAD)
80 Tailplane
81 Elevator
82 Gun turret housing two GSh-23 cannon
83 Tail gunner's position
84 Krypton tail radar antenna
85 Sonobuoy
86 TsOSAB-100 color marker bomb (TsOSAB = tsvetnaya orentirno-signalnaya aviatsionnaya bomba, colour marker air bomb)

© Aleksey Mikheyev

Tupolev Tu-16 'Badger'
Maid of all work

Like the Boeing B-47 Stratojet – its contemporary and Cold War rival – Tupolev's Aircraft '88' carved a unique niche for itself as its country's first successful swept-wing bomber and, like the B-47, was built in huge numbers to swell the ranks of the medium-range strategic bomber units. It also proved very adaptable to the needs of the reconnaissance and electronic warfare communities. More importantly, it adopted the role of missile-carrier, becoming for many years the backbone of the Soviet Union's answer to the 'blue-water' threat posed by the US Navy. Amazingly, 50 years after its first flight, the 'Badger' is still in widespread use in China, and still posing a significant threat to navies operating in the region.

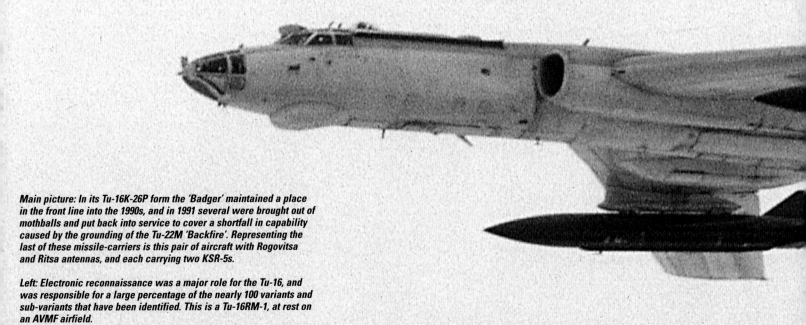

Main picture: In its Tu-16K-26P form the 'Badger' maintained a place in the front line into the 1990s, and in 1991 several were brought out of mothballs and put back into service to cover a shortfall in capability caused by the grounding of the Tu-22M 'Backfire'. Representing the last of these missile-carriers is this pair of aircraft with Rogovitsa and Ritsa antennas, and each carrying two KSR-5s.

Left: Electronic reconnaissance was a major role for the Tu-16, and was responsible for a large percentage of the nearly 100 variants and sub-variants that have been identified. This is a Tu-16RM-1, at rest on an AVMF airfield.

Unmistakeably a Tupolev design, the Tu-16 was an outstanding aircraft which far outlived its initially intended career span. As well as the basic soundness of the design, the key to this longevity was the airframe's tractability, allowing it to be tailored to a wide variety of roles. The wing pylons and Ritsa antennas above the flat-pane bombardier's window identify this as a Tu-16K-26P. The small antenna protruding from the lower port side of the nose was one of two which served the Rogovitsa formation-keeping system.

In 1954 and 1955, together with my crew, I ferried a number of Ilyushin Il-28 aircraft from Moscow, Voronezh and Irkutsk to the Pacific and Baltic Fleets, and to China. When we flew over or landed at the airfield of aircraft plant no. 22 at Kazan, we looked enviously at the big silver-coloured aircraft with an unusual swept-back wing. This was the Tu-16 – known in the West as 'Badger' – and at the time it was pouring from the production line at a prodigious rate.

In the mid-1940s the design bureau of general designer Tupolev started a careful study of 'foreign' (captured German) material, and undertook its own research to explore the characteristics of the swept-back wing. The aim was to evaluate the expediency and possibility of using it on large aircraft. There were numerous problems to solve. Paramount was the need to provide good aerodynamics at high subsonic speeds to meet flight range requirements and also satisfactory take-off and landing characteristics.

Location of the engines was another important consideration, and there were many more.

The concept of the swept-back wing was tested first on the experimental aircraft '82' powered by two VK-1 engines. Early work was begun on the initiative of the design bureau, but from June 1948 the activity came under government decree. In March 1949, '82' made its first flight, piloted by A. Perelyot. During the tests at the plant the aircraft reached a speed of 913 km/h (567 mph). The aircraft was not tested further and a proposed combat version was not built. However, the swept-back wing concept was proven.

During that period the Il-28 went into serial production. It perfectly met the requirements of both the Air Force and the Navy. Nevertheless, the need for a long-range aircraft existed, and a decree, dated 10 June 1950, assigned the Ministry of Aircraft Industry the task of creating a long-range bomber. The challenge was issued to design bureaux OKB-240 (Ilyushin) and OKB-156 (Tupolev).

An order issued by the ministry on 14 June 1950 required the Tupolev design bureau to develop an aircraft fitted with the domestic AL-5 turbojet engines, designed by A. Lyulka with a thrust of 53.96 kN (12,125 lb), and to meet the following characteristics: maximum flight speed – 900-1000 km/h (560-620 mph); range – 7000 km (4,350 miles) with a combat load of 2000 kg (4,410 lb); service ceiling – 11000-12000 m (36,090-39,370 ft). Defensive weaponry was to comprise seven guns. An option was agreed for installing the promising AM-03 engines – designed by A.A. Mikulin – which offered a thrust of 78.48 kN (17,636 lb).

Taking into consideration the time limit for building the aircraft, the relatively modest requirements and the lack of flight test data of swept-back wing aircraft, the OKB-240 design bureau decided to split the work into two stages. During the first stage it was to build the aircraft with a straight wing, like that of the Il-28, and subsequently replace it with a swept-back wing. Tests of the experimental Il-46 began on 3 March 1952 and were completed on 31 July of the same year. The tests proved the characteristics anticipated by OKB-240, and development of the swept-back wing variant accelerated.

Tupolev's approach

Tupolev's OKB-156 chose another way. After considering a number of intermediate concepts, in July 1951 a mock-up and a draft design of aircraft '88' were approved. Four months later, in compliance with the decree, the aircraft was fitted with two AM-3 engines, by then producing 85.84 kN (19,290 lb) thrust each. The prototype, with engines, was completed the following March.

Accommodating the AM-3 engines entailed a wide scope of alterations, due to its larger size as compared to the AL-5. Front-end diameter was 1.47 m (4 ft 10 in), length was 5.38 m (17 ft 8 in) and weight was 3700 kg (8,157 lb). Because of its size, the engine had to be located closer to the fuselage and attached to frames, partly sunk in the wing. Putting the engine in the root of the wing required placing the air intake in front of the wing near the side of the fuselage and then separate the flow into two channels,

Above: A unique feature of the Tu-16 was its elaborate and cumbersome wingtip-to-wingtip refuelling method. Here a Tu-16R reconnaissance aircraft prepares to refuel from a Tu-16Z.

Right: For much of the aircraft's career the bulk of the 'Badger' fleet was assigned to missile-carrying tasks. Large numbers of Tu-16K-10s were produced with the huge YeN ('Puff Ball') nose radar.

Perhaps more than any other Soviet aircraft, the Tu-16 confused Western analysts, resulting in some anomalies in the way reporting names were allocated by the Air Standards Co-ordination Committee. This was only to be expected, given that the assignation of such codenames was primarily based on visual and photographic intelligence reports from interceptor pilots and other human resources. Because they looked the same externally, several distinct variants with widely differing roles were grouped under the 'Badger-A' codename, while a string of letter suffixes were applied to the reconnaissance aircraft, despite the fact that they represented an ongoing modification process to the same aircraft. Continual equipment upgrades and additions throughout the Tu-16's long career, especially concerning electronics, further clouded the issue, as did the fact that AVMF and VVS Tu-16s often differed in their equipment fit.

'Badger-A': 'basic' Tu-16, covering Tu-16 and Tu-16A bombers, Tu-16N and Tu-16Z tankers, Tu-16PL ASW platform and Tu-16T torpedo-bomber
'Badger-B': Tu-16KS – first missile-carrier version armed with AS-1 'Kennel' missile
'Badger-C': Tu-16K-10 – missile-carrier with centreline AS-2 'Kipper' and large nose radome for 'Puff Ball' radar
'Badger-C Mod': Tu-16K-10-26 – 'Badger-C' modified to carry AS-6 'Kingfish' missiles under wing pylons
'Badger-D': Tu-16RM-1 – 'Badger-C' converted for reconnaissance duties with three additional radomes under belly
'Badger-E': Tu-16R – reconnaissance version with two radomes under belly
'Badger-F': Tu-16R – similar to 'Badger-E' but with Elint sensors in underwing pods
'Badger-G': Tu-16KSR/Tu-16K-11-16 – several similar versions converted from earlier aircraft (including Tu-16KS) to carry AS-5 'Kelt' under each wing. Undernose radar enlarged ('Short Horn')
'Badger-G Mod': Tu-16K-26/Tu-16KSR-2-5-11 – 'Badger-Gs' converted to carry AS-6 'Kingfish' missile under wing pylons. Tu-16K-26 retained undernose radome and is sometimes referred to as 'Badger-G'. Some aircraft had large belly radome
'Badger-H': Tu-16 Yolka – chaff-laying platform with chaff dispensers in belly
'Badger-J': Tu-16P – electronic warfare version with ventral canoe fairing covering jammers. Earlier Tu-16SPS jammer does not appear to have been given separate codename
'Badger-K': Tu-16R – reconnaissance update with two sizeable teardrop radomes under belly
'Badger-L': Tu-16R – reconnaissance version with two underbelly radomes and underwing sensor pods. Sometimes fitted with enlarged tailcone housing jammers and nose 'pimple' antenna

one being in the structural box of the wing and the other one below it. The AM-3-powered aircraft was expected to demonstrate the following performance: range – 6000 km (3,728 miles), speed – 1000 km/h (621 mph) and service ceiling – 14000 m (45,930 ft).

After completion, the experimental aircraft '88' was redesignated as the Tu-16 and passed over to the test team. On 27 April 1952 test pilot N. S. Rybko made the first flight that lasted just 12 minutes. In ensuing flights the aircraft reached a speed of 1020 km/h (634 mph) and demonstrated a range of 6050 km (3,760 miles). The performance advantage of the '88' over the Il-46 was readily apparent.

On 13 November 1952 the prototype was submitted for state testing which continued through late March 1953. Despite the aircraft initially failing to pass these state tests, as early as July 1952 Tupolev managed to obtain an approval for launching mass production in December 1952. In July 1953 plant 22 was to make the first series aircraft and work on the rival Il-46 was stopped.

The second prototype of project '88' was 3900 kg (8,598 lb) lighter and required 2000 kg (4,409 lb) less fuel to achieve its range requirement, reducing the maximum take-off weight from 77430 kg (170,701 lb) to 71560 kg (157,760 lb). For future use the outer wing panels were

fitted with additional fuel tanks, which increased capacity of the fuel system from 38200 to 43900 litres (8,403 to 9,657 Imp gal). Other modifications included extending the nose by 20 cm (8 in), reinforcing the spar caps, widening the engine nacelle, and installing defensive weapons with sighting stations and radar sights. The crew headed by N. S. Rybko flew the second prototype on 6 April 1953. This aircraft passed the state tests that concluded in April 1954 and was recommended for fielding operationally, endorsed by a decree dated 28 May 1954.

During the state tests the following characteristics were obtained: maximum speed at 6250 m (20,505 ft) – 992 km/h (616 mph); flight range with a 3-ton payload – 5670 km (3,523 miles); service ceiling – 12800 m (41,995 ft); maximum take-off weight – 72000 kg (158,730 lb) with a take-off run of 2000 m (6,562 ft).

Full-scale production

The first serial Tu-16 aircraft No. 3200101 was completed on 29 October 1953 at Kazan-based aircraft plant 22. In 1954 the output counted 70 aircraft. The aircraft number allocated by the plant indicated the following: the first digit – the year of manufacturing; the second one – the plant; the third – any digit; the fourth and the fifth – serial number, and the last two – the number in the series.

Electronic warfare variants of the 'Badger' were produced in sizeable quantities, and also exhibited many different configurations as equipment was upgraded. The main jamming variant was the Tu-16P Buket, with jammers housed in its canoe fairings, surrounded by heat exchanger inlets and exhausts to cool the equipment in the stores bay. Jamming platforms were procured either new from the factory or by conversion of other variants. This aircraft was probably a tanker previously.

Below: Without its deadly missile cargo, the Tu-16K-10 was often intercepted during navigation training sorties, or on missile launch simulation exercises.

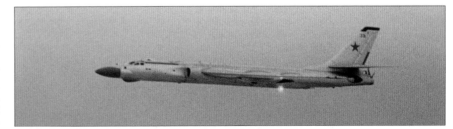

As with most other Soviet types of its era, the Tu-16 was exported readily to client states: China, Egypt, Indonesia and Iraq all received Soviet-built 'Badgers'. Clouding the issue in the United Arab Republic (Egypt) was the use of AVMF aircraft operating from Egyptian bases in spurious UARAF markings. This, however, is one of Egypt's Tu-16KSR-2-11s, purchased when the AVMF's 89 OMRAE departed the country in 1972.

'Badger-A' bombers were delivered in roughly equal numbers to both Long-Range and Naval Aviation. The AVMF also received a fleet of Tu-16T torpedo-bombers, although they did not differ externally. The Tu-16T had a very brief career in the late 1950s, as this mode of warfare was proved to be obsolescent. The Tu-16T fleet became available for conversion, and a handful were fitted with sonobuoy equipment to form an interim anti-submarine warfare capability (as the Tu-16PL) pending the arrival in service of the dedicated Il-38 maritime patrol aircraft. Another naval speciality was the Tu-16S rescue aircraft, which was designed to drop a boat to survivors.

Sometimes a short form of numeration was used. The first manufactured aircraft were widely used for test and research purposes. In this way, after undergoing check tests that increased its gross weight to 76000 kg (167,548 lb), production aircraft No. 4201002 was taken as a standard.

During the period 1953 through 1959 plant no. 22 at Kazan produced the Tu-16 and the Tu-16A bomber, the Tu-16KS missile-carrier and the Tu-16E jammer. The number of aircraft per series varied: up to series 11 – five aircraft per series; up to series 20 – 10 aircraft per series; from series 21 – 20 per series; and from 31 to 41 – 30 aircraft per series. In the period of 1958 to 1960 there was no production of the Tu-16, and in the period of 1961 through 1963 30 series of five aircraft each were built, comprising 150 Tu-16Ks for naval aviation. In total, plant no. 22 manufactured 800 Tu-16 aircraft of different versions.

On 19 September 1953 a decree was issued followed by the order of the Ministry of Aircraft Industry to launch production of the Tu-16 at plant no. 1 at Kuibyshev (now Samara). The first aircraft was assembled from components delivered from the Kazan factory. The following nine aircraft also used components received from plant 22. The numbers assigned to aircraft produced by the Kuibyshev plant indicate the following: the first digit – plant number; the second and the third ones – type of the article ('88'); the fourth and the fifth – series number; and the two last digits – number of the aircraft in the series.

Kuibyshev produced the Tu-16K, Tu-16SPS, Tu-16E, Tu-16 Yolka and the Tu-16R. Altogether, 40 series were made. The first series (up to the 11th) consisted of five aircraft each, series 11 – 20 ten aircraft each and from series 21 onwards 20 aircraft each. In total, plant no. 1 built 543 Tu-16s.

In July 1954 a decree was issued to start production of the Tu-16T for naval aviation at plant no. 64 at Voronezh. Tu-16s and Tu-16 Yolkas were also built there. The first aircraft, Tu-16T No. 5400001, was completed in May 1955. The first digit in its number indicated the year of manufacturing; the second one – plant number; the third – any digit; the fourth and the fifth – series number; the sixth and the seventh – number of the aircraft in the series. In 1957, production at Voronezh was stopped after 166 aircraft had been built,.

Combined, the three plants built 1,509 Tu-16, comprising 747 Tu-16 and Tu-16A, 76 Tu-16T, 107 Tu-16KS, 216 Tu-16K, 233 Tu-16 Yolka and Tu-16SPS, 75 Tu-16R and 52 Tu-16E (ASO-16). However, these far from represent the number of versions of the Tu-16, since the aircraft were modernised and modified by the VVS and AVMF aircraft overhaul plants.

According to their assigned tasks, the Tu-16s were divided into combat and special-purpose aircraft. The combat aircraft included bombers, missile-carriers, torpedo bombers, ASW aircraft and reconnaissance platforms. ECM jammers, tankers, rescue aircraft and some other variants are referred to as special-purpose aircraft.

'Badger-A' bombers

The basic variant of the Tu-16 bomber was under continuous upgrade, improving its airborne equipment and self-protection gear. The OPB-11 optical vector/synchronous bomb sight was subsequently replaced by the better OPB-15. Some aircraft were equipped with the A-326 Rogovitsa radar system, which provided station-keeping information for formation flying at a range of up to 20 km (12.4 miles), and gave warnings of potential collisions.

Prototypes for the Tu-16A nuclear bomb carrier were created through modifying the second and the third series Tu-16 aircraft nos 3200102 and 4200103. By 1958 453 similar aircraft had been built, 59 of which were equipped with an inflight refuelling system, becoming the Tu-16ZA. An almost equal number of aircraft was divided between long-range aviation and naval aviation units. Unlike the standard bomber, the stores bay of the nuclear carrier contained an electric heating system and featured an improved airtightness system. The crew cockpit was equipped with blinds. The bottom part of the fuselage had a special thermal protection skin.

Production of Tu-16 bombers stopped in 1958, but modifications continued and many were subsequently converted for other tasks. In the late 1960s the modification of aircraft no. 7203829 increased its capability to carry FAB-250 bombs from 16 to 24, and FAB-500s from 12 to 18. Some aircraft were equipped with SPS-100 jammers, while some individual aircraft carried Rubin radars required for the OPB-112 optic sights. In the 1960s, with the accent moving rapidly away from free-fall bombers, 156 Tu-16As were retrofitted to carry KSR-2 and KSR-11 missiles, becoming Tu-16KSR-2s or Tu-16K-11-16s in the process.

In compliance with a decree dated 28 March 1956, the

Few Western air arms saw more of the 'Badger' than the Svenska Flygvapnet (Swedish Air Force), for whom intercepts of 'Badgers' over the Baltic were an almost daily occurrence. Above is a pair of Tu-16K-10 'Badger-Cs', while at right is a Tu-16P Buket equipped with Geran nose jamming antenna. A rarely-seen variation on the Buket was the Fikus aircraft, which had five small radomes under the stores bay.

Tu-16B aircraft was developed. It was an attempt to improve the performance of the aircraft through the adoption of the 107.91-kN (24,250-lb) RD 16-15 engine that had been developed by OKB-16. Two aircraft were modified and were tested until 1961. The results were satisfactory but serial production was never launched.

As well as normal free-fall weapons, Tu-16s carried guided bombs. After a careful study of the characteristics of German guided bombs, from the early 1950s the UB-2F (Tchaika) and UB-5 (Kondor) bombs were developed. They were of two different diameters and weighed 2240 kg (4,938 lb) and 5100 kg (11,243 lb), respectively. The first one was intended for the Il-28 and the Tu-16, the second one only for the Tu-16. They utilised a three-point method of guidance – the navigator used the OPB-2UP optic sight to adjust the trajectory, watching the target and the tracer.

A thermal imaging guidance system was also tested. As a result, the fielding of Tchaika-2 with a thermal homing head was endorsed. In 1956 a UBV-5 5150-kg (11,354-lb) bomb with both high explosive and armour-piercing warheads was developed to fit the Tu-16. Gradually, a disadvantage of the guided bomb became obvious – it was necessary to get close to the target. The idea to equip the bomb with a missile engine for longer range complicated its design and made it almost as expensive as a normal missile.

Tu-16 bombers in service

Tu-16s served in many variants with dozens of aviation regiments of both long-range (DA – Dalnyaya Aviatsiya) and naval aviation (AVMF – Aviatsiya Voenno Morskogo Flota). Regiments could either be an independent part of a heavy bomber divisions (TBAD – Tyazhelaya Bombardirovochnaya Aviatsionnaya Diviziya) or mine-torpedo aviation divisions (MTAD – Minno-Torpednaya Aviatsionnaya Diviziya). In 1961 the latter were renamed naval missile carrier divisions (MRAD – Morskaya

Above: This 'Badger-A' rests at Zhukovskiy. The undernose radar has been removed.

Right: A 'Badger' refuels at Kamennyi Ruchey air base in the Soviet Far East during the Cold War. This was a major base for patrol and attack missions over the Pacific.

Left: A Tu-16 being shadowed by a US Navy F-4 Phantom highlights the undercarriage nacelles which were introduced by the 'Badger' and which became a Tupolev hallmark. The reasons for the nacelles were simple enough: to cater for the high weight of the aircraft a bogie undercarriage was required, and the high-speed wing was too thin to accommodate such a structure. To minimise the cross-sectional area of the nacelles, the bogies were designed to somersault so that they lay flat in the nacelle when retracted.

Below: This regular Tu-16 bomber is on display at the VVS museum at Monino, complete with an array of bombs. The Tu-16 could carry a 9000-kg weapon.

Raketonosnaya Aviatsionnaya Diviziya). The AVMF also had independent reconnaissance air regiments (ODRAP – Otdelnyi Dalniy Razvedyatelnyi Aviatsionnyi Polk) and squadrons (ORAE – Otdelnyi Razvedyatelnyi Aviatsionnyi

Eskadrilya). A TBAD or MRAD consisted of two to three heavy bomber regiments (TBAP – Tyazhelyi Bombardirovochnyi Aviatsionnayi Polk) or naval missile carrier regiments (MRAP – Morskoy Raketonosnyi Aviatsionnyi Polk). Both AVMF and DA aviation regiments consisted of three squadrons. Two squadrons operated combat aircraft while the third flew tankers and electronic countermeasures aircraft.

The first Tu-16s were received in February-March 1954 by 402 TBAP at Balbasovo and 203 TBAP at Baranovichi. Later they were fielded at Engels, while several Tu-16As deployed to Bagerovo.

Re-equipping the AVMF with Tu-16s was preceded by numerous appeals by the navy command for a long-range aircraft. On 24 June 1955 Minister of Defence of the USSR Marshal Zhukov, who did not favour the Navy much, forwarded a letter to the Presidium of the CPSU Central Committee reporting a decision to start re-equipment in the following year. It was planned to send the first 85 aircraft to the Northern Fleet, 170 aircraft of the 1957 delivery plan to the Black Sea and Pacific Fleets and only in 1958 provide 170 aircraft for the Baltic Fleet. In this way the AVMF was to receive 425 Tu-16s within three years.

The first four AVMF Tu-16s were delivered on 1 June 1955, and on 25 June the aircrew of 170 MTAR started flying at Bykhov airfield. In April 1956 Tu-16s were deployed with 5 MTAR of the Black Sea Fleet, and with the Northern Fleet. The Pacific Fleet received them only in 1957. In the initial service period the AVMF mastered bombing and, after receiving the Tu-16T, torpedo dropping, whose technique did not differ from bombing. In the middle of 1957, Tu-16s were delivered to the 4th naval aviation flight training centre, subordinate to the naval mine-torpedo air college at Nikolaev, where a squadron was organised. There were plenty of volunteers to fly the Tu-16 and the selection of candidates focused on age, education, health, level of training, morale and feedback from commanding officers. Pilots with experience of the Tu-4, Tu-14 and Il-28 at the level of class one with a total of not less than 600-700 flying hours were chosen as aircraft commanders, while pilots trained at the level of class two with a total of not less than 200 flying hours became assistant aircraft commanders.

For the Soviet Union the Tu-16 opened an era of heavy jets. It had a lot of peculiarities and a heavy emphasis was placed on the quality of flight training. As initial flying skills were acquired, the mastering of combat employment

followed. With the exception of bombing, the focuses of the DA and AVMF combat training were quite different.

Crews of nuclear weapon-carrying aircraft were selected in a special way. Besides being examined by different commissions, they made a signed statement of non-disclosure of top-secret information. Having been granted admission, the crews studied the physical properties of nuclear weapons and crew manuals, especially those covering emergency procedures. Then, endless training and flights with dummy bombs followed. The crews were trained to precisely reach the target at an appointed time and carry out a single bombing. Crews from the DA's 420 TBAP were the first to receive nuclear weapons for the Tu-16A. They were on combat duty at different airfields, including the naval base at Vesyolyi. With the coming of the Tu-16A, the Spetsnaz squadrons of Il-28s were disbanded.

Nuclear tests

DA Tu-16As were involved in nuclear tests on the ranges near Semipalatinsk and on Novaya Zemlya. In the period from 1957 to 1962, before the treaty banning nuclear tests came into force, 37 nuclear bombs had been dropped at Semipalatinsk. On 22 November 1955 the crew of a Tu-16A dropped the first RDS-37d nuclear bomb with half-filler (1.6 MT yield) over Semipalatinsk. Later, the Tu-16A participated in refining the bombs at Novaya Zemlya. Tu-16A crews not only dropped bombs, but in the interests of short-sighted scientists and dim-witted state-mongers passed through radioactive clouds to collect samples. On 30 November 1961, when the Tu-95V dropped a 'super-bomb' with a TNT equivalent of 57 MT, insulating sleeves of electric wire bundles of the escorting Tu-16 started smoking and the aft gunner received burns, while the aircraft was 55 km (34 miles) away.

In the early 1960s, with ICBMs not yet in service, both DA and AVMF units were ordered to be ready for nuclear retaliation, with targets designated and distributed. However, the limited capabilities of the Tu-16 did not let it reach the USA even from airfields in Amderm, Severomorsk and on Wrangel Island. By the early 1960s no fewer than 16 airfields had been built within the Arctic circle, including ones at Vorkuta and Tiksi. They were regularly used for inter-theatre manoeuvres, as well by the Tu-16s of naval aviation. The earlier experience of using ice airfields by

Il-28s was deemed to be suitable for the Tu-16. However, the first attempt of landing a Tu-16 on an ice airfield in May 1958 resulted in the loss of the aircraft.

After ICBMs took over combat duty, the significance of the 'pure' bomber evaporated and they began to be turned into missile-carriers and other variants. A few bombers were left in the long-range aviation combat training centre at Ryazan. However, major difficulties were to plague the rearming of the 'Badger' fleet missile systems as almost all of them, with the exception of the KSR-5, required considerable improvement and refinement.

As a postscript, during the war in Afghanistan the Tu-16A and Tu-16KSR-2-5 (a missile-carrier with bombing capability) once again became pure bombers to deliver attacks against congregations of Mujahideen, dropping bombs of 250 to 9000 kg (551-19,841 lb) in weight. Bombing was carried out in daylight with optic sights and support was provided by Tu-16Rs and Tu-16Ps for reconnaissance and jamming of Pakistani radars. The aircraft flew from Khanabad, Mary and Karshi airfields in either groups of three or four aircraft or in squadrons of eight to 10 aircraft. On 28 April 1984 a strike was delivered by a group of 24 aircraft, each carrying 24 to 40 FAB-250 bombs.

Tu-16T torpedo bomber

While the first Tu-16s were laid down as standard bombers, a decree issued on 12 July 1954 required that part of the production be converted into torpedo bombers. Plant no. 64 at Voronezh was charged with this task. The first Tu-16T, no. 5400001, left the factory in May 1955. In total, 76 Tu-16Ts were built.

Tu-16Ts did not look any different from their bomber counterparts. As well as bombs, provisions were made for carrying six 45-54 VT and four RAT-52 torpedoes, and six to 12 mines of different types. The entire load was accommodated in the stores bay. For suspending and releasing torpedoes a pneumatic torpedo control system was installed, which fed air to the torpedoes to start their gyros 0.6 seconds prior to release. There were circuits for charging capacitors and warming the weapons. To provide a clean release with minimum yaw, the weapons compartment of the aircraft was fitted with a central guiding girder and four rocking yokes that guided torpedoes from the moment of their release from the locks to the moment of exiting the bomb compartment.

A special circuit to ensure the torpedo's travel depth was added, drawing on the experience of the Pacific Fleet in operating the Il-28 aircraft with RAT-52s. In the incident in question, the torpedo exited the water, climbed 500 m (1,640 ft) and flew for 3.5 km (2.2 miles).

Deploying the Tu-16T added problems, while bringing little real advance to the capabilities of naval aviation other than torpedo bombing from altitude. Good results had been demonstrated during tests with the Tu-2 when torpedoes were released with a divergence angle ('fan' release). Calculations indicated that, if the RAT-52 torpedoes were released with a divergence angle, hit probability could increase by 40-50 percent. However, the optimists were outnumbered by the doubters, and attention shifted its focus to missiles. Torpedoes were not developed any further.

With the Tu-16KS entering naval service, Tu-16T training continued for some time, and trials exercises were conducted. One of them took place in June 1959 with the Black Sea Fleet's 943 mine torpedo air regiment. Three aircraft participated in the exercise, each aircraft packed with six 45-54 VT torpedoes. They undertook three group sorties but the exercise did not carry any practical value and the findings were only of theoretical use. Thus, the Tu-16T turned out to be the last torpedo bomber in the inventory.

Tu-16PL ASW platform

While anti-submarine systems were being developed and hopes for them were high, the situation in the fleets

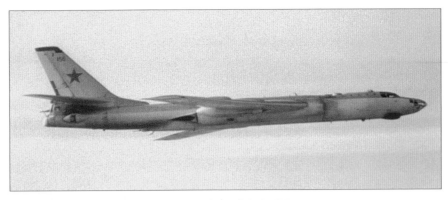

Above: 'Badger-As' continued in service as trainers and for general duties long after the front-line nuclear mission had passed to the missile-carriers. Many served at Ryazan to provide conversion training before crews moved to their operational version.

Left: Tu-16Ts were armed with up to 10 torpedoes, but they could also carry mines, like these AMD-2s.

was quite difficult. There were no assets capable of searching for submarines. Naval aviation possessed a considerable number of relatively new (by the date of manufacturing) and redundant Tu-16Ts, and it was decided to fit them with ASW equipment. The Northern Fleet was the priority, where a public design bureau was established. In 1962 a number of proposals were put forward as to how to equip the Tu-16T for the ASW role. The upgrade was to be co-ordinated with the Tupolev OKB.

In Soviet service the Tu-16 saw its moment of action during the occupation of Afghanistan in the 1980s. 'Badger-A' trainers – like this aircraft – were sporadically involved, as were some missile-carriers. The Tu-16KSR family carried its missiles on wing pylons, and consequently retained a bomb bay.

The black and white attachment projecting from the starboard wingtip of this 'Badger' identifies it as a Tu-16Z tanker, intercepted over the Baltic by a Swedish Saab Viggen in the 1980s. The aircraft is fitted with the SPS-5 Fasol ('kidney bean') jamming equipment, denoted by the small 'pimple' radome under the belly – a common sight on later tanker and Tu-16KSR aircraft. The 'shadow' is a JA 37 from 2./F13, the second squadron of the Bråvalla Flygflottilj at Norrköping.

Here a Tu-16R 'Badger-F' refuels from a Tu-16Z. Once the connection had been established between tanker and receiver the process asked only good formation-keeping of the receiver pilot, but getting hooked up in the first place involved a very demanding manoeuvre undertaken in close quarters to the receiver. By necessity the wingtips had to overlap for the hook-up to be successful.

Dwarfing even the sizeable 'Badger' is the immense bulk of a Typhoon SSBN. Tankers like this Tu-16Z usually served in mixed squadrons with EW aircraft, one squadron supporting two of missile-carriers in a regiment.

In 1962 Tu-16 aircraft from 9 MRAP (Naval Missile Air Regiment) were fitted with the Baku radio sonar system while the stores bay was configured to carry 40 sonobuoys and small bombs in cassettes, becoming Tu-16PLs in the process. In April 1966 the equipment of the Tu-16PL was refined to allow the employment of the AT-1 anti-submarine torpedo. Converting the Tu-16 into an anti-submarine platform was a forced measure. The Tu-16PL squadrons existed over five years before they were disbanded in 1967 in the Northern Fleet, and the following year in the Pacific Fleet.

Tu-16S: search and rescue

A decree of the Government dated 25 December 1955 committed the Ministry of Defence to create a search and rescue service in the Armed Forces, and to form search and rescue squadrons in all naval theatres by 1958. In particular, Minsudprom (the Ministry of ship building industry) was to build in the fourth quarter of 1956 two prototypes of self-propelled boats to equip the Tu-16. The Ministry of aviation industry was to equip the Tu-16 with a boat and present it for testing in the first quarter of 1957.

On 17 June 1958 a prototype evaluation commission examined a model of the project 647 rescue boat (code of the subject was 'Arkhangelsk'), featuring remote radio control. The model received an approval. However, a boat of different design entered service.

The Tu-16S was built on the basis of the Tu-16T, and was named 'Fregat naval aviation rescue system'. The system also included a transportable Fregat air-droppable boat which could be controlled manually or remotely from the aircraft. The aircraft was additionally equipped with boat attachment units, boat guidance and control equipment. The boat was made from duralumin and was of open design with folding tents and a watertight platform which ran along the entire length. The boat was fitted with a 25-kW (33-hp) petrol engine. The endurance of the boat (measured by food and water supply) was up to three days, and it could travel 1480 km (920 miles) in still water with a speed of 5 kt (9.2 km/h) and navigate sea states up to 5. The boat carried airbeds, dry clothes, canned water, fishing tackle, medicine, signalling equipment and a food supply.

Some 14 Tu-16S Fregats were produced by conversion, but they were scrapped in the early 1980s. They had never been used for their intended purpose.

Tankers

Fielding the Tu-16 brought with it the problem of how to increase its range: the only option was air refuelling. As well as range increase, it offered the advantage of an aircraft being able to make a lightweight take-off from a limited-size or muddy airfield, followed by a top-up refuelling. On 17 September 1953 the Ministry of Aviation Industry issued an order prescribing the Tupolev OKB-156 and other aircraft builders to design all bombers with air refuelling systems. At the same time, OKB-918 was ordered to continue working on the tanker for the Tu-16, and submit it for testing in the third quarter of 1954. The first Tu-16Z with the wing refuelling system arrived for testing in 1955 and was tested and refined for more than 18 months. From 1957 the refuelling system was installed on all Tu-16s. In total, 571 Tu-16s had the receiver kit installed, and 114 were converted into Tu-16Z tankers.

Any Tu-16 with a feed tank (10500-10800 litres/ 2,310-2,378 Imp gal) and additional equipment could be used as a tanker. From the starboard wing was extended a 37-m (121-ft 5-in) hose with an inner diameter of 76 mm (3 in) which was attached to a cable. For night refuelling, the right landing gear fairing had searchlights, three lamps and a manual searchlight operated by the gun operator. The left wing panel of the receiver had a contact unit with automatic control and monitoring devices. The unit gripped the feed hose and connected it to the fuel line.

Tanking was possible at an altitude of up to 11000 m (36,090 ft) and a speed of 480-500 km/h (298-311 mph). The fuel feed ratio was 2000 litres (440 Imp gal) per minute. Up to the automatic shutting of the fuel cocks, the refuelled aircraft could receive 17500-19500 litres (3,850-4,289 Imp gal), which increased the flight range by 1500-2000 km (932-1,243 miles).

It must have been hard to invent something as imperfect as the wing refuelling system, which ultimately killed dozens. The tanking process was complicated by the fact that the commander of the aircraft in his left-hand seat could not see the wing of his own aircraft and had to be guided by the marks on the hose and by commands from the gunner.

Both long-range aviation and naval aviation began mastering the art of tanking in 1958, and in 1961 the AVMF began night refuelling, although the procedure was identical. After it had established visual contact with the tanker, the receiver assumed an initial position 2-3 m (6.5-10 ft) above the hose and with 4-6 m (13-20 ft) between the wing and the hose. Relative speeds were then equalised. The pilot then stabilised at a distance some 45 m (148 ft) aft of the tanker, using the hose marks as a guide. Maintaining elevation and position aft, the receiver aircraft was then edged to the left so that the line of its port wingtip over-lapped that of the tanker by about 3-5 m (10-16 ft). Next, the receiver's port wingtip was lowered slightly over the hose to snag it, and then the receiver moved out to about 6-8 m (20-26 ft) separation to grip it.

Above: Over 100 tankers were converted to Tu-16Z or ZA standard (the latter converted from Tu-16A nuclear bombers). There were also a few Tu-16N conversions, which had hose-drogue refuelling systems.

Left: This view shows the limited separation between the two aircraft. Night refuelling greatly increased the risk of collision.

Below left: Laying the wing on top of the trailed hose was the first stage of refuelling, as demonstrated by a Tu-16K-10. The pilot then moved the aircraft out to snag the hose under the receiver's port wingtip.

Below: Having snagged the cable, the receiver had to close the distance between it and the tanker for fuel to flow. Here the receiver is a Tu-16R 'Badger-L'.

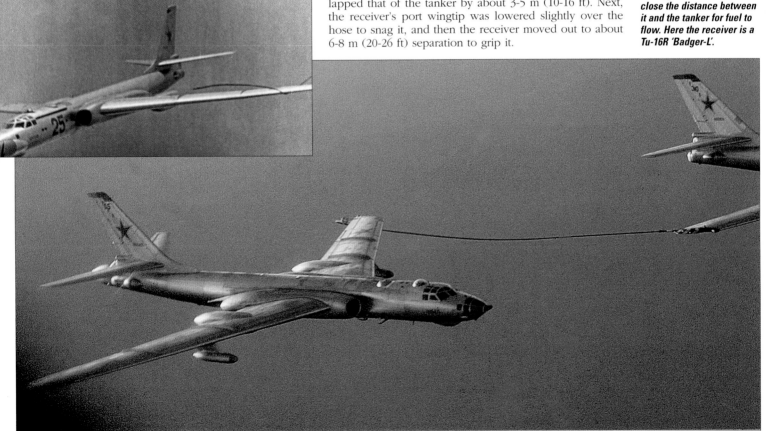

Above: A KS is seen at the moment of launch from a Tu-16KS, the Kobalt-1M guidance radar being clearly visible in its retractable 'dustbin'.

Above right: Tu-16KS aircraft were built as such from new, and featured strong pylons for carriage of the 2735-kg (6,030-lb) KS missile. They were subsequently modified to carry KSR-2s and, later, KSR-5s.

During the winching of the hose from the tanker until contact was established with the nipple, the gunner kept a running report, chiefly concerning the remainder of the rear end of the hose. Upon establishment of contact the refuelling system was activated, and the distance between the two aircraft was reduced by 10 m (33 ft). After that fuel feed started. Altitudes over 8000 m (26,250 ft) made refuelling complicated because of the aircraft's lack of manoeuvrability. Consequently, an altitude of 6000-7000 m (19,685-22,965 ft) was considered ideal.

There were other tanker versions: the Tu-16N was designed for refuelling the Tu-22 'Blinder' using a standard hose-drogue unit and probe receiver system. This was tested on Tu-16N no. 1882401 and several aircraft were

retrofitted in 1963. The Tu-16NN was based on the Tu-16Z but had a fuselage HDU and the wing refuelling system removed. It differed from the Tu-16N in having aerodynamic plates on the wingtips. Long-range aviation retrofitted a total of 20 aircraft. The Tu-16D was a Tu-16 retrofitted for receiving from a drogue-equipped tanker system. Tests were successful.

Tu-16K – missile-carriers

Of all the many tasks assigned to the Tu-16 throughout its long career, the most important was that of missile-carrier, leading to a wealth of variants. Work to create the Kometa aircraft missile system started in 1947. The cruise missile was developed by the A.I. Mikoyan OKB-155 headed by M.I. Gurevich, the carrier aircraft was the responsibility of the OKB headed by A.N. Tupolev, and SKB-1 headed by S.L. Beriya was charged with the development of control and guidance system. The missile system was intended to attack large surface ships at a range of 2000 km (1,243 miles) from the base airfield with the carrier aircraft beyond the reach of hostile air defences.

Mikoyan's KS missile (AS-1 'Kennel') was a smaller replica of the MiG-15 aircraft, with a maximum speed of 1100-1200 km/h (684-746 mph), range of 70-90 km (43-56 miles), length of 8.29 m (27 ft 2 in), launch weight of 2735 kg (6,030 lb) and a warhead of 1015 kg (2,238 lb). It was fitted with a single-mode (short-duration) RD-500K engine.

The control system consisted of equipment installed both on the carrier aircraft and the missile. Aircraft-mounted equipment included the Kobalt target detection, lock-on and auto-tracking radar, and the K-3 missile radio control equipment. The missile carried the K-2 radio control equipment, which was matched with the APK-5V autopilot. The K-2 receiving antenna was fin-mounted, and the K-1 homing equipment with its antenna was located in the forward part of the missile. Kometa was a radio command system, with semi-active homing in the terminal phase. When the target was detected and the carrier aircraft radar changed over to lock-on and tracking mode, the missile was launched and the operator guided its flight. As the signal reflected from the target was received by the aircraft's radar, the missile switched to homing mode using the K-1 system.

KS missile

Mikoyan's pug-nosed KS-1 missile was clearly based on the MiG-15 fighter. Guidance equipment consisted of the K-1 homing equipment, which was housed in the nose radome, and the K-2 radio command guidance equipment, the antenna for which was located in a bullet fairing at the tip of the fin (right). The Kometa system was originally tested on the Tu-4KS, but the operational missiles were fielded by the Tu-16KS aircraft of 124 TBAP in 1957.

Both Egypt and Indonesia received Tu-16KS aircraft and their associated KS missiles. These two are Indonesian machines, the aircraft above showing the Kobalt-1M radar extended on the ground for maintenance access.

A directive of the Main Staff of the Navy, dated 30 August 1955, was the starting point for the organisation of the 124 heavy bomber air regiment (TBAP) as a unit of the Black Sea Navy aviation. It was equipped with 12 Tu-4KS and two MiG-15SDK, plus sundry MiG-15UTIs, Li-2s and Po-2s. It was the first missile-carrier aircraft regiment in the air force. The MiG-15SDK (and subsequently the MiG-17SDK) was fitted with the equipment of the KS missile system, an autopilot and recording equipment.

For training, one or two MiG-15SDKs were suspended from the Tu-4KS and the latter took off and headed for the test range. Flying along a combat course, the crew of the Tu-4KS operated in the sequence identical to the missile launch procedure, although the engine of the converted fighter was started by the pilot. After separation from the Tu-4KS the receiving unit of the MiG-15SDK received guidance signals that were translated into control commands fed to the autopilot. The pilot did not interfere with the control of the aircraft until it dived and approached the target to a distance of 500-600 m (1,640-1,970 ft). Then he switched off the autopilot, took over control of the aircraft and flew to the landing airfield. The performance of the guidance system was analysed on the basis of data registered by the recorders in both the Tu-4KS and MiG-15SDK.

Tu-16KS 'Badger-B'

Taking into consideration the disadvantages of the Tu-4, it was decided that the missile system needed another carrier. The Tu-16 was the only alternative and, in 1954, along with some upgrade work, aircraft no. 4200305 was fitted with part of the Tu-4KS equipment. An improved Kobalt-1M radar was fitted and two external wing racks with locks and fairings were installed. Until the moment of their release the missiles were supplied with fuel from a 2300-litre (506-Imp gal) No. 1 tank, which was isolated from the aircraft's own fuel system.

At the same time, the crew gained one more member – a navigator-operator who was responsible for all operations related to the employment of the missiles. A suspended cabin was provided which was fitted to the lower attachment points of the bomb racks in the stores bay. The cabin had everything required for life support. Operating inside the cabin was quite difficult, especially in the summer. Besides, the operator in his box could not see anything and felt separated from the crew.

First deliveries of Tu-16KS aircraft with the Kometa missile system started in 1953, to naval aviation. In 1954, at the Black Sea Fleet aviation airfield at Gvardeiskoe in the Crimea, the 27th Separate Aviation Unit was formed. Live missile test launches were carried out at Bagerovo, the base of the Air Force R&D Institute. They ended in 1955 with the adoption of the missile. The tests indicated that the maximum flight speed of the Tu-16KS carrying two missiles dropped by 100 km/h (62 mph) and with one missile by 30 km/h (18.6 mph), while the take-off run became longer. The range of the Tu-16KS carrying two missiles and returning empty was 3250 km (2,020 miles) and 3560 km (2,212 miles) with one missile. The take-off weight of the aircraft carrying two missiles increased to 76000 kg (167,548 lb).

'Badger-Gs' carrying the KSR-2 missile were converted from either Tu-16KSs (Tu-16KSR-2) or from redundant free-fall bombers (Tu-16KSR-2A). The upgraded aircraft and its new missile entered service in 1963, but it was soon supplanted by the much better KSR-5 system.

This Tu-16KSR-2-11 has the SPS-5 Fasol EW system mounted in its belly. When upgraded to carry the KSR-11 anti-radar missile, the 'Badger-G' was known as either the Tu-16KSR-2-11 or the Tu-16K-11-16, depending on its former configuration. Aircraft with KSR-11 capability were fitted with the Ritsa radar-targeting system with characteristic nose antenna array.

Left: This Tu-16KSR-2 carries two missiles. From the calibration marks on the forward fuselage it can be assumed to be a test aircraft. KSR-2 tests were undertaken in 1960/61, although not without problems. KSR-11 tests were accomplished at much the same time. In 1968 the system was 'tweaked' and recertificated as the KSR-2M to allow launches from low altitude.

Series production of the KS missile with folding wings and increased fuel capacity was launched in 1957. With allowance made for the capabilities of the carrier aircraft's equipment, the missile upgrade provided a launch range of up to 150 km (93 miles).

Tu-16KSR

The KSR programme was created in accordance with an order of the Ministry of Aviation Industry dated 29 April 1957. It charged OKB-273 with the task of improving the Kometa system using new Rubikon airborne equipment, which combined the functions of the K-2M and the then up-to-date Rubin-1 radar (NATO: 'Short Horn'). In compliance with a decree issued 2 April 1958, a design bureau headed by A.Ya. Bereznyak was preparing the KSR version of the KS missile, equipped with a two-chamber liquid propellant engine designed by A.M. Isaev. The aim was to increase the altitude and launch speed range. The voracious engine required more fuel and the capacity of the tank for TG-02 fuel reached 666 litres (146.5 Imp gal). For the AK-20F oxidiser there was a 1032-litre (227-Imp gal) tank made of stainless steel. The fuel ignited when the two components reacted with each other. The warhead was taken from the K-10S missile developed by OKB-155. Since there was no air intake, the diameter of the KSR missile was reduced to 1 m (39.4 in) and the wings were made to fold. The missile radio control equipment included a K-1MR station and an APK-5D autopilot.

Between 1 July and 15 November 1959, 22 test sorties were undertaken, and KSR missiles were launched during nine of them. Out of six launches at a range of 90-96 km

KSR-2/11 missile

Although its roots lay in the KS, the KSR-2 missile was much cleaner aerodynamically thanks to the use of a liquid-propellant rocket motor. The motor had two chambers: one for boost and one for cruise. This example is seen on display under the wing of a Tu-16R reconnaissance aircraft.

(56-60 miles), four resulted in direct hits. The tests near Feodosia revealed low reliability of the guidance system and the missile was not endorsed for fielding. Nevertheless, the KSR missile entered service with the 5th Mine-torpedo Air Regiment of the Black Sea Fleet aviation and crews carried out launches.

Tu16K-16/Tu-16KSR-2

As a further development of the Tu-16KSR system, the Tu-16K-16 was developed in accordance with a decree dated 22 August 1959. OKB-283 updated the homing head of the missile by installing a larger antenna, covered by a radome which was almost the diameter of the missile, while the stabiliser was moved from the fin to the fuselage. The missile suite was designated K-16, while the system itself acquired the designation of Tu-16K-16. It included the Tu-16KSR-2 aircraft, the KSR-2 missile (AS-5 'Kelt'), Rubikon control equipment fitted to the aircraft and the missile, testing and measuring equipment, and servicing assets. The system was designed to attack targets such as large ships (with a displacement over 10,000 tons), railway bridges and dams. The guidance system used the missile's active radar from launch to strike, a principle later to be called 'fire-and-forget'.

Tu-16KSR-2 aircraft were fitted with the following equipment: upgraded radar designated Rubin-1k (Rn-1k), external store racks, and an AP-6E autopilot instead of the AP-5-2M. Changes were made in the fuel system. Missile guidance equipment consisted of the Tu-16's Rn-1k radar, the KS-2M homing radar of the cruise missile and its AP-72-4 autopilot. The Rn-1k searched for the target and commanded the KS-2M radar and the AP-72-4 autopilot before the release of the missile. During ground preparation of the Rn-1k radars it was possible to change the frequency range of their transmitters by up to 3 percent, which prevented interference during multiple launches. The navigator operated the Rn-1k radar in all its modes.

The KSR-2 missile was a mid-wing monoplane with a length of 8.65 m (28 ft 5 in), wingspan of 4.5 m (14 ft 9 in) and a sweep angle of the wing and the tail unit of 55°. The weight of the missile was 4000 kg (8,818 lb). In its forward part the missile accommodated the KS-2M radar and the warhead compartment, which could be fitted with either a conventional or nuclear charge. The 850-kg (1,874-lb) FK-2 high-explosive hollow-charge warhead was capable of penetrating steel armour 30 cm (12 in) thick. For attacking ground targets there was an FK-2N high-explosive warhead.

In the detachable tail section was the autopilot and a C5.6 liquid propellant engine which weighed 48.5 kg (107 lb). The engine developed 11.9 kN (2,674 lb) thrust operating in the boost mode and 6.93 kN (1,559 lb) in the cruise mode with the fuel consumption 5.4 and 2.3 kg (11.9 and 5.1 lb) per second, respectively. It started automatically 7 seconds after release. Power was supplied by a self-activating storage battery.

In June-July 1960 production Tu-16KS no. 720368 was fitted with additional equipment and acquired the designation of Tu-16KSR-2. Tests carried out from 20 October 1960 to 30 March 1961 revealed the need for further refinement and testing. A decree issued on 30 December 1961 endorsed the system for fielding by both naval and long-range aviation. With two missiles at a take-off weight of 76000 kg (167,548 lb), the Tu-16KSR-2 had a range of up to 1850 km (1,150 miles). The range of the missile's radar in detecting seaborne and ground targets was 220-290 km (137-180 miles), and launch range was 160-170 km (99 to 106 miles).

Beginning in 1962 some 205 aircraft were converted to 'Badger-G' configuration. These comprised 50 Tu-16KS, which became Tu-16KSR-2s, and 155 redundant Tu-16A bombers, which became Tu-16KSR-2As. Their wings were reinforced to accommodate external racks, the maximum flap setting was reduced by 5° and cutouts were made in the flaps for the missile fin. As well as the ability to carry

the KSR-2 missile, the 'Badger-G' retained its free-fall bombing capability. In the early 1970s some of the Tu-16KSR-2As were equipped with SPS-5 Fasol and SPS-100 Rezeda jammers. The latter was located in a special compartment in place of the tail gun.

Tu-16K-11 anti-radar system

Developed in accordance with a decree issued on 20 July 1957, the Tu-16K-11 system was intended as a development of either the KS or KSR missiles for the anti-radar role. Since the KSR provided for the installation of a larger diameter antenna it was selected as the preferable platform.

By the end of 1959 development of the Ritsa reconnaissance and target designation radar was completed. Components were housed in the nose landing gear bay, while a T-shaped direction-finding antenna was located on the upper framing of the navigator's canopy. To maintain the aircraft's centre of gravity the AM-23 nose gun was removed.

The KSR-11 missile was based on the KSR-2 and had much in common with it. The nose section of the missile was occupied by the 2PRG-10 (passive radio target seeker) with a gyrostabiliser and elements of the radar. Behind them there was a warhead, integral tanks with fuel and oxidiser, while the tail section housed the AP-72-11 autopilot, storage batteries and other equipment. A liquid propellant engine was installed under a detachable tail fairing. The weight of the armed missile was 3995 kg

(8,807 lb) with 1575 kg (3,472 lb) of oxidiser and 530 kg (1,168 lb) of fuel. The 840-kg (1,852-lb) warhead was of two types: FA-11 high-explosive fragmentation or FK-2 high-explosive hollow charge.

After the 2PRG-10 had completed tuning to the frequency of the target radar and had locked on to it, the missile was launched. The aircraft released the missile at a distance of 160-170 km (99 to 106 miles) upon receiving its readiness signal. Depending on the launch altitude, the missile dropped by 400 to 1200 m (1,312 to 3,937 ft) within the first 5 seconds. After 7 seconds the liquid propellant engine started operating and reached afterburning mode.

Forty seconds later an electronic time relay connected the output of the 2PRG-10 radar course channel to the autopilot, and from that moment its signals exercised directional control. Another 20 seconds later the engine changed

Although the full warload comprised two missiles, 'Badger-Gs' were mostly intercepted carrying one on the port wing. Above is an aircraft showing evidence of having been a Tu-16KS in a former incarnation. It is most likely a later Tu-16K-26 or Tu-16KSR-2-5, which retained the ability to launch the older KSR-2 missiles despite being equipped for the much better KSR-5.

Above left: This 'Badger-G' lacks the nose-mounted Ritsa antenna, and is probably a Tu-16KSR-2 or KSR-2-5. As well as anti-ship attacks, the KSR family of weapons could also be used against high-value and land targets with large radar returns such as bridges, dams or large buildings.

Tu-16KSR-2-5-11/Rn-1M

When the KSR-5 missile (AS-6 'Kingfish') was added to the Tu-16's arsenal, its increased range caused some operational problems. Chiefly, the range of the missile's active seeker was greater than that of the standard Rubin-1k radar fitted to Tu-16KSR aircraft. An initial attempt to overcome the shortfall involved fitment of Berkut radar (from the Il-38 'May') to the 14 aircraft of a single Baltic Fleet squadron. A more widespread upgrade, however, was the installation of a Rubin-1m radar in a large belly radome, while the undernose Rn-1k and nose cannon were removed. Rn-1m radar was retrofitted to both Tu-16KSR-2-5 and Tu-16KSR-2-5-11 aircraft, the numerical suffixes denoting which missiles the aircraft could carry. On at least one occasion a Tu-16KSR-2-5-11 with Rn-1m radar was spotted while carrying a KSR-5 and KSR-11 together.

Many of the problems associated with the earlier missiles were overcome with the adoption of the KSR-5, itself very closely modelled on the Kh-22 developed for the Tu-22 and Tu-22M. Its Mach 3 fly-out and terminal attack speed, combined with tactics which would involve the launch of several weapons against a single target, made it a very formidable system to defend against. Many of its Tu-16KSR-2-5, Tu-16KSR-2-5-11 and Tu-16K-26 carriers were upgraded with Rubin-1m radar to increase the effective range of the missile.

Right and below: Tu-16s carrying two KSR-5s were only rarely encountered, the normal load being one. Both of these aircraft have Ritsa nose antennas and Rubin-1m radar.

to sustainer mode and the missile was flying at the launch altitude. When the angle between the longitudinal axis of the missile and the direction to the target in the vertical plane reached 25°, it dived and the passive system guided it to the target. If the signal of the target radar disappeared, the 2PRG-10 switched into memory or search modes, depending on the conditions.

Kazan converted two Tu-16s into the carriers for the KSR-11, and they were designated Tu-16K-11. The first aircraft flew in January 1960. The system was tested for two years before a decree dated 13 April 1962 approved its fielding with the following performance: launch altitude range 4000-11000 m (13,123-36,090 ft), radar detection range 270-350 km (168-217 miles) and launch range 150-170 km (93 to 106 miles). The hit probability was estimated at between 0.8 and 0.9. Starting in 1962, the KSR-2 (article 085) and the KSR-11 missiles (article 086) replaced the KS and its variants in serial production.

Taking into consideration the specific employment of the KSR-11 it was decided to make it compatible with existing systems. The Tu-16KSR-2-11 system was approved for fielding in 1962 and included the modified Tu-16KSR-2-11 carrier aircraft, the KSR-11 and KSR-2 missiles, test and measuring equipment and ground equipment. The aircraft carried two KSR-2 or two KSR-11 missiles in any combination, and both conventional and nuclear bombs. Carrying two missiles the combat radius was 1900 km (1,180 miles) and 2300 km (1,429 miles) with one.

The similar Tu-16K-11-16 system included a carrier aircraft converted from the Tu-16KS. Sometimes it was designated as Tu-16K-11-16KS, and differed from the Tu-16KSR-2-11 in having riveted cutouts of the pressurised cabin entrance door and the Kobalt-P radar mounted on the bomb bay doors. At operating units the aircraft were known as the Tu-16K-11-16. Naval aviation deployed 130 aircraft and long-range aviation 211.

Tu-16K-26 'Badger-G Mod'

The Tu-16K-26 system (initially designated K-36) was developed in accordance with a decree issued on 11 August 1962 and was intended to destroy both radar contrast targets and operating radars on both sea and land. The system comprised the Tu-16K-26, Tu-16KSR-2-5 and Tu-16KSR-2-5-11 carrier aircraft, new KSR-5 missiles with conventional and nuclear warheads, and the older KSR-2 and KSR-11 missiles. The system was based on the use of the supersonic KSR-5 (AS-6 'Kingfish') with active homing in direction and pitch, and programmed control in altitude. This took the missile into the stratosphere for cruise, with a subsequent dive on to the target.

A smaller version of the Kh-22 (AS-4 'Kitchen') carried by the Tu-95 and Tu-22, the KSR-5 had a delta wing, tail-mounted elevons which controlled pitch and roll, and an upper fin for yaw control. A lower vertical fin remained folded until launch, and had no control surface. The propulsion system consisted of an S5.33A liquid propellant engine, and a fuel and air system. The two-chamber engine with turbopump injection had automatic mode control. The engine fuel consisted of two components: 660 litres (145 Imp gal) of TG-02 propellant and 1010 litres (222 Imp gal) of AK-27P oxidiser. The air system provided pressurisation of the waveguides, fuel and oxidiser tanks, and

Many 'Badger-Gs' already had an anti-radar capability thanks to the KSR-11 missile, but improvements in this field were introduced by the KSR-5P version of the AS-6 'Kingfish'. When modified to carry this weapon the aircraft were designated Tu-16K-26P, which became the final major variant of this missile-carrying family, and the last 'Badger' version to see widespread Soviet front-line service. All K-26Ps had the Ritsa direction-finding antennas on the nose.

power for the deployment of the lower fin and other operations.

Missile launch altitude varied between 500 and 11000 m (1,640 and 36,090 ft) and aircraft speed during launch ranged between 400 and 850 km/h (248 and 528 mph). Launched from 500 m the missile range was 40 km (25 miles), while from 11000 m it could reach 280 km (174 miles). The missile was 10.6 m (34 ft 9 in) long with a wingspan of 2.6 m (8 ft 6 in) and a body diameter of 0.92 m (3 ft). The fully tanked missile weighed 3952 kg (8,712 lb). It was equipped with either a 9A52 high-explosive hollow charge or a TK38 nuclear warhead.

The missile guidance system included VS-KN radio guidance equipment, autopilot, Mach switch and altitude switch. The VS-KN was a long-range active homing seeker which locked on to and automatically tracked the target while under the wing of the aircraft, following identification of the range and direction to the target. The missile was released at a rated distance. Two seconds later the engine ignited and the missile accelerated. After 15 seconds it began to climb and, upon reaching Mach 3, the booster chamber of the engine was cut off. At an altitude of 18000 m (59,055 ft) the missile began to level off and the engine switched to sustainer mode. After that the missile remained in a stabilised flight at an altitude of 22500 m (73,820 ft). As the slant range to the target reached 60 km (37 miles), a dive command was issued. At a distance of 400-500 m (1,312-1,640 ft) to the target, direction and pitch radio guidance was disabled. In case of jamming, the missile magnetron frequency was retuned and operation of the logic circuitry switched to the memory mode.

As time went by, a number of modifications were made to the basic KSR-5, such as the low-altitude KSR-5N (the K-26N system with a low-altitude radar) and the KSR-5M (the K-26M system for countering complex small-size targets).

Flight tests of the K-26 system started in October 1964 with two aircraft, a converted Tu-16K-11-16KS (no. 8204022) and a Tu-16KSR-2A no. 5202010, which was redesignated Tu-16KSR-2-5. Some flights of the programme were made by Tu-16K-26 no. 420073 and Tu-16K-10-26 no. 1793014. Tests were suspended several times, and it was not until 12 November 1969 that a decree approved the K-26 system for fielding.

From 1969 the overhaul plants of the Air Force and the Navy modified 15 Tu-16K-11-16KS into the Tu-16K-26, 125 Tu-16KSR-2A into the Tu-16KSR-2-5-11 and 110 Tu-16KSR-2A into the Tu-16KSR-2-5. By comparison with the Tu-16KSR-2-5-11, the latter lacked the nose-mounted antenna of the Ritsa system and could not use the KSR-11 anti-radiation missile.

KSR-5 missile

The KSR-5 missile appeared in the 1970s, and was far more capable of penetrating heavy defences than the KSR-2/11. After launch it accelerated and climbed to altitude, before diving at around Mach 3 on to its target. For the anti-ship mission a large conventional warhead was usually employed, while for land targets a nuclear TK38 was the warhead of choice. The KSR-5M was a low-altitude launch version.

Below: A KSR-5 is displayed on a Tu-16. The ventral fin would normally be folded until launch, but is seen here in flight position.

Above: Like its forebear, the KSR-5 employed a two-chamber motor. The large chamber accelerated and climbed the weapon to Mach 3 at around 18000 m (59,055 ft), while the smaller chamber sustained it in level flight.

Tu-16K-26 s/n 1883704
1st Squadron, 99th Guards Independent Reconnaissance Regiment (GvORAP)
Priozyorsk, Sary-Shagan air base, Kazakhstan, late 1980s

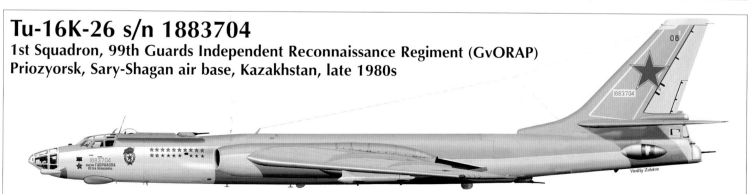

The Tu-16K-10 represented a major advance in Soviet missile warfare, for it introduced the first supersonic weapon in the form of the K-10S. The missile drew on elements of the MiG-19, including a version of its engine, and its guidance system was tested using MiG-19SMK surrogates. Installing the massive YeN radar in the Tu-16 necessitated moving the navigator from his nose compartment.

Above: This dramatic photograph captures the moment of launch of a K-10S. The missile was introduced to service in 1960, and was chiefly viewed as an anti-ship weapon.

Right: Crew inspect an armed Tu-16K-10. The missile was carried on a pylon which raised the weapon into the belly recess to provide ground clearance for take-off and landing, and to reduce drag in the cruise. For firing the pylon was lowered so that the missile could fly free from the aircraft.

Right: A Tu-16K-10 makes a pass with its K-10S missile in the lowered launch position.

Below: This view of a Tu-16K-10 at rest shows the missile in its raised position. The radome of the YeN radar actually improved the aerodynamics of the 'Badger'.

Problems emerged with retrofitting the Tu-16KSR-2 aircraft. It was discovered that the KSR-5 missile's radar surpassed the aircraft's Rn-1k in detection range. As an alternative, 14 aircraft of the naval aviation were equipped with the Berkut radar of the Il-38 aircraft, with a slight change in the shape of the radome. In 1973 some of the Tu-16KSR-2-5-11s were fitted with a Rubin-1m radar optic system with a longer detection range, increasing the launch range of the KSR-5 missile to 450 km (280 miles). The radome of the Rubin-1m radar was located under the forward part of the stores bay, and required the removal of the nose gun. Tu-16KSR-2-5s were also upgraded with Rubin-1m radar.

Tu-16K-26P

This system was developed in accordance with a decree issued on 7 February 1964. It was a modification of the K-26 system and was intended to destroy radar contrast targets with either KSR-2 and KSR-5 missiles, and radars operating in pulse mode with either KSR-11 and KSR-5P missiles. The KSR-5P missile radio guidance system consisted of the VSP-K equipment and an autopilot mounted in the missile, and elements of the aircraft-carried ANP-K radar and Ritsa direction-finding system. Two KSR-5Ps could be launched against one or two targets, provided they were within a 7.5° sector from the longitudinal axis of the aircraft. After the release of the missiles the aircraft made a turn.

State tests of the system began in April 1972. A decree issued 4 September 1974 approved it for fielding to the Navy. In the following year the naval overhaul plants started converting the Tu-16KSR-2-5-11 into the Tu-16K-26P. The aircraft retained its ability to launch the older missiles, and to deliver free-fall weapons.

Tu-16K-10 'Badger-C'

Development of missile-carrying 'Badgers' proceeded along two parallel lines. While the Tu-16KS/KSR family was developed, the Tu-16K emerged as a separate track with a very different mission fit. In the fullness of time, the two tracks were to move closer together with the common adoption of the KSR-5.

Initially intended for the '105' aircraft (Tu-22 'Blinder'), the K-10 system was intended to attack surface vessels with a displacement over 10,000 tons. Construction of the '105' aircraft was delayed, so it was decided to test the K-10 system on the Tu-16 instead. A decree issued on 3 February 1955 initiated development of the Tu-16K-10, with completion of tests scheduled for the third quarter of 1958. On 10 December 1957 plant no. 22 at Kazan completed the first Tu-16K (no. 7203805) and the second (no. 7203806) the following year.

Meanwhile, the first K-10 missile was sent to the test range at Vladimirovka in October 1957. From January 1957 two Tu-16Ks, two MiG-19SMKs and 36 missiles (34 with telemetry equipment and two live) were employed in tests. Initially, the test series encountered numerous unforeseen difficulties, and in the middle of 1958 a dilemma emerged as to whether it was expedient to proceed with the K-10 or not. In the event, a compromise was reached in which a new missile was to be developed for the Tu-22 (Kh-22) while the K-10 continued its development as a weapon for the Tu-16.

Following the guidelines of this decision, taken by the government commission for the military industry on 28 July

1958, another 10 aircraft equipped with telemetry equipment and two production Tu-16Ks were allocated for tests. In the course of testing 44 launches of missiles were made, including four launches against ground targets with corner reflectors and 34 against a target vessel on the air force's range no. 77 in the Caspian Sea. The ship was the half-submerged 9,100-ton tanker *Chkalov*, also equipped with corner reflectors.

From 5 September 1959 to 5 November 1960 the guidance system of the K-10 was tested. For that purpose ships of the Black Sea Fleet were employed as targets and the MiG-19SMK aircraft were used as surrogate missiles, having been equipped with the K-10's guidance system. In 1959, before tests were complete, large-scale production of the Tu-16K-10 was launched.

During state tests 20 K-10S missiles with production equipment were launched, of which eight missiles failed to reach their targets because of malfunctions and defects in design and manufacturing, and two missed their targets because of mistakes by the crews. Despite objections by the manufacturer, the results of the tests stated in the Act indicated that the technical serviceability of the system was rated as only 0.55. Later, on the basis of results of live launches carried out by the naval aviation, the hit probability in the Act of state tests was increased to 0.8. A decree of the Government of the USSR issued on 12 August 1961 endorsed the fielding of the K-10 system to naval aviation.

Production threatened

Overall, the Tu-16K-10 complex comprised the Tu-16K carrier aircraft, the K-10S air-to-ship missile, control system, ground preparation and servicing equipment. The Tu-16K differed from the Tu-16KS to such an extent that retrofitting the latter did not seem expedient. The first serial Tu-16K, no. 8204010, was built at Kazan in April 1958, but by the end of 1959 only seven Tu-16Ks equipped with refuelling systems had been built, and production was stopped. The destiny of the entire system was under threat as production of the Tu-16 was closed. Plant no. 64 at Voronezh was making the An-10, Kazan was preparing for production of the Tu-22, while plant no. 1 at Kuibyshev was transferring to the production of missiles.

On 6 June 1958, to save the situation, the Air Force commander-in-chief, deputy chairman of the Council of

Ministers D.F. Ustinov and the chairman of the State Committee for aviation, turned to the Central Committee of the CPSU with a proposal to continue building the Tu-16 at the Kuibyshev plant and make 173 aircraft (13 Tu-16s and 40 Tu-16Ks in 1958 and 60 Tu-16Ks during each of the following two years). By June 1960 the Kuibyshev plant had built 59 Tu-16Ks. In June next year Kazan began the manufacture of 150 Tu-16Ks, to add to seven produced earlier. A total of 216 Tu-16Ks was built.

To employ the K-10S missiles the Tu-16 was considerably upgraded: the nose section was redesigned with a large radome housing the antenna system for a target search and tracking channel, and the YeN radar (NATO: 'Puff Ball') transmitter. The radome slightly improved the aerodynamic characteristics of the aircraft and was necessarily large to accommodate the YeN's large antenna, which also traversed mechanically through 120° azimuth to continue guiding the missile even after the aircraft turned away. The missile guidance channel antenna was located in the fairing under the forward fuselage in the place of the standard Tu-16's radar.

The Tu-16K-10 was mainly operated by the AVMF, and it was commonly intercepted by Western air arms over international waters. Despite unreliability, the K-10 system offered significant advantages over the KS – notably the ability to launch up to 18 missiles simultaneously and the ability of the YeN radar to support the missiles at an angle up to 60° from the direction of flight.

K-10 missile

This K-10S is seen on its loading trolley, with wings folded. The RD-9FK turbojet engine had afterburning to propel the missile to supersonic speeds. The fin folded for carriage. Variants of the basic missile were the nuclear K-10SB, K-10SN low-level launch weapon, K-10SD with increased range, K-10SND low-level, increased-range weapon, and K-10SP jammer missile.

Production of Tu-16K-10s reached 216, making it the most numerous of the missile-carrying versions. Construction was handled at both Kuibyshev and Kazan to satisfy the demands for the type. However, according to plans the aircraft should not have been built at all: the K-10 system was destined to be fitted to the Tu-22 'Blinder', although delays with that programme meant that it was applied to the Tu-16 instead. The 'Blinder' eventually matured with the K-22 system with the Kh-22 (AS-4 'Kitchen') missile.

The crew of the Tu-16K consisted of six men. The navigator was moved to the navigator-operator station, and the stores bay was made longer. Tank no. 3 was removed, and the aircraft was fitted with a pressurised bay cabin for the navigator-operator of the YeN radar and missile guidance equipment. An additional 500-kg (1,102-lb) fuel tank provided a supply for the missile's engine while it was on the rack. Bombing capability was removed.

K-10S missile carriage was provided on an external rack under the fuselage. For take-off and cruise the rack was raised so that the upper half of the missile was inside the stores bay, but before launch the rack and missile were lowered by 55 cm (22 in) into the firing position. Despite somewhat better streamline characteristics than other variants, the cruising speed reduced to 780-820 km/h (485-510 mph) and combat radius to 1900 km (1,180 miles).

The capabilities of the Tu-16K-10 expanded over the years, mostly in the areas of increased missile range (K-10SD) and reduced launch altitude (K-10SN). The latter was of particular importance as all forms of aerial warfare moved to low-level to defeat ever more sophisticated defences. A novel idea was the use of the K-10SP missile, which had jammers instead of a warhead. It blinded hostile defences to allow armed missiles to penetrate.

Right: This cockpit view was taken aboard a Tu-16K-10 during a mission in 1961. In the centre of the dashboard is the missile control panel.

Below: Landing the Tu-16 with the missile retracted was no problem, as can be judged from this view. However, if the retraction mechanism failed there was very little ground clearance to land back safely with the weapon.

Known to NATO as the AS-2 'Kipper', the K-10S had a 7-m² (75-sq ft) wing with 55° sweep, and a folding tail unit. Power came from a short-endurance RD-9FK turbojet engine with an afterburner chamber, a version of the RD-9B engine used in the MiG-19 fighter. When not in use the engine was covered by a drop-down fairing. The engine provided a speed of 2030 km/h (1,261 mph), making the K-10S the USSR's first supersonic missile. Dimensions were 9.75 m (32 ft) length, 4.18 m (13 ft 8 in) wing span, 0.92 m (3 ft) body diameter and weight of 4500 kg (9,921 lb) with 780 kg (1,720 lb) of fuel. The missile could carry either a conventional or a nuclear warhead.

Missile guidance equipment was located in the extremities of the fuselage: the forward part housed the ES-2-1 antenna and elements of the ES-2 homing head, the tail part housed the ES-1 radio guidance equipment. The main tank was made from steel and was located between frames 15 and 19. The total capacity tank was 1573 litres (346 Imp gal). Behind the main tank there were elements of the ES-3 autopilot, hydraulic accumulator and hydraulic pump.

The high-energy YeN radar was used for searching for and tracking the target while the missile was on its trajectory. Frequency spacing of the radar allowed the simultaneous launch of 18 missiles. The K-10S missile was launched at a distance of 180-200 km (112-124 miles) from the target. Before launch, the navigator-operator locked on the target for auto-tracking, guidance equipment ran through self-test procedures, and the missile engine was run up to full afterburner.

Missile trajectory was divided into three phases: self-contained flight, stabilised altitude flight, and terminal dive. Depending on the launch altitude, 40 seconds after release the missile could have dropped by 600-1500 m (1,969-4,920 ft). It then climbed and flew horizontally at a stabilised cruise altitude. At a distance of 100-110 km (62-68 miles) to the target the carrier aircraft commanded the missile to dive at an angle of 12-17° and the missile attained its maximum speed. At an altitude of 2000 m (6,562 ft) the dive angle changed to 5-6° and the missile flew at its second stabilised altitude of 1200 m (3,937 ft). Some 15-20 km (9.3-12.5 miles) out from the target the missile homed in direction and altitude. 6.5 km (4 miles) short of the target the missile dived at an angle of 15-18°. The warhead exploded on impact with the target.

Meanwhile, 100 seconds after missile launch the Tu-16K's crew could turn 60° either side with a roll of 9-12°, the bank angle being limited by the stabilisation of the YeN antenna, which continued to guide the missile towards the target and monitored its flight by the signals from its transponder.

In 1963 the Tu-16K-10N with the low-altitude K-10SN missile was developed. A number of engineering solutions helped reduce launch altitude from 5000 to 1500 m (16,404 to 4,921 ft) and the second stabilised altitude from 1200 to 600 m (3,937 to 1,968 ft). Subsequently, the altitude of the last phase was successfully brought down to 90-150 m (295-492 ft).

Tu-16K-10SD

This upgrade employed an increased-range missile with an upgraded engine fuel system, which reduced fuel consumption per kilometre and added 65 km (40 miles) in range. The TK-34 warhead was replaced by a smaller TK-50 and it provided the possibility to install an additional 200-litre (44-Imp gal) tank. This gave a 40-km (25-mile) increment in range. Therefore, the maximum missile launch distance grew by 105 km (65 miles) to 325 km (202 miles). The launch altitude range expanded from 5000-10000 m (16,404-32,808 ft) to 1500-11000 m (4,921-36,090 ft). The retrofitted missile was designated K-10SD. The low-altitude missile, when retrofitted for a wider range of employment, was designated as the K-10SND.

Growing missile range in turn required increased capabilities of the carrier aircraft's YeN radar, a task which presented a challenge. Basic research was conducted at the

33rd Naval Aviation Centre. Detection range was increased through changing frequency and the length of outgoing pulses. The range of detecting typical sea-borne targets grew from 320 to 450 km (199 to 280 miles). These new advances meant that, after launching the missile from maximum distance, by the moment of impact the aircraft was 265 km (165 miles) away from the target, rather than 140 km (87 miles) as it had been before.

Tu-16K-10SP

This system was developed on the initiative of naval aviation, and featured a K-10SP jammer drone that protected armed missiles while they approached their targets. Navy overhaul plant no. 20 (in Leningrad) was charged with the job of retrofitting missiles, while tests were conducted at Centre no. 33. In fact, the K-10SP missile opened a completely new direction – ECM drones.

K-10SPs were fitted with one of the Azaliya jammers (SPS-61R or SPS-63R operating on a centimetric wavelength). Jamming characteristics could be changed before the flight, depending on the tactical situation. The jammer was first used during the Kvant electronic warfare exercises in the Pacific in 1976 and received positive responses. In accordance with the order of the Minister of Defense of the USSR dated 11 April 1979, the K-10SP jammer missile was endorsed for fielding for service.

K-10SPs were used again during the Ekran electronic warfare exercises by the Northern Fleet in 1981. That time six K-10SPs were covering an K-10SN missile, which the ship-borne Volna and Shtorm air defence systems were tasked to destroy. To avoid possible trouble, and taking into account the low effectiveness of the two systems, the K-10SN missile descended only to the second stabilised altitude of 1200 m.

Target designation for naval fire was provided by the MR-310A centimetric wave radar. It was discovered that, from a distance of 130-140 km (81-87 miles), the jammers produced a solid flash on the screens of the ship's radars and target designation did not seem possible. Only the MR-600 radar, operating in a different waveband, provided target designation and the K-10SN was destroyed 15 km (9.3 miles) short of the ships. However, the crews were in a high state of turmoil as they had not been informed that the K-10SN would descend.

Tu-16K-10-26 'Badger-C Mod'

This system was developed in compliance with a decree issued on 23 June 1964 and essentially added the KSR-5 missile to the K-10 system. It was intended for destroying ground and sea-borne targets with the KSR-5, KSR-2 and K-10SND missiles. The aircraft could carry two KSR-5Ns

The Tu-16K-10-26 introduced the KSR-5 missile, greatly expanding its capabilities. The ability to carry the K-10 was retained, and on rare occasions all three missiles were carried, albeit for short-range missions.

The Tu-16 was essentially a pack hunter. Firing one or two missiles each, a group of aircraft launching from different directions hoped to saturate the defences of a large ship and its air defence support vessels.

Tu-104Sh trainer for the Tu-16K-10

Two ex-Aeroflot Tu-104 airliners were converted with YeN radar and its large radome to serve as trainers for Tu-16K-10 'Badger-C' navigators and weapons officers, with operating stations in the cabin. They were designated Tu-104Sh and were delivered to the AVMF in 1964. In 1969 both aircraft were upgraded with the Ritsa radar direction-finding system, and had an antenna mounted on top of the nose forward of the windscreen. Subsequently, both Tu-104s were given Tu-22M 'Backfire' radar and had wing pylons added, becoming Tu-104Sh-2s in the process. They continued as 'Backfire' trainers until replaced by the Tu-134UBK. This aircraft – SSSR 42342 – was photographed at Pushkin in the early 1980s after it had been upgraded to Tu-104Sh-2 standard.

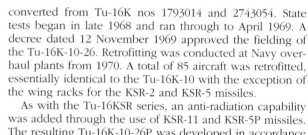

and one K-10SND. Additional missile carriage required reinforcing the wing, installing external store racks and limiting maximum flap setting to 25°. Addition of the KSR-5 greatly increased striking capabilities, although combat radius was cut to a third.

Factory tests of the system were carried out from November 1966 to March 1967 with two Tu-16K-10-26s

converted from Tu-16K nos 1793014 and 2743054. State tests began in late 1968 and ran through to April 1969. A decree dated 12 November 1969 approved the fielding of the Tu-16K-10-26. Retrofitting was conducted at Navy overhaul plants from 1970. A total of 85 aircraft was retrofitted, essentially identical to the Tu-16K-10 with the exception of the wing racks for the KSR-2 and KSR-5 missiles.

As with the Tu-16KSR series, an anti-radiation capability was added through the use of KSR-11 and KSR-5P missiles. The resulting Tu-16K-10-26P was developed in accordance with a decision of the military industrial complex issued on 21 January 1976. The KSR-5P radio guidance equipment included the VSP-K equipment installed on the missile, ANP-K equipment on the aircraft, and monitors for the I-41 and I-42 units of the Ritsa system.

Taifun upgrade

In 1980 the system was upgraded with the Taifun equipment, which had been installed in the production Tu-16K-10-26P no. 3642035 of naval aviation. The aircraft was fitted with LO-67 Taifun reconnaissance and target designation equipment, which was designed to operate together with the direction-finding element of the KSR-5P's homing head and identify characteristics of target radars. A naval overhaul plant was responsible for retrofitting. Check tests took place at Akhtubinsk and Nikolaev from 29 December 1979 to 18 June 1980. They indicated radar signals could be detected at a distance of 380-400 km (236-248 miles) with the aircraft flying at 9000-11000 m (28,528-36,090 ft), with lock-on range some 20-30 km (12.5-18.5 miles) less. The Taifun VSP-K system operated in two modes: reconnaissance and target designation.

Despite indifferent results, work on expanding the combat performance of the Tu-16K-10-26P with the Taifun equipment continued at Akhtubinsk and Nikolaev from 23 September 1984 to 14 January 1985. The final conclusion

Tupolev Tu-16K-10-26

Aviatsiya Voenno Morskogo Flota

'Badger-C Mods' mostly served with the AVMF (Aviation of the War Fleet), and were operated by all fleets (Baltic, Black Sea, Northern and Pacific). This version partnered the 'Badger-G Mod' throughout the 1970s and 1980s as the backbone of the missile-carrier force, even though the more capable Tu-22s and Tu-22Ms were in service. Each regiment had two squadrons of missile-carriers assigned, and they often exercised in squadron strength to practise mass attacks against high-value battle groups.

Armament
The radar nose of the 'Badger-C Mod' precluded the fitting of the fixed, forward-firing pilot's 23-mm cannon on the starboard side of the forward fuselage. Dorsal, ventral and tail gun turrets were retained, however, with two 23-mm cannon in each. The aircraft could carry a mixed load of one centreline K-10S (AS-2 'Kipper'), for which a recessed bay was provided, and two underwing KSR-5 (AS-6 'Kingfish'') missiles, although carriage of a single asymmetric K-26 was more normal.

Wingtips
Most 'Badgers' had asymmetric wingtips, dictated by the extraordinary inflight refuelling receptacle on the port wingtip, which incorporated a winch for the grapnel which was used to capture the refuelling hose.

Radar
The broad, flattened nose radome of the 'Badger-C' accommodated the giant YeN I-band search, mapping and target designation radar, which was known to NATO as 'Puff Ball'. This radar was similar to that which equipped maritime versions of the Myasishchev 3M 'Bison', the Tu-95K-22 'Bear-G' and the Kamov Ka-25 'Hormone-B'. The large parabolic dish antenna was suspended from a beam in the top of the aircraft's nose, and was mechanically traversed through 120° in azimuth to allow the aircraft to turn away from the target after missile launch. The undernose radome housed the antenna for the missile guidance system.

Observation blisters
Large bulged ports on the sides of the rear fuselage were used by the radio operator/gunner to aim the weapons. The blisters were also used as a good vantage point from which a running commentary could be given to the pilot during the dangerous refuelling process. At night the refuelling observer often used a hand-held flashlight to help illuminate the scene.

Markings
This aircraft carries typical AV-MF markings. A two-digit regimental code is carried on the fin and nosewheel doors, very small. The practice of painting large 'buzz number'-type codes was dropped early on, and this aircraft does not display its construction number. An 'Excellence' award (to recognise an individual aircraft's outstanding condition, as a reward to the crew chief) is worn on the nose.

Wing
The cantilever wings incorporated 3° of anhedral, 1° of incidence, and 41° of leading-edge sweep on the inboard panels and 35° on the outboard. The two-spar wing was of light alloy construction, and had two large aerodynamic fences on the top surface of each wing. Slotted flaps and mass-balanced ailerons (with trim tabs) occupied the trailing edge of each wing. The flaps had a maximum deflection of 35°.

The Tu-16K-10-26 'Badger-C' was built as a pure missile-carrier, and had no bomb bay. Despite the fact that free-fall bombing had little place in the Cold War maritime scenarios in which the 'Badger-C' was designed to operate, the AVMF desired a conventional bombing capability for its aircraft. Fuselage BD4-16-52 bomb racks could be added (above), while further racks could be mounted on the KSR-5 pylons, as seen on the aircraft at right (with bombs) and empty on the aircraft below. These could accommodate up to 12 from a range of small/medium FAB general-purpose bombs. With this upgrade the aircraft became known as the Tu-16K-10-26B.

stated that launch of the KSR-5P was possible in limited situations with the YeN-D radar monitoring distance to the target.

Tu-16K-10-26B

This system was prepared by naval aviation and developed at the naval overhaul plants during the period of 1974-1976 and gave the missile-carriers a bombing capability. Tu-16K-10-26 aircraft were fitted with 12 fuselage and wing external store racks, allowing the carriage of bombs from 100-500 kg (220-1,102 lb) in weight, to a total of

9000 kg (19,841 lb). A modernised OPB-1RU sight was fitted. An aircraft armed to the teeth with bombs looked quite impressive but, with hindsight, the Tu-16K-10-26B could hardly be seen as a great achievement, since bombs could only be delivered if the target was visible. Furthermore, bombing accuracy was low since the sight had its roots in the 1930s.

Missile-carriers in service

The Tu-16KS was first delivered to 124 TBAP of the Black Sea Fleet in June 1957 (from 3 October redesignated 124 MTAP). Its inventory included 16 Tu-16KS, six Tu-16SPSs, six Tu-16Zs and an An-2. The first missile was launched by the Tu-16KS in December 1957 against a target in the Caspian Sea. After 124 MTAR, the Tu-16KS rearmed 5 MTAP, also part of the Black Sea Fleet, and in 1958 joined the Northern and Pacific Fleets. The rate of assimilation of the new missile system can be demonstrated by 124 live launches in 1958, and 77 sorties by the Northern Fleet using the MiG-17SDK surrogate.

KS missiles had only one radio guidance frequency and, until 1959, launches had been practised from one, two or three directions to eliminate mutual interference. Under such conditions a combat formation of 12 Tu-16KSs was

900-1200 km (560-745 miles) deep and the strike dragged on for 1.5 hours. The study of the missile system discovered a possibility to increase the number of guidance channel frequencies to six and launch missiles from directions differing by 45-60°.

In 1958 launches and guidance of two missiles from one carrier aircraft were practised. In 1960 the option of launching missiles from four to six directions was tested. Four aircraft launched eight missiles and seven of them hit the target. An attack from six directions also turned out to be a success, and the strike lasted for just 40 seconds.

Improved systems

The Kometa system was slowly refined over the next few years. The improvement succeeded in reducing launch altitude from 4000 to 2000 m (13,123 to 6,562 ft), but despite all the tinkering the most reliable guidance of missiles was provided at a speed of no more 420 km/h (260 mph). The extending radome of the K-2M radar antenna was also a speed-limiting factor. In 1961 the Kometa system armed five air regiments of the AVMF: 9 MTAP of the Northern Fleet, 5 MTAP and 124 MTAP of the Black Sea Fleet, and 49 and 568 MRAP of the Pacific Fleet.

In December 1959 the flying and technical personnel of 924 and 987 MTAP of the Northern Fleet began mastering the Tu-16K-10. In May 1961 574 MRAP of the Northern Fleet and 170 MRAP of the Baltic Fleet's 57 MRAD began their retraining.

In 1959 the Tu-16K was delivered to the Northern Fleet and preparation for launches got under way. In July 1960 the crews of Colonels Myznikov and Kovalev were appointed to carry out the first AVMF launches of the K-10S. Myznikov's crew made the first launch against a target 165 km (102 miles) away, but the missile undershot. Then the second crew followed with a direct hit. Within two weeks a total of five launches had been made: one of them was considered to be abnormal (crew mistake), and one missile hit a wave crest 200 m (656 ft) short of the target.

In 1960-1962 the Tu-16K-10 was fielded to seven air regiments and the number of launches grew from 79 in 1960 and 126 in the next year, to a record figure of 147 in 1962. This year was marked by another event. On 22 August, in the course of the Shkval exercise involving the Air Force, Navy and Strategic Missile Forces, the crew of Lieutenant Colonel V.P. Krupyakov, commander of 924 MRAD, made the first launch of the K-10SB missile with a 6-kT nuclear warhead against a target (a barge with corner reflectors) from a distance of 250 km (155 miles) on a firing range near Basmachny bay (Novaya Zemlya).

In the process of mastering the Tu-16K-10, crews were often challenged with unusual situations. For example, in

1961 when the crew of captain G.A. Zimin flew a Tu-16K-10 to carry out simulated launches, the external rack did not retract the missile and left it in the lowered, firing position. The crew manual did not provide any recommendations as to what to do in such a situation. There was real concern that during landing the missile would brush against the runway, as the normal landing angle of attack was 8°. Thankfully, all ended well. After several research flights with extended missile landings (five of them were made by the crew of Zimin), the crew manual was amended with a relevant instruction.

Experience gained during the first years of operating the Kometa missile system and the Tu-16K-10 indicated that the latter was highly unreliable, though it had been considerably refined by 1961. Almost 50 percent of launches carried out in 1961 failed, 32 percent of which were through technical or manufacturing faults. Against that background, the design of the Kometa system looked more successful.

Sometimes, missiles chose targets on their own. In 1964 a crew from 169 MRAP of the Pacific Fleet launched a live K-10SND missile over a firing range at Cape Tyk. The missile homed in on a Japanese timber ship, the *Sine-Maru*, that had sailed from Nikolaevsk-na-Amure and had entered a prohibited area. The timber ship was saved due to the fact that the missile had been set for self-destruction 400 m (1,312 ft) short of the target. Only some fragments reached the ship. One crewmember was wounded and the timber ship called at the port of Holmsk for medical aid. The accident was followed by an investigation.

Naval aviation began training with the Tu-16K-16 (KSR-2) missile system in February 1963, the first units being 540 squadron the 33rd Naval Aviation Centre and 12 MRAP of the Baltic Fleet. In 1964 one squadron of 568 MRAP was retrained and in 1967 all of the Pacific

Above: The 'Badger-F' codename was applied to the Tu-16R equipped with SRS-3 Elint pods under the wings. The underfuselage radomes were retained.

Left: Photographed by another Tu-16R, this DA aircraft is fitted with a Geran nose jammer and Rezeda tail jammer.

Above: On 25 May 1968 this Tu-16R, captained by Major Pliev, crashed into the Norwegian Sea while snooping round a US Navy carrier.

Below: The large teardrop radomes under this Tu-16R signify fitment of the SRS-4 Elint suite.

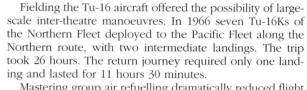

Fielding the Tu-16 aircraft offered the possibility of large-scale inter-theatre manoeuvres. In 1966 seven Tu-16Ks of the Northern Fleet deployed to the Pacific Fleet along the Northern route, with two intermediate landings. The trip took 26 hours. The return journey required only one landing and lasted for 11 hours 30 minutes.

Mastering group air refuelling dramatically reduced flight time. The tankers were flown to airfields along the route beforehand. This allowed Tu-16K missile-carriers from the Northern Fleet to simulate short-notice strikes against appointed targets in the Sea of Japan, including live launches at the firing range. In the beginning of 1970 nine Tu-16K-10-26s from 143 MRAD simulated a nocturnal tactical strike against a group of ships in the Pacific Ocean, with air refuelling from five Tu-16Zs. Missile-carrier units occasionally carried out tactical air exercises two to three days long, using US and NATO ship formations for simulated tactical launches.

From 1966 theatre exercises also involved non-nuclear operations, and directives were issued requiring missile-carrier crews to rediscover bombing skills. In August 1967 943 MRAP of the Black Sea Fleet, along with forces from Bulgaria and Romania, took part in a theatre exercise involving the 'organisation and execution of landing operations aimed at destroying the enemy in a coastal area'. In one of the scenarios the Tu-16s delivered a strike dropping 72 FAB-250 bombs. Centre no. 33 also obtained positive results from using the Tu-16 to bomb ships.

In April 1970 the large-scale Okean manoeuvres were undertaken. 13 MRAP undertook six successive launches of missiles on the firing ranges. On 20 April 10 Tu-16Ks of the Pacific Fleet's 169 MRAP deployed to the Northern Fleet, making an intermediate landing at Olenya and launching K-10S missiles on the Kolsky peninsula firing range.

Fleet's 49 MRAD was converted. The first live launches were performed by the crews of 12 MRAD from 25 October to 23 November 1963, at a firing range in the Caspian Sea. The target was acquired for steady tracking at a distance of 200-210 km (124-130 miles), launch following two or three minutes later.

With the fielding of the new system, trials were undertaken by Centre no. 33 to decrease launch altitude to 2000 m (6,562 ft). An order of the Minister of Defence of the USSR dated 22 April 1968 approved an upgrade for the missile allowing its employment in the 500-10000 m (1,640-32,808 ft) altitude range. They were designated KSR-2M. Research flights indicated that the minimum launch range at an altitude of 500 m was 70-80 km (43-50 miles), limited by the radar visibility of the target and pre-launch preparation time. The Tu-16K-16 had only a short career in the AVMF, being overtaken by the Tu-16K-26 system and its KSR-5 missile.

'Badgers' abroad

Following the earlier deployment of Tu-16Rs, at the end of 1970 a decision was taken to send an AVMF missile-carrier unit to the United Arab Republic. The squadron was named 89 Otdelnaya Morskaya Razvedovatelnaya Aviatsionnaya Eskadrila (OMRAE – independent naval missile air squadron). It consisted of 10 Tu-16KSR-2-11s from 9 MRAP. The aircraft were painted in Egyptian camouflage with UAR national insignia. On 4 November the first aircraft landed at Asuan airfield. The other aircraft arrived in accordance with the schedule, and an An-12 brought in technical personnel. Four Tu-16SPS from the Baltic Fleet came to provide ECM support for the squadron.

The squadron was charged with the task of retraining Egyptian crews (who had been flying the Tu-16KS) for the Tu-16KSR-2 aircraft. The Egyptians' previous experience and high level of general education made the task easy. Combat training flights were carried out by mixed crews: aircraft commander, navigator and the 'aft' were Arabic, while the pilot on the right seat and the second navigator were AVMF naval aviation instructors.

Initially, training required interpreters, but subsequently communication turned into a mixture of Russian, English and Arabic, aided by hand signals. By June 1972 all 10 Arab

Left: Operated by the AVMF's Northern and Pacific Fleets, 24 Tu-16RM-1s were produced by conversion of the Tu-16K-10. Here one overflies HMS Ark Royal at typically low level. Reconnaissance 'Badgers' aimed to approach ships under the radar to get the best intelligence.

Below: Primary mission equipment of the Tu-16RM-1 consisted of the two unequal-size SRS-1 Elint antennas found on early Tu-16Rs and a single SRS-4 in between them. The radar was 'tweaked' to give better performance in the reconnaissance role, and was known as the YeN-R.

crews had been trained for live missile launches. The following month, orders for the withdrawal of the Soviet staff arrived. The Egyptians purchased the Tu-16KSR-2-11s, along with ammunition, technical material and equipment.

The last overseas 'tour' for the Tu-16 took place in 1980 when an independent mixed air regiment (169 OSAP) was formed at Cam Ranh airfield in Vietnam. The regiment included 16 Tu-16Ks and Tu-16Rs, which periodically flew along prescribed routes, accumulating valuable data about operating the aircraft in conditions of high humidity. Further Tu-16s deployed to the base in 1982 and 1988, arriving direct (using inflight refuelling) or via Sunan in North Korea.

In 1989 the conclusion that basing the Tu-16 in Vietnam had little practical value was drawn. On 28 August 1989 the Minister of Defence of the USSR announced that 169 OSAP would disband in 1990, leaving an independent mixed squadron (OSAE). The Tu-16s left in two groups: one group landed at Pyongyang airfield for refuelling and the other group proceeded to the airfields of the Pacific Fleet.

Reconnaissance aircraft

Long range and a tractable airframe made the 'Badger' an ideal platform for reconnaissance, and a dedicated variant was planned from the outset. The Tu-16R was built in accordance with a decree of 3 July 1953. Several design bureaux were charged with developing equipment for it at the same time. Tu-16 no. 1880302 was additionally fitted with nine cameras for strip survey and mapping, and the SPS-1 jammer. State tests resulted in a decision to launch series production of the Tu-16R ('Badger-E'). In 1957 plant no. 1 at Kuibyshev manufactured 44 Tu-16Rs and 26 more with different sets of equipment the following year. In particular, the weapons bay accommodated a three-container automatic chaff-dispenser for ASO-16 and ASO-2b type chaff.

During production the equipment suite of the Tu-16R changed more than once. In the beginning, the aircraft was fitted with the SRS-1 and SRS-3 electronic intelligence stations, along with RBP-4 (RBP-6) radars. The SRS-1 was capable of detecting and identifying basic parameters of radars operating in the range of 10 to 500 cm (4 to 197 in). All operations were manual and a seventh crew member was required. He was called a special operator and occupied a suspended pressurised cabin, fitted with an ejection seat and the main units of the Elint suite, in the stores bay.

The SRS-3 automatic radio registered operations of 3- to 30-cm (1- to 12-in) band radars on a film that was decoded after flight. Cigar-shaped containers for the SRS-3 were attached to the pylons under the wings, leading to the NATO codename 'Badger-F'. Subsequently, the SRS-1 was replaced by the SRS-4 with teardrop-shaped radomes

bigger than those of the SRS-1. The Tu-16R had several cameras with lenses of 20 to 100 cm (7.9 to 38 in) focal length. For night time photography the NAFA-MK-75 camera was carried.

In the late 1970s some Tu-16Rs were upgraded to Tu-16RM configuration. Besides higher resolution cameras, they were fitted with the SRS-4 Elint suite and the Rubin-1k (Rn-1k) radar. The SRS-1 and SRS-3 were removed. Flight radius of the Tu-16R with a take-off weight of 75800 kg (167,108 lb) reached 2500 km (1,553 miles). Inflight refuelling increased the figure by 1300-1400 km (808-870 miles).

Tu-16RM-2

In 1962 the Tu-16K-16 (KSR-2) missile system entered service with naval aviation and the Tu-16RM-2 was developed to support it in 1965, on the initiative of the AVMF. Using the Tu-16R as a basis, the nose gun, bombing equipment and suspended pressurised cabin were removed, and

Intercepted by the Swedish air force over the Baltic, this 'Badger' is almost certainly a Tu-16R of some sub-variant, but could also be an electronic warfare aircraft. While EW-dedicated aircraft carried Elint sensors like the Tu-16Rs, so Tu-16Rs carried ECM equipment and chaff dispensers, clouding the division between the two. The distinctive fairing above the flight deck is part of the A-326 Rogovitsa system, which was used for station-keeping in formation flying and to alert of impending collisions with other similarly-equipped aircraft. This equipment was installed primarily for missile-carriers flying carefully structured mass attacks, but was also fitted to reconnaissance and EW machines.

A total of 75 Tu-16Rs was produced, shared by the AVMF and DA. Ongoing modifications and new systems dramatically altered the look of the aircraft throughout their long careers – none more so than the adoption of SPS-100 Rezeda jammers which replaced the tail gun turret of DA Tu-16Rs in the latter part of their service lives.

a container with a 7000-litre (1,540-Imp gal) flexible tank was installed in the cargo compartment, thus increasing capacity of the fuel system to 51000 litres (11,219 Imp gal). The RBP-4 (RBP-6) radar was replaced by the Rn-1k, capable of detecting large ships at a distance of 200-240 km (124-149 miles).

A platform with the receiving antennas of the SRS-4 system was installed under the entrance door of the pressurised cabin, while omnidirectional sector antennas of the SRS-4 were attached to the doors of the cargo compartment. Navigation equipment was improved with the addition of the DISS-1 ground speed and angle of drift Doppler computer, while the RSB-70 transmitter was replaced by the R-836 Neon. Only two cameras remained. The navigator-operator was responsible for the SRS-4 in flight.

Combat radius of the Tu-16RM-2 grew by 700 km (435 miles) and reached 3200 km (1,988 miles) at a 79000-kg (174,162-lb) take-off weight. One inflight refuelling raised it to 4200 km (2,610 miles). Naval aviation plant retrofitted a total of 12 aircraft.

Tu-16RM-1 'Badger-D'

In such a way, the Tu-16RM-2 aircraft was capable of reconnoitring, providing guidance and target designation for the Tu-16KS, Tu-16K-16/KSR-2 and Tu-16K-11-16. But the number of those aircraft remaining in service with naval aviation continued to shrink, and most of the units were being retrained for the Tu-16K-10 with a missile launch range of 220 km (137 miles), subsequently increased to 325 km (202 miles). The energy of the Tu-16K's YeN radar also grew, providing detection of large ships from as far as 450 km (280 miles).

Consequently, once again a disproportion arose between the capabilities of the Tu-16K and Tu-16RM-2 radars to detect seaborne targets, and the ability to provide target designation for missile systems became apparent. Thus, there was a need for an aircraft able to detect surface targets and offer target designation for employment of the Tu-16K-10SD and Tu-16K-26 missile systems. These reasons brought about a decision to develop a reconnaissance aircraft on the basis of the missile carrier.

The resultant Tu-16RM-1 was converted from the Tu-16K at a naval overhaul plant. All missile-related equipment was removed and an additional container with a flexible tank, like the one in the Tu-16RM-2, was installed in the cargo compartment. The capacity of the fuel system increased to 48000 litres (10,559 Imp gal). Two SRS-1M radomes were installed in the area of the stores bay, with one SRS-4 radome situated between them. The navigator-operator, located in the suspended pressurised cabin, controlled their operation.

Elements of the YeN-R search radar were fitted in the forward compartment at the navigator's station. The radar, with a pulse power of about 180 kW, was capable of detecting large surface ships at a distance of up to 480 km (298 miles). It was equipped to determine the largest ship for targeting prioritisation. The unrefuelled flight radius reached 3200 km (1,988 miles) and flight duration increased to 7 hours 45 minutes. The crew consisted of six, including the navigator who also operated the YeN-R. In 1966-1967 the naval overhaul plants converted 24 Tu-16K-10 aircraft into Tu-16RM-1s. They entered service with the Northern and Pacific Fleets.

Above: From 1968 six AVMF Tu-16Rs operated from Cairo-West wearing spurious UARAF markings. The aircraft and crews were drawn from the Northern Fleet's 967 ODRAP but were detached to the specially formed 90 ODRAE for the deployment, which was later bolstered by Tu-16SPS jammers. Here an Egyptian-marked Tu-16R is seen in Russia.

Above right: The Egyptian detachment was a constant thorn in the side of the US Navy's Sixth Fleet in the Mediterranean. This Tu-16R with SRS-1 ('Badger-E') passes an 'Essex'-class boat. This may not be an AVMF aircraft, for in October 1967 Egypt had acquired two Tu-16Rs (with SRS-1) of its own.

Right: Intercepted by a US Navy fighter over the eastern Mediterranean, this 90 ODRAE Tu-16R carries SRS-3 Elint pods under the wings. The blade antenna on the aircraft's spine just behind the wing trailing edge was one of the antennas for the SRS-2 system. A similar antenna was carried under the fuselage in a position slightly aft of the dorsal aerial.

Tupolev Tu-16R 'Badger-L'

Dalnyaya Aviatsiya

This 'Badger' is typical of the later reconnaissance versions, festooned with Elint systems and jamming pods. Aircraft fitted with the Rezeda tail are thought to have served only with the Soviet air force's DA (Long-Range Aviation).

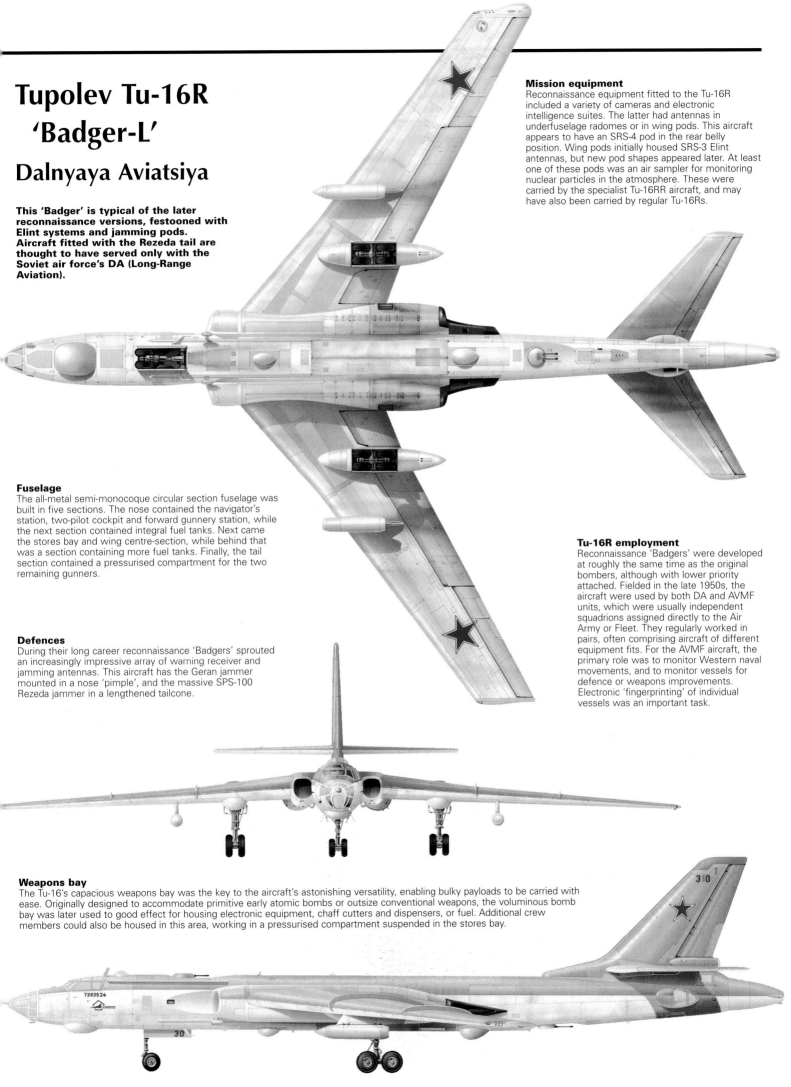

Mission equipment
Reconnaissance equipment fitted to the Tu-16R included a variety of cameras and electronic intelligence suites. The latter had antennas in underfuselage radomes or in wing pods. This aircraft appears to have an SRS-4 pod in the rear belly position. Wing pods initially housed SRS-3 Elint antennas, but new pod shapes appeared later. At least one of these pods was an air sampler for monitoring nuclear particles in the atmosphere. These were carried by the specialist Tu-16RR aircraft, and may have also been carried by regular Tu-16Rs.

Fuselage
The all-metal semi-monocoque circular section fuselage was built in five sections. The nose contained the navigator's station, two-pilot cockpit and forward gunnery station, while the next section contained integral fuel tanks. Next came the stores bay and wing centre-section, while behind that was a section containing more fuel tanks. Finally, the tail section contained a pressurised compartment for the two remaining gunners.

Tu-16R employment
Reconnaissance 'Badgers' were developed at roughly the same time as the original bombers, although with lower priority attached. Fielded in the late 1950s, the aircraft were used by both DA and AVMF units, which were usually independent squadrions assigned directly to the Air Army or Fleet. They regularly worked in pairs, often comprising aircraft of different equipment fits. For the AVMF aircraft, the primary role was to monitor Western naval movements, and to monitor vessels for defence or weapons improvements. Electronic 'fingerprinting' of individual vessels was an important task.

Defences
During their long career reconnaissance 'Badgers' sprouted an increasingly impressive array of warning receiver and jamming antennas. This aircraft has the Geran jammer mounted in a nose 'pimple', and the massive SPS-100 Rezeda jammer in a lengthened tailcone.

Weapons bay
The Tu-16's capacious weapons bay was the key to the aircraft's astonishing versatility, enabling bulky payloads to be carried with ease. Originally designed to accommodate primitive early atomic bombs or outsize conventional weapons, the voluminous bomb bay was later used to good effect for housing electronic equipment, chaff cutters and dispensers, or fuel. Additional crew members could also be housed in this area, working in a pressurised compartment suspended in the stores bay.

The original jamming platform was designated Tu-16SPS, and featured two large teardrop radomes for the SPS-2 jammers. Most were upgraded to Tu-16P Buket configuration, which had a canoe fairing and chaff dispensers in the reworked stores bay. This aircraft has the Buket modifications, but also retains the SPS-2 radomes, although they may well have been empty. A third radome is also mounted under the aft fuselage.

EW aircraft like this Tu-16P Buket served in missile-carrier regiments, and were intended to disrupt and blind enemy defences during missile attacks. As well as the Buket jammers, this aircraft carries additional EW antennas in small strut-mounted pods level with the engine intakes, also seen on other variants.

Radiological reconnaissance

Under a decree issued on 22 November 1967, the Tu-16RR was developed, designed to collect airborne samples of radioactivity. In 1969 Tu-16R no. 1883305 was fitted with two filter pods on the wing pods instead of the SRS-3 Elint pods, and dosimeters. Early in 1970 eight Tu-16Rs were converted into Tu-16RRs.

Another variant was the Tu-16RC, which was fitted with the MRSC-1 Uspekh airborne equipment suite to provide target designation for the missile systems of ships and submarines. Three aircraft were used to refine individual elements of the Uspekh system.

Reconnaissance 'Badgers' in service

Deployment of the Tu-16 boosted the capabilities of the DA and allowed the AVMF to reach wide expanses of ocean. The Tu-16 was to be arguably most important as a missile-carrier, but its successful employment in this role greatly depended on the reconnaissance aircraft, whose crews were characterised by high professionalism.

Tu-16Rs entered service with independent long-range reconnaissance air regiments (ODRAP). In the DA every corps had an ODRAP attached. In the AVMF the first Tu-16Rs were delivered to 967 ODRAP of the Northern Fleet aviation at the end of 1957, and to 50 ODRAP in the Pacific Fleet aviation in October 1958. In 1960 one squadron of 30 ODRAP of the Black Sea Fleet was retrained for the Tu-16R.

Tu-16Rs were delivered to the regiments that formerly operated the Il-28R, which made mastering equipment easier. In fact, AVMF Tu-16Rs were widely used in the surveillance of the fleets of neighboring countries almost from the very beginning of conversion, flying in pairs. The range/duration increase made possible through inflight refuelling became very important.

In the summer of 1961 the crew of the Tu-16R commanded by Major A.V. Uzlov, commander of 967 ODRAP, flew to the North Pole with two refuellings. Flight duration was 11 hours 48 minutes. With air refuelling, the crews of the Tu-16R from 317 independent mixed air regiment (OSAP – Otdelnyi Smeshannyi Aviatsionnyi Polk) flew from Yelizovo airfield (Kamchatka) and operated in the Pacific beyond the islands of Japan. In 1962 the crew of Colonel I.S. Pirozhenko, commander of 317 OSAP, flew a Tu-16R to Midway Island in the Pacific and back with two refuellings. Only those who understand that the crew had no alternate airfield can estimate the impact of this flight.

Crews were quite creative in developing techniques for the reconnaissance of carrier battle groups to discover their composition. The first contacts with the CVBG usually came with the interception of the Tu-16 by shipborne fighters, long before they managed to reach visual contact with the ships. To counter this, the Tu-16R crews descended to very low level after detecting the ship's radar, approaching under the radar lobe and often directly overflying the battle group.

Quite often AVMF and DA units worked together on reconnaissance missions. The following is an example, in which Northern Fleet aviation took initial information and, using its own assets, carried out additional reconnaissance, provided target designation and simulated a strike delivered by a regiment of missile-carrying aircraft against NATO ships participating in the Folex-64 manoeuvres.

The events unfolded in the following sequence: before entering the Norwegian Sea the group of NATO ships was under the surveillance of a Tu-95 'Bear'. Then a

Tu-16RM-1 from 967 ODRAP took over. The crew detected the ship's radars using Elint sensors and relayed positional information to a Tu-16R. At a distance of 450-460 km (280-286 miles) from the ships the crew of the Tu-16RM-1 established contact with the aircraft-carrier group using the YeN-R radar. Having ascertained the initial data, this was passed to the leaders of tactical (additional reconnaissance and strike) groups to set up the specified directions and appointed time of an attack. The crew of the Tu-16RM-1 simultaneously guided five Tu-16Rs and two groups of Tu-16Ks to the ships. The missile-carrying aircraft simulated tactical launches.

Tu-16Rs abroad

Following the mauling received by the Arab side in the 1967 Six-Day War, interest in Soviet aid increased. At the time the Soviet navy's 5th squadron of ships was in the Mediterranean. Its headquarters was housed in mother ships absolutely inadequate for command purposes, or on the command and control cruiser *Zhdanov*, which swarmed with rats and cockroaches. The squadron HQ encountered great difficulties in obtaining intelligence about the maritime situation.

In March 1968 the governments of the USSR and United Arabic Republic (Egypt) signed an agreement which would allow the deployment of an air group of six AVMF Tu-16Rs to conduct reconnaissance in the interests of both countries. The strength of the unit, named the 90th special-purpose separate long-range reconnaissance squadron (90 ODRAE) was determined as 170 men. The Tu-16Rs were drawn from the 967 ODRAP and were given UAR national insignia, the location being referred to as 'Object 015'. The 'Badgers' flew to 'Object 015' via Hungary and Yugoslavia, observing all international rules.

Cairo-West airfield was to become the base for the squadron. Flying and technical officers were accommodated in well-furnished cottages with conveniences that could only be dreamt of back in the Motherland. A systematic series of reconnaissance flights obtained a wealth of information about the activities of ships in the Mediterranean. Later, a detachment of Tu-16SPS ECM aircraft from the Baltic Fleet beefed up the group.

Some Tu-16P Buket aircraft featured extended wingtips. These may have been additional antennas, but more likely indicate that the aircraft were converted from tankers, which have the extended tips added as part of the tanker conversion process.

Electronic warfare aircraft

Electronic countermeasures provides both active and passive interference affecting enemy radioelectronic assets. A considerable number of Tu-16s were produced to perform this role, in several variants.

Known to NATO as the 'Badger-H', the Tu-16 Yolka was primarily a chaff-dispensing platform, equipped with a bellyful of chaff cutters and dispensing chutes. As with the reconnaissance aircraft, the EW family was reconfigured and upgraded several times, and Yolka aircraft were fitted with active jamming equipment to complement the passive chaff. The aircraft right has a large stick antenna aft of the stores bay, while the aircraft above has a small radome.

Officially designated Tu-16Gs (Grazhdanskiy – civil), but publicly known as Tu-104Gs, Aeroflot had a small number of disarmed 'Badgers' for crew training pending the arrival of the Tu-104 airliner. Nicknamed 'Krasnaya Shapochka' ('Little Red Riding Hood'), the aircraft also flew newspaper matrices (and other high-priority items) around the country until airliners assumed the role.

Below: Among the many Tu-16LL test aircraft which have served with the LII at Zhukovskiy, this former Tu-16K-10 was one of the most unusual, fitted with the nose section from the Myasishchev M-17 'Mystic'.

The Tu-16SPS was designed to create active noise interference of particular frequencies for jamming hostile radars. In 1955-1957 Kuibyshev built 42 Tu-16s equipped with SPS-1 jammers, and 102 Tu-16s with SPS-2 jammers. The first equipment created a 60-120 W interference in the 30-200 cm (12-79 in) band, while the SPS-2 produced 250-300 W interference in the 9.5-12.5 cm (3.7-5 in) band. The operator tuned to the frequency of the target radar using data provided by the SRS-1BV and SRS-1D high-precision radio reconnaissance systems. The SPS-1 and SPS-2 could jam only the radars selected by the operator. Tuning took 2-3 minutes.

In the Tu-16SPS the operator sat in a removable pressurised cabin in the rear part of the cargo compartment. Two SPS-2 jammer antennas under teardrop-shaped radomes were installed in the bottom part of the fuselage ahead and aft of the stores bay. Whip antennas of the SPS-1 jammer were mounted on top of the fuselage behind the operator's blister or in the bottom part of the fuselage forward of the cargo compartment. Subsequently, the Tu-16SPS was fitted with three ASO-16 chaff-laying systems, whose presence was indicated by dispensers in the bay

doors. From 1962 the SPS-1 and SPS-2 jammers began to be replaced by the Buket active jamming system.

Tu-16P Buket

This EW variant served the same purpose as the Tu-16SPS, but was equipped with the Buket system developed in the second half of the 1950s. This included SPS-22, SPS-33, SPS-44 and SPS-55 jammers, whose transmitters covered a wide frequency range, operated in automatic mode and were able to simultaneously jam several radars. Operation of the Buket equipment was powered by four additional PO-6000 AC converters and one PT-6000. The system was installed in the weapons bay, whose doors were replaced by a platform with units equipped with pressurisation and cooling systems. In its bottom part along the axis of the aircraft there was a long canoe radome covering the antennas.

Beginning in 1962, over 90 Tu-16s were equipped with the Buket suite. Ten years later, when it became clear that the Buket interfered with the aircraft's own operations, the radiation sector was narrowed.

Several Tu-16Ps were equipped with the Fikus system with five rotating directional antennas. They were installed under the fuselage and were covered by a radome. The equipment was tested on Tu-16P nos 1882409 and 1883117.

Under a decree dated 21 July 1959 the Tu-16P was developed with the RPZ-59 system. This used a K-5 air-to-air missile body to form the basis of a passive electronic countermeasures system. Six launchers in the cargo compartment fired missiles to create a cloud of chaff in front of the aircraft. Tests ran till 1964, and for safety reasons 12 launchers were placed under the wing. This led to the Pilon system which comprised 12 RPZ-59 missiles under the wing of a Tu-16P Buket. The system was not developed any further.

Yolka chaff-layers

Developed at the same time as the Tu-16SPS, the Tu-16 Yolka (fir tree) aircraft were fitted with an active electronic

M-16 Mishen drone

As 'Badger' airframes reached the end of their fatigue lives, many were converted to serve as full-scale targets for missile tests and practice launches. The Kazan factory performed the first conversions, which were known as the M-16 Mishen (target), or Tu-16M. All EW and navigation equipment was removed, and radio guidance equipment was installed. The first became operational in April 1965. From the early 1980s, as Tu-16s were retired in large numbers, conversions were performed by the VVS's 12 ARZ at Khabarovsk.

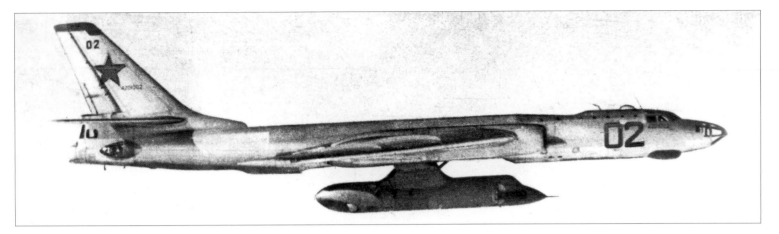

countermeasures system. The entire length of the stores bay housed seven ASO-16 chaff dispensers, with ejectors in the bay doors. Also, the aircraft were fitted with the SPS-4 Modulyatsiya jammer. The chaff dispenser used different types of chaff, covering most bands apart from 75-cm waveband radars. With a one-second dispensing interval, one load of ASO-16 was sufficient for 15-20 minutes operation (depending on the type of chaff). As well as new-build aircraft, some Tu-16Ts were modified to Yolka standard. In 1957-1958 naval aviation received 71 Yolka aircraft. They were modernised more than once, and carried both passive and active electronic countermeasures systems.

Some Tu-16 Yolkas were fitted with the SPS-61, 62, 63, 64, 65 and 66 jamming sets, which shared the common name of Azaliya. Aircraft carrying SPS-61, 62 and 63 were additionally equipped with SPS-6 Los, while those with SPS-64, 65 and 66 had SPS-5 Fasol. The antenna for Azaliya was located in the forward section of the stores bay.

Other equipment was also fitted to the jamming aircraft. At the end of the 1970s the Tu-16Ps were fitted with SPS-151, 152 and 153 jammers from the Siren series. With the fielding of heat-seeking missiles, the Tu-16P started to carry ASO-2 and ASO-7ER thermal noise equipment (IR flares), with dispensers located in the landing gear nacelles and rear fuselage fairings. There were two Tu-16Es designed for photographic, electronic, radiological and chemical reconnaissance, as well as ECM duties. They were equipped with the SPS-5 and SPS-151 jammers, and carried up to four containers of ASO-16.

Non-military Tu-16s

Tu-16s were widely used for purposes other than their originally intended ones. Many were converted for trials duties. Following are descriptions of the more important programmes.

■ In the 1950s an aircraft designated as the Tu-16KP was fitted with equipment for monitoring and adjusting the flight trajectory of missiles designed by S. Lavochkin. Equipment was housed in a suspended pressurised cabin as on the Tu-16R. In 1960 all work was stopped.

Ready availability of surplus aircraft and a capacious internal bay made the Tu-16 a sought-after trials platform, especially for powerplant trials. At least nine Tu-16LLs have been used for this task, carrying the test engine on a pylon which can be extended in mid-air (below). The most unusual of these platforms was the aircraft used to carry a complete Yak-38 fuselage section (above) to test the complicated propulsion system of the V/STOL fighter.

Above: H-6s take shape in the Xian factory, which has produced at least 150 'Badger' copies. The first wholly-Chinese aircraft was first flown by Xu Wenhong on 24 December 1968. The aircraft in the foreground is an H-6D missile-carrier.

Left: In standard form the H-6 differs in only minor respects from the Tu-16. As well as conventional bombers, the nuclear-capable H-6A was developed at an early stage.

During the course of its production, a number of improvements have been made to the basic H-6A, including the fitment of extended, rounded wingtips, as displayed by this aircraft. In PLAAF service the type equips several bomber regiments, which form part of bomber divisions that also operate the Harbin H-5 (Il-28 'Beagle'). Regiments are believed to be based at Shijiazhuang in the Hebei Military District, Datong (Shanxi MD), Xian and Wugong (Shaanxi MD), Nanchang (Jiangxi MD), Harbin (Heilongjiang MD) and one base in Guangdong MD. As well as free-fall bombers, the PLAAF is believed to have missile-carriers in service, possibly armed with the ramjet-powered YJ-16 missile. H-6s also perform reconnaissance and EW tasks.

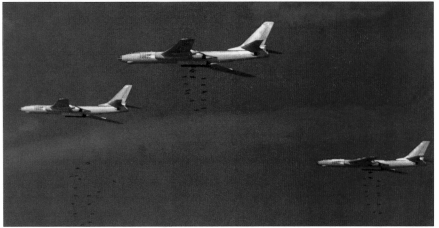

Above: H-6s conduct free-fall bombing. An unusual role for the type is breaking up the ice dams which form annually on the Yellow River.

Below: At least one H-6 serves as an engine testbed, using the same pylon arrangement as the Tu-16LL.

■ In the beginning of 1960 two Tu-16Ks were retrofitted for filming, and for a long time were used for monitoring the course of flight tests.

■ The Tu-16G and Tu-104G were variants of the Tu-16 outfitted for fast delivery of mail and matrices of central newspapers. With the arrival of airliners the aircraft were returned to the military.

■ The Tu-16 Tsyklon-N was used for weather modification and research, including the study of thermodynamic prop-

erties of the atmosphere. Naval aviation allocated two Tu-16KSR-2-5 aircraft, nos 6203203 and 6203208, which were modified by overhaul plant no. 20 at Pushkin in 1977. The aircraft were fitted with cassette holders for firing silver iodide, or containers with cement, for cloud-seeding. The external racks were also expected to carry containers with reagents. The crew included two meteorologists. The tests ran as long as 1980 and the aircraft, wearing Aeroflot colours, were handed over to the Air Force at Chkalovskaya airfield. They were used for rain-making over Moscow during the Olympic games of 1980. In 1986 the aircraft were used for dissipation of radioactive clouds in the wake of the Chernobyl disaster.

In November of the same year it was decided to use the aircraft in international programmes and to turn them into meteorological laboratories. In early 1990, during the course of modification at Pushkin, no. 6203203 was fitted with equipment for flying international airways. Tests were not completed, and the aircraft were later phased out as their service lives expired.

■ In 1970 two Tu-16Ns were modified for spraying carbonic acid. They flew from Chkalovskaya airfield.

■ The Tu-16AFS was retrofitted from a Tu-16 in 1970 for aerial photography of the Baykalo-Amurskaya trunk railway. Several photo cameras were located in the cargo compartment.

■ The Tu-16LLs were flying laboratories. They were converted in 1954 and were used for testing jet engines in an underslung pod. From 1957 for two years Tu-16 no. 1881808 was tested with engines featuring thrust reversal, which shortened the landing run by 30-35 percent. One of the aircraft was used for adjustment of the RD36-51V high-altitude engine. More recently, a Tu-16LL has flight-tested the GTRE GTX-35VS Kaveri engine developed for India's LCA fighter.

Tu-16s for export

People's Republic of China

Four years after the DA and AVMF received the Tu-16, it was decided to export the type. An agreement with the People's Republic of China for the manufacturing of the Tu-16 was signed in early 1956, with production entrusted to Harbin. The first aircraft was assembled from Soviet-made components and first flew on 27 September 1959. Designated H-6, it was handed over to the People's Liberation Army Air Force in December. At the same time a second aircraft was being assembled.

In 1958 production of the H-6 was assigned to a new aircraft plant at Xian. Aircraft assembled at that plant from Soviet components were built as H-6A nuclear bombers. On 14 May 1966 an H-6A dropped the third Chinese nuclear bomb. On 24 December 1968 the first H-6A made entirely from Chinese-built parts took to the air. Further versions were developed, including an inflight-refuellable reconnaissance platform and a tanker. The H-6I was a one-off trials aircraft powered by four Rolls-Royce Speys – two in the standard engine trunks and two in pods slung under the wings. In 1975 development of the H-6D anti-ship aircraft was launched. It was armed with two YJ-6 radar-guided missiles, based on the ship-borne P-15. The first flight was made on 29 August 1981. The H-6D entered service in 1985, and was later exported to Egypt and Iraq.

Egypt

In 1965-1966 Oktyabrskoe airfield of the Black Sea Fleet provided training for a group of flying personnel from the UAR, followed by deliveries of different versions of the Tu-16 to Egypt. For a year from 5 July 1966, Egypt hosted a group of 19 Soviet pilots, engineers and technicians, whose task was to train the flight crew and technical personnel of the UAR Air Force and pass on practical experience of servicing and operating the Tu-16KS. Six Tu-16KS crews were to be formed. By June 1966 four pilots, three navigators, as many navigators-operators and two gunner/radio operators had completed training in the USSR.

Preliminary training took five months and only by 12 December 1966 did training and test flights begin. The Soviet group performed its mission: by March 1967 three crews had been trained for live missile launches in both day and night, and the other three by April. During the Arab-Israeli war of 1967 most of the Tu-16s were lost on the ground.

A decree of the Government issued 24 January 1966 ordered the reallocation of Tu-16Ts from the Black Sea fleet to Egypt. On 26 September 1967 six Tu-16Ts were flown by the Black Sea Fleet crews to 'object 015' (as Egypt was codenamed) via Hungary and Yugoslavia. By 6 October instructor pilots had performed several training and test flights from Beni-Sueif, and subsequently returned to the Soviet Union. Further deliveries comprised two Tu-16Rs, which were flown to the UAR in early October 1967. They were equipped with SRS-1 Elint, RBP-4, ASO-26 and Sirena-2. The cost of each was estimated at 802,508 rubles. As recounted earlier, the Egyptian Air Force subsequently received ex-AVMF Tu-16KSR-2-11 aircraft.

During the October 1973 war the Tu-16s were based beyond the reach of Israeli fighter-bombers. Reports suggest that 25 missiles were launched with five of them allegedly reaching their targets, hitting two radars and a supply unit. After military co-operation with the Soviet Union ended, Egypt turned to China for spares, and additional H-6 aircraft. In July 1977, during a four-day conflict

with Libya, the Egyptian Air Force delivered strikes against a number of targets, including Tobruk, El Adem and Al-Kufr. Allegedly, two radars were destroyed. By early 1990 the Egyptian Air Force had 16 Tu-16s remaining: by 2000 they had been retired.

Indonesia

In 1961 crews of the Black Sea Fleet ferried 25 Tu-16KS 'Badger-Bs' to Indonesia and trained flight crews. Two squadrons were formed at an airfield near Jakarta. The AVMF group was headed by Lieutenant Colonel Dervoed, and members of the group proudly wore badges to show that they had crossed the Equator. After relations with Indonesia were broken off in 1965, the aircraft languished in a semi-serviceable state through a lack of spares, and were soon scrapped.

Iraq

By the beginning of the 1967 Six-Day War, Iraq had received eight Tu-16s, based at Habbaniyah, although they did not participate in active hostilities. Six Tu-16KSR-2-11s

Above and left: The most important version to be developed by the Chinese is the H-6D missile-carrier. It has maritime search/attack radar in an enlarged chin radome, and carries two YJ-6 missiles (export designation C-601, reporting name CAS-1 'Kraken').

Known as the HY-6, Xian has developed a tanker version with wing-mounted hose-drogue units (here refuelling a pair of J-8IIDs). Based on the standard bomber, the HY-6 is intended purely for the tanker role, and lacks the glazed bombardier's nose and armament.

The most successful of the Tu-16s operated by Egypt were the Tu-16KSR-2-11 'Badger-Gs' which, armed with KSR-2 missiles, were used in anger against Israel during the 1973 war, and in a brief border conflict with Libya. The aircraft had Ritsa antennas above the nose to assist with launching the anti-radar KSR-11.

Above: Egypt's 'Badger' force survived until 1999/2000, easily long enough to participate in regular exercises held jointly with US forces. Here two Tu-16KSR-2-11s taxi for a mission from their Cairo-West base. The survivors of the original batch of 10 Tu-16KSR-2-11s (plus survivors from the other variants delivered – Tu-16R, Tu-16T and Tu-16KS) were augmented by deliveries of a few H-6s from China.

Right and below: Indonesia's KS-armed 'Badgers' had the shortest career of any user, and were not used in anger, despite the confrontation with the UK in Borneo. They swiftly fell into disuse after the end of Soviet aid in 1965.

were delivered in 1970 and, again, they did not participate in the 1973 war. However, in 1974 they were used in Kurdistan. By the beginning of the Iran-Iraq war in 1980 the Iraqi AF had eight Tu-16s, which were used for delivering strikes against the airport in Tehran and other objectives. In 1987 Iraq bought four H-6Ds and C-601 missiles from China. By 1991 the Iraqi fleet was no longer operational, the majority having been destroyed on the ground during Desert Storm. At least three were destroyed on 18 January by F-117s at Al Taqaddum.

Twilight of the 'Badger'

For 37 years dozens of modifications maintained the strike potential of the Tu-16 in both DA and AVMF service. From the early 1970s the supersonic Tu-22M 'Backfire' began to replace the Tu-16, but the process was very protracted.

At the end of 1981 long-range aviation had 487 Tu-16s in service, while naval aviation had 350. By 1988 the combat component of the naval aviation included 14 missile-carrier regiments, and six of them were equipped with 212 Tu-16Ks. The grounding of the Tu-22M in 1991 because of design-manufacturing troubles saw the Tu-16 brought back to those units affected, since it was necessary to maintain operational skills. However, that year was to be the starting point of a wholesale retirement of the 'Badger'.

By 1980 106 Tu-16s, comprising 72 DA aircraft and 34 from the AVMF, had been lost for varying reasons. Most losses were attributed to human error. Naval aviation claimed an accident rate of 2.4 per 100,000 flying hours. Reliability of the aircraft was confirmed by the fact that, for a period of 15 years, only two breakdowns were caused by design-manufacturing troubles.

On the eve of the collapse of the USSR, the European sector of the country housed 173 Tu-16s, while a further 60 were deployed in the Far East. After the Belovezhsky deal, 121 aircraft were passed into Ukrainian possession, and 18 went to Belarus. Russia's share counted 34 aircraft in Europe. By 1994 the Tu-16 had been withdrawn from combat units, although the AVMF retained 62, of which 53 were Tu-16Ks held in reserve.

Lt Col Anatoliy Artemyev (Soviet/Russian Navy, Retired)

Top: Some of the 18 'Badgers' – mostly Tu-16K-26s – that were acquired by Belarus in 1991 are seen at Bobruysk air base. All were preserved in a flyable condition in the hope that they could be sold to various aviation museums. No aircraft were bought and all were scrapped.

Above: The Tu-16 had a long service life, its front-line career in the missile role being prolonged by delays encountered by the Tu-22M. This is a Tu-16K-10.

Bottom: This Tu-16 guards the entrance to Dyagilevo air base at Ryazan. This airfield is the home of the DA's long-range combat training centre, and had Tu-16s assigned throughout the type's service life.

'Badger' details

Wings and tail

The rigid two-spar wing had a torsion box structure, with high aspect ratio, and consisted of a wing centre section and wing panels. Sweep angle was 35° which increased critical Mach number and reduced shock stall. Since the aerofoil section of a swept wing is at an angle to the line of flight, local speeds along it are determined by the component of the airflow rather than the full velocity vector, as is the case with a straight wing.

Set an anhedral angle of 3°, the wing had an area of 164.65 m² (1,772 sq ft). For greater angles of attack, the wing tips (from rib seven) had profiles with stall-resistant characteristics. The trailing edge of the wing was equipped with single-slot Fowler extension flaps and sealed-type mass-balanced ailerons. The tail unit was designed with a higher critical Mach number than the wing. This was achieved through low aspect ratio and a higher sweep angle of 42°.

Fuselage and emergency egress

The fuselage of the aircraft was an all-metal semi-monocoque. The nose and aft sections housed pressurised cabins for the crew. The entrance to the front cabin was located under the seat of the navigator-operator, the entrance to the rear compartment was under the seat of the tail gunner. Jettisonable doors above and below allowed emergency escape. The pilots were ejected upwards after their seats reached the rearmost position, while other crew members escaped downwards. The pilots' control columns were pushed by the pneumatic system to the foremost position. Maximum g-force developed by the pilot seat ejection system was 18, with an initial seat velocity of 22 m (72 ft) per second. G-force of ejecting downwards reaches -3 to -5.

Powerplant and fuel

Two Mikulin AM-3 turbojets, with axial-flow compressors and two-stage turbines, formed the initial powerplant, each producing a maximum thrust of 85.84 kN (19,290 lb). From 1958 the more powerful RD-3M (93.79 kN/21,076 lb thrust) engines were fitted, and from 1961 the upgraded RD-3M-500 was installed, offering the same thrust but with a maximum take-off rpm of 4,700.

The engines were started by an engine-mounted starter using B-70 gasoline. The engines burned T-1, TS-1 or RT kerosene held in 27 flexible fuselage and wing fuel tanks separated into 10 groups (five per engine) with a total capacity of 43800 litres (9,635 Imp gal). With a normal take-off weight of 72000 kg (158,730 lb) the fuel load was 34360 kg (75,750 lb). Fuel consumption was controlled automatically and did not require attention from the crew apart from in an emergency. Fuel could be dumped from the wing tanks and nos 1, 2 and 5 fuselage tanks.

Control system

The aircraft featured a dual control system with mechanical push-pull control linkages without hydraulic actuators. The system included AP-5-2M autopilot servo units (subsequently replaced by AP-6E and AP-6B). The flap and trimmer drives were electromechanical with an alternate mechanical elevator control.

Undercarriage

The tricycle landing gear had a nose gear with twin wheels able to turn through 40° on either side. The nose wheels were controlled by the steering control wheel in the pilots' cockpit. The main landing gear, with four-wheel bogies, retracted back into the undercarriage nacelles. The tailskid was extended and retracted by an electric actuator. A brake chute was provided, roughly doubling the drag of the aircraft on landing.

Aircraft systems

The hydraulic system extended and retracted the landing gear, opened and closed the doors, and controlled the brakes. The hydraulic brake control system served as an alternate system for the primary when the stores bay doors were closed. The crew life support system included a liquid oxygen unit and individual oxygen masks. Wing anti-icing system was by hot air, bled from the engine compressor. Air was ducted through the wing and exited through gills at the wing tips. The leading edges of the tail unit were equipped with electric thermal heaters.

Above: The navigator could perform visual bomb drops from the glazed nose panel. This Tu-16KSR-2-11 has the Ritsa antenna installed.

Right: Access to the front crew compartment was made through this hatch (with drop-down ladder) between the nosewheel and the Rubin-1k radar.

Below: Detail of the two tail positions. Above the turret was the PRS-1 Argon gun-laying radar.

Aircraft converted or built to carry missiles on the wings had a cut-out in the flaps to accommodate the missile's fin, as well as two upper surface fences.

'Badger' weapons

This remarkable photo shows a Tu-16KSR-2-5-11 carrying a KSR-11 (port wing) and KSR-5 missile simultaneously. The KSR-11 was an anti-radar weapon, guidance for which did not interfere with the KSR-5. Below is a KSR-2 carried by an Egyptian Tu-16KSR-2-11.

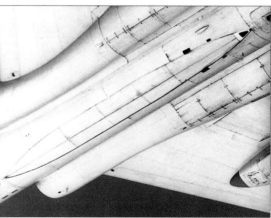

Above: Tu-16K-10s featured a recessed bay in the belly to house the K-10S missile. This was faired over when not in use.

The normal bomb load was 3000 kg (6,614 lb), although a maximum of 9000 kg (19,841 lb) could be carried. During bombing the aiming was carried out using the OPB-11R synchronous vector sight. If the target was not visible then the RBP-5 (or RBP-6) was used, coupled with the OPB-11R .

Gun armament consisted of seven 23-mm AM-23 guns located in the stationary nose mount and three movable mounts with remote electric control. The top guns were controlled by the navigator-operator from the top aiming post, or by the gun commander. The bottom DT-N7S guns were controlled by the gunner/radio operator from both blister posts or by the gun commander. The aft DK-7 guns could be controlled by the gun commander, navigator-operator or gunner/radio operator.

For firing under conditions of clear visibility the aircraft used four PS-53 aiming stations: one for the navigator-operator and one for the tail gunner, and two lateral blisters for the gunner/radio operator . The PRS-1 Argon radar allowed the crew to aim fire in the rear hemisphere under low visibility conditions.

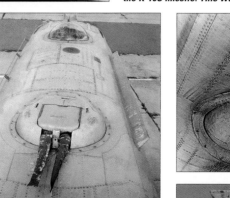

The seven guns of the 'Badger' were distributed between dorsal (above), ventral (above right) and tail (right) turrets, with one fixed gun in the nose (left). The nose gun was often removed during modification to make room for new equipment, or to help maintain the centre of gravity within limits. The tail guns were also removed when Siren or Rezeda jammers were installed.

Inside the Tu-16

Tu-16K-10-26 'Badger-C Mod'

1 Radome, 'Badger-C' and 'D'
2 Weapons ranging and search radar scanner
3 Radar navigator/bombardier's seat
4 Windscreen wipers
5 Pitot head
6 Windscreen panels
7 Cockpit eyebrow windows
8 Instrument panel shroud
9 Navigation radome
10 Pilot's seat
11 Co-pilot's seat
12 Cockpit roof escape hatches
13 Glazed nose section, all variants except 'C' and 'D'
14 Optically flat sighting window
15 Fixed forward-firing NR-23 23-mm cannon on starboard side only
16 Navigator/bombardier's seat
17 Navigation radome
18 'Towel-rail' aerial
19 Astrodome observation hatch
20 Forward gunner's swivelling seat
21 Cabin side window panels
22 Ventral entry/exit hatch
23 Extending boarding ladder
24 Retractable landing/taxiing lamps, port and starboard
25 Nose landing gear leg strut
26 Twin nose wheels, aft retracting
27 Nose wheel doors
28 Nose landing gear hydraulic jack
29 Electronics equipment racks, port and starboard
30 HF blade antenna
31 Remotely controlled dorsal gun turret
32 Twin NR-23 23-mm cannon
33 Communications aerials, port and starboard
34 Port engine air intake
35 Radar altimeter aerial
36 Intake duct divided around front spar
37 Forward fuselage fuel cells, maximum capacity approximately 45500 litres (10,009 Imp gal)
38 Starboard engine air intake
39 Aerial mast
40 Starboard inboard wing panel
41 Outer wing panel joint
42 Starboard missile pylon
43 AS-6 'Kingfish' air-to-surface missile, 'Badger-G Mod'
44 Starboard wing integral fuel tanks
45 Inboard wing fence
46 Outboard wing fence
47 Outer wing panel
48 Starboard navigation light
49 Wingtip fairing
50 Fuel jettison pipe
51 Starboard aileron
52 Aileron tab
53 Flap guide rails
54 Flap screw jacks
55 Starboard single-slotted track-mounted flap, down position
56 Starboard main landing gear fairing
57 Inboard flap segment
58 Starboard engine bay
59 Centre-section internal weapons bay, capacity 19,842 lb (9000 kg)
60 Rear fuselage fuel cells
61 Blade antenna
62 'Badger-D' electronic reconnaissance variant, ventral view
63 Ventral radomes

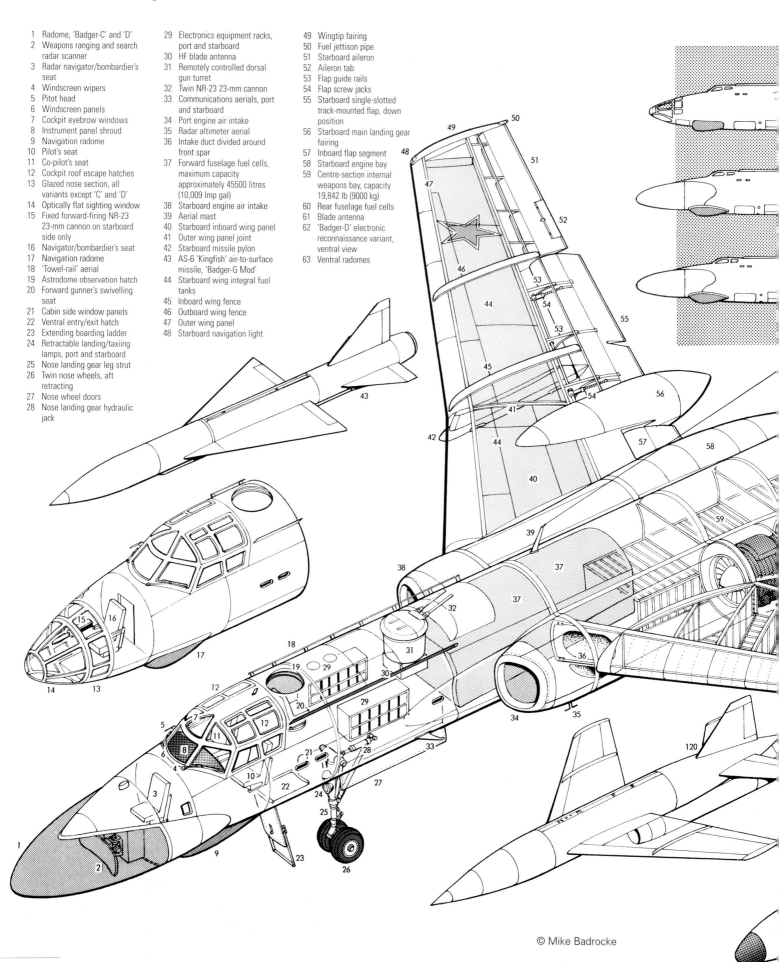

© Mike Badrocke

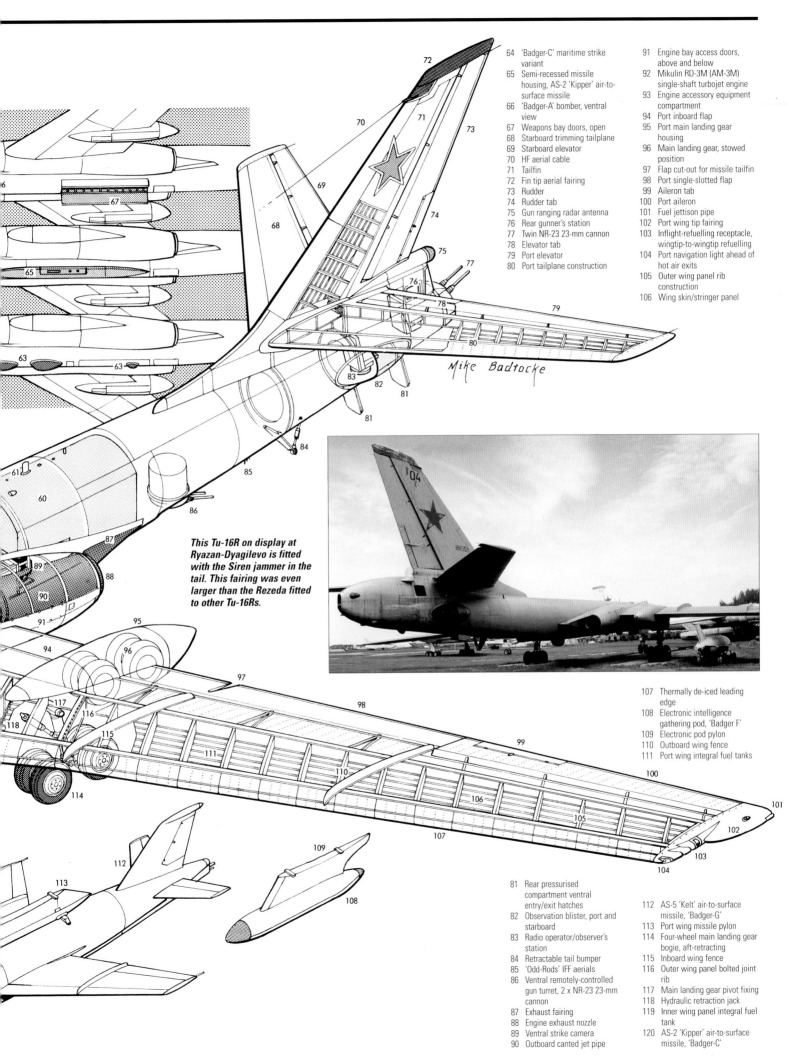

64 'Badger-C' maritime strike variant
65 Semi-recessed missile housing, AS-2 'Kipper' air-to-surface missile
66 'Badger-A' bomber, ventral view
67 Weapons bay doors, open
68 Starboard trimming tailplane
69 Starboard elevator
70 HF aerial cable
71 Tailfin
72 Fin tip aerial fairing
73 Rudder
74 Rudder tab
75 Gun ranging radar antenna
76 Rear gunner's station
77 Twin NR-23 23-mm cannon
78 Elevator tab
79 Port elevator
80 Port tailplane construction

91 Engine bay access doors, above and below
92 Mikulin RD-3M (AM-3M) single-shaft turbojet engine
93 Engine accessory equipment compartment
94 Port inboard flap
95 Port main landing gear housing
96 Main landing gear, stowed position
97 Flap cut-out for missile tailfin
98 Port single-slotted flap
99 Aileron tab
100 Port aileron
101 Fuel jettison pipe
102 Port wing tip fairing
103 Inflight-refuelling receptacle, wingtip-to-wingtip refuelling
104 Port navigation light ahead of hot air exits
105 Outer wing panel rib construction
106 Wing skin/stringer panel

This Tu-16R on display at Ryazan-Dyagilevo is fitted with the Siren jammer in the tail. This fairing was even larger than the Rezeda fitted to other Tu-16Rs.

Mike Badtocke

107 Thermally de-iced leading edge
108 Electronic intelligence gathering pod, 'Badger F'
109 Electronic pod pylon
110 Outboard wing fence
111 Port wing integral fuel tanks

81 Rear pressurised compartment ventral entry/exit hatches
82 Observation blister, port and starboard
83 Radio operator/observer's station
84 Retractable tail bumper
85 'Odd-Rods' IFF aerials
86 Ventral remotely-controlled gun turret, 2 x NR-23 23-mm cannon
87 Exhaust fairing
88 Engine exhaust nozzle
89 Ventral strike camera
90 Outboard canted jet pipe

112 AS-5 'Kelt' air-to-surface missile, 'Badger-G'
113 Port wing missile pylon
114 Four-wheel main landing gear bogie, aft-retracting
115 Inboard wing fence
116 Outer wing panel bolted joint rib
117 Main landing gear pivot fixing
118 Hydraulic retraction jack
119 Inner wing panel integral fuel tank
120 AS-2 'Kipper' air-to-surface missile, 'Badger-C'

Tupolev Tu-22 'Blinder' and Tu-22M 'Backfire'

Andrei Tupolev's instantly recognisable 'Blinder' and 'Backfire' bombers were two of the greatest Cold War symbols – on both sides of the Iron Curtain. The Tu-22 'Blinder' was an impressive achievement and had a surprisingly long service career. Surprising, as the aircraft faced bitter opposition in its early days from those in Moscow who believed the manned bomber was dead and the Tu-22 was not needed. Surprising also as the aircraft was hated by its crews and had an accident-ridden career. Nevertheless, the 'Blinder' paved the way for the Tu-22M 'Backfire', which was a very capable strike/attack aircraft, much feared by NATO planners. The 'Backfire' became one of the most controversial aircraft of its time, as the USSR and the USA argued endlessly about its capabilities during the SALT negotiations. Though the 'Backfire' also had its problems, the latest version – the Tu-22M3 'Backfire-C' – has largely solved these and is an important asset in today's cash-strapped Russian air force.

Right: Over its 35-year career Tupolev's Tu-22 has been developed into a series of mission-specific versions: the Tu-22B bomber, Tu-22R reconnaissance aircraft (as seen here), Tu-22K missile carrier, Tu-22P escort jammer and Tu-22U trainer.

Main picture and left: The 'Blinder' led to the swing-wing 'Backfire' which has evolved into the latest Tupolev Tu-22M3 'Backfire-C' version, optimised for low-level missions.

Tupolev Tu-22 'Blinder' and Tu-22M 'Backfire'

Above: Andrei Nikolaevich Tupolev was 70 years old when the Tu-22 (Project 105) made its maiden flight in 1958. As head of his Design Bureau, Tupolev oversaw the Tu-22 project, but the design team was led by chief designer Dmitri Markov. Tupolev's Design Bureau was famous for its bomber and large aircraft designs, whose lineage stretched back to the ANT-4/TB-1 of 1925. The four-engined ANT-6/TB-3 bomber of 1930 was one of the largest aircraft of its day. The five-engined ANT-16/TB-4 (1933) and eight-engined ANT-20 (1934) transports could carry 36 and 72 passengers, respectively. The ANT-25 set extraordinary long distance records, flying from Moscow non-stop to Washington state, in 1937. The Tu-2 (ANT-58) was the backbone of the Russian bomber force during the Great Patriotic War. After 1945, Tupolev developed his infamous B-29 copy, the Tu-4 'Bull', which led to the swept wing jet-propelled Tu-16 'Badger'. Other prototype jet bombers followed. The needle-nosed Tu-22 was thus not Tupolev's first jet bomber, but it was certainly his most adventurous.

The Tupolev Tu-22 'Blinder' and Tu-22M 'Backfire' represented a class of medium bombers that had largely disappeared in the United States Air Force by the 1960s. Although they were designed for strategic missions with nuclear weapons, they were not intended for intercontinental strike. Instead, they were intended for two distinctly different missions – continental strikes against strategic targets in Europe and Asia, and strikes against US Navy carrier battle groups.

The Tu-22 emerged during the most frigid years of the Cold War, the mid-1950s. Even in the wake of Stalin's death in 1953, and the end of the Korean War, relations between the superpowers remained tense. Complicating the confrontation were the enormous changes occurring in the very nature of modern warfare. The advent of nuclear weapons was at the heart of a revolution in military affairs that redefined the nature of military power. The Soviet Union had exploded its first atomic bomb, the RDS-1, in August 1949, and four years later exploded its first thermonuclear bomb, the RDS-6S. In spite of the power of these weapons and their American counterparts, there were serious problems with delivery. The United States had true intercontinental bombers – the B-36 and the new B-52 – but still depended on a significant number of medium bombers, the B-47 based in Europe, for any potential nuclear war with the Soviet Union. Britain also possessed a substantial strategic bomber force with its V-bombers. In addition, the US Navy provided the West with yet another possible means of delivery of nuclear weapons against the Soviet Union: its aircraft-carriers.

Early Tupolev bombers

In the face of these formidable forces, the Soviet Union possessed no reliable means of delivering its nuclear weapons, even within continental ranges against targets in Europe such as American and British bomber bases. As Soviet fighter regiments in Korea in 1950-51 had made clear, the World War II generation of piston-engined bombers, such as the B-29, were no match for modern jet fighters. At the time, the best-equipped regiments of the Soviet Long Range Aviation force were equipped with copies of the obsolete B-29, the Tupolev Tu-4. The Tu-4 was virtually worthless in the intercontinental delivery role due to its range limits and the lack of a significant refuelling

force. Harebrained schemes abounded to capture forward US bases for the Tu-4 in Greenland and in the Aleutians using a proposed new class of amphibious submarines, but they were more an indication of Soviet desperation than a realistic military option, and were not seriously pursued.

Shortly after World War II, Stalin established three secret organisations under the watchful eye of the sinister Lavrentiy Beria, head of the Soviet secret police. The First Chief Directorate was assigned the development of the Soviet atomic bomb, a programme which succeeded much sooner than American intelligence had anticipated. The Second Chief Directorate, under Dmitri Ustinov, was assigned the task of developing the platforms to deliver the nuclear weapons. The Third Chief Directorate was assigned the task of defending Moscow and other key cities against Anglo-American bomber attack.

The Second Chief Directorate sponsored at least four categories of weapons for the nuclear delivery task. Its most conventional programmes were two categories of bombers: an effort to develop medium bombers to strike Anglo-American bomber bases in Europe and Asia as well as US Navy carriers; and intercontinental bombers to strike the United States. The third programme was a revolutionary effort to develop nuclear armed ballistic missiles, first with ranges to strike targets in Europe, and eventually with the range to reach the United States. The fourth programme was to develop strategic cruise missiles to strike the USA and other objectives. This element remains the most secret to this day, as its projects, including the Lavochkin V-350 Burya, the Myasishchev RSS-40 Buran, the Ilyushin P-20 and the Tupolev Tu-121 Object S, were all failures.

One of the first successes of this effort was the Tupolev Tu-16 'Badger' medium bomber which began to enter serial production in 1954. This very durable aircraft would serve as the backbone of the Soviet Long Range Aviation regiments for many years, first carrying free-fall bombs, and later carrying stand-off missiles. However, in the mid-1950s, speed still remained the bomber's primary defence against fighters. Although the first crude air-to-air and surface-to-

air missiles had begun to appear, the bomber's primary opponent was the interceptor. A bomber's speed and high-altitude performance could drastically undermine the interceptor's chances of catching and engaging a bomber. Although the Tu-16 offered far superior performance to the Tu-4 in this regard, the subsonic 'Badger' emerged at a time when Britain and the United States were on the verge of fielding supersonic interceptors. It would grow increasingly vulnerable to its primary threat, so a supersonic medium bomber was needed.

Initial design efforts

Tupolev's Tu-22 was a response to the rapidly changing nature of strategic aerial warfare in the mid-1950s, intended as a supersonic replacement for the Tu-16 bomber much as the American B-58 Hustler was intended to replace the subsonic B-47 Stratojet. There is little evidence that any serious thought was given to competitive alternatives from Ilyushin or Myasishchev for this requirement. The early studies by the Tupolev OKB-156 design bureau in 1950-53 were not directed at a specific aircraft requirement, but rather at a variety of large supersonic aircraft that might have several roles, including as tactical strike aircraft, long-

range interceptors, medium and heavy bombers. This work began to coalesce in 1954 when the Tu-16 design was shifted into production. The supersonic aircraft programme received official government authorisation on 10 August 1954, in a decree from the Council of Ministers.

Wind tunnel studies were conducted at TsAGI in Zhukhovskii to determine the optimum configuration. Eventually, three preliminary design studies emerged: the Samolet 98 (Aircraft 98) tactical strike aircraft, the Samolet 103 medium bomber, and the Samolet 108 intercontinental missile carrier. Samolet 103 was the requirement that would result in the Tu-22, and was also known as Project Yu. The original conception of the Samolet 103 was an inexpensive evolutionary outgrowth of the Tu-16 with four Dobrynin VD-5 or VD-7 turbojet engines buried in the wingroot, stacked vertically two to a side. This design was far from satisfactory. In 1954 a design team under S. M. Yeger began to examine a more refined alternative, the Samolet 105, placing the twin jet engines in pods on either side of the tail. The fuselage and wing design was closer in conception to the Samolet 98 tactical strike aircraft than the Tu-16. Preliminary design was completed by the end of 1955, and detail design of sub-assemblies began.

Left: This is the prototype Tu-22R 'Blinder-C', the dedicated reconnaissance version of the the Tu-22, which entered service in 1962. Although the early-model Tu-22 was a disappointment in its intended role as a free-fall bomber, its high speed made it more suitable as a camera platform. When the Tu-22 was first seen by Western observers at the 1961 Tushino Aviation Day, it was assumed to be a product of the Myasishchev Bureau, and was allocated the NATO reporting name of 'Bullshot'. This was quickly changed to 'Beauty', on the grounds that it was 'inappropriate'. However, 'Beauty' was then changed to 'Blinder' on the grounds that it was too complimentary to the Soviet bomber.

Top: While the Tu-22, in all its many variants, is on the verge of complete withdrawal from service, the Tu-22M3 remains one of Russia's most important combat types – and virtually its only effective heavy bomber. Like the B-1 in the USA, the 'Backfire' will be too expensive ever to replace with a new improved bomber design and so its operational future seems assured.

Tupolev's Samolet 105, and the birth of the Tu-22 'Blinder'

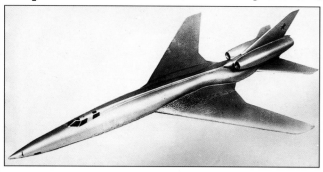

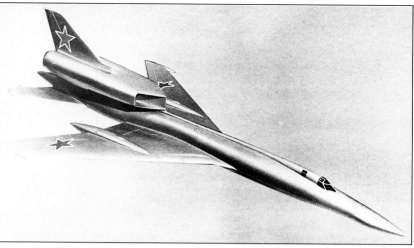

This Tupolev model (above) shows the original configuration of the Samolet (aircraft) 105, with its thicker wing and minus the undercarriage housings in the wing. The definitive Samolet 105A (below) had a reconfigured wing. An improved Mach 2-capable Samolet 106 design (right) was proposed, powered by Kuznetsov NK-6 engines housed in a common nacelle with a vertical 'shock wedge'. A T-tailed 106A with underwing engines was also proposed. Neither design proceeded.

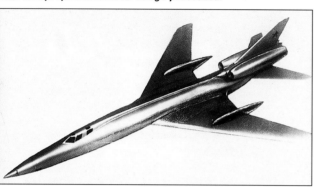

Above and below: The 105 prototype was completed in December 1957 and is seen here before its 1958 flight tests. Among the detail differences between it and production aircraft are the nose windows for the navigator and the main undercarriage design, which retracted into the wing.

The prototype of the Samolet 105 was completed in December 1957 at the experimental plant of the design bureau near Moscow, and transferred to Zhukhovskii for flight trials. Debate over the defensive armament for the aircraft was protracted. The initial conception was for a pair of aft-mounted TKB-494 cannon, and the second for a pair of twin 23-mm cannon mounted above.

The trials of Samolet 105

The 105 design was far more complicated than any previous Tupolev aircraft, and the first flight did not occur until 21 June 1958. As in other bomber designs of the day, the lack of maturity of contemporary jet engines was a continual handicap, and many alternative engines were considered. In addition, wind tunnel tests at TsAGI in Zhukhovskii were revealing the nature of area rule for supersonic flight. By the time the first prototype had flown, the new Kuznetsov NK-6 engines were completing their design phase. As a result, in April 1958 a Council of Ministers decree authorised a major redesign, completing the second prototype in the Samolet 105A configuration with the NK-6 engines and a fuselage redesigned with area rule. In the end, the NK-6 was not ready in time, and the Samolet 105A was built with the VD-7M engine instead. A

thinner wingroot on the aircraft led to the adoption of separate nacelles for the undercarriage, as on the Tu-16. Other changes in the 105A included yet another alteration of the defensive armament, this time to the DK-20 tail gun barbette system with the R-23 (261P) cannon, directed by a PRS-3 Argon-2 radar and a TP-1 remote television, for the gunner in the cabin. Two prototypes were built, one for flight trials and the other for static tests. The well known Tupolev engineer D. S. Markov assumed the role of chief designer in 1959.

The first test flight of the Samolet 105A took place on 7 September 1959. Flight trials proved so promising that the Samolet 105A was authorised to enter production at State Aviation Plant No. 22 in Kazan in 1959, replacing the Tu-16 on the assembly lines there. The programme was stalled on 21 December 1959 when the prototype was lost on its seventh test flight due to control surface flutter. Test pilot Yu. T. Alasheyev stayed with the aircraft in an attempt to save it, joined by the navigator, whose K-22 ejection seat had failed. Both crewmen were lost, but the radio operator ejected (at a speed of 1380 km/h; 857 mph) and was able to inform the investigation committee of what had occurred. In spite of the accident, production of the Samolet 105A continued at Kazan.

The first three series production Tu-22 bombers emerged from the Kazan plant in July-August 1960 and were sent to Zhukhovskii for further trials. They were in the Tu-22B configuration, which carried an armament of free-fall bombs. The first flight of a production Tu-22B took place on 22 September 1960, and early flights revealed more problems, including a tendency to pitch up. After the design bureau adjusted the control system, another flight was undertaken on 17 November 1960. This time, there was a fracture of an engine oil pipe, leading to the loss of power in one engine. The pilot, V. R. Kovalev, belly-landed the aircraft, splitting the nose off from the rest of the aircraft in the process and trapping the crew. However, they were rescued in spite of the fire which engulfed the rest of the bomber. An automatic pitch-damping feature was introduced, as well as other flight control improvements to compensate for effects caused by wing twisting. Subsequent flight trials revealed aileron reversal problems at high speeds, which led to a decision to limit flight speeds to Mach 1.4 and to introduce a flaperon system. Some of these upgrades were not ready until 1965, after the aircraft had already entered service.

Tu-22 enters service

The Samolet 105A aircraft was designated Tu-22 in Soviet air force service. The aircraft was first unveiled to the public on Aviation Day 1961, over Moscow. NATO originally codenamed it 'Bullshot', then 'Beauty' and finally 'Blinder'. In the Soviet air force, it was popularly nicknamed 'Shilo' (awl) by its aircrew for its metallic, pointed shape.

The first batch of aircraft was primarily composed of Tu-22Bs armed with free-fall bombs. The payload depended on the mission but could consist of 24 FAB-500 500-kg (1,102-lb) bombs or one of the massive FAB-9000 9-tonne (9.14-ton) blockbusters. It is doubtful that the aircraft was ever intended to actually carry the FAB-9000 bomb; this often stood in as a surrogate for large thermonuclear bombs in design studies.

The original Soviet air force plan called for the concurrent production of two variants of the Tu-22: the Tu-22B bomber, and the Tu-22R reconnaissance aircraft. Initial series production in 1961 was planned to be 12 Tu-22B bombers and 30 Tu-22R reconnaissance aircraft, trimmed back to seven and five, respectively. In the end, only 15 Tu-22B bombers were built, for reasons that will become apparent below.

The Tu-22B bombers produced were very trouble prone and they were used primarily for training. They were accepted for service in September 1962 and deployed with the 43rd Combat Training Centre (43 TsBP i PLS) in Dyagilevo near Ryazan. After a year of training, they were transferred to the 203rd Heavy Bomber Aviation Regiment of the 46th Air Army of the Long Range Aviation, commanded by Colonel A. Gamala, at Baranovichi.

All versions of the Tu-22 (this is a Tu-22K) were equipped with a twin cruciform braking chute. It was this variant which was first publicly seen, in 1961. The Tu-22B failed to adequately fulfil its intended role as a bomber – a role increasingly under threat from SAMs. The Tu-22K was, therefore, the first truly combat-capable 'Blinder'.

Below and below left: Few of the 15 Tu-22B bombers built ever entered service. Most were so trouble prone that they were quickly retired – the Tu-22Bs acquired by Libya and Iraq were rebuilt Tu-22Rs. The aircraft seen below left is preserved at the Monino museum, and has an early-model gun barbette plus VD-7M engine exhausts.

The Tu-22R was the next (front-line) production version to follow the Tu-22B. Confusingly, it was labelled 'Blinder-C' by NATO. This is a late-model Tu-22RDM, with refuelling probe, ventral SLAR fairing and ECM tail unit. Visible on the forward fuselage are an RWR antenna and the larger ESM fairing, particular to this variant.

The Tu-22B bomber was followed into trials by the Project YuR, the Tu-22R ('Blinder-C'), which was essentially similar to the bomber version, but with film camera equipment in the nose and in the weapons bay. There have been stories that this version was sponsored by the KGB for use in gathering strategic intelligence over Europe and Asia; however, by the early 1960s, satellites had arrived, and the aircraft's missions were oriented towards traditional military reconnaissance tasks, especially for the navy. The Tu-22R also retained free-fall bombing capability, and carried the optical bomb sight and weapons control system of the Tu-22B bomber.

The camera array in the Tu-22R depended on the mission and could include the AFA-40, AFA-41/20, AFA-42/20, AFA-42/75, AFA-42/100 and NAFA MK-75. In addition to the camera systems, it was fitted with the usual Rubin-1A surface-search radar, as well as the Romb electronic intelligence (Elint) system. For self-defence, the Tu-22R was fitted with KDS-16 dispensers at the rear of the undercarriage nacelles. The aircraft could also be adapted as an escort jammer, substituting the APP-22 palette in the bomb bay in lieu of reconnaissance equipment. A total of 127 of this type was built, making it the most common 'Blinder' model manufactured.

Tupolev Tu-22R 'Blinder-C'

Left: Wearing flight test photo calibration markings on its nose, this Tu-22R (2019012) was one of the very early production reconnaissance aircraft.

Above and below: Several attempts were made to improve the Tu-22's airfield performance. RD36-35 lift engines were fitted in the wheel wells of this Tu-22R (above). The same engines had previously been planned to provide boundary-layer control in the unbuilt Tu-22RTK. Rocket-assisted take-off trials using four SPRD-63 rockets were also conducted (below). They reduced take-off run from 2300 m (7,546 ft) to 1000 m (3,281 ft).

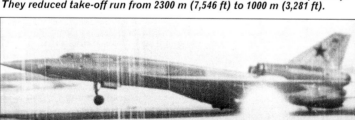

Above: The Tu-22RD (D=dalniy/long-range) was fitted with a refuelling probe. All aircraft were later refitted with VD-7MR engines.

Left: This Tu-22R of the 13th Heavy Bomber Aviation Division, based at Poltava, Ukraine, is fitted with the tail gun, later replaced by an ECM system.

Left: This early production Tu-22R, without a refuelling probe, is seen here departing on a training mission in November 1970. Not all Tu-22Rs were converted to Tu-22RD standard.

Above: This Tu-22RD of the 121st DBAP (Long-Range Aviation Regiment) was based at Machulishche, Byelorussia in the late 1980s. It has received the RWR upgrade (note the antenna housing beneath the navigator's window).

The first Tu-22R aircraft were issued in 1962 to the 290th OGDRAP (Separate Guards Long Range Reconnaissance Regiment) of the 46th Air Army at Zyabrovka near Gomel and the navy's 15th DRAP (Long Range Reconnaissance Regiment) at Chkalovskii near Kaliningrad with the Baltic Fleet. In 1965, two additional regiments were raised, the 199th OGDRAP in Nezhin northeast of Kiev with the 46th Air Army, and another naval DRAP at Saki attached to the Black Sea Fleet. In the case of the navy regiments, the Tu-22R replaced older Ilyushin Il-28R aircraft. As a result, the production run of the Tu-22R was split roughly equally between the regiments of the air force and navy. At peak strength in 1969-70, the two navy regiments had a total of 62 Tu-22R reconnaissance aircraft, a number which continued to decline until the mid-1980s when the type began to be withdrawn in favour of the Sukhoi Su-24MR. In total, the navy received about 80 of the 311 Tu-22 aircraft that were manufactured.

The Tu-22R was the first 'Blinder' to introduce a refuelling system into the series, in 1962, consisting of a nose-mounted refuelling probe system called *shtir-konus* (probe-and-drogue) in Russian. As a result of Tu-22R experiments with the refuelling system, all other Tu-22 aircraft were fitted with this system after 1965. Aircraft so-equipped had the suffix D (*dalni*/long range) added to their designation (*e.g.*, Tu-22RD, Tu-22KD). The refuelling capability of the Tu-22 led to a programme to convert obsolete Tu-16A bombers into Tu-16N tankers to support them, using the fuelling system first developed for the 3MS-2 'Bison' tankers.

Hunchback 'Blinder-D' and Tu-22K

The Tu-22R was followed into service by the hunch-backed Tu-22U trainer ('Blinder-D'), which was found necessary due to the radically different handling characteristics of the Tu-22 compared to its predecessor, the Tu-16. The state of the art in flight simulation was not particularly high at this time, and the standard KTS-22 simulator gave the new pilot only the roughest approximation of the handling characteristics of this very demanding aircraft. In the Tu-22U, a raised cabin for an instructor pilot was located above the station formerly occupied by the weapons officer. This version lacked the tail gun barbette, and fuel tankage was decreased. A prototype was completed at the end of 1960, and the type was accepted for service in 1962. The first production Tu-22U was deployed with the 46th Air Army in 1963 and a total of 46 Tu-22Us was eventually manufactured.

The Tu-22B bomber was quickly dropped from production after only 15 had been completed, due to a variety of factors. On the one hand, by 1960 it was appreciated that air defence had improved immeasurably since the aircraft had been conceived in the early 1950s. In many missions,

the primary threat would be radar-directed surface-to-air missiles (SAM), not interceptor aircraft. The Tu-22 was designed to operate at high altitudes, and low-altitude tactics to skirt under enemy radar were not considered to be realistic, given the design limits of the aircraft and the lack of a terrain-following radar. As an alternative, the Soviet air force decided to use stand-off tactics, firing a supersonic air-to-surface missile from outside the lethal envelope of enemy SAMs.

This led to the decision to develop a missile carrier version of the Tu-22, the Tu-22K ('Blinder-B'), an approach reinforced by the personal opinions of Soviet leader Nikita Kruschchev. Since the success of Sputnik in October 1957, and later Soviet space spectaculars,

In this view of a Tu-22RDM landing at Engels air base, the ventral housing for the Shompol sideways-looking radar is obvious. Between 1981 and 1982, a small number of RDs were modified to RDM standard. The existing camera fit was replaced by the SLAR and other IR sensors. Two AFA-42/100 cameras replaced a fuel tank and SPS-151 ECM and ASO-21 flare dispensers were also added.

Left: These Tu-22RDs were attached to the naval 'Blinder' regiment based at Saki, on the Crimean peninsula, that supported operations by the Black Sea fleet. The most obvious difference between these aircraft and the Tu-22KD cruise missile carriers comes in the nose configuration: the Tu-22KD's radome is bulged and extends over the tip of the nose.

Below: The added-on antenna housings of a late-model 'Blinder-C' are clearly visible in this view of a Ryazan-based Tu-22RD.

Not all Tu-22Rs ever made it to RD standard. This quartet of unmodified Tu-22Rs was destined for scrapping, in 1995, at the hands of the 6213 BLAT (base for the liquidation of aviation technology), Engels AB.

Kruschchev had become a great fan of missile technology. He was also intent on imposing substantial reforms on the Soviet military in the hopes of reducing the economic burden of defence. These views melded into a strongly-held belief that missile-armed systems were the wave of the future, and that smaller numbers of missile-armed aircraft, warships, and armoured vehicles would replace much larger inventories of more traditional weapons. Kruschchev viewed strategic bombers as an archaic concept, and prematurely terminated the Tupolev Tu-95M and Myasishchev 3M production programmes in favour of intercontinental ballistic missiles. To Kruschchev, bombers were the epitome of old-fashioned, costly and ineffective weapons.

In the early 1960s, there was a very real fear among Soviet air force leaders that the new Tu-22 bomber was the next item on the Kremlin's chopping block. Kruschchev had formed the new RVSN (Strategic Missile Force) in

December 1959 as the premier arm of the Soviet armed forces, and its first divisions were armed with R-12 and R-14 intermediate-range ballistic missiles – aimed at many of the same targets as were intended for the Tu-22. Two of the Long Range Aviation's proudest medium bomber units, the 43rd Air Army at Vinnitsa and the 50th Air Army at Smolensk, were disbanded in September 1960 and their personnel transferred to the new missile divisions. Kruschchev threatened to convert additional medium bomber divisions.

Naval role for the 'Blinder-B' and Kh-22

The design of a missile-firing version of the Tu-22 was absolutely essential to its survival in the halls of the Kremlin, as well as its survival in the new air defence environment. The one factor in favour of the Tu-22's survival was that it could be employed in maritime strikes against US naval carrier battle groups. This was a role for which ballistic missiles were ill-suited, although there were little-known Soviet experiments at this time for such missions. Kruschchev was very concerned about the nuclear power projection capabilities of the carriers, and so was expected to tolerate the continued production of the Tu-22 if modified. As a result, the Tu-22K was designated a missile carrier (*raketonosets*), and the term 'bomber' disappeared from the vocabulary of the Soviet air force for many years.

The Tu-22K ('Blinder-B') missile carrier was the most delayed of the 'Blinder' sub-types. It was armed with the K-22 (Kompleks-22) weapon system with its associated new supersonic, rocket-propelled, stand-off missile, the Kh-22 (AS-4 'Kitchen'). The delay in the Tu-22K's introduction into service was due to problems with both the missile and its integration into the aircraft. The aircraft had not originally been designed to accommodate such a large missile, and even when carried semi-submerged in the belly, it significantly altered the aircraft's flight characteristics.

The Kh-22 missile was powered by an Isayev liquid-fuel, two-chamber R201-300 rocket. The fuel was inhibited red fuming nitric acid (IRFNA) oxidant and hydrazine propellant. On launch, the missile was controlled by a preprogrammed APK-22A autopilot with a radio altimeter with Doppler input. During the cruise phase, the gyrostabilised autopilot also controlled the missile, unlike previous Soviet cruise missiles which tended to rely on command guidance, due to the shortcomings and cost of contemporary inertial guidance packages. There were at least two attack modes, depending on the target. For low-altitude attack to minimise radar detection, the missile climbed to 12000 m (39,370 ft) and made a shallow Mach 1.2 dive towards the target, under 500 m (1,640 ft) for the last portion of the flight. Against naval targets or certain land targets, the missile climbed to about 27000 m (88,580 ft) and made a steep Mach 2.5 dive. The anti-ship missile relied on contact fusing for the warhead detonation, while the nuclear warheads could be airburst, based on the guidance system. Tests found that even with a conventional warhead, the Kh-22 would blow a hole 20 m (65 ft) square in the side of a ship, to a depth of 12 m (39 ft). System range was dependent on the altitude and speed at which it was launched. When

Above and right: Both of these Tu-22RD 'Blinder-Cs' retain the DM-20 remotely-controlled tail gun position. Twin AM-23 guns (with 250 rounds per gun) were linked to the PRS-3A Argon-2 ranging radar, housed in the white radome immediately above the gun turret. Above the engines is the TSP-1 TV gunsight for close-in firing.

Tupolev Tu-22K 'Blinder-B'

Above: This prototype Tu-22K carrying a Kh-22 missile provided the first glimpse of either, at the 1961 Tushino Aviation Day. Only a partial refuelling system was fitted.

Below: The PN radar of the Tu-22K provides the distinctive nose configuration of this variant. Most 'Blinder-Bs' were built as Tu-22KDs.

Above: This early-production Tu-22K is carrying the nuclear-tipped version of the the Kh-22, the Kh-22N – as evidenced by the black dielectric panel of the PSI guidance system under the nose. The Kh-22N has a 350-kT warhead (estimated).

Right: The tarpaulin-covered ejection seats of this Tu-22KD are extended for maintenance.

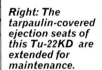

This Tu-22KD, in full afterburner, is not carrying its missile payload so the folding panels ahead of the bomb bay can be clearly seen.

Above: The bogies of the Tu-22's main undercarriage folded on retraction, allowing them to slot compactly into the podded undercarriage housings on the wing trailing edge.

Right: This 'Blinder-C' (Bort number 08) is a Tu-22KPD fitted with the Kurs ESM system to detect NATO surveillance radars.

released from 14000 m (45,930 ft) at 1720 km/h (1,070 mph), it could reach targets 550 km (340 miles) distant; at a release altitude of 10000 m (32,810 ft) and a cruise speed of 950 km/h (590 mph), it could reach 400 km (250 miles).

Initial tests of the K-22 system were conducted from a modified Tu-16 'Badger' medium bomber, designated Tu-16K-22. Missile fabrication for the Kh-22 programme was undertaken at state aviation plant No. 256 and the first test missiles were available in 1962. The first example of the

Tu-22K was completed in early 1961 and it, along with a model of the Kh-22, took part in the annual Tushino show.

The Tu-22K was fitted with the Leninets design bureau's PN radar (NATO 'Down Beat'), a modification of the widely-used Rubin-1A radar. Flight tests of the Tu-22K with the Kh-22 missile were conducted at the GNIKI VVS (Gosudarstvenniy nauchno-ispatitelniy Krasnozanmenniy institut VVS: State Red Banner Research Experimental Institute of the Air Force) in Akhtubinsk. The test

Above and top: During the late 1980s, a number of Tu-22KDs were rebuilt with an ECM system replacing the tail gun. This comprised the SPS-151, SPS-152 or SPS-153 system, in a streamlined fairing.

The Tu-22 had an accident-ridden early history and bad luck plagued it afterwards. In one incident, on 2 April 1976, a Guards unit aircraft was dropping FOTAB-250-215 bombs over the Karagaysky range. One of the six bombs exploded in the bomb bay, breaking the aircraft in half – although several of the crew managed to escape. However, during follow-on trials at the Akhtubinsk test centre – with the same bomb load – another Tu-22 was destroyed and the bomb was withdrawn from the inventory. This Tu-22KD is an aircraft of the 121st TBAP, previously based at Machulishche, in Belarus.

programme was plagued by problems, including fuselage deformation due to stress, fuel leaks, and onboard fires. It was found that during supersonic flight, the skin of the aircraft became overheated, deformed and passed some of the heat to the control booster rods. This led to erratic aircraft control. In addition, the new aircraft had problems with the autopilot, resulting in the loss of one test crew. A second crew was lost due to an engine fire. The Kh-22 missile was accepted for service use in 1964 before the Tu-22 aircraft trials were completed, as it was also intended to arm a new missile-carrying version of the Tu-95 'Bear' bomber. The state commission overseeing the Tu-22K aircraft test programme declared it to be a failure, but Andrei Tupolev himself was able to use his considerable political influence to avoid the programme being cancelled.

Production of the Tu-22K and the associated missile took place before the state acceptance trials were successfully concluded, and aircraft were issued to bomber regiments in 1965 while tests were continuing. The missile/aircraft

combination proved to be a hazard in service, due to unresolved problems with the basic Tu-22 aircraft, and the unreliability of the PN radar. A modification programme continued for several years, with no fewer than eight major modification programmes to bring the aircraft and missile complex up to acceptable standards.

The Tu-22K was finally accepted for service in 1967, about two years after it had actually been deployed. A total of 76 Tu-22K missile carriers was built at state aviation plant No. 22 in Kazan, including the improved Tu-22KD with the upgraded engines. This total was significantly below original plans, largely due to the protracted difficulties with the aircraft. Although intended to replace the Tu-16 in both air force and navy service, insufficient numbers were built to replace the air force 'Badgers'. Only a handful of Tu-22K missile carriers were delivered to the Soviet navy for trials, and no naval missile-carrier regiments were formed with the Tu-22K, the Tu-16K remaining in service instead. US intelligence estimated that about 700 Kh-22 missiles were built from 1961 to 1972, when initial production finally ended.

Although not officially accepted for service use, the first Tu-22Ks were issued to air force bomber regiments in 1965. Three regiments of Tu-22K became operational in 1965: the 121st DBAP (Long Range Aviation Regiment) at Machulishche near Minsk, the 203rd DBAP at Baranovichi, and the 341st DBAP at Ozernoye near Zhitomir, all attached to the 15th Heavy Bomber Division of the 46th Air Army of the Long Range Aviation. The Tu-22K appeared in service after the coup against Kruschchev in 1964, and there was some reconsideration of its mission as a result. Two combat roles for the Long Range Aviation's 15th Heavy Bomber Division predominated: nuclear strike missions against major strategic targets in NATO's Central Front or Southern Front, and a secondary role against NATO warships in the North Sea and Mediterranean. There have been reports that another air force 'Blinder' regiment operated in the Pacific area from Zavatinsk with the 30th Air Army.

Tu-22P: electronic snooper

The final major sub-series of the 'Shilo' was the Tu-22P ('Blinder-E'), designed as an electronics intelligence variant. This version employed the REB-K Elint system mounted in the bomb-bay area with a prominent ventral air scoop,

and sometimes had the aft defensive machine-gun barbette replaced with an SPS-100A Rezeda-A jammer station, although some Tu-22P carried the normal gun barbette. The role of the Tu-22P was to determine the location of targets – usually US Navy carrier battle groups – based on their radar and radio emissions. The Tu-22P also evolved into the role of stand-off-jammer, accompanying the Tu-22K strike aircraft and providing jamming support. A total of 47 Tu-22P-1s and Tu-22P-2s was built, the two versions varying in the precise configuration of the electronics package. As was the case with the other Tu-22 variants, the aircraft was upgraded with the RD-7M-2 engines and refuelling probe from 1965, and redesignated Tu-22PD. Eventually, the electronic warfare package was gradually improved, leading to the Tu-22P-4, Tu-22P-6 and Tu-22P-7 variants. The Tu-22PD was usually issued on the basis of one squadron per regiment of Tu-22K missile carriers, to provide EW support.

Tu-22 operational career

Although an aesthetically pleasing design, the Tu-22 was one of the least popular designs of its generation, and widely dreaded by the Long Range Aviation crews. It was dubbed 'unflyable' by some bomber pilots. The situation was by far the worst in the 1960s, due to uncorrected technical problems, and led to a number of instances of the crews refusing to fly the aircraft type. This was exacerbated when the Tu-22K missile carrier was pushed into service prematurely, with a resultant high accident rate. It was also due to inherent design flaws in the aircraft, which made it difficult to operate and difficult to fly, and a continual string of upgrade and modification programmes intended to fix

the lingering problems. Furthermore, the aircraft used downward-firing K-22 ejection seats, making ejection during take-off and landing impossible. This was an especially unhappy arrangement given the hazards of landing the Tu-22.

One of the most dangerous features of the Tu-22 was its high recommended landing speed of 310 km/h (192 mph) and a minimum speed of 290 km/h (180 mph), about 100 km/h (62 mph) higher than on the Tu-16, which made transition between the two aircraft especially troublesome. In the event that the speed dropped below the minimum, the aircraft had a tendency to pitch up and smash into the ground tail first. Once the aircraft safely touched down, the crew's troubles were not over. The undercarriage was spongy and tended to bounce. Inadequate shock absorption led to occasional undercarriage collapses, usually the nose-wheel. The Tu-22K had a high fatality rate during accidents due to the special hazard posed by the fully fuelled Kh-22 missile under its belly. Undercarriage failures would lead to spectacular explosions.

The pilot's perspective

The Tu-22, unlike its predecessor the Tu-16, had only a single pilot in order to reduce the frontal cross-section. Unfortunately, this was coupled with notoriously heavy flight controls. A pilot recalled that the aircraft was very tiring to fly even with both hands on the controls, and that even with the frequent use of the autopilot, no more than two missions a day could be flown because of pilot fatigue. The ergonomics of the crew stations were very poor. The pilot's seat was located slightly off-centre, to the left, to avoid the obstruction caused by the centre windscreen frame. However, when the pilot compensated for a cross-

The Tu-22K was not a success, although it was certainly more capable than the Tu-22B. The Kh-22 stand-off missile, its primary weapon, had a patchy development history and, even though the test programme ended with some successful launches, the Soviet state evaluation committee determined that the weapon was not an effective operational system. The PN radar guidance system was also flawed. Despite this, full Tu-22K production proceeded, as did Kh-22 deployment. The delays involved meant that the Tu-22K followed the Tu-22R into production and service, and so it was not until 1965 that the Soviet air force had any combat-capable 'Blinders' – albeit of limited effectiveness. It took another two years for the Tu-22K/Kh-22 combination to become operational. The Tu-22K was notoriously unpopular amongst crews, and there are several well-documented cases of pilots refusing to fly the aircraft. Over the course of its operational life the Tu-22K underwent eight major modifications, chiefly to its control systems, in an attempt to produce a better aircraft.

One of the rarest of Tu-22 sub-variants is the Tu-22KPD, the dedicated anti-radar/EW version, armed with the Kh-22P missile and fitted with the Kurs-N system. The only outward sign of this is a small twin-pronged 'pitchfork' antenna mounted above the nose, behind the radome, to starboard. It is just visible on the aircraft in the extreme right-hand side of this photograph.

Tupolev Tu-22 'Blinder' and Tu-22M 'Backfire'

features of the Tu-22 was the need for 450 litres (99 Imp gal) of pure grain alcohol for various hydraulic and de-icing systems – which the base personnel sometimes diverted for unofficial use. As a result, the Tu-22 was known as a '*spirtonosets*' ('booze carrier') by ground crews, a play on its official designation of *raketonosets* (missile carrier).

By the 1970s, many of the Tu-22's problems had been ironed out, and enough operational experience had been accumulated to reduce the accident rate. Nevertheless, the 'Blinder' was never a popular aircraft and continued to have one of the highest accident rates in the Soviet air force. Over 70 aircraft were lost in accidents through 1975, about 20 per cent of the total production, with an attendant high loss rate of crews. It was particularly unpopular compared the docile and dependable Tu-16 'Badger'. These losses were comparable to those suffered by the US Air Force's B-58 Hustler, although it should be pointed out that the Hustler was employed in the more demanding low-altitude environment, and had a higher operational tempo, giving it a lower loss-rate-per-sortie than the Tu-22.

Tu-22 mission profiles

The Long Range Aviation's 46th Air Army had two main missions: attack of high-priority NATO targets, and attack of aircraft-carrier groups of the US Sixth Fleet in the Mediterranean. For these missions, initial scouting was performed by the 46th Air Army's two Tu-22R 'Blinder' reconnaissance regiments, the 199th and 290th DRAP. The 199th DRAP operating out of Nezhin in Ukraine was assigned the task of operations over central Europe including Germany and Austria, as well as the southern region including Turkey, Greece, the Black Sea and the eastern Mediterranean. The 290th DRAP out of Zyabrovka was assigned strategic reconnaissance over the Baltic including Denmark, Scandinavia, and around 'the corner' beyond the Kola peninsula and down along the Norwegian coast. During peacetime, training missions for these two regiments were often conducted eastward along the Volga and towards the Caspian Sea. The Caspian Sea was also used for missile carrier training, with live missiles fired against hulks.

Seek and destroy the Sixth Fleet

In addition to acting as strategic scouts, these regiments would also serve as pathfinders during actual strike missions, especially strikes by the 15th Bomber Division against carrier battle groups. This was considered to be the 46th Air Army's most difficult and dangerous assignment. The strike mission would be cued by various intelligence assets, including land-based high-frequency direction-finding arrays (HF-DF, or 'Huff Duff'), intelligence trawlers shadowing the American warships, or other naval vessels like submarines. Although these systems could provide a rough indication of the location of the American carrier battle group, it would be necessary to determine the location with greater precision, and especially to distinguish the carrier from other ships in the battle group. This was the difficult assignment given to the Tu-22R crews. A typical mission against the Sixth Fleet in the Mediterranean would be preceded by a group of four Tu-22R reconnaissance aircraft, which would proceed to the target, usually over the friendly portions of the Balkans. If need be, some fighter escort could be provided part of the way. The carrier battle group would be approached initially at low altitude to avoid detection. As they neared the objective, a pair of Tu-22R reconnaissance aircraft would pull up while two more 'Blinders' proceeded into the heart of the carrier battle group. The pair that peeled off was assigned the mission of ECM activity against the fleet's surveillance radars, as well as acting as airborne relays for data from the penetrating pair. The penetrating pair was assigned the unenviable task of locating the precise position of the carrier within the group. This often required actual visual

wind from the left, the frame blocked his view of the runway. The accident rate was significant enough that less-experienced pilots were not permitted to take-off if crosswinds exceeded 12 m (39 ft) per second.

The cockpit was poorly designed, leading to some crews developing their own pull strings and hooks to operate controls that were out of reach. The navigator was located in 'a black pit' deep in the fuselage, and the visibility from the weapons officer's stations was poor. This prompted a sarcastic refrain among Tu-22R crews along the lines of 'it is a marvelous reconnaissance aircraft in which the pilot who should see the runway can only see the sky, the navigator who should see the terrain in front can only see it below, and the weapons officer who should keep an eye out over the tail can only see the wing.'

The Tu-22 was no more popular with ground crews. The combat readiness rate of the aircraft was low, which was attributable in part to difficulties in servicing the aircraft due to its design, such as the high-mounted engines. The location of the engines high above the fuselage required the use of special servicing scaffolds, which were not always available in the numbers needed. In addition, the aircraft had a relatively low durability, with a design life of only seven years or 1,000 landing cycles. The Kh-22 missile was especially unpopular with the ground crews because of its toxic oxidant. The fumes of the IRFNA oxidant were so toxic if breathed that the crew had to wear 'slime suits' (rubberised chemical protective ensembles with full face masks) when handling the weapon. One of the few prized

detection, since it could be difficult to distinguish the carrier from its escorts with the Tu-22K's PN radar in surface search mode. Once the carrier was identified, this data was immediately radioed back to the Tu-22R relays, which passed it on to the Tu-22K attack element.

Carrier hunting

The Tu-22K missile carriers of the 15th Bomber Division would carry out the attack in groups of up to a regiment in size, *i.e.*, 24-30 Tu-22K missile carriers, and four to eight Tu-22P electronic escort jammers. The attack would be conducted at stand-off ranges from the fleet, theoretically as far away as 550 km (340 miles) if the launch aircraft was at 14000 m (45,930 ft) or 400 km (250 miles) if launched from an altitude of 10000 m (32,810 ft). The usual launch range was 250-270 km (155-170 miles), since the aircraft had to acquire the target on its PN radar. For long-range

stand-off, the missile's autopilot was pre-programmed to fly to a cruise altitude of 22500 m (73,820 ft) and then begin a sharp supersonic dive on the target at speeds of 1400-1720 km/h (870-1,070 mph), relying on its active radar seeker for terminal guidance. The active radar guidance was not needed if the missile was the nuclear-armed version.

While the Tu-22K missile carriers were conducting their stand-off missile attack, the Tu-22P escort jammers would be attempting to mask the attack with various forms of electronic jamming. This jamming would be directed against naval air defence radars to pre-empt the use of Standard air defence missiles against the attacking bombers and missiles, and against fleet defence aircraft.

The viability of these tactics was severely undermined in the early 1970s with the advent of the F-14 Tomcat fighter. The F-14 was specifically developed to deal with the threat posed by Soviet bomber-fired anti-ship missiles. Due to its

The clean-lines of the Tu-22 were ruined in the ungainly Tu-22U 'Blinder-D' trainer conversion (which originally had the NATO name 'Blinder-C'). This aircraft wears the regimental badge of 121 TBAP.

Tupolev Tu-22U 'Blinder-D'

Above: The absence of a second pilot's seat in the Tu-22 made a trainer essential. This is the prototype Tu-22U, without refuelling probe.

Right: A small initial production series of Tu-22Us was built with provision for probes, which were added later. Note the open bomb bay doors.

Above: This is a Tu-22U of 121 DBAP. A few 'Blinder-Cs' were allocated to each 'Blinder' unit, in addition to the central training unit at Ryazan.

Above: The Tu-22U was not fitted with a tail gun and the instructor pilot sat where the gunner (navigator) used to be.

Right: The two small domes behind the second cockpit are for the BTs-63 astro-sextants, used for long-range navigation.

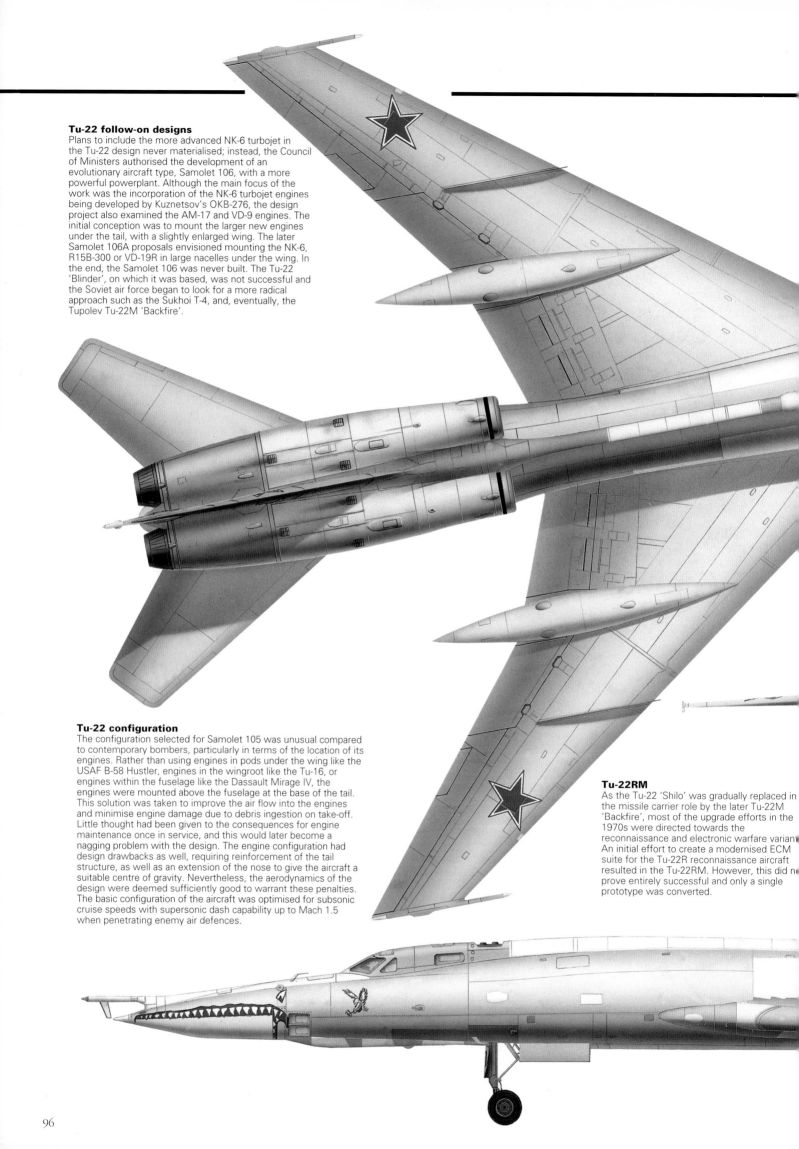

Tu-22 follow-on designs

Plans to include the more advanced NK-6 turbojet in the Tu-22 design never materialised; instead, the Council of Ministers authorised the development of an evolutionary aircraft type, Samolet 106, with a more powerful powerplant. Although the main focus of the work was the incorporation of the NK-6 turbojet engines being developed by Kuznetsov's OKB-276, the design project also examined the AM-17 and VD-9 engines. The initial conception was to mount the larger new engines under the tail, with a slightly enlarged wing. The later Samolet 106A proposals envisioned mounting the NK-6, R15B-300 or VD-19R in large nacelles under the wing. In the end, the Samolet 106 was never built. The Tu-22 'Blinder', on which it was based, was not successful and the Soviet air force began to look for a more radical approach such as the Sukhoi T-4, and, eventually, the Tupolev Tu-22M 'Backfire'.

Tu-22 configuration

The configuration selected for Samolet 105 was unusual compared to contemporary bombers, particularly in terms of the location of its engines. Rather than using engines in pods under the wing like the USAF B-58 Hustler, engines in the wingroot like the Tu-16, or engines within the fuselage like the Dassault Mirage IV, the engines were mounted above the fuselage at the base of the tail. This solution was taken to improve the air flow into the engines and minimise engine damage due to debris ingestion on take-off. Little thought had been given to the consequences for engine maintenance once in service, and this would later become a nagging problem with the design. The engine configuration had design drawbacks as well, requiring reinforcement of the tail structure, as well as an extension of the nose to give the aircraft a suitable centre of gravity. Nevertheless, the aerodynamics of the design were deemed sufficiently good to warrant these penalties. The basic configuration of the aircraft was optimised for subsonic cruise speeds with supersonic dash capability up to Mach 1.5 when penetrating enemy air defences.

Tu-22RM

As the Tu-22 'Shilo' was gradually replaced in the missile carrier role by the later Tu-22M 'Backfire', most of the upgrade efforts in the 1970s were directed towards the reconnaissance and electronic warfare variant. An initial effort to create a modernised ECM suite for the Tu-22R reconnaissance aircraft resulted in the Tu-22RM. However, this did not prove entirely successful and only a single prototype was converted.

Handling qualities

The Tu-22 did not have a reputation as a pilot's aircraft and could be very difficult and dangerous to fly. Remarking on its heavy controls, test pilot Alexey Nikonov once said, "two flights per day, without the autopilot, are enough for anyone." The Tu-22 could not be allowed to slow below 290 km/h (180 mph) on approach, without risking an uncontrollable pitch-up and stall. One such spectacular landing accident was captured for the opening sequence of the Soviet safety film 'Kindness to a roaring animal'.

Refuelling the Tu-22

Aerial refuelling was one of the most difficult operations for an inexperienced crew. Refuelling with the Tu-16 tanker took place at altitudes of 5000-8000 m (16,400-26,245 ft) and at a speed of 600 km/h (373 mph). The Tu-22 pilot would position his aircraft about 50 m (165 ft) to the right of the Tu-16, and gradually decelerate until behind the tanker. The bomber would then accelerate forward to connect the nose probe to the trailing drogue. The Tu-22 flight controls were not delicate, and many inexperienced pilots found themselves closing in on the drogue much too quickly and being forced to abandon the link-up with a fast descent to the right. Some less experienced pilots needed almost 45 minutes to secure a link-up. During the 1970s, the 199th OGDRAP at Nezhin developed a simpler technique to position the aircraft a few metres behind the drogue, and then use engine control alone to effect the link-up.

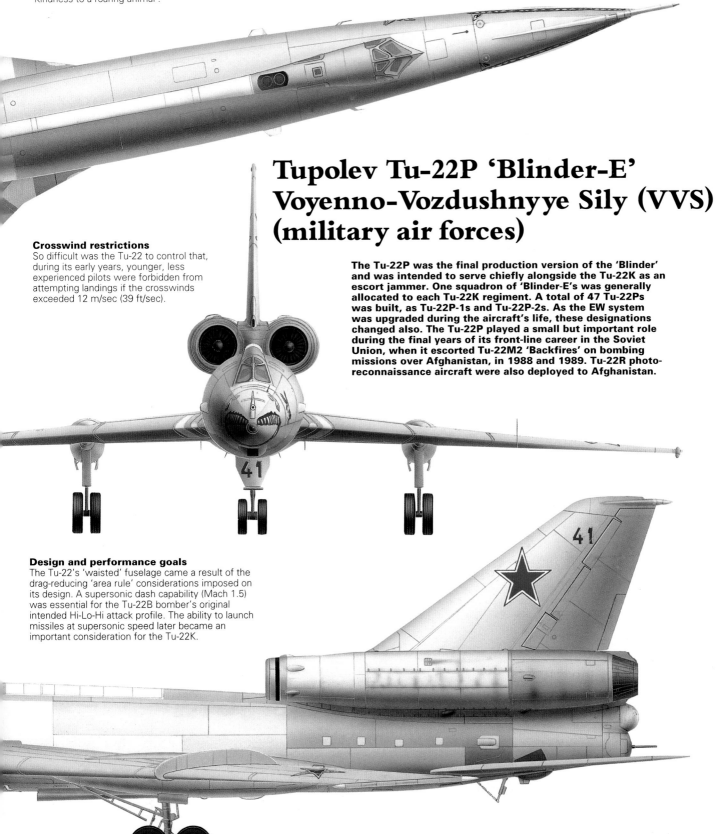

Tupolev Tu-22P 'Blinder-E' Voyenno-Vozdushnyye Sily (VVS) (military air forces)

Crosswind restrictions

So difficult was the Tu-22 to control that, during its early years, younger, less experienced pilots were forbidden from attempting landings if the crosswinds exceeded 12 m/sec (39 ft/sec).

The Tu-22P was the final production version of the 'Blinder' and was intended to serve chiefly alongside the Tu-22K as an escort jammer. One squadron of 'Blinder-E's was generally allocated to each Tu-22K regiment. A total of 47 Tu-22Ps was built, as Tu-22P-1s and Tu-22P-2s. As the EW system was upgraded during the aircraft's life, these designations changed also. The Tu-22P played a small but important role during the final years of its front-line career in the Soviet Union, when it escorted Tu-22M2 'Backfires' on bombing missions over Afghanistan, in 1988 and 1989. Tu-22R photo-reconnaissance aircraft were also deployed to Afghanistan.

Design and performance goals

The Tu-22's 'waisted' fuselage came a result of the drag-reducing 'area rule' considerations imposed on its design. A supersonic dash capability (Mach 1.5) was essential for the Tu-22B bomber's original intended Hi-Lo-Hi attack profile. The ability to launch missiles at supersonic speed later became an important consideration for the Tu-22K.

Tupolev Tu-22 'Blinder' and Tu-22M 'Backfire'

The Tu-22U was the least evolutionary of the entire Tu-22 family. It neither received, nor required, any of the ECM or systems upgrades applied to the other variants and so it remained free of antennas, fairings and other blemishes. Most Tu-22Us were based at Dyagilevo near Ryazan, the main training base for Long-Range Aviation. The 43rd training centre (43 TsBP i PLS) was located there, as was the main school for the 46th Air Army, which operated the 'Blinders'. Tu-22U production (totalling 46) was completed by 1960, acceptance and evaluation by 1962 and the first aircraft were issued to units in 1963. In practice, this meant that all early 'Blinder' crews had made the difficult transition to the Tu-22 without access to a trainer and had only a vague idea about how their dangerous new aircraft would perform.

long range, the Tomcat could provide combat air patrols a significant range from the carrier, forcing the 'Blinder' (or 'Bear' or 'Badger') to come within the lethal envelope of its Phoenix missiles. The tactic was to discover the incoming Tu-22R scouts or other similar aircraft using the E-2C Hawkeye, then vector the F-14s into the area. This could prevent the detection of the carrier and foil the attack before it started. Should the attack proceed anyway, the Tomcats were then expected to deal with both the missile carriers, and the Kh-22 missile if it had been released before interception of the bomber. The Phoenix missile was designed to reach targets at very high altitude – up to 18000 m (59,000 ft). The Kh-22 could be intercepted either in the early phase of flight, or in the terminal phase, but its high-altitude cruise regime was beyond the interception envelope of the Phoenix, if unclassified data is to be believed.

Upgrading the 'Blinder'

In addition to the development of new versions of the Tu-22, a significant rebuild programme for the Tu-22 was instituted throughout much of the 1960s to cure lingering problems. Aileron reversal problems were finally cured in 1965 with the addition of aileron fences. Additional hydraulic boosters were added to the flight control system to ease the pilot's handling problems. Improvements were made to the wing-mounted landing gear due to problems that had led to wing damage on landing. A string of engine upgrades was undertaken; the Dobrinin VD-7M was replaced from 1965 with an improved derivative, the Kolesov RD-7M2 engine, which offered 162 kN (36,375 lb) of static thrust compared to 159 kN (35,273 lb).

Following the development of an inflight-refuelling system for the Tu-22R reconnaissance aircraft, the system was adapted to the missile carriers due to the shortfall in their intended range compared to the official requirement. This upgrade programme began in 1965, with the missile carriers having a 'D' suffix added, such as Tu-22KD.

Electronic warfare systems were gradually improved through the career of the 'Blinder'. The basic defensive complex consisted of two passive radar warning receivers: the Avtomat-2 tuned to interceptor bands, and the Avtomat-3 tuned to ground-based radar bands.

New electronic systems for the Tu-22

The widespread deployment of the MIM-14 Nike Hercules and MIM-23 HAWK air defence missiles by NATO in the late 1950s presented a serious threat to any Soviet bomber strikes against high-value targets. GOSNIIAS, the main government avionics institute, began a detailed study of this problem under the codename Ekho. In 1962, experiments were conducted with a modified version of the Tu-22K adapted to attack key air defence radar installations with a special anti-radar version of the Kh-22 missile, the Kh-22P. The modified 'Blinder' was designated Tu-22KP and was fitted with the Kurs-N and later the Kurs-NM electronic intelligence system, which passively scanned for the emissions of standard NATO air defence radars. This version could be distinguished by a prominent 'pitchfork' antenna array carried on the right side of the nose. Most were built in the Tu-22KPD configuration with the standard refuelling system.

In the 1970s, some Tu-22R aircraft were upgraded with the Kub electronic intelligence system, with the antennas for the Elint system mounted in scabbed-on blisters on either side of the forward fuselage and in the wingroot. They were sometimes called Tu-22RK, but, since most were built with the refuelling probe, they were mostly designated Tu-22RDK. This was related to the system mounted on the MiG-25RBK reconnaissance aircraft.

In 1975, work began on another Tu-22R upgrade. A new reconnaissance package was developed, mounted in the bomb bay with a tub projecting under the fuselage for associated antennas and camera ports. The new centre package included M-202 Shompol side-looking radar, additional short focal-length cameras, and a new infra-red line scanner. The Shompol, developed by NPO Vega-M, was related to the type fitted to the MiG-25RBSh reconnaissance aircraft. The upgrade also included the addition of two AFA-42/100 cameras in place of one of the fuel tanks. Its ECM improvements included the incorporation of an SPS-151 jamming station (or the SPS-152 and SPS-153 Liutik jammers) and the addition of an ASO-2I chaff dispenser system. A small number were converted from Tu-22RD aircraft in 1981-82 as the Tu-22RDM.

A total of 311 Tu-22 and two prototypes was manufactured at Kazan through 1969, including 15 Tu-22Bs, 127 Tu-22Rs, 76 Tu-22Ks and 46 Tu-22Us.

Foreign exports and Libyan combat

In spite of its less than auspicious career in the Soviet air force, several air forces in the Middle East expressed interest in obtaining an aircraft more modern than the Tu-16. Sale of the new Tu-22M 'Backfire' was out of the question at the time, and the Tu-22 had been out of production for several years. After some discussion, the Ministry of Aviation Production decided to convert Tu-22R reconnaissance aircraft back to the Tu-22B configuration for export purposes. The total number converted is not certain, but Russian sources state it was over 20. In addition, a handful of Tu-22Us and Tu-22Rs were modified for export. One of the first requests was from Egypt, but this request was eventually turned down as its relations with the USSR cooled. Two export orders were approved: Libya and Iraq.

A Libyan squadron was the first to employ the Tu-22 in combat when, in 1979, Idi Amin of Uganda requested military support in his losing war with neighbouring Tanzania. On the night of 29-30 March 1979, a pair of Tu-22B bombers attacked the town of Mwanza in Tanzania, causing little damage. The Tu-22 bombers saw most of their combat action in the 1980s during the Libyan military campaigns in Chad. These air raids were seldom carried out by more than a pair of aircraft at a time, raising some questions about the availability of trained aircrews. In March 1980, civil war broke out again in Chad, with Colonel Muamar Khadaffi supporting Goukouni Oueddi's forces against those of defence minister Hissene Habre. On 9 October 1980, a small number of Tu-22B bombed Habre's forces

near N'djamena. The war eventually petered out and Khadaffi announced a union of Libya and Chad in January 1981. Habre managed to raise another insurgent army, and the civil war resumed in early 1982, with Habre's temporary victory. After a short interlude, the fighting broke out again in 1983, with Libya again supporting Goukouni against Habre. A number of bombing missions against Habre's forces from July to September 1983 used the Tu-22Bs, including raids on Fad, Faya-Largo and Umm-Shaluba.

International mediation brought the war to a close for three years until February 1986, when Goukoni's forces, with Libyan backing, attacked over the 'Red Line'. France decided to take a firmer line this time, and dispatched forces to assist Habre's forces. On 17 February 1986, a

This Tu-22U is seen connected to a a truck-mounted APA-50 electric 'start cart', as its crew prepare for a training sortie. All three crew K-22 ejection seats retract upwards into the fuselage. There are small emergency access hatches in the windscreen for the pilot and above the fuselage for the other crew.

Above and left: The Tu-22UD could be fitted with a complete refuelling probe, or the stubby housing for one above the nose. A Tu-22 typically refuelled from a Tu-16 tanker at heights between 5000 m (16,404 ft) and 8000 m (26,247 ft), and speeds of 600 km/h (373 mph). Air-to-air refuelling in the Tu-22 was a difficult and, in some cases, virtually impossible procedure. Reports tell of aircraft with inexperienced crews travelling 450 km (280 miles) together before achieving a successful hook-up.

Tupolev Tu-22P 'Blinder-E'

Above and left: The Tu-22P was the dedicated EW version of the 'Blinder'. Tu-22PDs of 341 TBAP saw action over Afghanistan, protecting bombers from Pakistani F-16s and SAMs. The dragon badge was adopted, in-theatre, in 1988.

Above: This view of the Tu-22P 'Blinder-E' escort jammer prototype shows the housings for the SPS-100A Rezeda-A ECM system. Some aircraft, however, retained the gun barbette. The Tu-22P also had antenna housings on the fuselage and in the wing root leading edge.

Right: Approximately 30 Tu-22P-1 and P-2 aircraft were built and each Tu-22K regiment was allocated a squadron of Tu-22Ps. The Tu-22P was designed to escort strike packages of missile carriers into and out of the target area. The baseline Tu-22Ps later evolved into Tu-22P-4/6/7s, with new equipment and antenna fits.

The air cooling scoop required by all its internal electronic equipment can be seen underneath this 'Blinder-E'. Also apparent are the problems faced by Tu-22 maintenance crews. The 'Blinder' sits high off the ground and none of its critical components – particularly the engines – is easily accessible.

single Tu-22B left Sebka air base, used terrain masking to approach N'djamena airport, and dropped three 500-kg (1,100-lb) bombs on it, hitting one of the main taxiways. Libyan forces were deployed in substantial numbers during this campaign, and the Tu-22B bombers were forward-deployed to Wadi-Dum air base to assist in supporting their operations. Bombing missions were carried out from October 1986 through March 1987. Habre's forces later captured Wadi-Dum, and found two derelict Tu-22B bombers there among other Libyan spoils. By August 1987, Habre's forces, supported by France, reached the disputed territory on the Chad-Libyan border. During the fighting near Aouza airbase on 8 August 1987, a Tu-22B was downed by a surface-to-air missile, apparently a Kub (SA-6) captured from the Libyans by Habre's troops. In response to a Chadian raid on the Maaten-es-Sara air base in Libya, on 5 September 1987, Khadaffi ordered a retaliatory raid on

N'djamena again. By this time, France had deployed an MIM-23 I-HAWK battery of the 402e Regiment Anti-Aérien. One Tu-22B was shot down, with the loss of its crew, and the other dumped its bombs and escaped.

The Tu-22Bs continued to launch pin-prick raids against Chadian forces at Wadi-Dum, Fada and Faya-Largo, until the ceasefire on 11 September 1987. Libya had been routed by the irregular Chadian forces, losing about $1.5 billion in equipment and a substantial number of troops.

While the war was going on against Chad, Libya became involved in border skirmishes with Sudan, which was supporting Chad in the conflict. As a result, Khadaffi ordered a Tu-22B bomber raid against Ondurman in March 1984, which caused civilian casualties. In April 1985, President Nimeiri was overthrown by forces friendly to Libya. As a result, the Libyan Tu-22B bombers were sent on several occasions in 1985 to support Sudanese forces in their campaigns against Christian insurgents in the southern regions of the country.

Iran-Iraq War

The second major conflict involving the Tu-22B bombers took place between Iran and Iraq in 1980. The Iraqi aircraft were heavily committed, and their range let them reach nearly any target in Iran. However, they faced much more serious opposition than their Libyan counterparts. When the war began on 19 September 1980, the Tu-22B bombers were committed to attacks against Teheran and Isfahan. During a 23 September 1980 raid on Teheran airport, the Iranians claim to have downed one Tu-22B bomber. After this initial onslaught, the Iraqi air force substantially reduced its operational tempo, returning only to carry out specific operations. In early October, the Tu-22B bombers returned in force, with fighter escort, to strike two automotive factories in Teheran. There have been reports that the Tu-22B bombers were occasionally allowed to operate from bases in Saudi Arabia and North Yemen, which served as a sanctuary from retaliatory Iranian strikes against their main operating base at Al-Walid.

The tempo of Tu-22 bomber strikes diminished when the Soviet Union imposed an arms embargo on Iraq. By 1984, Iraqi strength had been reduced to about eight Tu-22B

bombers, although it is not clear if the attrition was due to combat losses or accidents. The Tu-22B squadron continued to stage raids against key oil refineries and other military targets. Through 1982, Iran claims to have downed a further two Tu-22B bombers. In May 1985, the Iraqi air force resumed heavy air operations against Iranian cities, striking Teheran, Isfahan, and Shiraz with Tu-22 raids. This provoked the 'war of the cities' in which both sides pelted each other's cities with 'Scud' ballistic missiles. The Iraqi raids did not go uncontested and there were reports of at least one Tu-22B being damaged in an encounter with an Iranian F-4 Phantom, which severely damaged its stabiliser with an AIM-9 Sidewinder missile. Other aircraft suffered damage from MIM-23 HAWK missile batteries.

In March 1988, the Tu-22B bombers were used for the first time in maritime strikes during the 'tanker war'.

Tu-22Bs were credited with setting two supertankers on fire during a 19 March 1988 mission, the *Awai* and the *Sanandai*. By the end of the war in 1988, Iraq was reported to have only five Tu-22B bombers left in service. This suggests that as many as seven may have been lost in combat during the war.

Soviet 'Blinders' in combat

The Tu-22 was used in a limited support role during Soviet operations in Afghanistan. In October 1988, four Tu-22PDs of the 341st Heavy Bomber Regiment in Ozernoye were deployed to Mary-2 air base to provide electronic warfare support for Tu-22M3 'Backfire' bombers of the 185th Heavy Bomber Regiment from Poltava. The requirement for ECM support was prompted by the use of 'Backfires' near the Pakistani border, where there were

Sadly, this Tu-22PD 'Blinder-E', and its huge sharksmouth, is seen here withdrawn from service and awaiting its fate at the Engels dismantlement facility in 1995. It did not get broken up straight away, however, and survived at Engels for some years.

Tupolev Tu-22LL

A number of Tu-22s have served as trials aircraft for new engines and camera/reconnaissance systems. Of all these, the Tu-22LL stands out. In 1971, a single Tu-22R was converted at Tupolev factory N22 at Kazan (where all Tu-22 production was undertaken) to act as a high-speed equipment testbed. It was redesignated as the Tu-22LL (LL=letayuschchaya laboratoriya/flying laboratory). This Russian term is used indiscriminately and can be applied to an engine, avionics, equipment or weapons testbed or a research/survey aircraft. It is not known what functions the Tu-22LL and its modified (camera?) nose cone performed, but the aircraft ('Red 05') is still to be seen at the Russian flight test institute (LII), Zhukovskii.

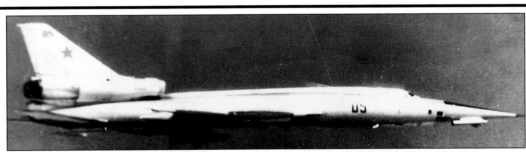

Tupolev Tu-22 'Blinder' production

1957	1958	1959	1960	1961	1962	1963	1964	1965	1966	1967	1968	1969
1	1	5	20	0	33	36	49	35	40	50	27	16

Tu-22K 'Blinder-C' technical data

(Tu-22KD data in parentheses)

Bureau designation:	Samolet 105A, Izd. YuK
Soviet air force designation:	Tu-22K
NATO designation:	'Blinder-C'
Powerplant:	two RD-7M2 (replacing VD-7M from 1965), each rated at 11000-kg (107.9-kN, 24,250-lb) thrust static and 16500-kg (161.9-kN, 36,376-lb) in reheat
Crew:	Three
Length:	41.6 m/42.6 m with refuelling probe (136.48 ft/139.76 ft)
Wingspan:	23.6 m (77.43 ft)
Height:	10.0 m (32.8 ft)
Maximum weight:	84000 kg (185,185 lb)
Maximum take-off-weight:	94000 kg (207,230 lb), with four RATO
Normal weight:	85000 kg (187,390 lb)
Fuel weight:	42500 kg (93,695 lb)
Maximum bomb load:	24000 kg (847,547 lb)
Effective range:	4900 km (3,045 miles)
Range, with one refuelling:	7150 km (4,443 miles)
Practical combat radius:	1300-2200 km (808-1,367 miles)
Maximum speed:	1510 km/h (938 mph)
Navigation/attack radar:	Rubin-1 (PN)
Optical bomb sight:	PSB-11
Defensive radar:	PRS-3 Argon II
Defensive weapons:	2x R-23 23-mm cannon
Active jamming system:	SPS-161 or SPS-162

Above and below: The Tu-22 was fitted with three K-22 downward-firing ejection seats (a Tu-22UB is seen above). Note the different configuration of the seats on the Tu-22KD below. The first seat is for the navigator, who sits in front of and below the pilot. The rear seat is occupied by the communications/navigation officer.

Above: The Tu-22RDM is fitted with the Shompol SLAR in its converted bomb bay.

Above right: The Tu-22R retained the bomb bay of the Tu-22B. Note also the pop-out emergency generator.

Right: Tu-22 crews can only access the aircraft by being raised and lowered on their seats.

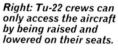

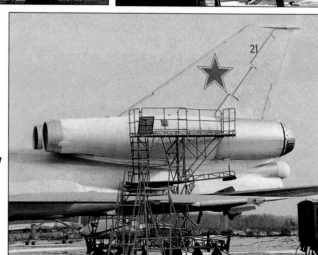

Above and left: The height of the Tu-22's engines from the ground presents considerable problems to its maintainers. Note the RD-7M engines fitted to the Tu-22RD above.

Right: By the mid-1980s, the Soviet air force had recognised the inadequacy of the tail gun and began refitting 'Blinder' with an ECM system instead. On the Tu-22RDM, this usually comprised the SPS-151 system.

Tupolev Tu-22

Tu-22 'Blinder' Operators

Soviet Union

Upon the dissolution of the Soviet Union in December 1991, 'Blinder' strength had shrunk to less than half of its original production levels, through attrition, export and retirement. The Soviet navy began retiring its Baltic Fleet Tu-22R regiment in the mid-1980s and it was disbanded in 1989. Likewise, the reconnaissance regiment at Saki in the Crimea was in the

process of disbanding in 1991, and had gone by 1994. Only six were still operational at Oktybrskoye in 1991, the remnants of the Black Sea Fleet regiment.

Most of the Soviet air force 'Blinder' regiments were outside of Russia in 1991. Prior to the USSR break-up, the Soviet air force was still operating 100 Tu-22Ks and Tu-22Ps with the 13th Heavy Bomber Division, and 55 Tu-22R reconnaissance aircraft with the two regiments of the 46th Air Army.

Above: In this line-up of Tu-22KDs, at Engels air base, the aircraft closest to the camera is wearing a Guards badge, while the second 'Blinder' is wearing a Tupolev emblem.

Below: This eagle and shield badge was worn by the 'Blinders' of the 121st Heavy Bomber Regiment, formerly stationed at Machulishche air base, in the newly independent republic of Belarus.

Tupolev Tu-22 'Blinder' Inventory, 1991		
Unit	Location	Inventory
46th Air Army, Long Range Aviation		
199 DRAP	Nezhin, Ukraine	26
290 DRAP	Zyabrovka, Belarus	29
15th Heavy Bomber Division, HQ Ozernoye, Ukraine		
121st Heavy Bomber Regiment	Machulishche, Belarus	34
341st Heavy Bomber Regiment	Ozernoye, Ukraine	32
203rd Heavy Bomber Regiment	Baranovichi, Belarus	32
Soviet Naval Aviation	Oktybrskoye, Ukraine	6

Russia

The heaviest concentration of the surviving 'Blinders' was actually in Belarus. However, the newly independent Belarussian government allowed Russian armed forces to maintain control over strategic forces on

its soil, and this included the regiments of the 15th Heavy Bomber Division. Russia eventually withdrew the regiments back to Engels air base for disbandment, and, as of 1997, there were 92 Tu-22 aircraft at the 6213 BLAT (Base for the Liquidation of Aviation Technology) being 'demilitarised'.

Ukraine

The status of Tu-22 regiments on Ukrainian soil remained uncertain for several years, especially those under Black Sea Fleet control. Ukraine eventually took control of most of the 'Blinders' on its soil in 1993-94. In 1994, the total number of Tu-22s was 55, comprising 33 at the 18th Aviation Base, six at the 1339 ABR (Aviation Repair Base) in

Belaya Tserkov, and 22 Tu-22Rs with the 199 DRAP at Nizhin. By 1995, the inventory had fallen to 50 Tu-22 aircraft in Ukraine subordinate to the 13th Heavy Bomber Division, including 17 Tu-22Rs attached to the 199 DRAP in Nezhin, and 27 aircraft being retired at the 18th Aviation Base in Ozernoye. These aircraft will remain in service until attrition and a lack of spare parts finally force their retirement.

Iraq

Iraq ordered the Tu-22 'Blinder' in 1973, with an initial order for 12 aircraft. The exact mixture is unknown, but is believed to have included at least 10 Tu-22B bombers. Iraqi pilots began training at Zyabrovka in 1973-74. Most of these crews were experienced pilots who had already trained in the Soviet Union. The Soviet instructors found their pupils very conscientious when it came to practical flight training, but very nonchalant in their academic studies. The 'Blinder' bomber squadron was based at Al-Walid. Iraqi Tu-22B bombers saw extensive combat use during the 1980-88 war with

Iran, but there is no reliable figure for the number of losses. The Iraqi inventory after the war is variously reported as five to eight aircraft, which suggests four to seven losses, unless the Soviet Union provided additional aircraft. Some of the Iraqi aircraft were returned for overhaul to the Soviet plant at Ryazan.

Most sources suggest that at the beginning of Operation Desert Storm in January 1991, Iraq still had five to eight Tu-22s in service, although they saw no combat in that action. Reports conflict about the number of these aircraft lost during the war, but Iraqi reports claim that 'a handful' remained operational after the war.

Above: The dragon badge of the 341st TBAP was first worn in Afghanistan but was retained on its Tu-22Ps in later years.

Below: This 1977 photo is one of very few available that depict Libyan Tu-22s. It was taken during their delivery flight, by a VF-51 Phantom.

Libya

Considerable mystery surrounds the 'Blinder' in Libyan service. Many sources claim that as many as 12 to 18 'Blinders' were sold to Libya, but other sources put the number as low as seven to eight. Delivery of the aircraft took place from 1977 to 1983, and training of the Libyan pilots reportedly took place at Zyabrovka from 1976. However, repeated reports indicate that there were never sufficient numbers of qualified Libyan pilots for these aircraft, and that foreign mercenary pilots were employed. These aircrew have been described as coming from Pakistan, Syria, the Soviet Union and North Korea, though details remain sketchy. The Libyan 'Blinder' squadron was based at Obka Ben Nafi Air Base near Tripoli. At least four were lost in combat in Chad and elsewhere in the 1980s. Sources vary about the number still in inventory, with the consensus being six to eight. It is doubtful if many are actually serviceable, given the low level of pilot training, shortage of spares, and the Tu-22's notorious maintenance problems.

concerns that Pakistani F-16 fighters or radar-directed SAMs might be employed. After three months of operations, this unit was replaced by four Tu-22PD stand-off jammers from the 203rd Heavy Bomber Regiment from Baranovichi in January 1989. They saw very little action as, by this time, bombing operations had shifted to the Salang pass area where there was no need for ECM support. As a result, the last Tu-22PDs were sent back to their bases in February. There had been plans to use Tu-22Rs of the 199th OGDRAP for photographic reconnaissance missions over Afghanistan in November 1988 from Mozdok, but they never took place.

Andrei Tupolev himself regarded the Tupolev Tu-22 as one of his "less fortunate creations." Its troubled history can be linked both to design problems and to the rapidly changing military environment in the later Kruschchev years. Although intended to take over the continental strike mission from the Tu-16, this never transpired. Much of the role was assumed by the Yangel design bureau's R-12 and R-14 (SS-4 and SS-5) intermediate-range missiles. In addition, the high cost and troubled early career of the Tu-22 led to a scaling-back of production compared to earlier plans. In its primary combat role as a stand-off cruise missile launcher, the 'Blinder' was inferior to the Tu-16, which could carry two missiles to the Tu-22's one, had better range, and was more dependable. The Tu-16 remained in service many years beyond its presumed life-expectancy, in part to make up for the problems with the Tu-22. The Tu-22's primary role in its later career was long-range reconnaissance, which it performed well after its teething problems had been overcome in the mid-1970s.

At the moment, the Tu-22 is on the brink of retirement. Given its shaky start, it is surprising it lasted this long. All Russian 'Blinders' are waiting for disposal. Ukraine possesses a small number of aircraft, but their long-term prospects for continued operational use seem poor. 'Blinders' in Iraq and Libya are likewise on the verge of extinction, if for no other reason than a lack of spare parts.

The same fate probably awaits the Tu-22's predecessor, the hardy and dependable Tu-16.

Taking the Tu-22's place has been a far more durable and successful aircraft, the Tu-22M 'Backfire'. The similarity in designation of the two aircraft is slightly misleading, but was not aimed at spy agencies in NATO. It was prompted by a complex power struggle in the halls of Kremlin in the late 1960s over the future of Soviet heavy combat aircraft development.

Tupolev Tu-22M 'Backfire'

The Tupolev Tu-22M 'Backfire' bomber was one of the most controversial Soviet aircraft of the 1980s. Intended as a follow-on to the Tu-22 'Blinder', it represented such a significant leap in capabilities that some intelligence analysts in the United States thought it was an intercontinental strategic bomber rather than a mere medium bomber. This led to protracted arguments at the strategic arms limitation talks between the USA and USSR. Its origins and missions stemmed from unusually intense rivalries within the Soviet military industrial complex.

In 1959, the 3rd Directorate of the NII-VVS (Scientific Research Institute of the Air Force) developed the tactical-technical requirements document (TTT) for a new-generation supersonic strategic bomber. The requirement was clearly influenced by the US XB-70 project, and the Soviet document referred to the need for a "reconnaissance strike complex" reflecting the US conception of this aircraft. As in the American case, the requirement pushed the state of the art, requiring a high level of performance and considerable advances in aircraft avionics including an automated astro-navigation system and fly-by-wire flight controls. The new design was intended to serve as a follow-on to the Tu-22 'Blinder'; it would have an effective combat radius of 2000 km (1,243 miles) and would carry two 1500-kg (3,310-lb) nuclear-armed Kh-45 Molniya stand-off missiles. The aircraft was designed to attack US Navy carrier battle groups, as well as key regional targets in Europe and the

Tupolev Tu-22 'Blinder' and Tu-22M 'Backfire'

chairman of the State Committee for Aviation Engineering (GKAT), who headed the Soviet aviation industry. The requirement was issued instead to three other bureaux, two of them fighter bureaux: Myasishchev's OKB-23, Sukhoi's OKB-51 and Yakovlev's OKB-115. Myasishchev's bureau had been working on a string of successor designs to its failed M-50 bomber (NATO's 'Bounder'), including the M-56 design. This bureau was quickly eliminated, quite literally, as Kruschchev's frustration over the bureau's past failures led to his decision to close the design bureau and turn over its assets to Chelomey's missile design bureau to assist with the new UR-100 (SS-11 Sego) missile programme.

Sukhoi was not as closely attuned to Kremlin politics as Tupolev, and threw the full weight of his bureau into the effort, coming up with the radical T-4 design. This sophisticated titanium aircraft was also called izdeliye 100 or T-100 due to its 100-tonne (98-ton) take-off weight. Yakovlev offered the Yak-33 design. Although not officially invited, Tupolev offered his Samolet 135 for the requirement, a 205-tonne (202-ton) design that strongly resembled the American XB-70 in configuration and grossly exceeded the design weight of the requirement. The designs were evaluated by a state commission in the spring of 1962, at which point it became apparent to Tupolev that the scales had been rigged and that his aircraft was far too large to compete with the Sukhoi or Yakovlev designs. As a result, Tupolev quickly came up with a substantially pared-down design, the Project 125, with a take-off weight of 130 tonnes (128 tons) and a cruising range of 6000 km (3,728 miles). However, the competition had been loaded in favour of his challengers, and Sukhoi's elegant T-4 design was selected to proceed.

The Sukhoi bureau was at first entrusted with the development of both the Molniya missile system and the aircraft itself. As the magnitude of the task became clear, the missile project was split off and delegated to the more experienced MKB Raduga design bureau in Dubna. The Molniya missile was to be powered by a solid rocket engine, with an effective range of 1500 km (932 miles), about three times

Pacific, but did not have the range for strategic strikes against the USA. The aircraft was required to have a top speed of Mach 3 and a cruising speed of Mach 2.8, a significant challenge given both structural airframe life and engine fuel economy issues.

The obvious choice to undertake the programme would have been Tupolev's OKB-156 design bureau, which had designed most post-war Soviet strategic bombers. However, Kruschchev was becoming disenchanted with Tupolev, in part due to his arrogant assumption that his bureau would be entrusted with all future bomber designs, as well as problems with the Tu-22 design that were becoming more evident. Nevertheless, Tupolev had continually bested all his rivals, emerging on top in contests with the experienced Ilyushin and the hapless Myasishchev. Kruschchev was also unhappy with Tupolev's design conservatism and reluctance to examine novel technologies.

Kruschchev made his views known to the Pyotr Dementyev,

Far left and below: By the late 1970s, the 15th Bomber Division's 'Blinders' were growing increasingly obsolete in one of their primary roles, that of attacking US Navy carrier battle groups. By this time, however, the 'Blinder' was being supplemented by the more modern Tu-22M 'Backfire', which was assigned the same mission. The first 'Backfires' entered service in 1971/1972, but it was not until 1976 that the first real operational variant, the Tu-22M2 'Backfire-B', was ready. The aircraft seen here are the latest model Tu-22M3 'Backfire-C'. In addition to the new bomber, a new family of Kh-22 missiles was introduced, the Kh-22M (AS-4 'Kitchen'), which incorporated features aimed at improving the probability of the missile 'leaking' through a carrier battle group's increasingly tough defences.

Tupolev T-22M0 and Tu-22M1 'Backfire-A'

Left: Wind tunnel tests at TSAGI revealed that the Tu-22M0 had several shortcomings, including its inadequate range. This tunnel model is a Tu-22M1, with bomb racks.

Below: Nine pre-production Tu-22M0s were built. This one survives at the Irkutsk military engineering academy.

Above: Redolent with Cold War intrigue, this photo shows one of the Tu-22M0s during test operations. Note the distinctive tail configuration and refuelling probe.

Right: Another preserved Tu-22M0 is now at the Kiev military aviation academy. Its probe was removed after SALT II.

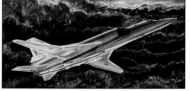

Above: This is how the 'Tu-26' was revealed by the US DoD in 1982.

Left: The large undercarriage fairings of the Tu-22M0 were dropped on production aircraft.

Below: This Tu-22M1 is carrying a single Kh-22 and is equipped with the OPB-15 optical bombsight ahead of the nose gear.

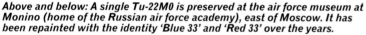

Above and below: A single Tu-22M0 is preserved at the air force museum at Monino (home of the Russian air force academy), east of Moscow. It has been repainted with the identity 'Blue 33' and 'Red 33' over the years.

the range of the contemporary Kh-22. The missile would be command-guided during the cruise phase, with an active terminal guidance system. There were also plans to develop a separating warhead section for the missile, to improve its survivability against SAMs. The missile would be lofted on a semi-ballistic trajectory and its warhead would separate upon re-entry into the upper atmosphere, with an active radar seeker on the re-entry vehicle providing terminal guidance. In some respects, this missile was similar to the Skybolt missile being developed at the time for the US Air Force and the RAF. The T-4 bomber would carry two Molniya missiles in internal bomb bays.

With preliminary design of the T-4 complete, Dementyev called Sukhoi to his office and crudely remarked, "the Negro has done his job, the Negro can leave." With his task of chastening Tupolev accomplished, Dementyev saw no further need to proceed with the T-4 programme. However, Sukhoi had became enamoured with the engineering challenge posed by the T-4 effort, and had won some support within the Military Industrial Committee (VPK) to continue the work, even if not fully funded. While Sukhoi was struggling through the early phase of the T-4's development, Kruschchev was ousted from power in the autumn of 1964.

Tupolev's lack of favour with Kruschchev rebounded to his benefit after the coup, and he enjoyed strong support from the new Brezhnev regime. In late 1964 Tupolev was able win approval to proceed with his new Samolet 145 design as a follow-on to the Tu-22. The project had the strong endorsement of the air force commander, General P. S. Kutakhov. Unhappy about the limitations of the new Tu-22 'Blinder', the Soviet air force wanted a more capable aircraft. The requirement for the new bomber included a range of at least 5000 km (3,106 miles), a speed of at least Mach 2 at high altitude, a speed near Mach 1 during low-altitude penetration missions, a payload of at least 20 tonnes (19.7 tons) to include missiles and bombs, and the ability to operate from forward air bases. The Samolet 145 had been conceived without government backing in 1962 as a lower-cost alternative to either the Tupolev Samolet 125 or the Sukhoi T-4. Development of the Samolet 145 was opposed by Kruschchev, who regarded manned aircraft as inferior to

The addition of a refuelling probe to the Tu-22M2 was the most controversial point in the history of the 'Backfire' and photos of such aircraft are rare. This photograph was taken by an SH-37 Viggen, in 1980.

Tupolev Tu-22M2 'Backfire-B'

Above and left: The Tu-22M2 was in flight test while SALT II negotiations were being conducted, but development aircraft were never fitted with refuelling probes. Note the early bullet-shaped fairing for the Argon-2 fire control radar above the tail guns.

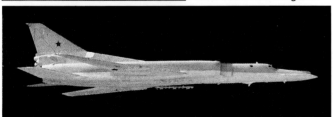

Above: This Tu-22M2 has the revised, squared-off, PRS-3 Argon-2 radome and multiple ejector rack mounted on its ventral hardpoint.

Below: The complete deletion of the probe housing from some M2s led to a smoother nose profile.

Above: The most distinctive feature of the Tu-22M2 – the enlarged and revised air intakes feeding the NK-22 engines – is evident in this view of an aircraft on its take-off run.

Above: A Tu-22M2 carrying a live Kh-22 missile – the type's primary armament for virtually all operational missions.

Right: This overhead view of a Tu-22M2 is one of those required for release under the terms of the CFE (Conventional Forces in Europe) arms reduction treaty. Like all its predecessors, the Tu-22M2 had a wing sweep range of 20° to 60°.

Right and below: By late 1969, Western intelligence agencies had determined that a 'new variant' of the Tu-22 existed and the first US satellite images of a Tu-22M on the ramp were taken over Kazan in July 1970. Russian hackles were raised when photos of the Tu-22M2 appeared – they had been taken at Poltava air base by a West German 'tourist'. It it was not until 1979 that the first good photographs, taken by the Swedish air force and others, began to appear. The photos seen here are both US Navy intercept shots, of Tu-22M2s, taken in 1989.

This Tu-22M2 is one of those operated by the training centre at Ryazan. The complete removal of the refuelling probe housing from the nose considerably alters the profile of the 'Backfire-B'. When the 'Backfire' became an issue during the SALT talks, its estimated maximum range, coupled with its refuelling capability, became a hugely contentious issue. The CIA and independent US industry sources (chiefly McDonnell Douglas) maintained that Soviet figures were correct and the aircraft had a range of approximately 3,000-3,500 nm. The US Air Force and the DoD steadfastly attributed an unrefuelled range of 5,000-6,000 nm to the aircraft. The Soviet Union was permitted only 2,400 'strategic delivery systems' under the terms of the Ford-Brezhnev Vladivostok agreement that established the SALT II guidelines. Ultimately, the Soviet position that the 'Backfire' was a medium-range theatre bomber was accepted, but only with the removal of its refuelling capability.

missiles for nuclear strike missions. When resubmitted to the new Brezhnev administration, the aircraft was depicted as a mere upgrade of the existing and seriously flawed Tu-22 'Blinder'. If the Samolet 145 had not been offered as a safe and cheap alternative to the T-4, it also might have been armed with the highly sophisticated Molniya missile. Instead, it was to be equipped with the existing Kh-22 and K-22 weapon system that armed the Tu-22K bomber.

The selection of the older Kh-22 missile for the new bomber, rather than a new weapon such as the Kh-45, was tied to Tupolev's marketing strategy with Brezhnev and the Council of Ministers. The competitor for the requirement was the struggling Sukhoi T-4 programme, an entirely new and expensive aircraft. In contrast, Tupolev was offering his

Samolet 145 as a less expensive alternative, linked to the existing Tu-22. The internal bureau designation reflected that relationship; the Tu-22 had been Project Yu, the new design was Project YuM (later, more honestly, Project A). The Samolet 145 would use an upgraded version of the K-22 system, designated K-22M, based around the Leninets PN-A radar (NATO's 'Down Beat'), derived from the radar used in the earlier Tu-22K.

Samolet 145 wins out

Brezhnev's decision to permit Tupolev to proceed with Project 145 meant that in the late 1960s the Soviet air force was funding the development of two parallel intermediate-range bombers armed with two entirely different missile systems. In November 1967, the Council of Ministers decided to proceed with engineering-manufacturing development of the Samolet 145 instead of the T-4. The decision was based on several factors. To begin with, the Tu-22 'Blinder' had proved very disappointing in service and a new aircraft was needed to replace it on the production lines. The Tu-22 never came close to replacing the Tu-16, which was one of the original goals of the programme. Secondly, there was some concern about the cost of the T-4. It was pointedly nicknamed '100 tonnes of gold' due to the high cost of its titanium structure. The Samolet 145 appeared to be a more reasonable compromise in terms of performance and cost. Thirdly, the new Brezhnev administration was becoming increasingly concerned about the threat posed by China. Strikes against China posed a different set of requirements than those

against the more technologically advanced threat of NATO, and an aircraft with a hefty payload was more attractive than the elegant but more lightly armed T-4.

Although promoted as a mere upgrade of the Tu-22, the Samolet 145 was in fact an entirely new aircraft, sharing only a common weapon system. In the end, the only structural assemblies in common between the two aircraft were the front landing gear and the bomb bay doors. The construction of the first prototype was accomplished fairly quickly, with the first Tu-22M0 being delivered to the Flight Test Institute (LII) at Zhukhovskii in the summer of 1969, hardly two years after the project had officially been blessed. The first test flight took place on 30 August 1969. In order to hasten the testing, it was decided to build a somewhat larger pre-series batch than the normal five aircraft, 10 being planned. Trials revealed some problems in the design, but they were to be addressed in the early production aircraft. The problems included flexing and deformation problems with the wing fillet, excessive landing gear weight and complexity, and the lack of utility of the planned arrester hook. The prototype employed the Kuznetsov NK-144-22 engine, derived from the engine on the Tu-144 supersonic transport. It was not sufficiently fuel efficient, and the Tu-22M0 was below the range requirements at only 4140 km (2,573 miles). A total of nine of the pre-series Tu-22M0 was manufactured at Kazan in 1969-71. The final production aircraft incorporated some of the features intended for the series production aircraft, including the rear UKU-9K-502 defensive machine-gun position designed by I. Goropov's Vympel OKB-43 in place of an electronic warfare station and braking parachute housing of the original aircraft. The decision to add the defensive station was not applauded throughout the air force, and it came at a time of increasing doubts about the usefulness of such weapons as a defence against fighters. As a concession to critics, the role of the machine-gun position was changed. Instead of firing conventional ammunition, it sprayed out a stream of special PIKS anti-IR projectiles with a thermite fill, and PRLS anti-radar projectiles which dispensed small chaff dipoles.

Troubled Tu-22M1

The series production aircraft received the evolved NK-22 engine, which offered about 10 per cent more thrust. This engine was developed by the N. Kuznetsov design bureau and manufactured at the Trud Plant in Kuibyshev (now Samara). Production was scheduled to begin at the State Aviation Plant No. 22 in Kazan in 1971, after the conclusion of Tu-22 'Blinder' production there.

The initial production type was designated Tu-22M1. This production batch used a simplified landing gear retracting into the wingroot, and the wing span was increased. Design problems persisted with this version of the aircraft as well, and only nine Tu-22M1s were manufactured in 1971-72. Operational trials were conducted by the 185th Guards Heavy Bomber Aviation Regiment, 13th Guards Heavy Bomber Aviation Division in Poltava, Ukraine, commanded by the later head of the Russian Air Force, P. S. Denikin. There has never been a detailed explanation of the full extent of the problems with the Tu-22M1, but it was not accepted for series production. Russian accounts state that the Tu-22M1 was specifically intended for naval applications and that seven of the nine aircraft manufactured were deployed with naval regiments.

The improved design required additional work, and official service acceptance did not take place until 1976. It incorporated the modified ABSU-145M flight control and NK-45 flight navigation systems, plus improvements to the weapons system. The revised design can be identified by the change in the configuration of the air inlets, the intake

This page, clockwise from top left: The first clear photos of the 'Backfire-B' came in 1979 when 'Red 78' was photographed by the Swedes. 'Red 43' was next seen in 1980, again over the Baltic. Eventually the Tu-22M became a common sight – particularly in the northern European region. The Flygvapnet brought back the first clear images of the AS-4 'Kitchen' missile (Kh-22), carried by 'Red 76'. In this case (three photos) it is a silver training ('uchebniy') round of the Kh-22MA low-level nuclear-armed version. The missile-carrying Tu-22M2 is seen escorted by a Flygvapnet J 35F Draken. In 1980, two Danish air force RF 35 reconnaissance Drakens intercepted a gaggle of Tu-22M2s over the Baltic. The Drakens left the scene upon the arrival of Soviet MiG-23s sent to shepherd the 'Backfires'. The Tu-22s then went on to make the first observed (but only on radar) air-to-surface firings of the Kh-22 against shipping and ground targets (on the East German island of Rugen). The 'Backfires' were operating as part of of exercise Brotherhood in Arms-80, supporting amphibious landings. The RNAF 331 Skv F-16A is seen escorting Tu-22M2 'Red 41' which is carrying a standard Kh-22 training round – containing all the missile avionics, but no fuel or warhead.

Tupolev Tu-22M3 'Backfire-C'

Above and left: The prototype Tu-22M had a refuelling probe stub which was removed from all subsequent M3s as part of the Soviet concessions to SALT II. The aircraft seen left is one of the pre-production batch.

Above: A clandestine photograph of an early Tu-22M3 'Backfire-C', seen landing at Zhukhovskii.

Left: The M3 routinely carries its missile armament under the wing, on BD-45K pylons, unlike earlier 'Backfires' or the 'Blinder'.

Below: A Tu-22M3, armed with a single Kh-22M, departs on a training mission.

Above: The boundary-layer intakes over the main engine intakes are visible in this overhead CFE view of a Tu-22M3.

Left: Free-fall bombs are rarely seen on the 'Backfire', particularly on the Tu-22M3.

Below: A Tu-22M3 in landing configuration.

and venting ports for an APU added in the dorsal fin, and reshaping of the dielectric cover over the Argon-3 aft-facing defensive radar. The standard production version was designated Tu-22M2 ('Backfire-B'), and it was nicknamed the 'Dvoika' (deuce) by its crews. Total production of the Tu-22M from 1972 to 1983 was 211 aircraft, all manufactured at the State Aviation Plant No. 22 in Kazan.

The standard payload of the Tu-22M2 was a single Kh-22 (AS-4 'Kitchen') in a recessed central bomb bay under the fuselage. For short-range missions, the Tu-22M2 could increase its payload at the expense of range, typically a pair of Kh-22N missiles, one under each wing pylon. As many as three Kh-22s could be carried simultaneously, at the expense of range, but this configuration appears to have been rarely used with this version of the aircraft.

The Tu-22M2 was received with enthusiasm by its crews, in contrast to the earlier Tu-22 'Blinder'. It had far better handling characteristics and cockpit ergonomics. In addition to their deployment with the Long Range Aviation branch of the air force, Tu-22M2s were also issued to Naval Aviation regiments of the Northern and Black Sea Fleets to replace the Tu-16K. In this role, they could be fitted to deliver aerial mines. Training for both branches was undertaken at the 43rd Flight Personnel Combat Training and Conversion Centre at Ryazan. Tu-22M2 regiments were organised around 18 bombers, although regimental strength was sometimes as high as 20. In addition, the accepted practice was to deploy at least a squadron of Tu-16P escort jammers with each Tu-22M2 regiment for electronic warfare support. Due to the high

cost of the aircraft, it was decided to develop a conversion trainer for crews, the Tupolev Tu-134UBL, based on the common twin-engined airliner.

Early service troubles

The reputation of the Tu-22M2 began to suffer as the aircraft aged. The design was quite complicated, which led to servicing problems. The mean-time-between-overhauls (MBTO) of the NK-22 engines on the initial aircraft was an appallingly low 50 hours, and led to a service-wide edict to limit turbine temperatures and, therefore, engine thrust. The ECM system had not been well integrated with the aircraft avionics, leading to interference problems which sometimes shut down the automated flight control system, forcing the crew to fly the aircraft manually. The Tu-22M2 was not well suited to low-level tactics, even though they were supposed to be its primary combat envelope. Rivets in the air intake would pop off, causing cracks in the fuselage and potentially leading to engine ingestion of parts and subsequent engine disintegration. A programme of strengthening the intake splitters alleviated some of these problems. The aircraft was ruefully referred to as the

'*vsepogodniy defektonosets*' (all-weather defect-carrier) a play on its official designation of *vsepogodniy raketnosets* (all-weather missile-carrier).

Range controversy

The international controversy over the role of the 'Backfire' bomber had already begun by 1975 when the bombers were first entering widespread service. At the time, negotiations were underway between the US and USSR on the SALT II (Strategic Arms Limitation Treaty) talks.

The Tu-22M3 was fitted with more powerful NK-25 engines, which necessitated revised (and very distinctive) forward-raked air intakes. It also had an improved and strengthened main wing, with an increased maximum sweep angle of 65°. The 'Backfire-C' was optimised for low-level operations, down to 50 m (164 ft), and intended for use in conjunction with A-50 'Mainstay' AWACS and MiG-31 or Su-27 escorts. The Tu-22M3 has never been seen by Western observers in such an operational setting, even though the first aircraft specifically intended for low-level missions entered service in 1983 (with the 185th Guards heavy bomber air regiment).

This is the Tu-22M3 exhibited at the 1992 Minsk-Machulishche military exhibition, held for visiting heads of state and defence ministers. It was the first 'public' showing of the 'Backfire-C'. Note the redesigned vertical cannon installation refitted to late-model 'Backfire-Cs'.

Weapons of the Tu-22M3 'Backfire-C'

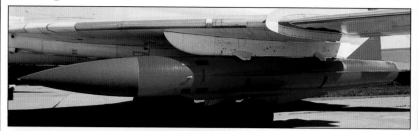

Above, left and below: The primary weapon of the 'Backfire', particularly in the anti-shipping and land attack role (against large targets), is the Kh-22 (AS-4 'Kitchen') missile. The Tu-22M3 can carry up to three Kh-22s (two underwing on BD-45K pylons) over a short range. Kh-22 was only carried recessed by the Tu-22M2. The missiles seen here are Kh-22M training rounds.

Above and left: The Tu-22M3 was modernised to carry the Raduga Kh-15 missile (AS-16 'Kickback') on a six-round internal rotary launcher.

Left, above and below: When first seen by Western observers, the Tu-22M's MBD3-U9-68 multiple ejector rack was identified as 'ECM equipment'. Up to four racks can be carried. The Tu-22M served as a bomber in the Afghan and Chechen conflicts. The aircraft seen here is carrying nine 250-kg FAB-250 HE fragmentation bombs.

The Tu-22M2 (above) was fitted with the UKU-9K-502 gun barbette, comprising two twin-barrelled GSh-23 23-mm cannon. The Tu-22M3 (left) adopted a single GSh-23 installation in a UK-9A-802 housing. The 'Backfire-C's guns are equipped to fire IR decoys and small chaff-dispensing projectiles.

The 'Backfire-A' was first spotted by US intelligence satellites in July 1970, and the 'Backfire-B' in May 1973. The US Air Force's intelligence branch took the hardest line on the 'Backfire', arguing as early as 1971 that the bomber was being developed for both the intercontinental and peripheral attack missions. 'Peripheral attack' was the US's phrase at the time for strategic missions not directed at the continental United States, but against objectives in Europe and Asia. The initial CIA assessment in 1970 was that the 'Backfire' had a maximum combat radius of 5550 km (3,450 miles) when flying a subsonic high-altitude mission with refuelling, similar to that of the 3M 'Bison' bomber. As more data on the 'Backfire' became available, CIA estimates of the aircraft's effective radius dropped, and by 1976 it was down to 3380 km (2,100 miles).

USAF versus the CIA

Other intelligence organisations, and the US Air Force in particular, strongly disagreed. The USAF argued that it was intended for intercontinental missions, while the CIA and Navy argued it was intended primarily for peripheral attack missions in Eurasia. Contemporary US Air Force intelligence assessments estimated that the 'Backfire-B' had an unrefuelled combat radius of 5650 km (3,510 miles) (10450-km/6,495-mile range), and with a single refuelling a combat radius of 7780 km (4,835 miles) (14350-km/8,915-mile range). The argument continued in earnest in the mid-1970s during the SALT deliberations, with the CIA and the

State Department leaning toward the lower estimates, and the Defense Intelligence Agency (DIA), Air Force and Army leaning toward the more alarmist estimates. The high Air Force assessments were in part due to overestimates of fuel stowage, which USAF and DIA analysts put at 68040 kg (150,000 lb) and the CIA at 49895 kg (110,000 lb). Recent Russian accounts indicate that for the Tu-22M3 the figure was 53525 kg (118,000 lb). Air Force estimates also posited a more fuel-efficient engine than was the case, estimating that at its maximum static thrust with afterburner of 55,500 lb (247 kN), it had a specific fuel consumption of 1.99 lb/hr/lb, while at its maximum thrust without afterburner of 33,000 lb (147 kN), its specific fuel consumption was 0.61 lb/hr/lb.

The 'Backfire' compromise

The Soviets argued equally vehemently that the 'Backfire' was not intended for the intercontinental role and therefore should not be classified as a 'heavy bomber' in SALT terminology. At first, the Soviet negotiators believed that the US position was simply a negotiating ploy due to the sharp disparity between the US assessment of the 'Backfire' and its stated performance. However, given Minister of Defence Marshal A. A. Grechko's hardline views on the arms control treaties, the Soviet Union was unwilling to release any significant documentation on 'Backfire' performance to the Americans. Indeed, Grechko even refused to give the Soviet negotiators the aircraft's true designation, using the NATO

name 'Backfire' instead. As a result, the service designation for the 'Backfire' was something of a mystery for many years, with Tu-26 being one of the more popular mistakes. The Soviet negotiators' failure to supply any data rendered any detailed discussion of the issue impossible.

In spite of opposition from the Soviet General Staff, the Kremlin finally decided to make a concession in the 'Backfire' controversy. During the course of negotiations on SALT II in Vienna in 1979, Leonid Brezhnev provided a formal letter to President Jimmy Carter. It stated that any significant increase in the range or payload of the 'Backfire' would be inconsistent with the terms of the treaty, and that production would be frozen at the current annual rate of 30. The Soviet side also agreed to remove the nose refuelling probe from the 'Backfire', to put to rest the contention that the bomber could reach intercontinental ranges if refuelled. In recognition that the aircraft could be easily retrofitted with the refuelling probes, assurances were given that the size of the Soviet tanker force would not be enlarged sufficiently to support the use of the 'Backfire' in an intercontinental role.

In 1985, the DIA conceded that the CIA's lower combat radius estimate of 4825 km (3000 miles) was substantially correct. Ironically, this concession came just as evidence began to emerge that the new 'Backfire-C' variant might have range advantages over the standard 'Backfire-B'.

Recent Russian accounts indicate that the combat range of the Tu-22M1 was 5000 km (3,106 miles) unrefuelled with a 3-tonne (2.9-ton) payload and that the Tu-22M2 was 5100 km (3,169 miles), and that combat radius was only 2200 km (1,367 miles) unrefuelled when carrying a single Kh-22. Range figures are highly contingent both on fuel/payload mixes and flight profiles, and Russian range data has seldom been accompanied by any explicit description of these criteria. However, the Russian and later American estimates may not be as divergent as they seem at first, since the US estimates considered an aircraft flying at economical cruise at high altitude with an internal load of bombs, while the Russian figures apparently refer to a more realistic combat mission consisting of a payload of a single Kh-22 missile with higher drag than internal bombs, and a hi-lo mission profile.

Mission profile

As in the case of the Tu-22 'Blinder', the Tu-22M 'Backfire' was used on two principal types of missions: attacks on strategic land targets, and attacks on US Navy carrier battle groups. In contrast to the 'Blinder', the majority of 'Backfires' were of the missile-carrying versions. Instead of only a single 'Blinder' missile-carrier division, there were five 'Backfire' missile-carrier divisions – three with the Long Range Aviation branch of the Air Force and two with the Navy – plus independent regiments in the Pacific. As a result, the operating environment of the 'Backfire' was considerably larger than in the case of the 'Blinder', including much of the North, Baltic, Black and Mediterranean Seas. 'Backfires' also operated in the Far East against the US Pacific Fleet and Japan.

The Tu-22M3's new NK-25 engines were test flown on a Tu-142 testbed, before being fitted to the Tu-22M2Ye trials aircraft, which integrated the fuel system and other related equipment. The Tu-22M3 made its maiden flight on 20 June 1977.

This Tu-22M3 was involved in weapons trials from Zhukhovskii air base, Moscow. Note the unusual serial presentation (9804) on the forward nosewheel door – most Tu-22s carry a service 'Bort' number on the tail. This 'Backfire-C' is carrying a heavy load of two Kh-22 (AS-4) missiles – both missiles are test versions of the Kh-22 anti-shipping variant with the full dielectric nosecone, indicating that the round is fitted with the active radar seeker.

Tupolev Tu-134UBK and Tu-134UBL

The Tu-134UBL is intended to train Tu-22M3 'Backfire-C' and Tu-160 'Blackjack' crews, who have never had a dedicated trainer, like the Tu-22U. The Tu-134 and Tu-22M have a similar thrust-to-weight ratio and comparable low-speed handling. The Tu-134UBL is a purpose-built aircraft, not a conversion, and is instantly recognisable by its long pointed nose, housing a ROZ-1 radar. Each aircraft has only nine cabin windows, and all Russian air force aircraft are grey painted, with a red lightning bolt. By late 1983, 90 aircraft had been built. Tu-134UBLs serve with the pilot's schools at Orsk and Tambov. A single Tu-134UBL was converted to Tu-134UBK standard, in 1982, to train Tu-22M3 for anti-shipping missions. This aircraft has a small undernose fairing to house the re-located ROZ-1 radar, and the nosecone instead housed the bomber's PN-A attack radar. A fixed Kh-22 acquisition round was installed under the fuselage and the 'Backfire's OPB-15T electro-optical targetting system was also fitted. This aircraft was delivered to the naval conversion training centre in Nikolayev, on the Black Sea, and was taken over by the Ukrainian air force.

Top: The standard operational load for the Tu-22M3 is a single Kh-22 missile – to provide maximum range for the launch aircraft. The 'Backfire-C' can easily carry two Kh-22s, however, along with (theoretically) a full load of Kh-15 short-range attack missiles. Despite its age, and the many problems that plagued its early development, the Kh-22 remains an important weapon in the Russian inventory. It is the primary weapon of the 'Backfire' and the Tu-95 'Bear-G'. It is also believed to be in the Ukrainian, Belarussian and Kazakh inventories. When allegations of a Tu-22M sale to Iran surfaced in 1994, the most controversial aspect of the 'sale' was the suspected supply of Kh-22 and Kh-26 (AS-6 'Kingfish') missiles with the aircraft.

The 'Blinder' made its terminal approaches to the carrier battle group at relatively high altitudes, which made it easily detectable by both surface-based naval radars and airborne radars such as the E-2C Hawkeye. The Tu-22M 'Backfire' was designed to address this problem by using low-altitude approaches which reduced its vulnerability of detection. It was not nap-of-the-earth flying, but rather low-altitude flying. Most peacetime training missions were not carried out at such altitude since it placed greater stress on the airframe and increased the likelihood of training accidents. However, in wartime, most attack missions would have been conducted in a hi-lo-hi profile: high-altitude economical cruise into the target area to conserve fuel and extend range, low-altitude approach and egress when within radar range, and high-altitude return.

The tactics and force structure of the 'Backfire' regiments differed from the 'Blinder' regiments due to important changes in intelligence gathering. While a very large percentage of 'Blinders' had to be devoted to the naval reconnaissance mission, by the late 1970s this mission was being assumed by satellites. The reasons behind this are fairly apparent, as the description of the Tu-22R 'Blinder' tactics makes it quite clear that such missions would be almost suicidal with the advent of improved US Navy air defences, especially the F-14 Tomcat.

The first efforts to develop an MKRT (*sistem morskoy kosmicheskoy razvedki I tselkazaniya* – naval reconnaissance and targeting space system) had begun in the late 1950s

when the 'Blinder' was still on the drawing boards. The programme was a co-operative effort between the Chelomey OKB-52 missile design bureau (onboard targeting system, satellite bus); A. I. Savin's KB-1 MRP/OKB-41 design bureau (satellite); and I. Ya. Brukhanskiy's NII-17 GKRE design bureau (radar and electronic intelligence sensors). The MKRTs was much delayed due to the enormous technological challenge it presented. A small series of test satellites was launched from 1965 but the lack of a sufficiently high-energy power source continued to hinder the programme. A number of compact nuclear power sources were developed, from which the Topaz system from TsKB Mach in Leningrad was selected. The first successful element of this system, the new nuclear-powered US-A RORSAT (Radar Ocean Reconnaissance Satellite), was finally launched in October 1970. The US-A was fitted with a NII-17 active surveillance radar powered by the Topaz nuclear reactor, which gave it enough power to detect and track naval formations. Sufficient US-A satellites were launched for the system to be accepted into service in October 1975. The second element of the MKRTs system was the US-P naval EORSAT (Electronic Intelligence Ocean Reconnaissance Satellite), which began launches in 1975. The US-P was a new generation of Elint satellites fitted with passive electronic sensors to locate naval formations by their radar emissions and radio communications transmissions. The US-A and US-P satellites were the space-based elements of an extensive naval reconnaissance system codenamed Legenda (legend), which was finally accepted for service use in 1978. The satellites were managed by the GRU military intelligence arm of the Soviet General Staff for the regiments of the Long Range Aviation, and by the Department of Satellite Intelligence of the Naval Intelligence Directorate of the Main Navy Staff for the naval 'Backfire' regiments.

The Legenda system gradually replaced the fleet of Tu-22R 'Blinder' aircraft. Data from the system was analysed at primary command centres and transmitted to the 'Backfire' bombers via conventional radio or the Molniya satellite communication datalinks. The advent of the Legenda maritime reconnaissance satellites removed the need for large numbers of reconnaissance 'Backfires', and this hazardous task was conducted from the relative security of space, instead.

New versions of the Kh-22

With data on the location of the carrier battle group, the Tu-22M 'Backfire' squadrons would conduct their final approach to the target at low altitudes. This necessitated changes in the Kh-22 missile to enhance its survivability against US naval air defences. The new system was designated K-22M, and new missile variants as Kh-22M and Kh-22MA. The Kh-22M was intended to attack naval targets and high-radar-contrast land targets. It had two flight profiles: an aero-ballistic profile like the earlier Kh-22 intended to take the missile over the lethal envelope of the F-14 Tomcat, and a new low-altitude approach to reduce the missile's vulnerability to detection. The Kh-22MA was specifically designed for low-altitude attack at minimal approach heights. Both versions had improved electronic counter-countermeasures (ECCM) and datalinks for midcourse corrections from the launching 'Backfire'. The other major advantage of the 'Backfire' over the 'Blinder' was its ability to carry several Kh-22 missiles per mission. As a result, on short-range missions, a 'Backfire' regiment could fire about 50-75 missiles against the carrier battle group, saturating the battle group's defences even if many missile were shot down by Phoenixes from the F-14 Tomcat or other naval air defences.

The viability of 'Backfire' tactics was never proven, and a constant cat-and-mouse game continued between both sides in an attempt to determine each other's weaknesses.

After the fall of the Shah of Iran in 1979, the Soviet Union managed to obtain one or more F-14 Tomcat fighters and Phoenix missiles. This gave them a better appreciation of the strengths and limitations of this element of the defence, and provided the final evidence of the need for a more modern missile to arm the 'Backfire'.

Tu-22M3 'Backfire-C'

As production of the Tu-22M2 was underway, a comprehensive modernisation of the aircraft was initiated in the mid-1970s, under the internal designation Project AM. The shortcomings of the initial NK-22 jet engines prompted efforts to improve their service life and other features. The evolved engine type was designated NK-25. The new engines, as well as previous problems with the initial vertical variable compression air intakes, led to a new 'scoop' horizontal air intake design, which was trialled on a modified Tu-22M2Ye testbed. A variety of other improvements were incorporated at the same time. The maximum wing sweep was extended back to 65°, a feature so secret that crews were forbidden to leave the aircraft on the ground with the wings locked in this position for fear it would be photographed by US satellites. A vigorous weight trimming programme took 3 tonnes (2.9 tons) off the aircraft. Combined with the more powerful and fuel-efficient engines, the new version offered a 33 per cent extension in range (from 5100 to 6800 km/3,170 to 4,225 miles), and doubled the practical combat load from 3 to 6 tonnes (2.9 to 5.9 tons). The new propulsion system improved the

thrust-to-weight ratio from 0.33 on the Tu-22M2 to 0.4 on the Tu-22M3, and maximum speed at altitude increased from Mach 1.65 to Mach 2.05. The only deficit of the new design was a 20 per cent increase in radar cross-section at some view angles caused by the new intakes.

By the 1970s, the K-22 weapons system of the Tu-22M2 was obsolete. Its evolutionary improvements had petered out, and the missile had a lessening probability of success when faced with typical defences of the period, especially in the naval arena when facing Phoenix-armed Tomcats. The Kh-22 missile was nearing the end of its practical life. It had proved to be an enduring hazard in service due to its use of inhibited red fuming nitric acid (IRFNA) oxidiser, a chemical that was highly lethal if the fumes were inhaled, and was extremely prone to starting fires when in contact

The battered appearance of these naval aviation Tu-22M3s is an indication of the use that Russian forces are still getting from their 'Backfires'. Evident in this view are the row of (six) auxiliary inlet doors on the main engine intake and the rectangular APU intake on the main fin fillet.

Above: This 'Backfire-C' is one of the early developmental airframes, still in use with the LII flight test centre. The APU auxiliary inlet is open on this aircraft.

The Tu-22M3 has a pair of folding landing lights under the nose, and one under each air intake.

Tupolev Tu-22M3(R) 'Backfire'

Though the role has been largely adopted by satellites, a small number of Tu-22M3s were modified to act as quick-reaction reconnaissance platforms for the Soviet/Russian navy. This version of the 'Backfire-C', the Tu-22M3(R), sometimes referred to as Tu-22MR, has a large sensor package built into the bomb bay. This equipment resembles that of the Tu-22RDM and so may include the Shompol side-looking radar, or a similar system. The Tu-22M3(R)'s primary role is believed to be as an Elint gatherer and it may be fitted with the Miass EW system. Approximately 12 Tu-22M3s were rebuilt to this configuration and there may be plans to convert some additional older Tu-22M2s to augment those in service.

The Tu-22M3 has been dubbed the 'Troika' (trio) by its crews. The earlier Tu-22M2 was the 'Dvoika' (deuce). The Tu-22M3 is notionally still in production at Kazan, although in reality no new aircraft have been delivered since 1993. As a result, export orders for the aircraft have assumed ever-increasing importance, and perhaps only substantial outside political pressure has halted sales to customers such as Iran and China.

with any type of hydrocarbon including normal fuels, oils and plastics. A solid-fuel missile was desired, like the Kh-45 that had been abandoned as a short-cut in the early 1970s.

A major study programme codenamed 'Pleyada' was launched by the GOSNIIAS air weapons institute in the early 1970s to examine future air-to-surface missiles for strategic aircraft. One of the conclusions of the study was that a missile was needed that could climb to very high altitudes to avoid the lethal envelope of the Phoenix. This study, and its follow-on codenamed 'Chetkost P', urged the services to concentrate on a smaller number of multi-role missile systems instead of the plague of separate sub-types being developed. Several different contenders for the Tu-22M3 armament system were considered, including designs from the Zvezda, Novator and Raduga design bureaux. The Raduga Kh-22 was retained as one option for the Tu-22M3, since there was an available inventory of the missiles, supplemented with a single new type.

The new weapon selected for the Tu-22M3 was MKB Raduga's Kh-15 (AS-16 'Kickback'). The origins of this weapon can be traced to 1967, when it was first called Kh-2000. The Kh-15 uses a solid fuel rocket engine which, after release, boosts it to altitudes up to 40000 m (131,000 ft), well over the operational envelope of the F-14's Phoenix missile. It then dives on its targets at speeds of up to Mach 5. The very high speeds and steep dive angle are intended to reduce its vulnerability to air defence missiles and air-to-air missiles such as the AIM-54 Phoenix, as well as reducing its vulnerability to ship-based defences such as the RIM-67 Standard missile. A missile with this flight profile is sometimes called an aero-ballistic missile due to its terminal flight profile. The basic strategic version of the missile is the nuclear-armed Kh-15P and its guidance system is purely inertial, with no terminal guidance. Due to its planned use on the navy Tu-22M3, a conventionally-armed anti-ship version, the Kh-15A (export designation:

Kh-15S) was developed with a millimetre-wave active radar seeker for the terminal phase of the dive.

The new Tu-22M3 version was accepted for service in 1983; it was called 'Backfire-C' by NATO. It was first deployed, again, with the 185th Guards Heavy Bomber Aviation Regiment. In service, it was nicknamed the 'Troika' (Trio). A total of 268 Tu-22M3s was manufactured when production ground to a halt for lack of funding in 1993.

Electronic warfare

The original ECM system for the Tu-22M2 was unsatisfactory, as mentioned earlier, due to integration problems, leading to a variety of exploratory studies on improvements. Among the alternatives considered was the SPS-55 Buket (Bouquet) system, already in use on Tu-16P escort jammer aircraft. Eventually, the Tu-22M3 was fitted with the new Ural system consisting of the SPS-171 and SPS-172 jammers, the AG-56 noise jammer, the L-082 Mak IR-missile warning systems and the Sirena-3 radar warning system. Although the Ural system doubled the ECM effectiveness of the aircraft compared to the earlier Tu-22M2, the electronic warfare system on the Tu-22M3 was still not considered to be entirely satisfactory. At least some Tu-22M2 were later upgraded with the Ural system.

In the mid-1980s a dedicated EW escort-jammer aircraft to accompany the Tu-22M3 was sought to replace the old and much slower Tu-16P aircraft used in Tu-22M2 regiments. Two options were developed. The Tu-22MP was a Tu-22M3 airframe fitted with the Miass electronic warfare system. The first prototype was completed at Kazan in 1986, followed by two more in 1992. It had not entered service at the time this article was written. This version can be distinguished by the use of a dielectric fairing at the base of the tail, a dielectric fairing on the side of the air intake tunnel, and a semi-recessed 'canoe' under the belly of the aircraft. The second option was a more sophisticated electronic warfare platform based on the Il-76 transport, called the Il-76PP. This system was developed by the G. M. Beriev design bureau in Taganrog on the basis of a modified Il-76MD transport. The electronic warfare complex used was the Dandish system, which required far more power than could be provided on a modified 'Backfire'. The prototype was tested at the main electronic warfare proving ground at Chernaya Rechka near Tashkent, but no series production took place. As a result, Tu-22M3 regiments were forced to retain earlier escort jammer aircraft, mainly older Tu-16P types.

Navy scout

The Soviet navy largely abandoned the use of aircraft such as the Tu-22R for strategic reconnaissance due to the advent of reconnaissance satellites in 1975-78. The navy still perceived a need for a modest number of aircraft, since it was found that a real-time intelligence source with the strike force was necessary to distinguish the carrier from other warships in the battle group. Attention turned –

obviously enough – to the Tu-22M. A single Tu-22M3 was modified to the Tu-22M3(R) (or Tu-22MR) configuration in 1984 and was accepted for navy use. A total of 12 was built, and their manufacture is included in the Tu-22M3 figures presented here. Details of the exact sensor fit on these aircraft is lacking, although the ventral tub bears some resemblance to the system on the Tu-22RDM with its Shompol SLAR. In 1994, it was decided to begin converting some older Tu-22M2s into reconnaissance versions, designated Tu-22M2R. As is evident from their small numbers, they do not begin to match the large number of Tu-22R 'Blinders' that were formerly in service.

Crew station

The Tu-22M has a crew of four: commander (left front), co-pilot (right front), communications officer (radio-*telegrafist*: left rear) and navigator (*shturman*: right rear). The crew is seated on KT-1 ejection seats which are effective at all altitudes at speeds of 130 km/h (80 mph) or greater for a single ejection, and a speed of 300 km/h (186 mph) for a simultaneous ejection of all four crewmen, because of the need for separation. They are fired upward, and so avoid the problems encountered with the downward-firing seats

After the break-up of the USSR, Russia was deprived of several of its most important weapons which had been based in the newly independent republics. For example, a large proportion of the Tu-22 fleet was based in Belarus. A well-known dispute arose over the Tu-160s left in the Ukraine – but Ukraine also inherited a force of Tu-22M3s. While the handful of Tu-160s soon became unserviceable, the 'Backfires' and their well-trained crews were retained. Lt Gen Vladimir Antonets, the air force chief, stated that the Ukraine must have "forces of strategic deterrence" and the Tu-22M3 was "the most potent weapon of the air force."

long-range missions, a problem that is not solely confined to Tupolev's 'Backfire'.

Combat use

The Tu-22M was used in combat in at least two conflicts. Two Tu-22M2 squadrons from the 185th Heavy Bomber Regiment were used to provide air support in breaking the siege of Khost in Afghanistan in December 1987, operating from Mary-2 air base in Turkestan. The attacks were conducted against Mujahideen bases and storage areas, often in massed formation. On occasion, the squadrons conducted simultaneous drops of 200 tonnes (196.8 tons) of ordnance against single objectives. In January 1988, they were replaced with Tu-22M3 squadrons from the 402nd Heavy Bomber Regiment. The final operations by the 'Backfire' over Afghanistan took place in October 1988 during the withdrawal of Soviet forces. A total of 16 Tu-22M3 bombers was committed to the operation, which was aimed at preventing Mujahideen attacks on withdrawing Soviet columns. The Tu-22Ms were initially armed with normal FAB-500 bombs, but later switched to FAB-1500 1.5-tonne and FAB-3000 3-tonne conventional bombs for these missions. Attacks were conducted against bases, or carried out as pre-emptive strikes against likely

This page: These Tu-22M3s are operated by the Russian navy's 240th Sep. Composite Aviation Regiment, based at Ostrov. This unit is one of naval aviation's primary training centres.

of the 'Blinder', which were not safe below 250 m (820 ft). During Tu-22M3 production, consideration was given to substituting the new Severin K-36D zero-zero seats, but this did not pass beyond the test stage. Although a substantial improvement over the Tu-22 'Blinder', the Tu-22M cockpit is not a model of comfort. Toilet facilities are limited to a hospital-style bed pan. Russian crews have long complained of the lack of decent prepackaged food for

Tupolev Tu-22M3 'Backfire-C' Aviatsiya Voyenno-Morskoyo Flota

The Tu-22M 'Backfire' resembles few other aircraft of its size, combining a variable-geometry wing with engines buried deep in the fuselage. The former feature is common to other heavy strategic bombers, including the American B-1B and the Tupolev Tu-160. The latter feature is found more commonly on tactical strike aircraft, however, and most heavy bomber designs since the 1960s have had the engines mounted in pods below the wing. The M3 version, seen here, introduced several important changes over previous 'Backfire' versions, most noticeably its reprofiled nose, redesigned main intakes, lengthened fuselage and increased wing sweep back.

Avionics and systems

The Tu-22M3's flight control system includes the basic Bort-45 system and the ABSU-145M automatic flight control system, linked to the NK-45 navigation system. The NK-45 navigation complex includes two high-altitude RV-5 radio altimeters, a low-altitude RV-18G radio altimeter, an ARM-15M radio compass, a UHF ARK-U2 radio compass, a short-range RSBN-PKV radio navigation system, and the OSh-1 instrumented landing system. The aircraft communication system includes an onboard SPU-7 intercommunication system, two R-832M radios, one R-847 radio, one R-876 receiver, and a R-855-9M emergency transmitter in the LAS-5M dinghy. The basic aircraft sensor is the Leninets PN-A radar in the nose (PN-AD on the Tu-22M3). This radar, although permitting low-altitude target approaches, does not provide nap-of-the-earth capability. The Tu-22M retains optical bomb aiming capability, accomplished with a forward-pointing OPB-15T television sight.

Samolet 145

The aircraft design that became the 'Backfire' was designed to carry a substantially greater maximum bombload than either the earlier Tu-22 or Tu-16: 24 tonnes (23.6 tons) versus 9 tonnes (8.8 tons) for the earlier medium bombers. The configuration of the aircraft bore a slight resemblance to the Tu-22, having been based on studies of evolutionary versions such as the Samolet 106K. However, the new design developed under chief designer D. S. Markov mounted the engines inside the fuselage and employed vertical compression 'cheek' air intakes. The Samolet 145 was also the first Tupolev heavy bomber design to use variable-geometry wings, due to the demanding speed and range requirements of the new aircraft.

What's in a name?

In its early years, and particularly throughout the SALT controversy, the Soviet Union refused to confirm the exact designation of its new swing-wing bomber. For many years, the type was mistakenly referred to as the Tu-26, because Western 'experts' refused to accept the Tu-22M designation – which simply a modified 'Blinder'. It was inferred that the 'Backfire' was not until 1990, the last year of its publication, that Soviet Military Power (the US DoD's chronicle of the Soviet Union's armed forces) finally attached the designation Tu-22M to the 'Backfire'. Mischievously, the Soviets played the West at its own game. For example, the newspaper Izvestiya continually referred to the Tu-22M as "the aircraft referred to in the West as the 'Backfire'.' Ironically, the NATO name was later adopted by the Russian crews themselves (and not for the last time), who preferred it to the awkward Russian 'Tu-dvadcat-dva-em-dva' (Tu-22M2).

Radar warning receiver

The fairings on the trailing edge of the Tu-22M3's fintip are the antenna for its Sirena-3 radar warning receiver.

Satellites v 'Backfires'

'Backfire' crews considered missions against US carrier battle groups to be their most demanding assignment. This was because the aircraft could not use terrain masking for the final approach phase of the mission, which made it more vulnerable to detection by US Navy Hawkeyes, or other surveillance systems. Although not widely known, the US examined the possible use of satellites, such as the DSP infra-red missile early warning satellite, under a programme codenamed Slow Walker, to detect 'Backfire' take-offs and terminal approaches when the use of its afterburner provided an IR signature detectable from space. The data from the satellite could then be passed to the carrier battle groups to provide an approximate early warning of approach of hostile forces.

ambush positions. Some missions were conducted at night, and, in one mission the city of Herat was severely damaged. A witness to one of the raids remarked, "the mountains turned into valleys." The final missions in January 1989 were conducted near the vital Salang tunnels.

The Tu-22M3 was later used in operations in the 1995 Chechen conflict, mainly in bombing attacks near Groznii. Although the Russian press referred to mass carpet bombing attacks by 'Backfires' against the city, General P. S. Deneikin – the commander of the Russian air force and himself a former 'Backfire' pilot – stated that there had been in fact only a few Tu-22M missions. Ironically, the Chechen leader, Dzhokar Dudayev, was also a former Tu-22M3 pilot.

'Backfire' replacement?

In 1983, preliminary design work began on a possible successor to the Tu-22M 'Backfire' bomber. It took two parallel paths: a new version of the Tu-22M armed with a new weapon system, and an entirely new Sukhoi design. The Sukhoi OKB had been working on a follow-on to the Su-24 'Fencer' frontal strike aircraft called Su-24BM, grew too large and was cancelled in 1983. However, the concept was revived shortly afterward as a possible successor to the Tu-16, Tu-22 and Tu-22M. The new aircraft was called T-60S. The preliminary design studies were for a large 80-tonne (78.7-ton) aircraft with twin engines, using air intakes mounted over the wing. The design was intended to incorporate stealth characteristics. Work began on a prototype aircraft at the Komsomolsk-na-Amur plant in the mid-1990s, with an aim to begin flight trials around 2000. However, by 1997 it had become apparent that the Russian air force would not have the funding for such an aircraft. Although the T-60S has not been cancelled, its budget has been slashed so severely that it may become simply a technology demonstrator until the budget improves.

In its place, the Long Range Aviation is considering an upgrade programme for the Tu-22M3 'Backfire'. A prototype of an improved version was completed in 1990 as the Tu-22M4, but, by the time it entered trials, production of the Tu-22M at Kazan had almost ended due to a lack of funding. The 1997 plan called for an upgrade rather than new construction. The development effort is designated project 245 or Tu-245, and full details of the effort had not been clarified at the time this article was written. The new aircraft is expected to be armed with the new Kh-101 stealth cruise missile being developed by MKB Raduga.

'Backfire' exports

Repeated reports of attempted sales of the Tu-22M have circulated since the early 1990s. The aircraft was displayed at the 1992 Farnborough air show, lending credence to the reports. At Farnborough, Tupolev representatives stated that government clearances to export the bomber were expected 'very soon'. At least two countries – China and Iran – showed serious interest in purchasing the Tu-22M. China's interest was reported as early as 1993, and there have been rumors that construction of bomber bases for Chinese Tu-22M 'Backfires' had been spotted in 1997. Iran first approached Russia about the Tu-22M in 1992. Its interest took a new twist in January 1994 when a Ukrainian delegation turned up in Teheran in an effort to sell used Tu-22M 'Backfire' bombers from existing Ukrainian inventory. Iran was unwilling to agree to such a sale in the absence of Russian assurances about obtaining spare parts, and the deal fell through.

Back to the future?

Ironically, the changing nature of the world situation may give the 'Backfire' a more central role in future Russian strategic planning than at the height of the Cold War. In the past, US intelligence agencies referred to the role of the 'Backfire' as the 'peripheral attack mission'. Although appropriate in the geographic sense of the word, its mission really was 'peripheral' to main confrontations along the Central Front in Europe, or in the event of the ultimate confrontation of strategic thermonuclear war. Scenarios of a NATO-Warsaw Pact clash, or an all-out Soviet-US thermonuclear exchange, no longer seem plausible. In their place, regional conflicts grow more likely. The 'Backfire', with its impressive conventional bomb capacity, has already been demonstrated in this role during the Afghanistan war. Russia is still embroiled in border conflicts along its southern periphery in the Caucasus and Central Asia, and future employment of the 'Backfire' in this troubled region remains likely.

The collapse of the Soviet Union has also seen the collapse of the Soviet army, and over the past five years the Russian army has atrophied due to a lack of funding. Its greatly diminished combat capabilities were all too evident from its embarrassing performance in the war in Chechnya. It seems unlikely that funding to rejuvenate the army will be available until well into the next century. At the

moment, the Russian General Staff is examining various options. One option that has emerged in 1996-97 as a realistic answer to the budget shortfalls is to place greater reliance on tactical nuclear theatre forces. This is in many ways reminiscent of the US Army's tactical nuclear doctrine under the Eisenhower administration's 'New Look' policy in the 1950s when the drain of funds into strategic nuclear forces threatened to render the army a hollow force. Russia's option is to declare its intention to use theater nuclear forces in response to any serious threat, even if only conventional, rather than relying on a large conventional army. At the moment, no such threat to Russia is plausible, be it from NATO, Ukraine or China. Nonetheless, military planning must consider a changing world situation, and prepare solutions. Under this doctrine, the 'Backfire' will play an important role. Its most likely technological competitor for deep-theatre nuclear strikes – theatre nuclear missiles such as the Pioner (SS-20) – were eliminated in the early 1990s as part of the Intermediate Nuclear

Forces (INF) treaty with the United States. The 'Backfire' remains the only major element of the former Soviet Union's theatre nuclear forces.

At the moment, it seems improbable that Russia will be able to afford a 'Backfire' replacement for this role. The Sukhoi T-60S is likely to remain in limbo given current budget realities. The Russian air force is barely able to afford enough funding for spare parts to keep the Tu-22M flying, and has had insufficient funding for adequate pilot flight time. Under the optimistic scenarios, the Russian air force will be able to fund a significant upgrade programme for the Tu-22M such as the Tu-245 proposal. This is not implausible, as the Russian air force and navy both have a significant number of the more recent Tu-22M3 aircraft in inventory. However, even this modest option may not be affordable, and from recent trends evident in the figures presented here, the Russian 'Backfire' force may continue to atrophy and shrink, starved of necessary funding.

Steven J. Zaloga

The 'Backfire' probably scoops the prize as the greatest of the West's Cold War bugbears. Few aircraft have been as feared or as mocked, as overestimated and as dismissed. A look back through the pages of Soviet Military Power, *the great US chronicle of the USSR in the 1980s and early 1990s, shows that the Tu-22M was always considered to be a long-range strategic system. However, both it and the 'Blinder' have only ever been used in the medium-range theatre role, and no doubt will be so again.*

Tupolev Tu-22M 'Backfire' production

	1972	1973	1974	1975	1976	1977	1978	1979	1980	1981	1982	1983	1984	1985	1986
Tu-22M2	3	14	15	17	17	21	22	26	23	23	20	10			
Tu-22M3					1	1	3	5	7	7	10	20	30	28	30

	1987	1988	1989	1990	1991	1992	1993
Tu-22M3	28	27	25	20	17	6	3

A total of nine Tu-22M0 prototypes was manufactured in 1969-71 and nine Tu-22M1s in 1971-72

Above and right: The Tu-22M dispensed with the cumbersome entry system of the Tu-22 and uses conventional access doors on the upper fuselage. The Tu-22M has a crew of four: commander (left front), co-pilot (right front), communications officer (radio-telegrafist: left rear) and navigator (shturman: right rear). The typical crew uniform is the VKK-6MP flight suit, TZK-2M jacket and GSh-6A helmet, although the older VMSK-4 flight suit with ZSh-5A helmet can still be seen in use.

Left: The Tu-22M3 retains an optical bomb aiming capability, using a forward-pointing OPB-15T television sight, fitted behind the radome of the Leninets PN-A attack radar.

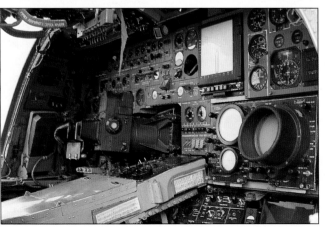

Above and left: The front and rear cockpits of the Tu-22M2 and M3 differ only in minor details (these views are of an M2). The crew all sit on KT-1 ejection seats, which are not 'zero-zero'. Very little modern avionics are in evidence and the instruments are almost all electro-mechanical 'clockwork' dials. Although the rear crewmen have no forward visibility, they do have a surprisingly large side window each, which contrasts sharply with the Tu-22.

Above and left: The Tu-22M3 is powered by NK-25 engines, replacing the earlier NK-22s. Coupled with its new intake design, this boosted maximum speed from Mach 1.65 to Mach 2.05.

Tu-22M 'Backfire' Operators

Russia

The 'Backfire' has been deployed in both air force and navy heavy bomber regiments since it reached operational status in 1975. 'Backfire' regiments were generally organised into heavy bomber divisions. Three air force divisions comprised the 326th Heavy Bomber Division near the Baltic, the 22nd Heavy Bomber Division in the Pripyat region straddling Belarus and Ukraine, and the 13th Heavy Bomber Division in Ukraine. At least one Long Range Aviation 'Backfire' regiment was deployed near Irkutsk in Siberia and oriented towards The People's Republic of China.

An initial Northern Fleet 'Backfire' regiment was deployed near Olenya, and a second regiment began to be added in late 1991. The first Pacific Fleet 'Backfire' heavy bomber regiment became operational at Alekseyevka in 1979-80. The naval regiments were also organised into divisions: the 2nd Missile Carrier Division with the Black Sea Fleet, and the 5th Missile Carrier Division with the Northern Fleet. Overhaul of the 'Backfires' was undertaken at the 150th ARZ (Aviation Repair Plant) near Kaliningrad, and the 328th Aviation Repair Plant near Nikolayev, Ukraine for the Black Sea Fleet.

In order to minimise the wear and tear on the bombers, the Soviet air force deployed special training aircraft alongside the bombers, based on a modified version of the Tu-134 airliner fitted with the Tu-22M's radar and weapon control system. The air force version of these aircraft was designated Tu-134UBL and the navy's single Tu-134UBK. A total of about 90 Tu-134UBLs was completed between 1981 and 1983.

In 1988, 321 'Backfires' were in service, comprising 178 in air force regiments and 143 in navy regiments. As of time of the disintegration of the Soviet Union in 1991, about 370 'Backfires' were in service, with 210 in nine air force regiments and 160 in eight navy regiments. The 'Backfire' regiments were heavily concentrated in the European portions of the former USSR; about 315 of the 370 aircraft were west of the Urals in 1991. By 1991, the 'Backfire' fleet was beginning to suffer from serious maintenance problems due to shortages of spare parts. One estimate in 1991 put the operational rate at only 30-40 per cent of the force.

As of 1991, only 40 per cent of the 'Backfire' force was based on Russian soil, the other aircraft being based in Ukraine (26 per cent), Belarus (15 per cent) and Estonia (19 per cent). The CIS Ministry of Defence tried, with varying degrees of success, to place these types of aircraft under central control. The aircraft stationed in Estonia were returned to Russia, while those in Belarus remained in place but under Russian control. Ukraine attempted to retain control of all of its 'Backfires', although the naval regiments became embroiled in the controversy over the fate of the Black Sea Fleet. As of 1995, only 52 Tu-22Ms were in Russian air force service, and 79 in Russian navy service, for a total of 131 in European Russia. By 1996, these figures had fallen again to only 59 in air force service and 46 in navy service, for a total of 105 in European Russia, and perhaps 40 more in the Far East.

Tu-22M Deployment in the European former USSR*

Unit	Location	Strength		
Air Force (Long Range Aviation)		*1991*	*1994*	*1995*
43rd Training Centre	Ryazan, Russia	19	26	0
49th Heavy Bomber Regiment	Ryazan, Russia	0	0	1
52nd Heavy Bomber Training Regiment	Shaikovka, Russia	19	26	29
840th H. Bomber Regiment (326 HBD)	Soltsi, Russia	19	20	22
132nd H. Bomber Regiment (326 HBD)	Tartu, Estonia	18	0	0
402nd H. Bomber Regiment (326 HBD)	Balbasovo, Belarus	17	11	0
200th H. Bomber Regiment (22 HBD)	Bobruisk, Belarus	20	19	0
260th H. Bomber Regiment (22 HBD)	Striy, Ukraine	18	0	0
184th H. Bomber Regiment (13 HBD)	Priluki, Ukraine	0	14	12
185th H. Bomber Regiment (13 HBD)	Poltava, Ukraine	18	16	14
328th Aviation Repair Plant	Nikolayev, Ukraine	0	0	4
Sub-total		148	132	82
Navy		*1991*	*1994*	*1995*
240th Sep. Composite Av. Regiment	Ostrov, Russia	0	6	?
574th Missile Carrier Regiment (5 MCD)	Lakhta, Russia (Northern Fleet)	18	20	20
924th Missile Carrier Regiment (5 MCD)	Olenya, Russia (Northern Fleet)	32	20	20
5th Missile Carrier Regiment (2 MCD)	Veseloye, Ukraine (Black Sea Fleet)	22	19	7
943rd Missile Carrier Regiment (2 MCD)	Oktyabrskoe, Ukraine (Black Sea Fleet)	21	20	32
540th Missile Carrier Regiment (6 AB)	Kulbakino, Ukraine (Black Sea Fleet)	18	24	23
Sub-total		111	109	102
TOTAL		259	241	184

*west of the Urals and accountable under the CFE Treaty; there are at least two additional 'Backfire' regiments in the Far East

Soviet Tu-22M 'Backfire' Operational Strength

	1975	1976	1977	1978	1979	1980	1981	1982	1983	1984	1985	1986	1987	1988	1989	1990	1991
Air Force	10	20	30	50	65	75	90	100	115	130	145	160	165	175	195	195	210
Navy		30	35	50	65	75	85	90	100	120	115	115	120	130	125	130	160

Right: This Tu-22M3 was photographed at Shaikova air base and, like many current VVS aircraft, it wears the modern Russian flag along with its red stars.

Below right: This aerial view of Shaikova shows a typical Soviet/Russian airbase, hidden in a wooded area with the aircraft dispersed among large revetments.

Below: A Tu-22M3 of the Ostrov-based 240 Sep. Composite Aviation Regiment.

Inside the Tu-22M3

Tu-22M2 'Backfire-B'

The 'Backfire-B' was the definitive production version of the Tu-22M, although it was supplanted by the more capable Tu-22M3 'Backfire-C'. Production ran from 1972 to 1983 and a total of 211 was built, for both air force and navy units. The best-known aspect of this variant was its refuelling probe, or the lack of it. In its early service days the Tu-22M2 was fitted with a probe but this was subsequently removed by stipulation of the SALT treaty in order to ensure that the aircraft did not have true intercontinental range. The truth of the matter was that the probes could be reinstated within a matter of hours, but the Soviet Union simply did not possess the tanker assets to make such missions possible, at least not on any large scale. The probe housing was eventually removed from some aircraft, although most retained the characteristic bulge. Other salient features were the intakes with conventional boundary layer splitter plates, and the side-by-side twin 23-mm cannon installation.

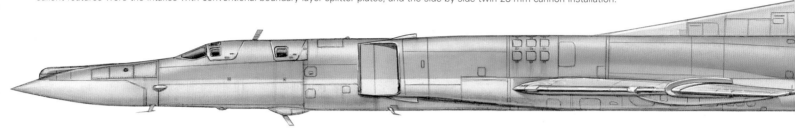

Tu-22M3 'Backfire-C'

1 Ventral nose radome
2 Flight refuelling probe installation (not fitted post SALT agreement)
3 Radar electronics equipment
4 PNA navigation and attack radar scanner
5 Retractable landing/taxiing lamps
6 Pitot head, port and starboard
7 Flight refuelling floodlights
8 Front pressure bulkhead
9 Windscreen panels
10 Folding nuclear 'flash' screens
11 Instrument panel shroud
12 Rudder pedals
13 Control column and handwheel
14 First Pilot's ejection seat
15 Second Pilot's seat
16 Jettisonable 'gull-wing' cockpit hatches
17 VHF aerial
18 Rear cockpit instrument console
19 Navigation and Weapon Systems Officer's ejection seats
20 Canopy emergency release
21 Static ports
22 Ventral visual periscopic sighting cupola
23 Lower VHF aerial
24 Twin-wheel nose undercarriage, aft retracting
25 Nose wheel bay doors
26 Hydraulic retraction jack
27 Nose wheel bay access hatch to avionics equipment

28 Dinghy stowage
29 Avionics equipment racks, port and starboard
30 Missile launch alert receiver
31 Starboard engine air intake
32 Intake ramp bleed air spill duct
33 Anti-collision light
34 Forward fuselage fuel tank
35 Boundary layer spill duct
36 Intake ramp bleed air perforations
37 Port engine air intake
38 ECM antenna
39 Retractable landing/taxiing lamp
40 Variable-area intake ramp doors
41 Bypass air spill duct
42 Ramp door hydraulic jacks
43 'Blow-in' heat exchanger air intake
44 Environmental control system pack, port and starboard
45 Heat exchanger exhaust duct
46 Wing centre-section carry-through structure with integral fuel tank
47 Ventral AS-4 'Kitchen' missile cut-out doors
48 Intake suction relief doors
49 Port main undercarriage, stowed position
50 Ventral keel structure alongside weapons bay
51 Internal weapons bay
52 Centre fuselage fuel tankage
53 Fin root fillet flush aerial panel

54 Starboard intake suction relief doors
55 Leading-edge EW aerials
56 Starboard fixed wing panel integral fuel tank
57 Wing pivot bearing
58 Fixed wing fence
59 Outer, swinging, wing panel integral fuel tank
60 Three-segment leading-edge slats
61 Starboard navigation lights
62 Starboard wing fully forward, 20° sweep, position
63 Three-segment asymmetric double-slotted flaps
64 Three-segment spoiler panels
65 Starboard wing fully swept, 65°, position
66 Wing sweep control screw jack
67 Extended fin root fillet
68 Hydraulic equipment bay
69 Auxiliary Power Unit (APU)
70 HF flush aerial
71 APU air intake
72 Fin root integral fuel tank
73 Leading-edge EW antenna
74 Short-wave communications antennas
75 Fin tip aerial fairing
76 ILS aerial
77 Tail navigation light
78 Radar warning antenna

79 Static dischargers
80 Rudder
81 Rudder hydraulic actuator
82 Radar cooling air scoop
83 EW antenna
84 Ammunition magazine
85 Ammunition feed and cartridge case return chutes
86 Tail gun control radar
87 Twin-barrel GSh-23 cannon
88 Remotely controlled gun turret
89 Variable-area afterburner nozzle
90 Nozzle control jacks
91 Afterburner cooling air scoop, above and below
92 Port all-moving tailplane
93 Tailplane pivot mounting
94 All-moving tailplane hydraulic actuator
95 Tailplane fairing 'expendables' launcher (chaff or flare cartridges)
96 Kuznetsov NK-25 afterburning turbofan engines
97 Engine mounting main frame

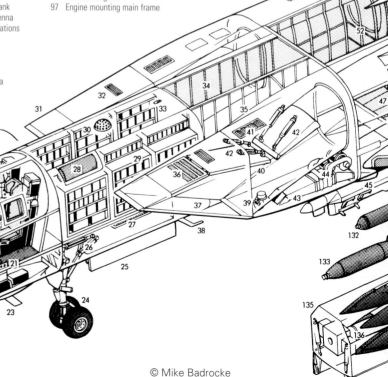

© Mike Badrocke

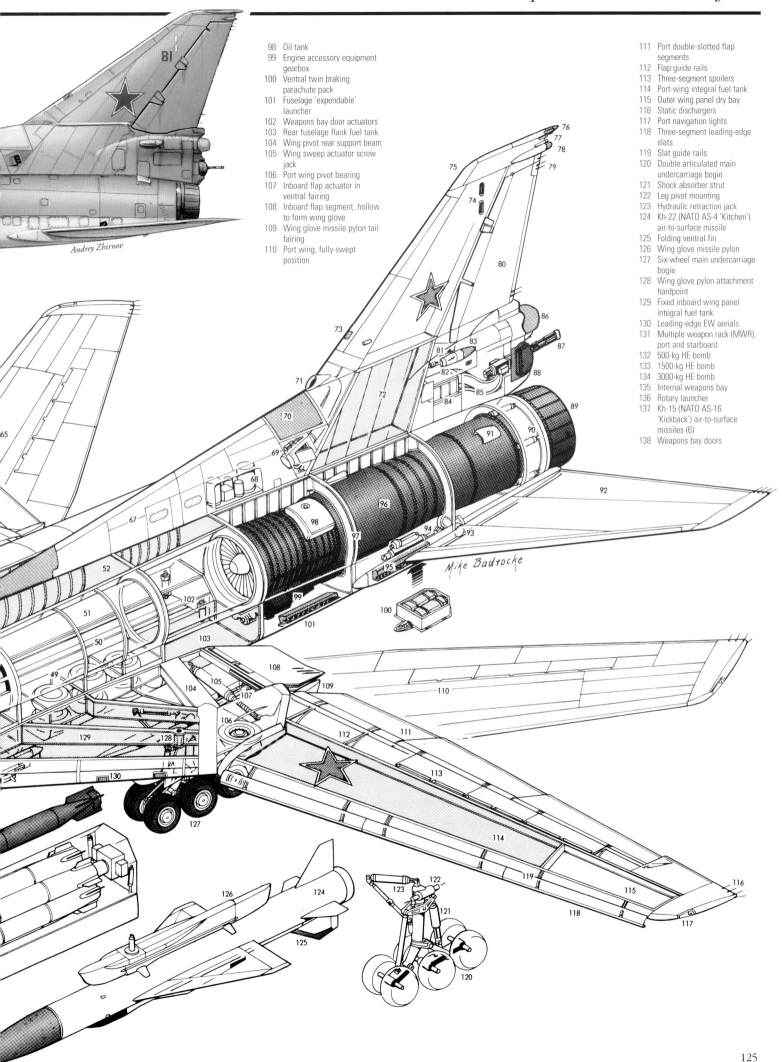

98 Oil tank
99 Engine accessory equipment gearbox
100 Ventral twin braking parachute pack
101 Fuselage 'expendable' launcher
102 Weapons bay door actuators
103 Rear fuselage flank fuel tank
104 Wing pivot rear support beam
105 Wing sweep actuator screw jack
106 Port wing pivot bearing
107 Inboard flap actuator in ventral fairing
108 Inboard flap segment, hollow to form wing glove
109 Wing glove missile pylon tail fairing
110 Port wing, fully-swept position

111 Port double-slotted flap segments
112 Flap guide rails
113 Three-segment spoilers
114 Port-wing integral fuel tank
115 Outer wing panel dry bay
116 Static dischargers
117 Port navigation lights
118 Three-segment leading-edge slats
119 Slat guide rails
120 Double articulated main undercarriage bogie
121 Shock absorber strut
122 Leg pivot mounting
123 Hydraulic retraction jack
124 Kh-22 (NATO AS-4 'Kitchen') air-to-surface missile
125 Folding ventral fin
126 Wing glove missile pylon
127 Six-wheel main undercarriage bogie
128 Wing glove pylon attachment hardpoint
129 Fixed inboard wing panel integral fuel tank
130 Leading-edge EW aerials
131 Multiple weapon rack (MWR), port and starboard
132 500-kg HE bomb
133 1500-kg HE bomb
134 3000-kg HE bomb
135 Internal weapons bay
136 Rotary launcher
137 Kh-15 (NATO AS-16 'Kickback') air-to-surface missiles (6)
138 Weapons bay doors

Andrey Zhirnov

Mike Badrocke

Tu-160 'Blackjack'
Russia's 'Big Stick'

The vast bulk of Tu-160 no. 05 Ilya Muromets settles on to the Engels runway. In the background is a row of around 30 Tu-22 'Blinders' which await the scrapman's torch. In the bleak economic reality of the 1990s, the 'Blackjack' seemed to be doomed to be just another footnote in the history of the Soviet/ Russian military machine, despite its awesome capabilities. Yet at the end of the decade a hardening of Russian foreign policy and a strengthening of the resolve to maintain capable military forces has breathed new life into the programme, although the required funds have yet to filter through to the operational fleet in any significant amount.

Following the end of World War II, a bipolar political system was established in the world in which the US and the USSR represented opposite ideologies. The military priority for both countries was the possession of intercontinental weapons capable of hitting the other on its own territory, which became even more urgent when arsenals were supplied with nuclear bombs having devastating effect yet comparatively light weight. The 1950s was a time of particularly hectic activity into means of intercontinental delivery for nuclear bombs, and over the next dozen or so years many options for achieving this task were proposed. The Soviets began work on an intercontinental supersonic bomber in 1952.

In a task assigned to aircraft designers on 19 July 1955, the range of the future aircraft was stipulated as 11000 to 12000 km (5,940 to 6,480 nm) at a supersonic cruising speed of 1700 to 1800 km/h (918 to 972 kt), or 14000 to 15000 km (7,560 to 8,100 nm) with inflight refuelling. Myasishchev's design bureau built a prototype of the M-50 'Bounder' supersonic bomber, but it could hardly be considered a success. The M-50A, first tested in flight on 27 October 1959, made only 23 flights, and its maximum performance figures were a speed of 1050 km/h (567 kt) and a range of 3150 km (1,700 nm). Further tests were cancelled.

The contemporary stage in the history of Soviet strategic bombers began in 1967. Two years before this date, Nikita

Khrushchev, who did not think highly of air forces and who stopped many developing aviation programmes, left active political life. Also, in 1965, the US formulated a specification for a new AMSA (Advanced Manned Strategic Aircraft), the future B-1. With consideration to the existing XB-70 Valkyrie bomber, as well as the new AMSA, the Soviet government announced on 28 November 1967 a competition for a strategic bomber with very high technical parameters. The aircraft was to reach 11000 to 13000 km (5,940 to 7,020 nm) and have a supersonic cruising speed of 3200 to 3500 km/h (1,728 to 1,890 kt) at an altitude of 18000 m (54,864 ft). The maximum range at subsonic speed was to be 16000 to 18000 km (8,640 to 9,720 nm) at high altitude or 11000 to 13000 km (5,940 to 7,020 nm) at sea level. The basic armament of the aircraft was to be nuclear missiles, including heavy Kh-45s and small Kh-2000s. New types of conventional and nuclear bombs were options for alternative armament.

Sukhoi's proposal

The design bureaux of Pavel Sukhoi and Vladimir Myasishchev contested the first stage of the competition. Sukhoi's design bureau in Moscow, formally named at the time as Moscow Engineering Plant 'Kulon' (Coulomb) (and before 1966 known as OKB-52, Opytno-Konstruktorskoye Byuro, Test-Design Bureau), specialised in tactical aircraft, and this work on heavy bombers was a one-off. The first

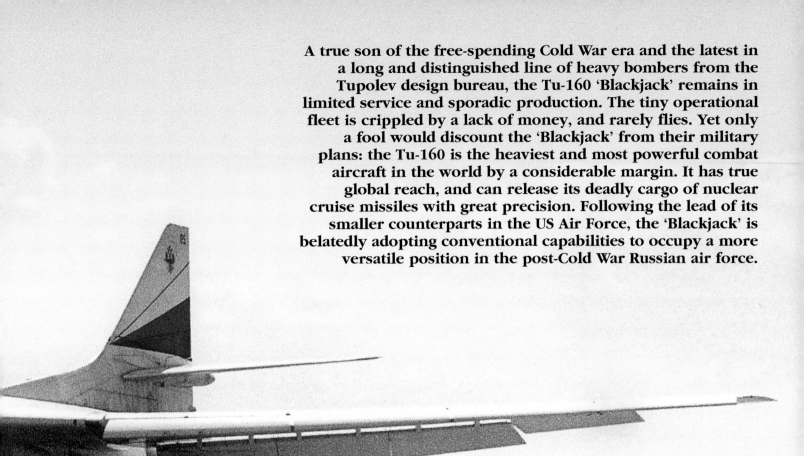

A true son of the free-spending Cold War era and the latest in a long and distinguished line of heavy bombers from the Tupolev design bureau, the Tu-160 'Blackjack' remains in limited service and sporadic production. The tiny operational fleet is crippled by a lack of money, and rarely flies. Yet only a fool would discount the 'Blackjack' from their military plans: the Tu-160 is the heaviest and most powerful combat aircraft in the world by a considerable margin. It has true global reach, and can release its deadly cargo of nuclear cruise missiles with great precision. Following the lead of its smaller counterparts in the US Air Force, the 'Blackjack' is belatedly adopting conventional capabilities to occupy a more versatile position in the post-Cold War Russian air force.

Sukhoi design made maximum utilisation of components already prepared for the T-4 (*izdeliye* 100) Mach 3 medium bomber. Recognising the necessity of a variable-geometry wing in the optimum design of a heavy multi-purpose aircraft, Sukhoi's designers simply replaced the delta-shaped wing of the T-4 aircraft with a variable-geometry one. In this form, and named T-4M, the project was ready in 1968.

The T-4M (M standing for modification) had a length of 50 m (164 ft), wingspan ranging from 22.5 m (73 ft 10 in) (at sweep of 72°) to 43.4 m (142 ft 5 in) (sweep of 15°); the take-off weight was from 131000 kg (288,800 lb) (normal) to 149000 kg (328,483 lb) (maximum), including an armament weight of 4000 kg (8,818 lb) for a single Kh-45 missile to 18000 kg (39,682 lb) for bombs. With four Kolesov/Rybinsk RD36-41 turbojet engines, the aircraft's maximum speed was 3200 km/h (1,728 kt), whereas the cruising speed would be 3000 to 3200 km/h (1,619 to 1,728 kt) at an altitude of 20000 to 23000 m (65,620 to 75,460 ft). The designed supersonic range was 7000 km (3,780 nm); subsonic range was 10000 km (5,400 nm) at high altitude and 3500 km (1,890 nm) at low altitude. The maximum range of 16000 km (8,640 nm) required by the armed forces was possible at subsonic speed only with two inflight refuellings.

Drawbacks of the T-4M's design were soon disclosed. The whole armament had to be carried outside the airframe because the packet arrangement of the engines meant that the internal armament chamber could not be installed without increasing the aircraft's size. The necessary rigidity of the long outer parts of the wings could not be attained. The T-4M project was subjected to design corrections up to the end of 1969, but eventually Sukhoi gave it up in favour of the next aircraft.

Although the new project was named T-4MS (S for strategic), or *izdeliye* 200, it had nothing in common with the original T-4. As the result of research work, a variable-

'Blackjack' crews are the elite of the Russian long-range air force, but they receive very little flying due to lack of funds. The cockpits of early production aircraft were only partially pressurised, requiring the use of pressure suits for high-altitude operations.

geometry flying wing was conceived, with high lift-to-drag ratio and great airframe capacity that could be used for fuel and equipment. The airframe of the T-4MS consisted of a middle wing and small movable wing ends. The mid-wing aspect ratio was 0.5 and the relative thickness was 6 per cent. The aerodynamic torsion, equal to -3.5 per cent at the mid-wing ends, was selected for minimum balancing drag at a speed of 3200 km/h (1,728 kt). The relative thickness of movable parts of the wings varied from 11 per cent near mid-wing to 7 per cent at the ends. The sweep could be adjusted from 30º to 72º. Model tests of the aircraft in the TsAGI (Central Aero- and Hydrodynamics Institute) wind tunnel revealed a very high lift-to-drag ratio: 17.5 at Mach 0.8 and 7.3 at Mach 3.0. The propulsion system of the T-4MS was to consist initially of four RD36-41 turbojet engines rated at 156.9 kN (35,280 lb thrust) each, which later were to be replaced by K-101 engines of Nikolai Kuznetsov design, each 196.1 kN (44,094 lb thrust). The crew, consisting of two pilots and a navigator/system operator, was located in a common cockpit in the aircraft nose.

The dimensions of the T-4MS were as follows: length 41.2 m (135 ft 2 in), maximum wingspan 40.8 m (133 ft 1 in) (at sweep angle of 30°), minimum wingspan 25 m (82 ft) (at sweep angle of 72°), height 8.0 m (26 ft 3 in), lifting surface area 482.3 to 506.5 m² (5,191.6 to 5,452.1 ft), undercarriage track 6.0 m (19 ft 8 in) and undercarriage base 12.0 m (39 ft 4 in). The 170000-kg (374,780-lb) design take-off weight of the aircraft included 63000 kg (138,890 lb) for the airframe, 97000 kg (213,845 lb) of fuel and 9000 kg (19,841 lb) of armament. Maximum design speed

was 3200 km/h (1,728 kt), cruising speed at high altitude was 3000 to 3200 km/h (1,620 to 1,728 kt), maximum speed at low altitude was 1100 km/h (594 kt), and cruising speed at low altitude was 850 km/h (459 kt). The aircraft's practical ceiling was 24000 m (78,740 ft). Its range at 3000 km/h (1,620 kt) and an altitude of 20000 to 24000 m (65,618 to 78,740 ft) was 9000 km (4,860 nm) (or 7500 km/4,050 nm with temporary RD36-41 engines), range at subsonic speed and an altitude of 11000 m (36,090 ft) was 14000 km (7,560 nm) (or 11000 km/5,940 nm with RD-36-41s), its take-off run was 1100 m (3,609 ft) and landing run was 950 m (3,117 ft).

On strategic missions, typically two Kh-45 missiles were to be carried inside the bomb bay (total weight 9000 kg/ 19,840 lb). Two other missiles of the same type could be carried externally, between the engine nacelles. An alternative variant of the aircraft was to carry 24 short-range Kh-2000 missiles externally. Total maximum warload was to be 45 tonnes (99,180 lb) (at the cost of the fuel, since the maximum take-off weight was limited to 170 tonnes/ 374,680 lb).

Myasishchev's proposal

Myasishchev's design bureau, which disbanded in 1960 at the same time as it stopped work on the M-50 'Bounder', was reinstated in October 1966 under the new name EMZ (Experimentalnyi Mashinostroitelnyi Zavod, Experimental Engineering Plant). In 1967-68 Myasishchev worked under the designation M-20 on four different projects for supersonic strategic bombers. He started with variable-geometry winged aircraft in a classical configuration, with engines installed in the rear part of fuselage and air intakes at the sides or under the fuselage. This configuration was similar to prototypes of the F-111 or MiG-23 flying at the time (but much larger) and covered projects M20-1, M20-2, M20-5 and M20-6, all known by the common name of M-20 variant I.

The next configuration – M-20 variant II – was a canard with a considerable mid-wing sweep and less-swept wing panels. A characteristic feature of this project was wingtips that deflected down when flying at high speed. The variants of this project featured different engine arrangements (e.g., a packet at the rear part of the fuselage or in separate nacelles under the mid-wing), as well as different tailfins (single or double). Such variants as M20-7, M20-10, M20-11, M20-12, M20-14 and M20-15 fell within this project. The next series of projects included the M20-16, M20-17, M20-18, M20-19 and M20-21 (known collectively as M-20 variant III), which were canards with variable-geometry

Sukhoi Mach 3 bomber projects

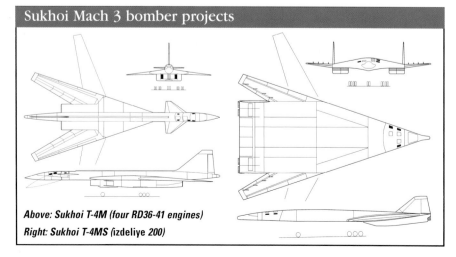

Above: Sukhoi T-4M (four RD36-41 engines)

Right: Sukhoi T-4MS (izdeliye 200)

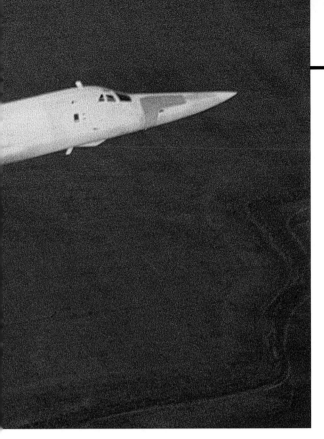

Myasishchev M-20 studies

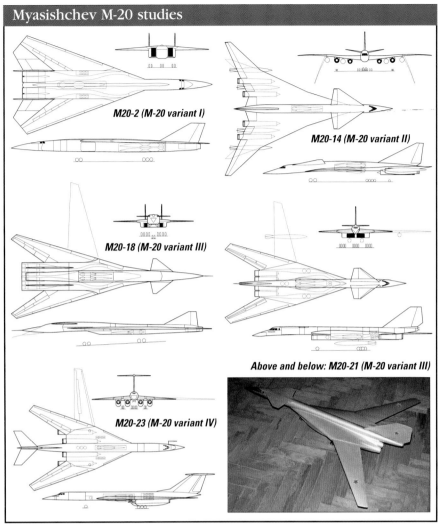

M20-2 (M-20 variant I)

M20-14 (M-20 variant II)

M20-18 (M-20 variant III)

Above and below: M20-21 (M-20 variant III)

M20-23 (M-20 variant IV)

wings and four to six engines under the rear part of fuse-lage or inside it. The differences between these variants were insignificant. The fourth configuration, M-20 variant IV (variants M20-22 and M20-23), was an aircraft with a variable-geometry wing in conventional configuration and with four engines located in separate nacelles under the mid-wing, very similar to both the American AMSA design and to later Tu-160s .

The idea of wing flow laminarisation via blown air on the wing surface appeared in two Myasishchev project vari-ants: M20-9 with a triangular wing, and M20-4 with a swept wing. All the M-20 variants had a take-off weight of 300 to 325 tonnes (661,200 to 705,280 lb) (or up to 345 tonnes/760,380 lb with additional fuel tanks).

Tupolev's Mach 2.3 bomber

Tupolev (formally the Moscow Engineering Plant 'Opyt', meaning experience or test) had been known as OKB-156 before 1966. In 1970 the design bureau joined Sukhoi and Myasishchev in the quest for a supersonic strategic bomber. His design team stood the best chance of building the

aircraft, given the bureau's familiarity with such types dating to the 1930s. Tupolev began designing his aircraft in quite a different way – less concerned about the require-ments of the air forces, and demanding that the specifica-tions be adjusted to feasible limits. The essential change concerned the aircraft speed. According to Tupolev, the increase in combat potential of an aircraft at Mach 3.0 to

Aircraft '29', one of the 'Blackjack' prototypes, blasts off in front of a packed house at the MosaeroShow at Zhukovskiy. With a light fuel load and no weapons the Tu-160 has power in abundance. At a typical light take-off weight (150 tonnes) the Tu-160 has a very healthy thrust:weight ratio of 0.66:1. This combines with the battery of high-lift devices on the wing to produce astonishing climb performance at low speeds, making for an impressive airshow spectacle. More importantly, from an operational point of view, it allows the Tu-160 to fly heavyweight missions from relatively short airfields, although the amount of specialist ground equipment required hinders the aircraft's mobility considerably.

Tupolev 160M (*izdeliye* L) designs

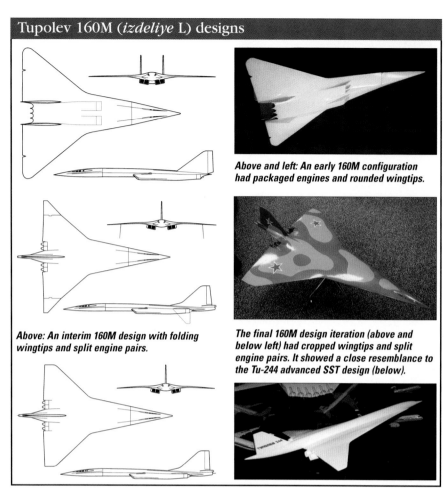

Above and left: An early 160M configuration had packaged engines and rounded wingtips.

Above: An interim 160M design with folding wingtips and split engine pairs.

The final 160M design iteration (above and below left) had cropped wingtips and split engine pairs. It showed a close resemblance to the Tu-244 advanced SST design (below).

airliner, developed in parallel, were very similar; they shared the requirement for as great a range as possible when flying at supersonic speed at high altitude. Both aircraft took the form of a triangular flying wing with a smooth blending between the wing and fuselage, which ensured, according to calculations, a lift:drag ratio of 7 to 9 at supersonic speed and up to 15 for subsonic speed. In August 1972, Tupolev ordered the Rybinsk RD36-51 (*izdeliye* 61) non-afterburning turbojet engine for both the Tu-160 bomber and the passenger-carrying Tu-144D. The engine's thrust was 225.6 to 235.4 kN (50,727 to 52,931 lb), its weight was 4200 kg (9,260 lb) and fuel consumption was 1.23 to 1.24 lb/lbfh (pound of fuel burned per pound aircraft weight per flying hour) (when flying at Mach 2.2 at an altitude of 18000 m/59,055 ft). The engine was ready in 1978; it passed ground tests but was never used for flying because, in the meantime, other engines were chosen for the Tu-160 and the Tu-144 programme was cancelled.

In 1972 the air forces assessed Sukhoi's T-4MS and Myasishchev's M-20 projects, and decided that Sukhoi was the winner. Nevertheless, none of the projects met the air forces' requirements (and it may be supposed that the actual performances would have been even worse than those calculated in the designs). It was obvious that aircraft able to meet the required characteristics could not be made. The second stage of the competition began in the same year, when the air forces approved a reduction of the maximum speed to Mach 2.3. Tupolev's projects were compatible with this speed, enabling his flying-wing project 160M to take part in the second stage of the competition. Myasishchev proposed an M-18 bomber with a variable-geometry wing, apparently identical to the last, fourth variant of the M-20 project but made of aluminium instead of titanium, and capable of a maximum speed of Mach 2.3. Sukhoi decided to concentrate on fighter aircraft, giving up the competition for the strategic bomber.

Project gains form

The air forces chose Myasishchev's M-18 project with its variable-geometry wing, a project also supported by TsAGI and the Technological-Scientific Council of the Ministry of Air Industry. Tupolev's proposal lost because a flying wing is a single-mode aircraft, optimised for a specific speed and altitude (in this case, 2500 km/h; 1,350 kt at an altitude of 18000m/59,055 ft). The air forces approved the reduction of the maximum speed, but the requirement for a maximum range of 14000 to 16000 km (7,559 to 8,639 nm) was, for them, beyond discussion. Moreover, the aircraft was to

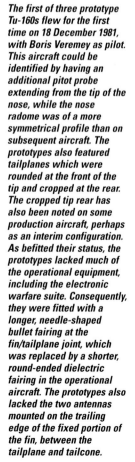

The first of three prototype Tu-160s flew for the first time on 18 December 1981, with Boris Veremey as pilot. This aircraft could be identified by having an additional pitot probe extending from the tip of the nose, while the nose radome was of a more symmetrical profile than on subsequent aircraft. The prototypes also featured tailplanes which were rounded at the front of the tip and cropped at the rear. The cropped tip rear has also been noted on some production aircraft, perhaps as an interim configuration. As befitted their status, the prototypes lacked much of the operational equipment, including the electronic warfare suite. Consequently, they were fitted with a longer, needle-shaped bullet fairing at the fin/tailplane joint, which was replaced by a shorter, round-ended dielectric fairing in the operational aircraft. The prototypes also lacked the two antennas mounted on the trailing edge of the fixed portion of the fin, between the tailplane and tailcone.

3.2 (3200 to 3500 km/h; 1,728 to 1,890 kt), compared with an aircraft at Mach 2.3 (2500 km/h; 1,350 kt), did not offset the cost of its construction and the associated technological risk. Therefore, his project – named Aircraft 160 (but initially known as Aircraft 156) – was designed for the maximum speed of Mach 2.3 (2500 km/h).

In 1970-72 Tupolev prepared a series of designs for the 160M (*izdeliye* L) bomber, designated L-1, L-2, etc., configured as a delta-shaped flying wing. At the same time, he continued tests of the Tu-144 supersonic airliner and began preliminary work on a second-generation supersonic transport known as Tu-244. The 160M bomber and the 244

be capable of getting to the target following a compound flight profile: most of the route was to be flown at subsonic speed at high altitude, but the 2000-km (1,080-nm) zone of anti-aircraft defence was to be circumvented by flying at 2500 km/h (1,350 kt) at high altitude or at 1000 km/h (540 kt) near the ground. The aircraft could not be too particular about airfields and had to be capable of deployment to more than the longest airstrips in the Soviet Union.

All these demands could only be met by an aircraft with a variable-geometry wing. Its medium position ensured long range at subsonic cruise speed, full sweep enabled high supersonic speed, and full spread during take-off allowed an increase in the weight of fuel and armament. Calculations indicated that, at supersonic speed, the range of an aircraft with a variable-geometry wing was similar to that of an aircraft with a fixed delta wing – but at subsonic speeds, range was 35-35 per cent greater. The aerodynamic configuration, which eventually was accepted for the Tu-160, has a lift:drag ratio of 18.5 to 19 when flying at subsonic speed and 6.0 at supersonic speed.

The use of a variable-geometry wing, particularly in such a heavy aircraft, led to a more sophisticated structure and increased weight due to structural nodes and pivoting gear. A new quality of technology was necessary for the application of variable geometry in the Tu-160, and a special state programme co-ordinated directly by Piotr Dementyev, Minister of Air Industry, was launched to create a new metallurgic technology. Production of large, very strong components was prepared, as was unique tooling to produce structural details, including vacuum welding of titanium alloys.

Myasishchev's winning design was completed by Tupolev because the former's team was just too small to bring it to fruition. In 1973 Tupolev prepared the first design of the Tu-160 (*izdeliye* K) with a variable-geometry wing using the general layout of Myasishchev's M-18. In successive projects, the design was gradually improved and began to resemble more closely the present Tu-160. After selection of the general layout and basic parameters of the new bomber, the Tupolev bureau, plus the scientific institutes of the air forces and Ministry of Air Industry, began selecting aircraft systems and structural elements.

The engine parameters specified according to the expected profile of flight were to be afterburning turbofans with a bypass ratio between 1 and 2. At first, NK-25 engines from the Tu-22M3 'Backfire-C' bomber were tried for the new bomber (the flight tests of this engine began in 1974).

The NK-25's thrust (245.18 kN/55,130 lb with afterburning) was sufficient, but its great consumption of fuel gave no expectation that it would attain the required range. Therefore, in 1977, the design team of Nikolai Kuznetsov of Samara (then Kuibyshev) began work on the NK-32 three-shaft turbofan engine that made use of many elements of the NK-25; it would have the same thrust, but fuel consumption rates of 0.72 to 0.73 lb/lbfh in subsonic cruise flight and 1.7 lb/lbfh at supersonic speed. The first flying tests of NK-32 engines were carried out in 1980 under the fuselage of a Tu-142 testbed, and series production began in 1983. Plans to install the modern and economical Kuznetsov NK-74 engines in the Tu-160 did not extend beyond the design stage.

Powerplant configuration

Tupolev considered 14 different variants of engine arrangement, including four engines arranged in pairs one above the other, four engines in a common nacelle under the fuselage, and three separate engines with round air intakes. Eventually, four engines were arranged in pairs and installed under the mid-wing (with a free space between them for armament bays) with two-dimensional vertical-wedge inlets.

The formal documents ordering construction of the Tu-160 by Tupolev's design team comprised two resolutions of the USSR Council of Ministers, dated 26 June 1974 and 19 December 1975. According to these documents, the Tu-160 was to be a multi-mode strategic missile carrier powered by four NK-32 engines. Its practical range with two Kh-45 missiles (a weight of 9000 kg/19,840 lb) at subsonic speed was set at 14000 to 16000 km (7,560 to

Bort 29, a 'sting'-tailed prototype, turns sharply as the gear cleans up after take-off. Despite its size the Tu-160 is surprisingly agile at low speeds. In this regime roll control is effected by outboard ailerons (which also droop for extra lift) and overwing spoiler sections. At medium/high speeds, when the flaps are retracted and the wings are swept back to the intermediate or full-swept position, roll control is handled by the differentially moving tailplanes. This view emphasises how far back the engines are mounted, necessary for centre of gravity requirements, and also shows the unusual wing fence surface in its low-speed, flat position. Hinging this surface solves the problem of where to 'park' the trailing-edge section of the outer panel when it is swept back: in the Boeing B-1B the same portion fits into a slot fitted with an inflatable rubber seal and a hinging cover.

Myasishchev M-18 design

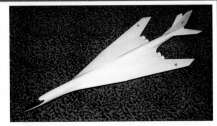

The M-18 was the eventual winner of the advanced bomber competition, although its development was subsequently entrusted to Tupolev. The M-18 was very similar to the final M-20 configuration, but was designed for Mach 2.3 flight rather than for the Mach 3 demanded of the earlier series.

Above: The first prototype Tu-160 is seen how it appears today at Zhukovskiy, derelict and missing its tailplanes, among other components.

Right: The original weapon envisaged for the Tu-160 was the massive Raduga Kh-45 missile, of which two were to be carried internally, as shown in this model. Two more were planned to be carried on wing pylons on short-range missions. The Kh-45, of which a handful were built and tested, was a supersonic weapon which employed inertial mid-course guidance and active radar over the final 90 km (56 miles) or so of its flight. The 'Blackjack' was again considered for carrying two giant missiles in the Tu-160M project of the early 1980s, which involved a lengthened fuselage to house a pair of 5000-km (3,107-mile) 3M25 Meteorit-As. Both missile projects were cancelled.

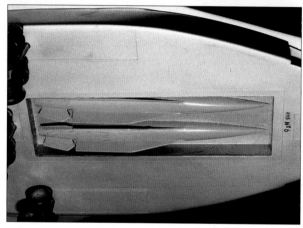

During the drawn-out process which resulted in today's Tu-160, the design underwent many changes. One of the main areas of contention was the engine configuration. This model, while resembling the final form in many areas, has large wedge-shaped variable-area ramp intakes at the wing roots. The wedge shape was retained for the final iteration, but was turned on its side so that the intakes could be positioned beneath the wings.

Kazan factory. All these men contributed considerably to the development of the Tu-160.

In January 1975 Tupolev's team began the next stage: preparation of preliminary design and construction of a full-size mock-up, for which the Tu-160 had been given the name *izdeliye* 70. In 1977 the preliminary design and mock-up bomber were submitted for state committee acceptance. In this form, the weight of the Tu-160 with a normal warload of 9 tonnes (19,840 lb), comprising two Kh-45 missiles, was to amount to 260 tonnes (573,040 lb), the empty weight was 103 tonnes (227,012 lb) and fuel weight was 148 tonnes (326,192 lb). As can be seen from later data, the Tu-160 gained weight in the process of design and construction so that eventually its empty operating weight became 117 tonnes (237,868 lb) and its take-off weight, 275 tonnes (606,100 lb).

The name 'Tu-160' appeared in the press several years before the aircraft came into being – probably the one such event in the history of Soviet combat aircraft. During the Strategic Arms Limitation Treaty 2 talks in the late 1970s, Leonid Brezhnyev, or someone on his team, informed the Americans of preparations for a new heavy bomber. No details were given other than the name of Tu-160 and that it would be manufactured in a Kazan factory extended for that purpose. This leaked information subsequently appeared in *Air Force Magazine* in November 1978 in an article about 'Backfire' aircraft.

Weapon controversy

For a long time, there were no doubts concerning the bomber's weaponry. Former Soviet long-range bombers were armed with one or two heavy missiles, initially the subsonic KS (AS-1 'Kennel'), then the supersonic K-10S (AS-2 'Kipper'), Kh-20 (AS-3 'Kangaroo'), and finally the excellent Kh-22 (AS-4 'Kitchen'), which is still in use. In a continuation of this line for the strategic bomber, the Soviets prepared new Kh-45 missiles. The normal variant of the Tu-160 was to carry two such weapons inside the bomb bay and, if necessary, two more missiles suspended externally, at the cost of performance.

The Raduga (Rainbow) design bureau in Dubna near Moscow, which until the mid-1960s had been branch office OKB-2-155 of the Mikoyan design bureau, began work under Alexander Bereznyak's direction on the Kh-45 missile in July 1965, at the same time as the programme for Sukhoi's T-4 medium strike aircraft was launched. Over the next 10 years, Raduga built a dozen or so Kh-45 missiles (or *izdeliye* D-4) for testing. The missile was made of titanium alloys, had a length of 10.8 m (35 ft 5 in), weighed 4500 kg (9,920 lb) and reached a range of 500 to 600 km (270 to 324 nm). It was guided to the target by an inertial navigation system and in the final part of the flight by an active radar seeker known as Garpun (Harpoon), with a search range of 150 km (81 nm) and a lock-on distance of 90 km (49 nm). Short-range Kh-15 strike missiles, developed within the Kh-2000 programme that also launched in 1965, were an alternative armament for the new bomber.

Other missile variants were proposed. In 1968, soon after the first competition for the strategic bomber was announced, a new research and development programme – Echo – was launched to develop a low-altitude strategic stand-off missile. There were many ideas for supersonic missiles, but the contractors of this programme, GosNIIAS (Gosudarstvennyi Nauchno-Issledovatelskiy Institut Aviatsionnykh Sistem, State Scientific-Research Institute of Aviation Systems) and the Raduga design bureau suggested the then-unfashionable, small subsonic Kh-55 with an absolutely new terrain-following navigational system. This idea was rejected as pure fantasy by the committees of the air forces and Air Industry, which held that two Kh-45 supersonic missiles were the only armament for the Tu-160. Work on the Kh-55 missile went ahead only on the medium-range version with a traditional homing system, i.e., inertial navigation during its path to the target and active radar seeker in the terminal phase.

8,640 nm), and range in variable-profile flight (including 2000 km/1,080 nm at supersonic speed or at high subsonic speed at an altitude of 50 to 200 m/164 to 656 ft) was to be 12000 to 13000 km (6,480 to 7,020 nm). Maximum speed was specified in the resolution at 2300 to 2500 km/h (1,242 to 1,350 kt) and speed at low altitude was 1000 km/h (540 kt), ceiling was 18000 to 20000 m (59,055 to 65,617 ft), and maximum weight of the armament was 40000 kg (88,183 lb).

Aleksei Tupolev (son of Andrei Tupolev, founder of the design bureau) was in charge of the work on the Tu-160 during its early period. At the initial design phase, in 1975, Valentin Bliznyuk was appointed as chief designer (and is still in charge of this programme); his closest assistant was Lev Bazenkov. During work on the Tu-160, Georgiy Cheryomukhin was in charge of the aerodynamic department, Vyacheslav Sulimenkov – structural strength department, Vadim Razumikhin – control system department, and Semyon Vigdorchik – engineering department. Construction of the mid-wing and wing pivoting node was under the direction of Daniil Gapeyev, construction of landing gear – Yakov Livshits, construction of airframe structure – Iosiph Nezval. Valentin Klimov was the head of the Tupolev branch office at Zhukovskiy near Moscow, Anatoliy Yashukov was the prototype test engineer, Andrei Misheykov was the chief engineer at Tupolev's experimental workshop in Moscow, and Vitaliy Kopylov managed the

As such, the armament provided for in the preliminary design of the Tu-160 of 1976 constituted two Kh-45 missiles for the basic variant, and alternative variants carrying 24 Kh-15s, or 10 to 12 Kh-15Ms (these missiles remained in the design stage), or 10 to 15 of the new Kh-55s.

These plans were turned upside-down in 1976-77 when the Soviets learned about American work on the AGM-86 (ALCM-B) strategic cruise missile. The Kh-45 was deleted from the Tu-160's armament list and Raduga resumed work on a strategic version of the Kh-55. The basic armament of the Tu-160 was fixed as six to 12 subsonic strategic Kh-55 missiles in revolving MKU6-5U launchers, with 12 to 24 Kh-15s being the alternative. Consideration was also given to other types of medium- and short-range missiles, guided and unguided bombs but, as yet, they have not been realised.

Raduga's cruise missile

The Raduga Kh-55 (*izdeliye* 120) was launched for the first time in 1978 and series production began in 1981; the missile was officially commissioned in 1983, together with the Tu-95MS 'Bear-H'. Several years later, in 1986, series production began of the strategic version, Kh-55SM (*izdeliye* 125), intended for Tu-160s and later versions of the Tu-95MS bomber. More than 3,000 Kh-55 missiles were built in two production plants, in Smolensk and Kharkiv (Ukraine). The Kh-55SM strategic cruise missile (AS-15B 'Kent' to NATO), also designated RKV-500B (given officially by the Soviets during the SALT-2 negotiations), can be used for attacking targets with known co-ordinates and is equipped with a homing system comprising an accurate INS updated by a terrain-reference system that compares the terrain below to a map stored in the missile's memory. Its BSU-55 flight control system uses the terrain-following feature when flying at low altitude, and during anti-intercept manoeuvres in a horizontal plane. The Kh-55SM has a 200-kT nuclear warhead. It weighs 1500 kg (3,309 lb) (including an additional conformal fuel tank), its length is 6.04 m (19 ft 10 in) and its wingspan is 3.1 m (10 ft 2 in). Cruising speed is between Mach 0.48 and 0.77. Official maximum range of the Kh-55SM is 3000 km (1,620 nm), or 2500 km (1,350 nm) without the additional tank. The missile has straight wings which unfold and control fins, and is propelled by an R95-300 turbofan engine lowered after launch from the bottom rear part of the fuselage.

When Kh-15s are the armament, 24 of these nuclear short-range attack missiles can be installed in four short revolving MKU6-1U drums (six missiles per drum). The drums are located in a line inside the armament bays. The Tu-160 has been adapted to carry such weapons (there are suitable fasteners and connectors in the bay) but, according to reliable sources, this type of armament was not implemented in service aircraft.

The Kh-15 (*izdeliye* 115, NATO AS-16 'Kickback'), developed by the same Raduga design team as the Kh-55, is an analogue to the US AGM-69 SRAM commissioned in 1980.

It has an inertial navigation system (although without correction) and carries a 350-kT nuclear warhead. In the first phase of flight the missile climbs to about 40000 m (131,230 ft) and then dives, accelerating to Mach 5. The Kh-15 has a launch weight of 1200 kg (2,646 lb), a length of 4.78 m (15 ft 8 in) and a diameter of 0.455 m (1 ft 6 in); its maximum range is claimed to be between 150 and 300 km (81 and 162 nm).

An anti-radar version of the missile, designated Kh-15P, was commissioned in 1988. This missile has a passive final homing system and a conventional 150-kg (330-lb) high-explosive warhead. It is very probable that Kh-15Ps are used by Tu-160s to destroy enemy radar sites, thereby breaking through the air defence system.

No other weapons are mentioned in official materials or publications, but the actual set of missiles carried by the Tu-160 remains a mystery. The length of the armament bay – 11.28 m (37 ft) – remained the same as that designed to accommodate Kh-45 missiles (which are 10.8 m/35 ft 5 in long), much longer than necessary for Kh-55s, which are 6.04 m (19 ft 10 in) in length. Kh-45s were dispensed with in 1976/77, so there has been enough time to redesign the bomber. That this has not been done suggests that, apart from the Kh-55, other large missiles were considered for the Tu-160, perhaps Meteorit-A missiles, although these did not pass their tests.

A traditional self-defence system proposed initially for the Tu-160 included a tail turret with a six-barrelled, 30-mm GSh-6-30 cannon (GSh, Gryazev Shipunov). However, the designers later replaced the gun with a Baykal self-defence system, most of the components for which – some 80 per cent – are located in the aircraft's tail, in a so-called 'carrot'. A Mak (Poppy) infra-red missile launch and approach sensor is installed at the very end of the tail, as are a radar warning device, electronic jammer and a battery of 24

Above: The Tu-160's undercarriage retracts rearwards. The mainwheel bogies are angled nose-down so that the forward wheel touches first. The main strut is slightly angled to absorb the full impact at the Tu-160's normal landing incidence.

Right: At the heart of the Tu-160's attack capability is the Obzor-K nav/bombing radar in the nose. Mapping fixes from the radar are used to update the inertial navigation system. There is also a terrain-following radar fitted under the large radome. The forward-looking optical sight is visible behind the window of the undernose fairing.

Although the 'Blackjack' began life as a Myasishchev design, Valentin Bliznyuk of the Tupolev OKB can rightly be regarded as the aircraft's father. As head of the large design team, Bliznyuk turned a paper and tunnel model study into the world's largest combat aircraft.

APP-50 three-round 50-mm chaff/flare dispensers. Initially, the system's failure rate was very high due to extreme vibration in this region of the airframe, and it often generated false indications, e.g., the radar of an F-16 fighter could be interpreted as a ground-based anti-aircraft radar. In the course of production, the fairing projecting aft at the intersection of the tailplane and tailfin was shortened, thereby reducing tail vibration.

Not all plans for the self-defence system have been executed. For instance, the implementation of R-77 medium-range missiles proposed for self-defence was not pursued.

Prototypes under test

After acceptance of the project in 1977, the experimental workshop of Tupolev's design bureau in Moscow began construction of three prototypes from sub-assemblies mostly supplied from other production plants, such as Kazan (fuselage), Novosibirsk (outer wings and tailplanes), Voronezh (bomb chamber doors) and Gorkiy (landing gear). The first Tu-160 prototype, designated 70-01 and intended for testing the basic flight characteristics, had incomplete equipment. Prototype 70-02 was used for static tests, and 70-03 was practically an equivalent of serial aircraft. Prototype 70-01 was eventually assembled in Zhukovskiy in January 1981. After many months of testing the aircraft's systems and equipment, on 14 November a Tu-160 taxied for the first time to the airstrip and made the first high-speed taxi.

On 25 November 1981 the aircraft, being prepared for its next test taxi, was parked near two Tu-144 airliners. This was the image of the Tu-160 that appeared in the first photo published in the world's press. It caused quite a sensation. The media speculated that the aircraft had been revealed for purposes of propaganda, in order to be photographed by American satellites (according to general opinion, the photograph was taken by a reconnaissance satellite). The truth is more prosaic: a passenger on an airliner landing at nearby Bykovo airport took the picture and passed it to the West. The aircraft was then temporarily named 'Ram-P' (from Ramenskoye, which was a common name used in the West for the Zhukovskiy test airfield) and then 'Blackjack' by NATO. In this way, the world became acquainted with the heaviest combat aircraft of all time.

The maiden flight of prototype 70-01 was made with Boris Veremey at the controls on Friday 18 December 1981, the eve of the 75th birthday of Leonid Brezhnyev, General Secretary of Communist Party of the Soviet Union. Today, the designers argue about the connection between these two dates, saying their convergence was incidental. It may be true: in the history of Soviet aviation, many aircraft were first tested in flight in December in order to satisfy the year's schedules. In this case, the flight's date was probably changed by a few days to match the official anniversary. The duration of the first flight was 27 minutes; the aircraft climbed to 2000 m (7,217 ft) and – according to Veremey's memoirs – flew 150-220 km (81-119 nm) from the airfield (which is doubtful in such a short flight). With Veremey in the cockpit were co-pilot Sergey Agapov and navigators Mikhail Kozel and Anatoliy Yeremenko.

Three months after the maiden flight, in February 1982, Boris Veremey first exceeded the speed of sound with the Tu-160. During one of the experimental flights he also achieved the top speed of 2200 km/h (1,188 kt). Some critical situations arose during test flights, for example when Veremey landed with the front leg of the landing gear still retracted; after his masterful landing and a small repair, the tests continued. One of the most interesting tests was the flight by Nail Sattarov in which the upper covers of the cockpit were removed in order to test the effect on the crew of a broken cockpit canopy.

Prototype 70-01, partly dismantled, stands at Zhukovskiy. Externally, it differs very little from later aircraft, the most conspicuous change being a long probe at the nose tip. The internal differences are greater: not only are some parts of equipment absent, but some structural elements are makeshift, e.g., made of substitute materials. Prolonged work on the new materials and engineering of their treatment was the main reason for delay in the construction of the second flying prototype, 70-03, which did not take off until 6 October 1984. The first stage of Tu-160 testing was carried out at Zhukovskiy, then, after investigations into systems and armament began, trials were gradually moved to Akhtubinsk to the NII VVS (Nauchno-Issledovatelskiy Institut Voenno-Vozdushnikh Sil, Scientific-Research Institute of the Air Force; today it is known as 929th GLITs VVS, Gosudarstvennyi Lyotno-Ispytatelnyi Tsentr, State Flight-Test Centre of the Air Force). During Tu-160 armament tests, the launched missile was followed by an Il-76SKIP (Samolyotnyi Komandno-Izmeritelnyi Punkt, Airborne Command-Measuring Post) gathering telemetry information.

Serial production starts

Under the personal patronage of Dmitriy Ustinov, Soviet Minister of Defence, construction began in 1976 at Ulyanovsk on the Volga River of a new production plant intended for series production of the Tu-160. However, several years later, the plans were changed (reportedly under the influence of then-Prime Minister Aleksei Kosygin) and Ulyanovsk was re-roled for production of the world's heaviest transport aircraft, the An-124. The Tu-160 prototypes were made in co-operation with the Kazan factory, a traditional manufacturer of Tupolev bombers. Eventually, series production was also located in Kazan, which was extended for this purpose and which implemented new production tooling.

Construction of Kazan aircraft factory No. 124 began in 1932 and its first aircraft left the production line in 1938. In October 1941, soon after the German invasion of the USSR, the factory – located 700 km (435 miles) east of Moscow – was evacuated to Moscow factory No. 22, which specialised in the production of bombers (e.g., Tupolev's TB-3 and SB) and was one of the biggest factories of the Air Industry. Both factories were merged to become factory No. 22. During the war it undertook mass production of Pe-2 light bombers, as well as small numbers of heavy TB-7s (Pe-8). Still heavier Tu-4 'Bulls' (copies of the B-29 Superfortress) were manufactured after the war. In the jet age, the factory made Tupolev's medium bombers – Tu-16 'Badger', Tu-22 'Blinder' and Tu-22M 'Backfire' – as well as such passenger aircraft as the Tu-104 and Il-62. Now the factory bears the name Kazanskoye Aviatsionnoye

Proizvodstvennoye Obyedineniye (KAPO, Kazan Aviation Production Association) named after S.P. Gorbunov and, apart from Tu-160s, builds Tu-214 airliners.

The first series Tu-160 took off from Kazan on 10 October 1984 (only four days after the first flight of prototype 70-03), but it was two and a half years before the first aircraft was handed over to the air forces. The fourth aircraft built in Kazan (number 2-03, i.e., the third aircraft of the second production batch) took off for the first time on 15 August 1986 and became the first aircraft commissioned into service (together with number 3-01).

In Pryluky

At mid-day on 23 April 1987 (or, according to some sources, on 17 April), the first two Tu-160 aircraft, numbers 2-03 and 3-01, landed at Pryluky airfield, 130 km (81 miles) east of Kiev. One of these aircraft was piloted by Major General Lev Kozlov, deputy commanding officer of 37th Air Army (Long Range Aviation), and the other by a factory pilot from Kazan. A few weeks later, on 12 May, Lev Kozlov

Bort 87 is one of the test aircraft. Early trials, which were primarily concerned with aerodynamics, performance and systems, were conducted from Zhukovskiy. As the trials programme moved towards testing the aircraft from an operational standpoint, the focus shifted to Akhtubinsk. In 2001 four Tu-160s remained in airworthy trials status at Zhukovskiy – two assigned to the air force and two with the Tupolev OKB, although they fly only sporadically.

Left: The first picture revealed in the West was this 1981 image showing a Tu-160 parked at Zhukovskiy next to two Tu-144 airliners. At the time, the airfield was thought to be named Ramenskoye, and new new types were assigned 'Ram-' designations. The Tu-160 became 'Ram-P'.

Below: In August 1988 US Secretary of Defense Frank Carlucci was shown the 'Blackjack', along with other Soviet hardware, at Kubinka. This was one of two aircraft which flew past during the demonstration.

took off for the first time from Pryluky in a Tu-160, marking the start of training of the regiment's pilots. On 1 June then-commanding officer of the regiment, Colonel Vladimir Grebennikov, and commander of the Tu-160 squadron, Major Alexander Medvedyev, made their first independent flights.

Originally, Tu-160s were to serve with the Myasishchev 3M 'Bison' bomber-equipped 1096th Heavy Bomber Regiment stationed in Engels on the Volga estuary, the greatest base of the Soviet strategic air forces. However, these plans were changed, and the first Tu-160s were assigned to the 184th GvTBAP (Heavy Bomber Regiment of Guards) at Pryluky. Preparation of Pryluky and this regiment to operate the Tu-160s had started a few years earlier: the airstrip was strengthened and extended to 3000 m (9,843 ft), and in 1984 the regiment had obtained Tu-22M3 'Backfire-Cs' to accustom the crews to heavy supersonic aircraft with variable-geometry wings. One squadron remained equipped with Tu-16P 'Badger' electronic warfare aircraft. The future Tu-160 pilots undertook theoretical training in Kazan and Kuibyshev (now Samara).

The 184 Gvardeyskiy Ordena Lenina Boyevogo Krasnogo Znameni Poltavsko-Berlinskiy Tyazholo-bombardirovochnyi Aviatsyonnyi Polk (Poltava-Berlin Heavy Bomber Regiment of Guards awarded with Lenin's Order and Combat Red Banner) was one of the oldest Soviet bomber units. Its first combat mission – as the 9th Long Range Heavy Bomber Regiment of Guards – was made on the first night of the Soviet-German war, 22/23 June 1941; a month later the regiment made the first Soviet air raid on Berlin. During World War II, the regiment was equipped with Il-4 and Yer-2 aircraft. After the war it

briefly used 'Lend-Lease' B-25 bombers, and then was the first Soviet regiment to be equipped with the Tu-4 'Bull', a copy of the B-29 Superfortress. From the 1950s to the 1980s, the regiment flew several versions of the Tu-16 'Badger'.

Intensive Kh-55SM cruise missile-firing exercises began soon after the 184th received the Tu-160, at the end of July 1987 (the first aircraft to launch the missile was crewed by pilot Vladimir Grebennikov with navigator Igor Aninkin). By November 1991, one of the aircraft had launched seven missiles, and others had three or four launchings each. The first firing exercises were made on the NII VVS firing ground in Kazakhstan (later, other firing grounds were also used). Telemetry-monitoring Il-76SKIP aircraft always followed the launching aircraft and the missile.

At the end of 1987 there were three Tu-160s at Pryluky, and before the end of 1988 the first squadron of 10 aircraft was complete, with Alexander Medvedyev as the commanding officer. At the end of 1991 – also the time of the disintegration of the USSR – the regiment had two squadrons of Tu-160s, totalling 19 aircraft, as well as one squadron of Tu-134UBL training aircraft. As new 'Blackjacks' arrived, older Tu-16s were transferred to other units, or retired. The Tu-22M3s were also withdrawn, since they were expensive to operate as training aircraft, and at the beginning of 1991 the 'Backfires' were replaced by Tu-134UBL training aircraft (the last Tu-22M3 left Pryluky in March 1991).

Typical routes for Tu-160s flying from Pryluky air base were over Soviet territory to Baikal and back again, or across the North Pole. During the longest flight made by Colonel Valeriy Gorgol, who was commanding officer of the regiment from 1989 to 1993, his Tu-160 flew for 12 hours and 50 minutes over the North Pole, to within 450 km (243 nm) of the Canadian coast, and back. In May 1991, during one such flight, the first contact between 'Blackjacks' and Western aircraft occurred: over the Barents Sea, two Tu-160s deviated from their usual westerly route along the Norwegian coast near Tromsø, and were escorted by F-16A fighters from the 331st Squadron of the Royal Norwegian Air Force.

Presentations

On 2 August 1988, Frank C. Carlucci, then-US Defense Secretary, became the first foreigner to go inside a Tu-160, at Kubinka air base near Moscow. The Soviets had prepared the aircraft wearing tactical number 12, onboard which Carlucci spent 15 minutes examining the cockpit. When he stood up from the left pilot seat, he hit his head hard against the upper console (it is now called 'shchitok Karluchi', Carlucci's console). At Kubinka, Carlucci was also shown two other 'Blackjacks', which flew above the airfield at low altitude (one piloted by V. Grebennikov and the other by A. Medvedyev), each with one engine off (see below). Carlucci was given basic data on the aircraft, and was told its maximum range without refuelling was 14000

The most notable feature of the Tu-160's flight deck is the stick control column, which gives the aircraft a 'fighter' feel while obscuring the instrument panel less than a conventional yoke. Otherwise, the Tu-160's flight deck is entirely conventional with a mixture of dial and strip instruments. The centre of each pilot's display has an attitude reference display, compass display, vertical speed indicator and airspeed indicator. Between the two pilot displays is a variety of nav/comms data entry panels and auxiliary displays such as wing sweep and undercarriage indicators. The dashboard is painted in the blue colour favoured by Russian psychologists for cockpits, with the vital flight instruments framed in white.

'Blackjack' cockpit

Below: The central console has the thrust levers offset to starboard for primary operation by the co-pilot. The console also has fuel transfer controls and flap selection levers.

Below: This is the electronic warfare console, dominated by the circular threat warning display. The pilot has a similar, but simpler, display on the far left of the instrument panel.

km (7,560 nm). Next year, the aircraft was shown to then-Chairman of the Joint Chiefs of Staff, Admiral William Crowe. This presentation also took place at Kubinka, on 13 June 1989, and the aircraft had the side number 21.

The Tu-160 was shown to the public for the first time on 20 August 1989, flying over Tushino airfield in Moscow. The first public ground presentation was at MosaeroShow '92 held in August 1992 at Zhukovskiy. The first international presentation of the Tu-160 was in June 1995, at the Paris air show, where it was presented with a wooden mock-up of the Burlak space missile suspended under its fuselage.

Records

In 1989-90 the Tu-160 set a series of 44 world air records. The first were set by a military crew under the command of Lev Kozlov in the aircraft with side number 14, and two other series were set by the crew of the Tupolev design bureau under Boris Veremey in prototype 70-03. On 31 October 1989, L. Kozlov achieved 1731.4 km/h (934.88 kt) on a 1000-km (540-nm) closed circuit with a load of

30000 kg (66,138 lb) in class C-1-r (aircraft weighing 240 tonnes/528,960 lb). It was also the record for loads of 25, 20, 15, 10, 5, 2 and 1 tonnes, and without a load. In the same flight, Kozlov set the altitude record in level flight, 12150 m (39,862 ft); the load record – 30471 kg (67,176 lb) – raised to an altitude of 2000 m (6,562 ft); and reached 13894 m (45,584 ft) altitude with a 30-tonne (66,120-lb) load. On 3 November 1989, B. Veremey flying with a take-off weight of 275 tonnes (606,100 lb) (class C-1-s) achieved 1678 km/h (906 kt) on a closed 2000-km (1,080-nm) circuit with a load of 25 tonnes (55,100 lb). On 15 May 1990, B. Veremey reached 1720 km/h (929 kt) on a 1000-km (540-nm) circuit with a load of 30 tonnes (66,120 lb) (as well as 25, 20, 15, 10, 5, 2 and 1 tonnes, and without load). This time the aircraft weight was 251 tonnes (553,204 lb) and the performances were recorded in class C-1-s.

Service problems

Under a decision by the Soviet Minister of Defence, the aircraft was handed over to the combat unit in Pryluky before completion of state acceptance tests (which were

The wing joint fences aid directional stability when the wings are swept to their 65° supersonic position. The fences actually consist of three separate surfaces. When the wing is fully forward the three sections are: the leading, independently raising, section lies flat to cover most of the gap between wing and engine nacelle; the central section forms part of the outer wing section, maintaining the wing's aerofoil shape, and has a simple hinge set at 45° to the direction of flight (45° + 20° minimum wing sweep = 65° maximum sweep); the rearmost section forms part of the drooping main flap.

Bort 24 lands at Pryluky on a murky day. The aircraft has a full ILS system installed. The navigation system is based on an inertial unit, which provides a continuous plotted position on a moving map. The system's accuracy is refined using radar fixes against known points or automatic celestial sightings. The system interfaces with the inertial system of the Kh-55SM missile, so that the missile 'knows' its exact position and attitude at the point of launch. The aircraft's system also prepares the digital terrain map for the missile.

All weapons are carried in two similar-sized bays located either side of the wing carry-through structure. Each bay is covered by four doors, the forward pair of which are longer – corresponding to the length of the MKU6-5U launcher – allowing Kh-55SM weapons to be launched by opening just one set of doors.

completed in 1989) and before official commissioning of the aircraft into service. In a situation known as 'trial service', each take-off and landing was recorded on film from a special stand near the airstrip, and changes were constantly introduced into the aircraft's construction and equipment. This trial service was supervised by a group of experts, sometimes as many as 300, from the Tupolev design bureau and the Kazan factory. With the regiment, the aircraft was equipped with an INS featuring astro correction, which improved accuracy when overflying oceans and other terrain devoid of pinpoints. Due to problems with starting the engines, the number of additional inlets at the sides of the air intakes was increased from five to six, and at the same time their control was simplified to improve air inlet conditions and reduce noise. The tailplanes were changed: metal honeycomb filling in some structural parts was replaced by composite filling.

Three serious breakdowns happened during the aircraft's service in Pryluky, fortunately all with happy endings. In the first case, a 1.5-m (4-ft 11-in) tailplane section was torn off in the air due to excessive stress, but the aircraft was landed successfully by pilot A. Medvedyev. After this accident, Tu-160 flights were halted for some time and the tail units were improved on all aircraft: the tailplane structure was strengthened and made 50 cm (19.69 in) shorter. The new tailplanes were delivered from Kazan to Pryluky as 'oversize' load in the fuselage of Il-76 cargo aircraft. In the second mishap, the wheel brakes were blocked on take-off, tearing open the tyres. In the third instance, in May 1993, the undercarriage bogie rotating gear failed, but Valeriy Gorgol managed to land successfully. All the disclosed defects were addressed in successive production series, and retroactively in existing aircraft.

Pilots are satisfied with the Tu-160 and with its impres-

sive combat potential. It is the most powerful combat aircraft built in the USSR (several years ago, the commanding officer of a Tu-160 regiment, Valeriy Gorgol, told the author that "my regiment of Tu-160s outweighs the remaining armed forces of Ukraine"). The aircraft is very pleasant to handle, much simpler than its Tu-22M3 forerunner, and the earlier control wheel has been replaced by a control stick. This stick was at first strongly criticised and was not accepted, until it was realised that the aircraft could be controlled without physical effort; it is much more convenient, does not obscure the instrument panel and allows simultaneous control of the throttle. Thanks to its excellent thrust-to-weight ratio, the aircraft climbs easily (once it even took off with accidentally-open wing spoilers). The thrust margin allows take-off even with one engine stopped (not, of course, at maximum take-off weight) and the flight can be continued with two engines only. This feature proved to be very useful when the Tu-160s were displayed in flight for Frank Carlucci. One engine in each of the two selected aircraft refused to start and, after brief consideration, the pilots took off with only three engines running. The aircraft's landing characteristics are excellent, 'holding onto the air' until it reaches the landing speed of 260 km/h (140 kt). The failure rate of the Tu-160 – which, for obvious reasons, was high during the first phase of service – is no greater than for other aircraft, including the American B-1B Lancer.

Seat problems

The assessment of the crew comfort, unfortunately, is not so favourable. Tu-160 crews, when questioned at Pryluky about the conditions of their work in the air, had reservations about the equipment that related directly to their personal comfort and safety. In the first aircraft delivered to the regiment, crews criticised the emergency ejection system. The pilots' seats are movable for easier ingress and for better comfort during the flight, but can be ejected only in the extreme forward position. In the first aircraft, if the seat was in another position, the navigator had to push it forward manually. Now, the aircraft are equipped with a pneumatic cylinder that pushes the seat automatically prior to ejection. The seats, designed for fighter aircraft, were not suitable for bomber pilots spending 10-plus hours in a seated position. Only after some time were the seats equipped with pneumatic pulsating cushions that provide massage during long flights. In the first aircraft, cockpit pressure was equivalent to the ambient pressure at an altitude of 5000 m (16,404 ft), meaning that oxygen masks had to be used all the time; this inconvenience has been remedied. The noise level in the cockpit is so high that crew seated side-by-side can hear each other only via intercom. On a more positive note, a small corridor leads to a galley and toilet, equipment that had not previously been installed in a Soviet bomber.

There were also reservations concerning the cockpit ergonomics of the first 'Blackjacks'. For instance, the indicators for main and stand-by instruments were of different types, so the pilots had to switch between two 'mind-sets'; they are now uniform. The cockpit equipment is of conventional type, the result of a conscious decision to use the equipment of other aircraft to ease crew training and to allow alternate flying in different aircraft types. This decision limited the aircraft's abilities – which could be justified in the initial period of aircraft service – and will probably be changed in the course of a planned modernisation if it is deemed economically viable.

The most critical remarks came from ground personnel. Preparing a Tu-160 for flight requires 15-20 special vehicles with running generator units, resulting in smoke and noise levels that far exceed acceptable standards (the noise level is 130 dB). This problem was analysed and an easy solution was offered by the design bureau, which suggested adopting the American solution applied to the B-1B, i.e., organising special maintenance areas with underground installations and power supply units. However, the armed forces rejected this solution, maintaining that the whole system is required to be mobile.

The complexity of ground service practically ties an aircraft to its airfield. Several times, aircraft from Pryluky air base were forced by bad weather to land at stand-by Uzin airfield (170 km/106 miles southeast of Pryluky), home of the 182nd Heavy Bomber Regiment with Tu-95MS and the 409th Air Tanker Regiment with Il-78s. In each case, a long column of vehicles had to be brought from Pryluky to Uzin, including tank trucks with liquid nitrogen and equipment for nitration of the fuel with hydraulic oil. Similar situations happened during shows for VIPs at Kubinka, Ryazan, Machulische and other places.

Where the Tu-160 mainly differs from the B-1B is in its Mach 2+ performance. This is largely due to the complex variable-area intakes, which were deleted when the B-1 design was resurrected. Downstream of the main intake is a set of six (five in early aircraft) large auxiliary louvre intakes which admit extra air at low air speeds. The mass flow of the NK-32 engine is reported as 365 kg (805 lb) per second, and its dry power is more than the full afterburning power of the B-1B's F101.

Tu-134UBL pilot trainer

The Tu-134UBL (Uchebno-Boyevoi dlya Lyotchikov, combat trainer for pilots) is a special version of the Tu-134 'Crusty' airliner designed for training pilots and navigators of Soviet Long Range Aviation. It features special equipment and its most conspicuous external detail is the long, sharp front fuselage containing the radar antenna. Tu-134s were transformed into training versions by the factory in Kharkiv. The Tu-134 is very similar to the Tu-160 in its flying characteristics, particularly the thrust load, take-off and landing path. The cost of one hour of flying a Tu-134 is one-quarter that of a Tu-160 flight.

Tu-160s served at Pryluky with the 184 GvTBAP for five years, forming the spearhead of the Soviet Union's strategic deterrent. Although the greater 'muscle' of that deterrent lay under the oceans in submarines, or in ICBM silos, the bomber fleet offered far greater flexibility, chiefly on account of its ability to deploy swiftly, to re-target rapidly and to be recalled in flight after launch.

With their red stars crudely obliterated, four Tu-160s await their fate at Pryluky. Transferred by default to the Ukraine in 1992, the 184 GvTBAP fleet effectively lost its combat capability, as many pilots returned to Russia and technical support was withdrawn. The 'Blackjacks' made only a few flights under the Ukrainian flag, and were held in open storage throughout the 1990s. Their greatest value was as a bargaining chip with Russia, although the initial round of talks concerning their sale broke down. Subsequently, eight were returned to Russia and the remainder scrapped.

Tu-160 operations impose very strict requirements for runway cleanliness. After rejecting five engines damaged by impurities sucked from the ground, the regiment had to form a so-called 'fourth squadron' for cleaning, in addition to the three normal ones. This additional squadron, equipped with vehicles with old jet engines installed on them, was responsible for blowing all dirt from the concrete surface.

In Engels

Prior to the disintegration of the USSR, 19 'Blackjacks' entered service with the air forces, all stationed at Pryluky. On 24 August 1991 the Ukrainian parliament decreed it was taking under its control all military units stationed on Ukrainian territory; the Ukrainian Ministry of Defence was created on the same day. For several months, these events had no effect on the life of the 184th Heavy Bomber Regiment in Pryluky. Air military units did not begin to swear allegiance to Ukraine until spring 1992. The day for this for the Pryluky regiment was 8 May 1992, and it caused a split among members. About 25 per cent of the pilots and most of the ground personnel swore the oath for Ukraine, the first being the regiment's commanding officer, Colonel Valeriy Gorgol.

A group of about 30 pilots went to Engels air base in Russia, where the first Russian Tu-160 unit was forming, the 121st Sevastopol Heavy Bomber Regiment of Guards. At that time, Russia had just three Tu-160s at the Kazan factory, and several others used for tests at Zhukovskiy. On 16 February 1992 the first of the Kazan aircraft arrived at Engels airfield, the remaining two being ferried before May, but they spent several months on the ground because there were no pilots. On 29 July 1992, Alexander Medvedyev took off for the first time in a Russian Tu-160 from Engels. On 22 October 1992 the crew of the regiment's commander, Lieutenant Colonel Anatoliy Zhikharyev (currently the commanding officer of the 22nd Division of Strategic Bombers), made the first Russian test launch of a Kh-55SM from a service Tu-160, followed the next day by the crew

of Lieutenant Colonel A. Malishev. In mid-May 1993 a pair of Russian Tu-160s participated in the first large-scale exercises of the Russian Air Force, Voskhod-93 (Rising).

Engels, the greatest air base of the Russian strategic air forces, had previously housed Myasishchev 3M 'Bison' aircraft, originally used as bombers and subsequently as air tankers. The last flight of a 3MS-2 'Bison' from Engels occurred on 23 March 1994. Afterwards, these aircraft were stored, and their destruction began in August 1997.

The production of Tu-160s at Kazan continued for some time, but the air force soon ran out of money and in June 1994, the sixth – and, for a long time, the last – aircraft destined for the Engels regiment left the factory. At Kazan, four unfinished airframes remained in various states of completion.

Meanwhile, the Pryluky regiment, in a very brief time, virtually lost its combat value. Nineteen Tu-160s from the 184th Heavy Bomber Regiment were grounded because of lack of technical support from the design bureau and manufacturer, lack of spare parts and lack of appropriate fuel. Flights, made sporadically, lacked a combat element for many reasons, not least of which was the lack of areas suitable for exercises with strategic missiles. From the very beginning, Ukraine considered the Tu-160 bombers to be a

Above: An Engels-based aircraft cruises at high altitude. With wings in the intermediate 35° position, the aircraft is optimised to cruise at Mach 0.77. It can theoretically fly for nearly 14000 km (7,560 nm) in this configuration without refuelling, with an endurance of about 15 hours. When launched from bases in the Russian Arctic, it has the range to cover all of the United States on a two-way over-the-Pole trip.

Left: The 121 GvTBAP was the unit chosen to operate the Russian Tu-160s, although it was scheduled to adopt the historic 184 GvTBAP number. The Tu-160s are currently operated by a single squadron, although this should increase to two when the eight ex-Ukrainian aircraft are cleared for service (they are currently going through an overhaul programme at the Kazan factory). At present the 121 GvTBAP also operates the Tu-95MS 'Bear-H' which, like the Tu-160, employs the Kh-55 cruise missile as its primary weapon.

'trump card' in talks with Russia. Economically, the aircraft were unsustainable for Ukraine, and militarily, they were completely unnecessary to its armed forces. From 1991, Russia and Ukraine held talks about transferring the strategic aircraft to Russia, the main bone of contention being money. Russian experts, who examined the aircraft in Pryluky and Uzin (home to Tu-95MS 'Bear-Hs') in 1993 and 1996, assessed the aircraft's technical condition as good, but the price of US$3 billion initially demanded by Ukraine was not acceptable to Russia. In April 1998, when it became apparent that negotiations would yield no results, the Ukrainian Council of National Security and Defence decided to scrap the aircraft, with the exception of several destined for civil research programmes and for museums. In November 1998 at Pryluky, the first Tu-160 was ostentatiously cut up.

Bombers for gas

In April 1999, immediately after the commencement of NATO air attacks against Yugoslavia, Russia resumed talks with Ukraine about the strategic bombers. This time, Russia proposed buying back eight Tu-160s and three Tu-95MS 'Bears' manufactured in 1991, in the best technical condition, as well as 575 Kh-55 and Kh-55SM missiles (in total,

1,068 examples of various Kh-55 missiles remained in the Ukraine following the break-up of the USSR), documentation and ground equipment. Finally, at Yalta on 6 October 1999, Russia and Ukraine signed an agreement to sell the aircraft, according to Russian conditions. The contract's value of US$285 million was deducted from Ukraine's outstanding payments to Russia for the supply of natural gas.

On 20 October a group of Russian military experts went to the Ukraine to take possession of the aircraft, and on 5 November 1999 the first two ex-Ukrainian bombers – a Tu-160 and a Tu-95MS – landed at Engels. In a solemn welcoming ceremony, the pilots received gifts from the commander of Russian Long Range Aviation, Lieutenant General Mikhail Oparin, and the aircraft were dressed with Russian flags. During successive months, all eight 'Blackjacks' in the purchase agreement arrived at Engels, the last two on 21 February 2000. The Russians are pleased with the technical condition of the aircraft, although in 2001 all the Tu-160s will be overhauled at the Kazan factory.

Along with buying back the aircraft from Ukraine, the Russian Ministry of Defence signed a contract with the Kazan factory at the end of June 1999 to transfer to the

Above: Accompanied by Su-27 'Flankers' from the 'Russian Knights' aerobatic display team, Tu-160 Bort 01 thunders past the gallery at the Zhukovskiy air show. Such flypasts have become one of the highlights of the MAKS show, which has become the main occasion that a 'Blackjack' can be seen in public. The type has only ventured once to the West – to Paris in 1995 – perhaps indicative of the air of security that still surrounds this bomber or, more prosaically, a reflection of the huge logistic effort required to move the specialised ground equipment.

Above right: Bort 01 was the first aircraft delivered to the 121 GvTBAP at Engels, arriving in February 1992 to initiate Russian air force service with the type (at the time the other operational aircraft were all in the Ukraine). Visible in the background is a line of Myasishchev 3M 'Bisons' which had previously equipped the regiment. After a period in open storage, the 3Ms were sectioned in situ from 1997, and slowly carted away for scrap.

Right: When the wings are fully swept, the curving planform of the fixed wing portion combines with the straight-edged swivelling portion to highlight the prominent 'knuckle' which marks the wing pivot point. The two pivots form the tips of an immensely strong wing box section which lies at the heart of the aircraft's structure. All available portions of the aircraft, including inside the wing box, are used for fuel carriage.

armed forces a nearly-complete Tu-160 bomber that had been languishing at the factory for some time. This aircraft, number 8-02, took off from Kazan on 10 September 1999 and on 5 May 2000 it was commissioned into service with the Engels regiment as '07'.

Current organisation

Russian Long Range Aviation is now organised in the 37th Air Army of the Supreme High Command (with head-quarters in Moscow), itself consisting of five divisions: the 22nd and 73rd Divisions with Tu-160 'Blackjack' and Tu-95MS 'Bear-H' bombers, and the 31st, 55th and 326th Divisions with medium-range Tu-22M 'Backfire' bombers. The 22nd Donbass Red-Banner Heavy Bomber Air Division at Engels consists of three air regiments: the 121st

Sevastopol Heavy Bomber Regiment of Guards (Engels) with Tu-160 and Tu-95 bombers, the 182nd Heavy Bomber Regiment (Engels) with Tu-95s, and the 203rd Air Tanker Regiment of Guards (Ryazan) with Il-78 ' Midas' air tankers. After the incorporation of the eight aircraft from the Ukraine, Russian Tu-160s will be organised in a new regiment, which will probably be given the historical number of '184' (the former 184th Regiment of Ukrainian Air Forces at Pryluky was disbanded on 1 December 2000).

Russian long-range aircraft – in common with the nation's other military aircraft – fly very little. In 2000, the average annual flying time of a 37th Army pilot was merely 10 hours (down from 20 to 25 hours in previous years). Nevertheless, Russian strategic aircraft, for the first time in many years, have begun to venture on long-distance flights. On 25-26 June 1999, during Exercise Zapad-99 (West), a pair of Tu-160 bombers (one piloted by Igor Sitsky, the other by Vladimir Popov) made a 12-hour flight from Engels, along the Norwegian coast, reaching almost to Iceland. On the way back, one of the aircraft launched a Kh-55SM missile over the exercise ground in the Caspian Lowland. Exercises in April 2000 were restricted to Russian territory, but in February 2001 a pair of Tu-160s from Engels again travelled along the Norwegian coast and over the North Sea, approaching to within 150 km (81 nm) of Great Britain. On the way, they were intercepted by Norwegian F-16s and British Tornados.

The current number of Tu-160 bombers in the Russian Air Force – 15 – may increase over the next few years. According to basic directives of technological policy for 2001-2010, approved by the Russian Air Force in December 2000, Tu-160 production at Kazan will be continued –

although it is unclear if this means only that the three aircraft started before 1994 will be completed, or if new aircraft will be ordered. The transfer of at least two 'Blackjacks' from Zhukovskiy to the air forces is also under consideration. Little publicised talks about buying back three more bombers from Pryluky were undertaken, although the Ukraine eventually scrapped all of its remaining aircraft.

The total number of Tu-160 aircraft built to the end of 2000 was 35, comprising three prototypes built in Moscow and 32 series aircraft built in Kazan; another three (unfinished) aircraft are at the Kazan factory. Presently, 15 aircraft are at Engels and 11 have been scrapped by the Ukrainians: one was on display at Poltava museum in Ukraine since April 2000 (under international treaty, Ukraine was required to dispose of its strategic bombers by October 2001). Six aircraft are at the test centre at Zhukovskiy

Top: A Tu-160 nudges into the drogue trailed by an Il-78 'Midas' tanker. Il-78s form part of the same heavy bomber division as the Tu-160s, and their primary role is to extend the range of the Tu-160 and Tu-95MS 'Bear-H' strategic bombers.

Above: Ilya Muromets takes part in an air show flypast with the MiG-29s of the 'Swifts' aerobatic team.

Left: Bort 07 is the most recent aircraft to be delivered to the 121 GvTBAP, entering service with the Engels-based 'Blackjack' regiment in May 2000.

Ilya Muromets *demonstrates the intermediate wing sweep position. While Western observers have dismissed the Tu-160's low observable characteristics, Russian authorities claim that they are better than those of the B-1B, citing the blended wing/fuselage as being of low-RCS design. The large intakes would appear to be an obvious source of radar returns, but it has been suggested that there is some sort of radar blocker in front of the engine compressor face. In the Cold War scenario, low RCS was always of lesser concern to the Soviet Union, as the US did not have the same scale of multi-layered air defence system as employed by the USSR.*

(including four airworthy ones: two belonging to Tupolev and two to the air force). Another two airframes were intended for static and fatigue tests. One Tu-160 (the second series aircraft) crashed in March 1987 after suffering an engine fire soon after take-off from Zhukovskiy; the crew, commanded by Valeriy Pavlov, ejected and survived.

Non-nuclear 'Blackjack'

Modernisation of the aircraft, which was pointless when Russia had only six Tu-160s, may be justified for 15-plus examples. The upgrade would consist of extending service life, upgrading equipment and introducing new missiles. Tu-160 bombers are relatively young; the oldest of them were made just 10 years ago. Their service life was originally designed to be 20 years, but under this programme it would be doubled, allowing the aircraft to remain in service until at least 2030. Navigation, communication, self-defence and other systems would certainly be the subject of upgrades, too. The Kh-55SM missiles would be repaired and their service life prolonged.

The task formerly assigned to Tu-160s was nuclear attack in a global conflict, or nuclear deterrence (these aircraft are armed only with nuclear 200-kT Kh-55SM cruise missiles).

Aviation is the most effective means of power projection: a nuclear missile carried by a bomber can be launched to hit its target, or return to base in the bomb bay. Neither intercontinental ballistic missiles nor strategic nuclear submarines can achieve this.

Now that the Cold War is over, though, one vital potential application of Russian Long Range Aviation is participation in non-nuclear regional conflicts. For this purpose, the Tu-160s are to be armed with several new types of conventional weapons currently under test. Although new conventional missiles are being commissioned only now, work on them began much earlier, in the late 1980s. Added impetus came from the experience of Desert Storm operations in 1991 and from later operations of the US Air Force, which proved spectacularly the effectiveness of long-range aviation coupled with smart conventional weapons. All information about new missiles for the Tu-160 is vague, but it seems likely that at the end of October 1999 a decision was made to start series production of new Kh-101 and modernised Kh-555 missiles. Anatoliy Kornukov, commander in chief of the Russian Air Force, announced at a press conference on 11 January 2001 that a "modernised version of the Kh-55 missile with non-nuclear warhead" (i.e.,

'Blackjack' names

Some time ago, the Russians began to give names to their strategic aircraft. The first, at the beginning of 1995, were the aircraft with side numbers 05 and 06, named after mythical Russian popular hero *Ilya Muromets* (these aircraft were prepared for an air parade over Moscow on the occasion of the 50th anniversary of victory over Germany on 9 May 1945; aircraft No. 05 took part in the parade piloted by then-Commander In Chief of the Russian Air Force, Colonel General Piotr Deynekin, while 06 was a reserve aircraft). Subsequently, other aircraft received names: 01 (*Mikhail Gromov*), 02 (*Vasiliy Reshetnikov*) and 04 (*Ivan Yarigin*). Bort 05 was subsequently renamed *Alexander Golovanov*. 07 was named *Alexander Molodchiy*. At the time of writing, the aircraft from Ukraine had not been incorporated into service, so had not received names.

Above: **Alexander Molodchiy (07).**
Below: **Vasiliy Reshetnikov (02) at Engels.**

Above: **Ivan Yarigin (04) at Engels.**
Left: **Mikhail Gromov (01) with Kh-55SM cruise missile.**

Kh-555) would be launched for the first time in the same month.

Long-range stealthy cruise missile

The most important new weapon for the Tu-160 – the non-nuclear Kh-101 cruise missile developed by the Raduga design bureau – is now being tested and is scheduled to begin series production in 2003. The missile has a 400-kg (882-lb) high-explosive/penetrating warhead, and a total weight of 2200 to 2400 kg (4,850 to 5,290 lb). It is equipped with an electro-optical terrain-reference navigation system similar to that of the Kh-55 missile, as well as a TV seeker for terminal homing to ensure impact accuracy within 12 to 20 m (39 to 66 ft) (or, according to other sources, within 6 to 9 m/20 to 29 ft). Russians boast of the missile having an unusually small radar cross-section of about 0.01 m² (0.108 sq ft). Its flight profile varies from a minimum altitude of 30 to 70 m (98 to 230 ft) to a maximum of 6000 m (19,685 ft). Cruising speed is 190 to 200 m (623 to 656 ft) per second (Mach 0.57-0.60); maximum speed is 250 to 260 m (820 to 853 ft) per second (Mach 0.75-0.78). According to Russian sources, the range of the Kh-101 is 5000 to 5500 km (2,670 to 2,970 nm). A modernised Tu-160 could carry 12 Kh-101 missiles inside its weapon bays.

Successive new types of armament are coming into being, such as the Kh-555 missile, a variant of the Kh-55SM with a conventional warhead and a homing system borrowed from the Kh-101. Under development is a subsonic, low-altitude medium-range Kh-SD missile that also borrows the navigation and homing systems and onboard software of the Kh-101. The Kh-SD (Sredney Dalnosti, medium range) will have a launch weight of 1600 kg (5,250 lb) and will carry a conventional penetrating or cassette warhead. Work on this missile is much less advanced than that of the Kh-101 or Kh-555, and it will be developed only upon completion of the Kh-101 and will rely on Kh-101 elements. The Tu-160 will be able to carry up to 12 Kh-SD missiles (its size is similar to that of the current Kh-55).

Tu-160 versus B-1

The question of similarities between the Tu-160 'Blackjack' and the earlier American B-1B Lancer arises with the first glance at a Tu-160. The B-1A took off for the first time on 23 December 1974, but on 30 June 1977 then-US President Jimmy Carter decided to stop work on the aircraft and focus on the development of cruise missiles. When it became apparent that both types of weapon could be used jointly, in November 1979 the Americans began

If the conventional upgrade reaches fruition, the Tu-160 fleet can expect more flying as it trains for new roles.

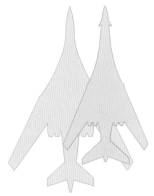

Above: Size comparison of the Tu-160 (red) and B-1B.

Below: Overwing spoilers dump lift on landing. Lightly laden, the Tu-160 can stop in about 1200 m (3,940 ft).

Hypersonic successors

Even at the beginning of the 1980s, as the Tu-160 was starting flight tests, work on its successor began. It was expected to be a hypersonic strike aircraft. Two successors to the Tu-160 were designed, named Tu-260 and Tu-360. Design work on the Tu-260 (or Aircraft 230) began in 1983 against an order for a Mach 4 bomber. According to the preliminary design completed in 1985, the Tu-260 was to be a tailless aircraft with delta-shaped wing. Design take-off weight was 180 tonnes (396,720 lb), including 106 tonnes (233,624 lb) of fuel for the four Soloviev D-80 turbojet engines. Flying at Mach 4 at an altitude of 25000 to 27000 m (82,020 to 88,580 ft), the Tu-260 was to cover a distance of 8000 to 10000 km (4,320 to 5,400 nm).

Unlike the Tu-260, which was designed for Mach 4, the Tu-360 (or Aircraft 360) was to reach Mach 6 and cover a distance of 15000 km (8,100 nm) carrying 10 tonnes (22,040 lb) of armament. The general layout of the Tu-360 was similar to that of the Tu-260, but its size was much greater, and it required a brand new propulsion arrangement. The maximum speed available from kerosene-fuelled engines is 4500 km/h (2,430 kt), above which cryogenic fuel is the optimum solution. As such, six variable-cycle turbojet/ramjet engines fuelled with liquid hydrogen were provided for the Tu-360. Design take-off weight of the aircraft was 350 tonnes (771,400 lb), empty weight was 200 tonnes (440,800 lb), length was 100 m (328 ft), wingspan was 40.7 m (133.53 ft) and lifting surface area was 1250 m² (13,455 sq ft). The required range could not be guaranteed: according to its design, the Tu-360 could manage only 9000 to 10000

Tupolev Tu-360 Mach 6 bomber

km (4,860 to 5,400 nm) at Mach 6. Armament was to be carried inside two weapon bays located in the wingroots. Crew consisted of two pilots.

In the first stage of development a small (70 to 90-tonne/154,280 to 198,360-lb) model of the Tu-360 was to be built, but work was stopped in the aftermath of the USSR's collapse and the prolonged economic crisis in Russia. Before financing ceased in 1992, a nickel-alloy wing torque box measuring 10 x 4 x 0.8 m (32.8 x 12.1 x 2.6 ft) was built, as were some elements of the fuselage, tanks for the liquid hydrogen and fuel pipes made of unique composite material.

The Tu-160's first outing to the West was in 1995, when a 'Blackjack' appeared at the Paris air show (below) masquerading as a Tu-160SK with wooden mock-up Burlak space vehicle. The concept was to provide a low-cost method of placing small satellites into orbit. The Burlak dummy was carried to the show in sections, stowed in the aircraft's weapons bays (above). The 'Tu-160SK' was subsequently displayed at Zhukovskiy (below right).

redesigning the B-1A into the cruise missile-carrying B-1B. The first B-1B prototype (converted from the second B-1A prototype) took off on 23 March 1983 and the first series aircraft flew on 18 October 1984. Production of the B-1B came to an end in 1988 after the construction of 100 aircraft.

There are many similarities between the B-1B and Tu-160: both have blended fuselage/wing centre-section airframes and variable-geometry wings. The interior arrangement of the fuselage is similar, with two armament chambers, as is the arrangement of engines in two double underwing nacelles near the fuselage, and the cruciform empennage.

There are also some significant differences. The Tu-160 is 27 per cent heavier than the B-1B and the thrust of its engines is 79 per cent greater. The B-1B is practically a subsonic aircraft (it can fly Mach 1.2 at high altitude, but this feature is not very useful). To reach its required maximum speed of 2200 km/h, the Tu-160 has adjustable air intakes (the non-adjustable intakes of the B-1B are simpler in design and have a smaller radar cross-section), its transverse section was made as small as possible, and the crew cockpit extends forward in front of the landing gear (the B-1B's cockpit is located above the landing gear bay and its fuselage is considerably thicker at this point). The 'Blackjack' has relatively small aerodynamic drag and radar cross-section, both believed to be much smaller than those of the B-1B. The Americans adapted their aircraft to carry armament on external pylons, whereas the Soviets located all the armament inside the airframe.

Moreover, the aircraft are optimised for different roles. The B-1A was designed as a specialised long-range penetration aircraft, attacking targets from low altitude with SRAMs carried in three small bays inside the fuselage. Later, with the advent of ALCMs, two front armament bays of the B-1B were interconnected to accommodate eight cruise missiles. The type's emphasis was changed again, to conventional mission enhancement, in August 1993 when Rockwell/Boeing initiated the Conventional Mission Upgrade Program (CMUP). In contrast, the 30-year-old Tu-160 has remained a nuclear strategic stand-off platform all its life, and only now is a Russian programme similar to the CMUP being implemented.

	Tu-160 'Blackjack'	B-1B Lancer
Wingspan, fully swept	116 ft 9.5 in (35.6 m)	78 ft 3 in (23.85 m)
Wingspan, fully spread	182 ft 9 in (55.7 m)	136 ft 8 in (41.66 m)
Length	177 ft 6 in (54.1 m)	145 ft 9 in (44.42 m)
Empty operating weight	257,941 lb (117000 kg)	192,000 lb (87090 kg)
Max. take-off weight	606,270 lb (275000 kg)	477,000 lb (216367 kg)
Thrust-to-weight ratio	36 per cent	26 per cent
Maximum Mach number	2.05	1.2
Maximum speed at s/l	556 kt (1030 km/h)	520 kt (963 km/h)
Maximum range	7,532 nm (13950 km)	about 6,500 nm (12040 km)

The Tu-160 and B-1B met face-to-face on 23-25 September 1994 in Poltava, Ukraine, during celebrations marking the 50th anniversary of Operation Frantic, the shuttle flights of American bombers between western Europe and the USSR (bombing Germany on the way).

'Blackjack' projects

Only the standard Tu-160 (Aircraft K, *izdeliye* 70) has so far been built, but a number of proposals have been made.
■ **Tu-160M:** this was to have been armed with two large supersonic missiles, one in each weapon bay, dating from the beginning of the 1980s. It is very probable that the Tu-160M was to be armed with two 3M25 Meteorit-A missiles (also known as Grom (Thunder), or as AS-X-19 'Koala' by NATO) developed by the NPO Mashinostroyeniya design bureau of Vladimir Chelomey. Work on Meteorit in ground-based (-N), submarine (-M) and airborne (-A) versions followed from a government resolution dated 9 December 1976, when the Tu-160 armament system was being formed and the dimensions of the weapon bays were known. Nevertheless, for unknown reasons, the missile was too long (12.8 m/41.99 ft), so the Tu-160M's bays had to be lengthened by the insertion of additional segments into the fuselage. The Meteorit-A missile, weighing 6300 kg (13,889 lb), was to fly up to 5000 km (2,670 nm) at 3000 km/h (1,620 kt) at an altitude of 22000 to 24000 m (72,180 to 78,740 ft). The homing system was similar to the Kh-55's, i.e., inertial with terrain-reference correction. The first test launching of a Meteorit missile from the ground took place on 20 May 1980, and from the air (a Tu-95MA test aircraft) on 11 January 1984. Unfortunately, the tests were unsuccessful from the beginning and work on Meteorit was soon stopped.
■ **Tu-160PP:** When designing the Tu-160, consideration was given to the problem of bomber survivability in a long, lonely flight across a zone of enemy fighter activity and air defence. Therefore, in 1979 the Tu-160PP (Postanovshchik Pomekh, jammer) was proposed, an escort aircraft designed to protect a group of bombers beyond the range of friendly fighters. In addition to a powerful set of elec-

tronic countermeasures, the aircraft was also to carry medium- and long-range AAMs. Work on the Tu-160PP did not proceed beyond the mock-up stage.

■ **Tu-160R:** projected strategic reconnaissance aircraft.

■ **Tu-160 Voron carrier:** In the wake of the capture in Vietnam of an American D-21 unpiloted reconnaissance vehicle, and its shipment to the USSR, in 1971 Tupolev's design team was ordered to build a Russian equivalent. The project's codename was Voron (Raven) and work on it continued for many years, with varying degrees of intensity. The Voron and its Tu-160 carrier (or maritime Tu-142) were to form a strategic reconnaissance system. After being launched from the carrier aircraft, the Voron was to accelerate to a cruising speed of 3500 to 3800 km/h (1,890 to 2,052 kt) at an altitude of 23000 to 24000 m (75,460 to 78,740 ft) by means of a powerful rocket engine suspended under its fuselage. Then, after dropping the empty accelerating engine, the vehicle was to cover a distance of 4600 km (2,484 nm) powered by an RD-012 ramjet engine. After completion of its task, the Voron was to parachute a capsule with reconnaissance material. The Voron vehicle was to be 13.06 m (42.85 ft) long, its design wingspan was 5.8 m (19.03), wing area was 37 m² (398 sq ft) and launch weight was 6300 kg (13,889 lb) (or 14120 kg/31,129 lb with the rocket booster).

Work continues on a strategic reconnaissance project incorporating a Tu-160 aircraft and a Voron unpiloted vehicle, but the vehicle is very different to its 1970s counterpart.

■ **Tu-160V:** The Tu-160V (Vodorod, hydrogen) of the 1980s was a project with a liquid hydrogen powerplant. Since cryogenic fuel needs much more space than kerosene, the Tu-160V's fuselage had to be enlarged to accommodate hydrogen tanks.

■ **Tu-161:** A long-range intercepting fighter was designed as a development of the Tu-160PP escort aircraft. It was intended to hunt transport aircraft carrying supplies from the United States to Europe, and was to patrol the Atlantic, receiving initial indications of targets from reconnaissance satellites. The Tu-161 was to be equipped with a powerful radar and 12 long-range air-to-air missiles.

■ **Tu-170:** In the late 1980s, the Soviets were designing a Tu-160 variant adapted for carrying only conventional weapons. The objective of this conversion was to circumvent the SALT-2 limitations. Material for the Tu-170 project is now being used for the current modernisation programme of Tu-160s.

Space launch

A possible civil application of the Tu-160 was presented at the Le Bourget air show in 1995. A Tu-160SK (the original designation was Tu-160SC, for space carrier, but it was somehow changed to SK) could act as the launch platform

Next-generation strategic bomber project

In addition to hypersonic aircraft, a new subsonic bomber similar to the American B-2 was designed. Preliminary work began in the mid-1980s on the B-90 (bomber for the 1990s), a subsonic flying wing with an aspect ratio of about 7, made of composite materials. High-bypass ratio (about 5-6:1) turbofans and the size of the airframe are intended to achieve a record range.

Keeping in mind the considerable parallelism between Tupolev's airliners and its bombers (e.g., the Tu-16 and Tu-104 of the 1950s, and the first designs of the Tu-160 and Tu-244), an examination of one of the developments of the new Tu-404 airliner could shed light on the new bomber. Tupolev presented the model at the Paris air show of 1993, showing a giant 700/850-seat airliner with a flying wing layout, having wide fuselage/wing centre-sections, moderately swept outer wings and a twin tailfin. The essential difference between the layouts of bomber and airliner is the arrangement of the engines. In the airliner they are located outside, above the rear part of fuselage, whereas in the bomber they will be installed inside and have air intakes arranged in the wing's leading edge. For shorter take-off and landing (or for increasing the take-off weight by 10-15 per cent), the engine nozzles will be flat with thrust vectoring. Analytic work on this bomber continues and its commissioning is expected after 2015.

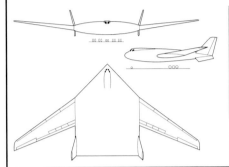

A model and drawing show the Tu-404 airliner study. A stealthy subsonic bomber project is thought to be based on a similar design.

for the Burlak space vehicle developed by the Raduga missile design bureau, analogous to the American Pegasus system. The Burlak was designed as an inexpensive low-Earth orbital vehicle able to carry a load of 825-1100 kg (1,819-2,425 lb), depending on the orbital altitude. The Burlak-M, with an additional hypersonic ramjet engine, was to carry 50 per cent more payload. Weighing 32000 kg (70,546 lb), the Burlak is suspended beneath the Tu-160's fuselage, between the engine nacelles. According to the design, the Tu-160SK is capable of carrying the Burlak 5500 km (2,970 nm) from the airfield. The space vehicle is launched at an altitude of 13500 m (44,291 ft) at a speed of 1800 km/h (972 kt). Work on this system continued for some time in co-operation with Germany (the vehicle was called Burlak-Diana), but this joint effort later ended.

In 1999 the project returned in another form. Three Ukrainian Tu-160s were to be sold to Platforms International Corporation of Mojave, in the US, to be used as a launch platform for a two-stage '2001' spacecraft developed from the Burlak. Other, heavier rockets were later suggested for the Tu-160, but eventually the whole project was abandoned. Tupolev still presents the Burlak at expositions, but practically no work on it is ongoing.

Piotr Butowski

Six Tu-160s are at Zhukovskiy, including four theoretically airworthy aircraft, of which two are earmarked for upgrade to operational status. These two remain derelict outside the Tupolev complex. The aircraft with its wings missing has the pointed tailplane fairing of early test aircraft. In President Putin's more hawkish Russia, the chances for further 'Blackjack' production, or at least the completion of three unfinished airframes still at Kazan, are high.

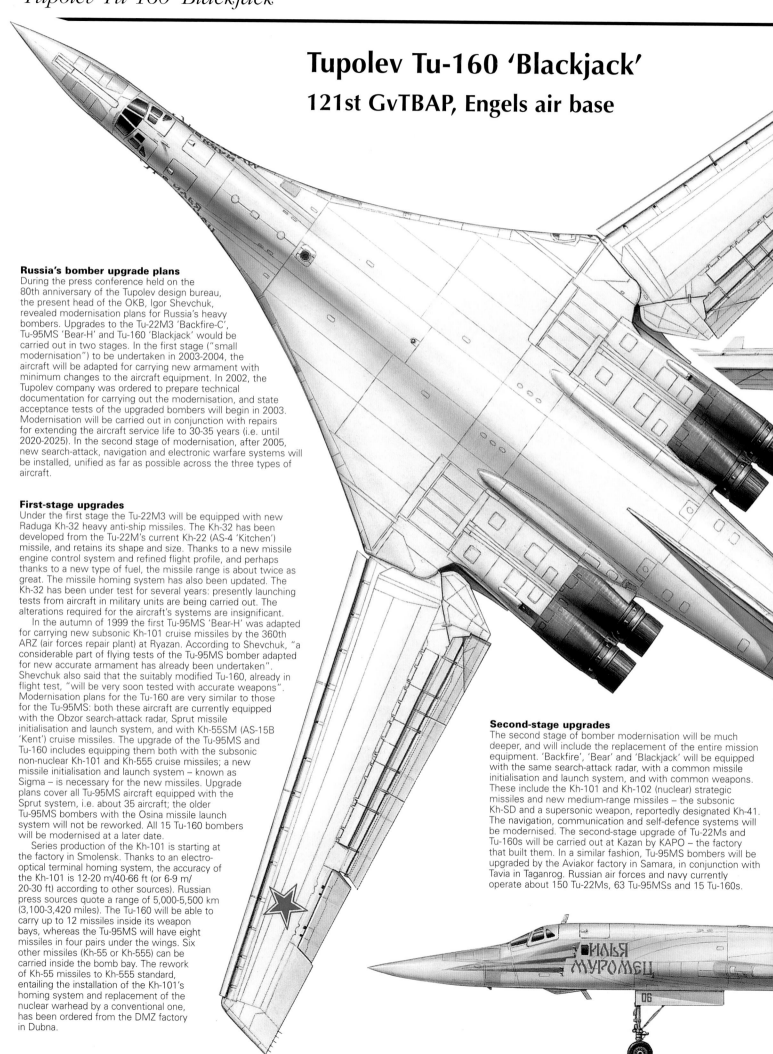

Tupolev Tu-160 'Blackjack'
121st GvTBAP, Engels air base

Russia's bomber upgrade plans

During the press conference held on the 80th anniversary of the Tupolev design bureau, the present head of the OKB, Igor Shevchuk, revealed modernisation plans for Russia's heavy bombers. Upgrades to the Tu-22M3 'Backfire-C', Tu-95MS 'Bear-H' and Tu-160 'Blackjack' would be carried out in two stages. In the first stage ("small modernisation") to be undertaken in 2003-2004, the aircraft will be adapted for carrying new armament with minimum changes to the aircraft equipment. In 2002, the Tupolev company was ordered to prepare technical documentation for carrying out the modernisation, and state acceptance tests of the upgraded bombers will begin in 2003. Modernisation will be carried out in conjunction with repairs for extending the aircraft service life to 30-35 years (i.e. until 2020-2025). In the second stage of modernisation, after 2005, new search-attack, navigation and electronic warfare systems will be installed, unified as far as possible across the three types of aircraft.

First-stage upgrades

Under the first stage the Tu-22M3 will be equipped with new Raduga Kh-32 heavy anti-ship missiles. The Kh-32 has been developed from the Tu-22M's current Kh-22 (AS-4 'Kitchen') missile, and retains its shape and size. Thanks to a new missile engine control system and refined flight profile, and perhaps thanks to a new type of fuel, the missile range is about twice as great. The missile homing system has also been updated. The Kh-32 has been under test for several years: presently launching tests from aircraft in military units are being carried out. The alterations required for the aircraft's systems are insignificant.

In the autumn of 1999 the first Tu-95MS 'Bear-H' was adapted for carrying new subsonic Kh-101 cruise missiles by the 360th ARZ (air forces repair plant) at Ryazan. According to Shevchuk, "a considerable part of flying tests of the Tu-95MS bomber adapted for new accurate armament has already been undertaken". Shevchuk also said that the suitably modified Tu-160, already in flight test, "will be very soon tested with accurate weapons". Modernisation plans for the Tu-160 are very similar to those for the Tu-95MS: both these aircraft are currently equipped with the Obzor search-attack radar, Sprut missile initialisation and launch system, and with Kh-55SM (AS-15B 'Kent') cruise missiles. The upgrade of the Tu-95MS and Tu-160 includes equipping them both with the subsonic non-nuclear Kh-101 and Kh-555 cruise missiles; a new missile initialisation and launch system – known as Sigma – is necessary for the new missiles. Upgrade plans cover all Tu-95MS aircraft equipped with the Sprut system, i.e. about 35 aircraft; the older Tu-95MS bombers with the Osina missile launch system will not be reworked. All 15 Tu-160 bombers will be modernised at a later date.

Series production of the Kh-101 is starting at the factory in Smolensk. Thanks to an electro-optical terminal homing system, the accuracy of the Kh-101 is 12-20 m/40-66 ft (or 6-9 m/ 20-30 ft) according to other sources). Russian press sources quote a range of 5,000-5,500 km (3,100-3,420 miles). The Tu-160 will be able to carry up to 12 missiles inside its weapon bays, whereas the Tu-95MS will have eight missiles in four pairs under the wings. Six other missiles (Kh-55 or Kh-555) can be carried inside the bomb bay. The rework of Kh-55 missiles to Kh-555 standard, entailing the installation of the Kh-101's homing system and replacement of the nuclear warhead by a conventional one, has been ordered from the DMZ factory in Dubna.

Second-stage upgrades

The second stage of bomber modernisation will be much deeper, and will include the replacement of the entire mission equipment. 'Backfire', 'Bear' and 'Blackjack' will be equipped with the same search-attack radar, with a common missile initialisation and launch system, and with common weapons. These include the Kh-101 and Kh-102 (nuclear) strategic missiles and new medium-range missiles – the subsonic Kh-SD and a supersonic weapon, reportedly designated Kh-41. The navigation, communication and self-defence systems will be modernised. The second-stage upgrade of Tu-22Ms and Tu-160s will be carried out at Kazan by KAPO – the factory that built them. In a similar fashion, Tu-95MS bombers will be upgraded by the Aviakor factory in Samara, in conjunction with Tavia in Taganrog. Russian air forces and navy currently operate about 150 Tu-22Ms, 63 Tu-95MSs and 15 Tu-160s.

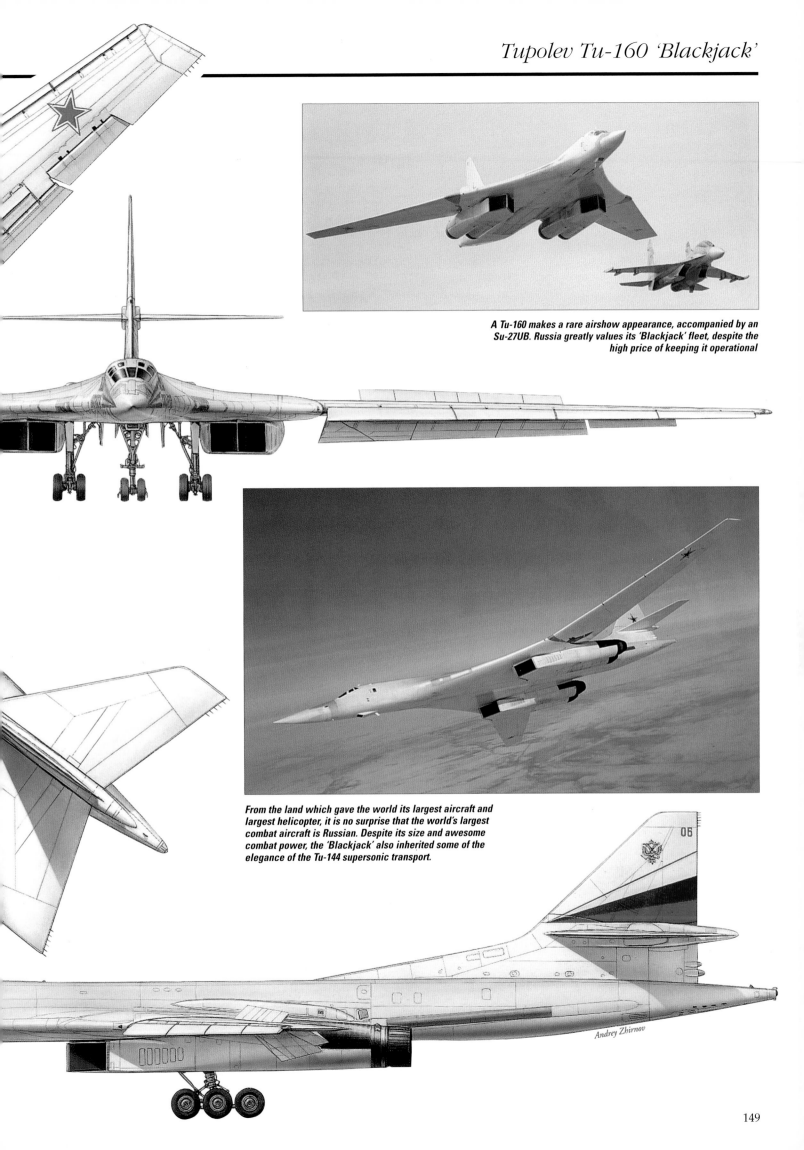

A Tu-160 makes a rare airshow appearance, accompanied by an Su-27UB. Russia greatly values its 'Blackjack' fleet, despite the high price of keeping it operational

From the land which gave the world its largest aircraft and largest helicopter, it is no surprise that the world's largest combat aircraft is Russian. Despite its size and awesome combat power, the 'Blackjack' also inherited some of the elegance of the Tu-144 supersonic transport.

Andrey Zhirnov

The primary weapon of the Tu-160 is the Raduga Kh-55SM cruise missile (AS-15B 'Kent'), of which up to 12 can be carried on two six-round MKU6-5U rotary launchers. The missiles are carried with their wings folded back and their tailfins folded. The missile is powered by an R95-300 turbofan which is lowered from the rear fuselage after launch. The warhead has a yield of 200 kT. Test and training launches are nearly always tracked by an Il-76SKIP aircraft. Five of these 'airborne measuring and control station' aircraft are in use, fitted with Shmel radar in a 'toadstool' rotodome and superficially resembling the A-50 'Mainstay'. In line with the Tu-160's projected conventional roles, Raduga has developed the Kh-555, a version with a conventional warhead. Whether production missiles would be newly built or converted from Kh-55SMs is unknown. Large numbers of the latter are held by Russia, which purchased the entire stock held by the Ukraine.

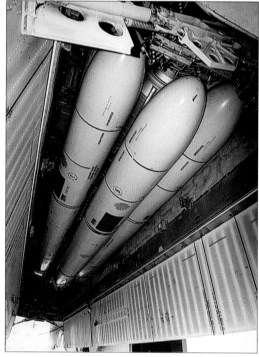

This is the standard Kh-55SM, shown in flight configuration with its turbofan, wings and control fins deployed. Note the conformal fuel tank which can be scabbed on to the side.

The Kh-65SE is a proposed version of the Kh-55 associated with the Su-34/35, but has 'Blackjack' potential. This version is an anti-ship weapon with active radar seeker and conventional warhead.

The Tu-160 can carry 24 Kh-15s on four MKU6-1U launchers. This weapon is available in either standard form with a 350-kT nuclear warhead, or Kh-15P conventional anti-radiation configuration.

Tu-160 'Blackjack' technical details

Only one standard version of the Tu-160 has been manufactured, the other versions being no more than projects. The Tu-160 is a four-engined, all-metal, low-winged monoplane with variable-geometry wings. The **fuselage** and central wing section form a common shape with appended empennage and movable wing panels. The long, narrow fuselage/wing centre-section (LERX type), blended for maximum radar deflection, is subdivided into four compartments: nose (radar unit, crew cockpit and nosewheel undercarriage unit), front (fuel tanks and front weapon bay), centre (main undercarriage units, engine nacelles and rear weapon bay) and rear (fuel tanks and equipment).

The aircraft can carry 148000 kg (326,279 lb) of **fuel** in the 13 tanks installed inside the fuselage/wing centre-section and in the movable wing panels. The fuel transfer system is used to balance the aircraft when accelerating to supersonic speed. The retractable probe of the inflight-refuelling system is mounted in the upper part of the aircraft's nose.

Located inside the nose is the Obzor-K (Survey) **radar**, used for ground observation as well as detection of air targets. Another radar – Sopka (Hill) – used for terrain following when flying at low altitude is installed below the same fairing. Under the front fuselage is a forward-looking OPB-15T optical sight and video. The aircraft is equipped with the K-042K astro-inertial long-range navigation system that plots the current position on the map.

Weapons are carried inside the fuselage in two tandem **weapon bays**, each 11.28 m (37.00 ft) long and 1.92 m (6.29 ft) wide. Basic armament comprises six (maximum 12) Raduga Kh-55SM (AS-15B 'Kent') cruise missiles installed on six-round MKU6-5U revolving launchers (MKU stands for Mnogozaryadnaya Katapultnaya Ustanovka, multi-round catapulting device). Each missile is dropped by pneumatic-hydraulic catapult from the lowest point of the revolving drum, and then fired. The drum is then revolved by 60° into position for the next launch. An alternative weapon is the Raduga Kh-15 (AS-16 'Kickback') short-range attack missile, but reportedly it has not been implemented on service aircraft. Twenty-four Kh-15 missiles can be carried in four short MKU6-1U revolving drums (in tandem pairs). The Tu-160 is theoretically capable of carrying 40000 kg (88,183 lb) of free-falling nuclear or conventional bombs.

A new airborne **navigation/attack** system – Sprut-SM (Octopus) – had to be developed for the strategic Kh-55SM. Sprut-SM includes the computerised SURO-70 (Sistema Upravleniya Raketnym Oruzhyem, missile weapon control system) sub-system that exactly aligns the co-ordination axes of the inertial navigation systems of both aircraft and missile. It also generates a digital map of the terrain along the planned itinerary of the missile, which is transmitted from the aircraft to the missile prior to launching.

For the first time, Russian aircraft were equipped with the Sigma pre-flight data management system. About 100 **computers** are used to control various onboard systems (including 12 computers for the fire control system). A single central computer concept was considered and abandoned during the course of aircraft design, the designers opting instead for a multi-computer system which was considered to be "more reliable".

From the front the blending of the fuselage and wing is apparent, providing the Tu-160 with an enormous internal fuel volume despite its slender lines. Like the B-1B, the shape is optimised for low radar cross section.

Tu-160 'Blackjack' specification

Dimensions
Wingspan: 35.6 m (116 ft 9.5 in) at 65° sweep, 50.7 m (166 ft 4 in) at 35° sweep, and 55.7 m (182 ft 9 in) at 20° sweep
Maximum length: 54.1 m (177 ft 6 in)
Maximum height: 13.1 m (42 ft 11 in)
Length of engine nacelle: 13.28 m (43 ft 7 in)
Tailplane span: 13.25 m (43 ft 6 in)
Wing area: 293.15 m² (3,155.4 sq ft) fully spread, 232 m² (2,497.2 sq ft) fully swept
Aspect ratio: 10.58 fully spread, 5.46 fully swept
Sweepback: fixed at 20°, 35° or 65°

Weights
Empty operational: 117000 kg (257,937 lb)
Maximum take-off: 275000 kg (606,261 lb)
Maximum landing: 155000 kg (341,710 lb)

Performance
Maximum operating Mach number: Mach 2.05
Maximum speed: 2200 km/h (1,188 kt)
Maximum speed at sea level: 1030 km/h (556 kt)
Cruise Mach number: Mach 0.77
Minimum speed at 140000 kg (308,642 lb): 260 km/h (140 kt)
Take-off distance: 900 and 2200 m (2,953 and 7,218 ft) at 150 and 275 tonnes (330,600 and 606,100 lb) weight, respectively
Landing distance: 1200 and 1600 m (3,937 and 5,250 ft) at 140 and 155 tonnes (308,560 and 341,620 lb) weight, respectively
Maximum climb rate: 4200 m (13,780 ft) per minute
Practical ceiling: 15600 m (51,181 ft)
G limit: 2
Practical range without inflight refuelling, at Mach 0.77, carrying six Kh-55SM missiles dropped mid-range: 12300 km (6,641 nm), with 5 per cent fuel reserve
Maximum theoretical range: 13950 km (7,533 nm)
Maximum duration without inflight refuelling: 15 hours
Combat radius at Mach 1.5: 2000 km (1,080 nm)

Above and right: The tail section houses a considerable array of rear-facing antennas for the passive warning system and active jamming system. The small dark panels are three-round APP-50 chaff/flare dispensers. Scabbed on to the side of the rear fuselage is a fairing which may be a side-facing antenna, or a waveguide/conduit serving the tail-mounted jammers and antennas. In the underside of the tailcone is the housing for the brake chutes, seen with doors open above. There is no rudder, directional control being provided by an all-moving fin which pivots above the tailplane.

Wing structure and control surfaces

The main structural strength element of the aircraft is the central wing stringer, 12.4 m (40.68 ft) long and 2.1 m (6.89 ft) wide, that connects both wing-pivoting nodes. The stringer is made of two halves, upper and lower, milled of titanium alloy and welded together in a vacuum chamber according to a unique engineering process. Outer, movable wing panels are set for three manually-selected positions: 20° for take-off and landing, 35° for Mach 0.77 cruising speed, and 65° for supersonic flight. Each movable wing panel has four-section leading-edge slats, a three-section double-slotted trailing-edge flap, and an aileron. Five-section spoilers are installed ahead of the flaps.

With the wings fully swept, the inner section of each three-section trailing-edge flap is raised to become a large aerodynamic fence between the wing and the fixed glove to improve directional stability. A mid-mounted slab (taileron) tailplane may be deflected symmetrically or differentially. The all-moving upper section of the tailfin, above the tailplane, forms the rudder. The flight control system is quadruple fly-by-wire, and has a stand-by mechanical mode. The usefulness of a mechanical control system is considerably limited, since the aircraft is statically unstable.

This Tu-160 (above) is seen with all its wing surfaces fully deployed. The four-sections of leading-edge slats (right) extend across nearly the full span of the pivoting wing section. The three sections of double-slotted flaps (left) are augmented by drooping ailerons (further outboard) and five sections of spoilers immediately ahead of the flaps. The ailerons are only used for roll control at low speeds: at high speed differential tailplane movement is employed.

Unique to the 'Blackjack' is the unusual folding inner portion of the pivoting wing section trailing edge (above left). With the wing fully forward the section lies flat to fill in the 'missing' segment of the trailing edge, but with the wing swept back it is raised to the vertical to provide additional directional stability (above right).

Crew accommodation

The crew of four is seated in the aircraft's nose in a common pressurised cockpit. The commander-pilot occupies the front left seat, with the co-pilot to his right. The rear seats are occupied by the navigator/offensive weapons operator and the navigator/EW and communications operator. All the crew have Zvezda/Tomilino K-36LM 'zero-zero' ejection seats. Access to the cockpit is via the nosewheel undercarriage bay.

The K-36LM ejection seats can be removed through the upper escape hatches (right), using a hoist (below). Note the doors covering the retractable refuelling probe, centrally mounted forward of the windscreens.

Above and left: An OPB-15T optical bombing sight iand video are mounted under the forward fuselage, covered by a drop-down window fairing.

Right: The Tu-160 crew accesses the aircraft by climbing a ladder to a hatch in the nosewheel bay. A narrow corridor leads forward to the flight postions

Powerplant

The propulsion system consists of four NK-32 (or *izdeliye* R) engines designed by Nikolay Kuznetsov's design team at Kuibyshev (now Samara), in widely separated pairs under the wing centre-section, with the nacelles protruding far beyond the wing trailing edge. The NK-32 is a turbofan with a bypass ratio 1.36:1, compression of 28.2 and temperature at the turbine entry of 1630° K (1357° C/2,473° F). Maximum thrust is 137.3 kN (30,872 lb) dry or 245.18 kN (55,140 lb) with full afterburning. The engine weighs 3650 kg (8,047 lb), its inlet diameter is 1.455 m (4.77 ft), and its overall length is 7.453 m (24.45 ft). The engine has three shafts, with a three-stage low-pressure compressor at the front, aft of which is a five-stage medium-pressure compressor followed by a seven-stage high-pressure compressor. The low- and medium-pressure turbines are single-stage, whereas the high-pressure turbine has two stages. The engine has automatically adjustable nozzles.

Above: The nozzles of each NK-32 engine are enormous to handle the huge mass flow. The area is automatically controlled for optimum thrust at all settings and conditions.

Left: Access to the engines for in situ maintenance is easy thanks to hinged cowling panels. These also facilitate removal of the engines.

Along with the Tu-22M3's NK-25, the NK-32 is the most powerful engine to have been installed in a combat aircraft. The nacelles project far behind the wing trailing edge to maintain the centre of gravity. Electric controls are fitted, with hydromechanical back-up, although a FADEC (full authority digital engine control) system is under review.

This cutaway exhibit shows the inner workings of the NK-32. The combustion chamber and afterburner are optimised to produce maximum thrust, but at minimum temperature to reduce IR signature, and to produce no smoke. It has been reported that the first compressor stage is designed for minimum radar reflectivity to reduce frontal RCS.

Undercarriage

The tricycle landing gear is retracted and lowered hydraulically. The front double-wheel leg (far left) retracts aft; its wheels measure 1080 x 400 mm (42.5 x 15.7 in). The main landing gear (below and left) consists of two six-wheel bogies (three tandem pairs), retracted into the mid-wing, between the fuselage and engine nacelles. The main wheels measure 1260 x 425 mm (48.4 x 16.7 in), and the track is relatively narrow, only 5.4 m (17.72 ft); the wheelbase is 17.88 m (58.66 ft). Three braking parachutes with a total surface area of 105 m² (1,130 sq ft) are located in the tail.

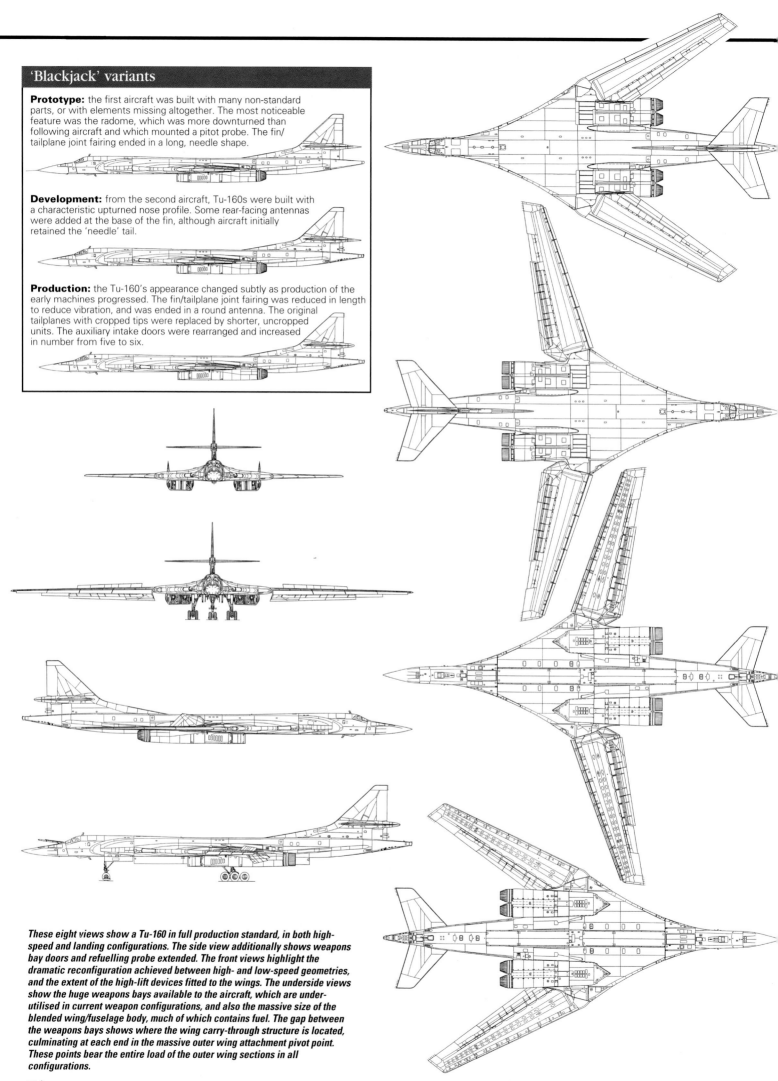

'Blackjack' variants

Prototype: the first aircraft was built with many non-standard parts, or with elements missing altogether. The most noticeable feature was the radome, which was more downturned than following aircraft and which mounted a pitot probe. The fin/tailplane joint fairing ended in a long, needle shape.

Development: from the second aircraft, Tu-160s were built with a characteristic upturned nose profile. Some rear-facing antennas were added at the base of the fin, although aircraft initially retained the 'needle' tail.

Production: the Tu-160's appearance changed subtly as production of the early machines progressed. The fin/tailplane joint fairing was reduced in length to reduce vibration, and was ended in a round antenna. The original tailplanes with cropped tips were replaced by shorter, uncropped units. The auxiliary intake doors were rearranged and increased in number from five to six.

These eight views show a Tu-160 in full production standard, in both high-speed and landing configurations. The side view additionally shows weapons bay doors and refuelling probe extended. The front views highlight the dramatic reconfiguration achieved between high- and low-speed geometries, and the extent of the high-lift devices fitted to the wings. The underside views show the huge weapons bays available to the aircraft, which are under-utilised in current weapon configurations, and also the massive size of the blended wing/fuselage body, much of which contains fuel. The gap between the weapons bays shows where the wing carry-through structure is located, culminating at each end in the massive outer wing attachment pivot point. These points bear the entire load of the outer wing sections in all configurations.

Bort 01/ Mikhail Gromov Gromov, after whom the LII is also named, was a famous pilot and Hero of the Soviet Union. The Tu-160 was named on the day of his 100th birthday in 1999.

Bort 02/ Vasiliy Reshetnikov Bort 02 is named for Reshetnikov, who was an influential commander of Long-Range Aviation.

Bort 04/ Ivan Yarygin Yarigin was a wrestler who took Olympic Gold in 1972 and 1976, and many other titles. He was proclaimed by the Soviets as the strongest man in the world.

Bort 05/ Aleksandr Golovanov Bort 05 was renamed after Golovanov, who was commander of Long-Range Aviation during 1942-1944, and 1946-48.

Borts 05-06/ Ilya Muromets The name of the hero of Russian folklore – who protected the nation from all kinds of enemies – adorned two Tu-160s, although 05 was later renamed.

Bort 29 This prototype aircraft has appeared sev[...] all-over white. During peacetime nose art has bee[...] War of 1941-45 and, more recently, in Afghanista[...] fingers', as the Russian expression goes. In 1995[...]

Bort 07/ Aleksandr Molodchiy The last aircr[...] legendary bomber pilot and Hero of the Soviet Un[...] sport a Russian flag and double eagle insignia on[...]

Tu-160 'Blackjack' cutaway

1 Glass-fibre radome
2 Flight refuelling probe, extended
3 Probe housing
4 Navigation/attack radar scanner
5 Scanner tracking mechanism
6 Sopka terrain-following radar scanner
7 Radar mounting bulkhead
8 Obzor-K radar equipment
9 Windscreen panels
10 Instrument panel shroud
11 Conventional control column and rudder pedals actuating quadruplex digital fly-by-wire flight control system
12 Cockpit sloping front pressure bulkhead
13 OPB-15 optical bombsight in ventral fairing
14 First pilot's Zvezda K-36DM ejection seat
15 Pilot's jettisonable roof hatches
16 Co-pilot's ejection seat
17 Upper VHF antenna
18 Rear crew member's seat jettisonable hatches with rear-view periscopes
19 Electronic warfare officer's ejection seat
20 Crew galley unit
21 Navigator/bombardier's ejection seat
22 Instrument consoles, port and starboard
23 Nosewheel leg-mounted taxiing lights
24 Lower VHF antenna

25 Nose undercarriage leg struts with hydraulic steering jacks
26 Twin nosewheels, aft retracting
27 Nosewheel spray/debris deflectors
28 Rear breaker strut
29 Hydraulic retraction jack
30 Avionics equipment racks, port and starboard, foldaway supernumerary seat and crew rest bunk between
31 Flush antennas
32 Cockpit rear pressure bulkhead
33 Crew entry hatch via nosewheel bay, open
34 Toilet
35 Nose undercarriage wheel bay
36 Weapons bay retractable spoilers
37 Forward weapons bay doors
38 Forward fuselage chine fairing
39 Port forward/oblique EW antenna
40 Port forward fuselage integral fuel tank
41 Starboard undercarriage six-wheel bogie
42 Weapons bay door actuator
43 Forward weapons bay, six Kh-55SM on rotary launcher
44 GPS antenna
45 Starboard forward oblique EW antenna

46 Starboard forward fuselage integral fuel tank
47 Starboard engine air intakes
48 Centre-section wing pivot box carry-through structure
49 Wing pivot bearing
50 Wing sweep actuator
51 Variable-sweep wing sealing fairing
52 Starboard position light
53 Starboard wing integral fuel tank
54 Four-segment leading-edge slat
55 Slat guide rails
56 Starboard navigation light
57 Wing fully forward, 20° sweep position
58 Starboard wing in cruise position, 30° sweep
59 Starboard drooping aileron
60 Three-segment double-slotted flap
61 Spoiler panels (five)
62 Slat guide rails and screw jacks
63 Wing root segment folded to vertical fence position
64 Starboard engine nacelles
65 Main undercarriage stowage fairing
66 Starboard engine exhaust nozzles
67 Starboard wing in maximum sweep position, 65°
68 Fin root fairing
69 Flush antenna panels
70 Lower fin segment
71 Rudder hydraulic actuators
72 Rudder pivot mounting
73 Tailplane hydraulic actuators

74 Tailplane bearing and sealing plate
75 All-moving upper fin segment/rudder
76 Starboard all-moving taileron
77 Fin tip antenna fairing
78 Titanium honeycomb core control surface construction
79 Rear EW antenna
80 Navigational antennas
81 IFF antenna
82 Tail navigation light
83 RWR antenna
84 Static dischargers
85 Port all-moving taileron
86 Chaff/flare launchers
87 Brake parachute housing and doors
88 Aft equipment bay
89 Fin/tailplane mounting main bulkheads
90 Aft fuselage integral fuel tanks
91 Rear weapons bay door actuator
92 External cable duct
93 Rear weapons bay doors
94 Auxiliary power unit (APU)
95 Rear weapons bay with 12 Kh-15 missiles on dual tandem rotary launchers

96 Electrical systems equipment
97 Main undercarriage stowed position
98 Port hydraulic reservoir
99 Wing pivot box integral fuel tank
100 Main undercarriage pivot mounting
101 Hydraulic retraction jack
102 Flap and slat drive unit
103 Telescopic flap and slat drive shaft
104 Port wing root seal/vertical fence, retracted position
105 Engine fuel control equipment
106 Bleed air system pre-cooler
107 Engine accessory equipment gearboxes
108 Fire suppression bottles
109 Trud/Samara NK-32 afterburning turbofan engines
110 Engine bay centre keel
111 Exhaust nozzle actuators
112 Variable-area exhaust nozzles
113 Port wing fully swept position
114 Three-segment double-slotted trailing-edge flap

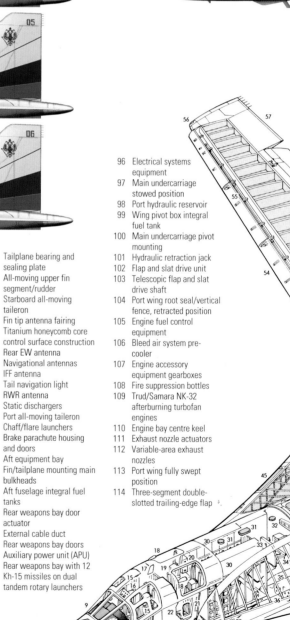

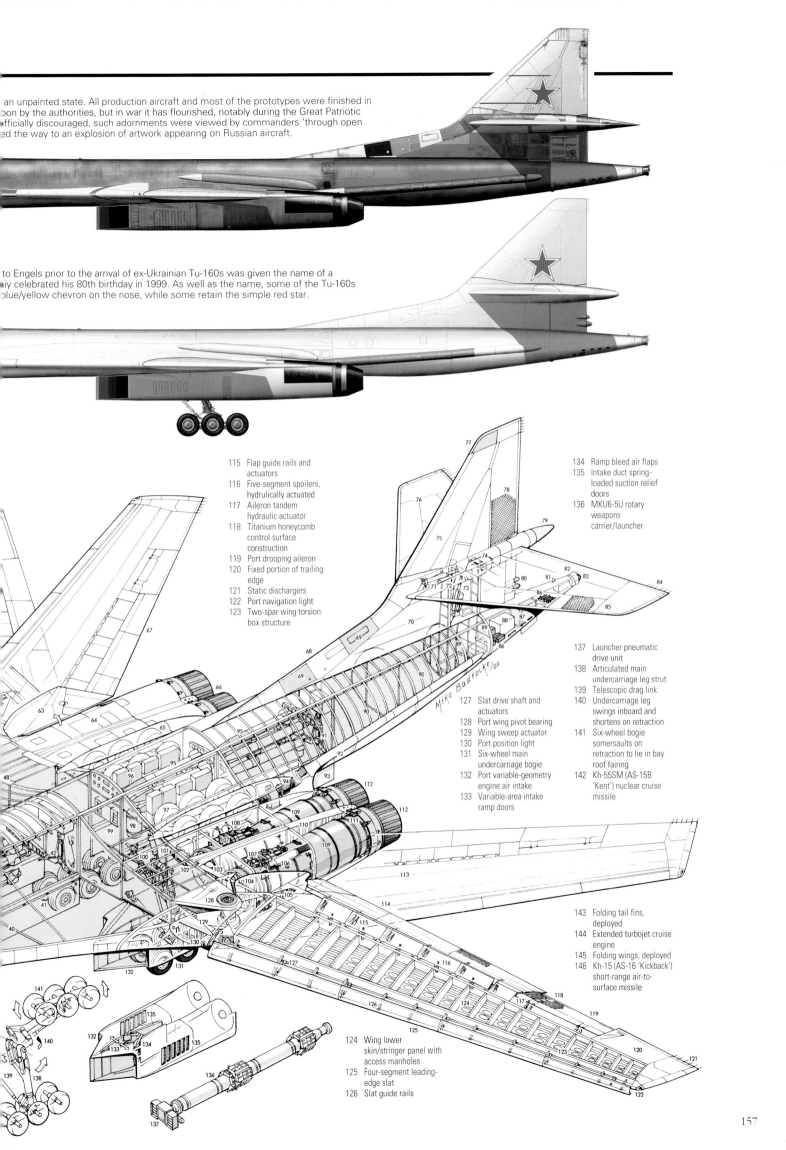

an unpainted state. All production aircraft and most of the prototypes were finished in
~~on~~ by the authorities, but in war it has flourished, notably during the Great Patriotic
~~ffi~~cially discouraged, such adornments were viewed by commanders 'through open
~~ed~~ the way to an explosion of artwork appearing on Russian aircraft.

~~to~~ Engels prior to the arrival of ex-Ukrainian Tu-160s was given the name of a
~~ily~~ celebrated his 80th birthday in 1999. As well as the name, some of the Tu-160s
~~blue~~/yellow chevron on the nose, while some retain the simple red star.

115 Flap guide rails and
actuators
116 Five-segment spoilers,
hydraulically actuated
117 Aileron tandem
hydraulic actuator
118 Titanium honeycomb
control surface
construction
119 Port drooping aileron
120 Fixed portion of trailing
edge
121 Static dischargers
122 Port navigation light
123 Two-spar wing torsion
box structure

127 Slat drive shaft and
actuators
128 Port wing pivot bearing
129 Wing sweep actuator
130 Port position light
131 Six-wheel main
undercarriage bogie
132 Port variable-geometry
engine air intake
133 Variable-area intake
ramp doors

134 Ramp bleed air flaps
135 Intake duct spring-
loaded suction relief
doors
136 MKU6-5U rotary
weapons
carrier/launcher

137 Launcher pneumatic
drive unit
138 Articulated main
undercarriage leg strut
139 Telescopic drag link
140 Undercarriage leg
swings inboard and
shortens on retraction
141 Six-wheel bogie
somersaults on
retraction to lie in bay
roof fairing
142 Kh-55SM (AS-15B
'Kent') nuclear cruise
missile

143 Folding tail fins,
deployed
144 Extended turbojet cruise
engine
145 Folding wings, deployed
146 Kh-15 (AS-16 'Kickback')
short-range air-to-
surface missile

124 Wing lower
skin/stringer panel with
access manholes
125 Four-segment leading-
edge slat
126 Slat guide rails

Mike Badrocke/00

INDEX

The publishers would like to thank the following individuals and organisations for their assistance in providing photographs for this book.

Front cover: Sergey Skrynnikov (three), Anatoliy Andreyev. **6-7:** US Navy, Sergey Skrynnikov. **8:** Piotr Butowski (four). **9:** via Terry Panopalis, Sergey Skrynnikov. **10:** Mikhail Kuznetsov, Piotr Butowski, USAF. **11:** Hugo Mambour, David Donald, Sergey Skrynnikov. **12:** Gary Bihary, USAF, David Donald, Cees-Jan van der Ende. **13:** Sergey Skrynnikov (two), Eugène Gadet (two). **14:** USAF, Piotr Butowski (two). **15:** Piotr Butowski (six). **16:** Piotr Butowski (two), Mikhail Kuznetsov. **17:** Sergey Skrynnikov, Hugo Mambour, Eugène Gadet. **20:** Lt Col Anatoliy Artemyev, Jeremy Flack/API. **21:** Sergey Skrynnikov, Piotr Butowski. **22:** Aerospace, US Navy. **23:** Aerospace, US Navy. **24:** Aerospace, via Sergey Skrynnikov, Cees-Jan van der Ende, Hugo Mambour. **25:** Victor Drushlyakov, via Eric Hehs/Code One. **26:** Gennadiy Petrov, Piotr Butowski. **27:** US Navy, Jeremy Flack/API. **28:** USAF, Alexey Mikheyev. **29:** Sergey Skrynnikov, MoD. **30:** Indian Navy (two), via Terry Panopalis. **31:** Indian Navy, Simon Watson. **32:** US Navy, Victor Drushlyakov. **33:** Piotr Butowski, Alexey Mikheyev. **34:** Piotr Butowski (two), Sergey Sergeyev via Piotr Butowski. **35:** Victor Drushlyakov, Piotr Butowski. **36:** Piotr Butowski, US Navy (two). **37:** Victor Drushlyakov, Alexey Mikheyev. **38:** Lt Col Anatoliy Artemyev (two), Gennadiy Petrov, Piotr Butowski (two), Andrey Salnikov. **39:** Victor Drushlyakov, Lt Col Anatoliy Artemyev (nine), Piotr Butowski. **40:** Victor Drushlyakov, Jeremy Flack/API (two). **41:** Victor Drushlyakov, Lt Col Anatoliy Artemyev (two). **42-43:** Piotr Butowski, Sergey Skrynnikov. **44:** Sergey Skrynnikov, Sergey Skrinnikov via Jon Lake, Swedish Air Force. **45:** Swedish Air Force (two), Aerospace. **46:** US Navy, Swedish Air Force (two). **47:** Hugo Mambour, Anatoliy Artemyev, US Navy, Sergey Skrynnikov. **48:** Swedish Air Force, Sergey Skrynnikov, US Navy, Aerospace. **49:** Swedish Air Force (three), Anatoliy Artemyev. **50:** Sergey Skrynnikov, via Jon Lake. **51:** via Jon Lake, Anatoliy Artemyev, Sergey Skrynnikov. **52:** Anatoliy Artemyev (three), Aerospace (three). **53:** Sergey Skrynnikov, Swedish Air Force, Anatoliy Artemyev. **54:** Swedish Air Force (two), Alexey Mikheyev. **55:** Swedish Air Force (three). **56:** US Navy, Swedish Air Force (two). **57:** Swedish Air Force, Anatoliy Artemyev, Sergey Skrynnikov. **58:** Gennady Petrov, TASS, Anatoliy Artemyev (two), Aerospace. **59:** Swedish Air Force, US Navy, Anatoliy Artemyev (two). **60:** Swedish Air Force (two), Anatoliy Artemyev, Peter Batuev Collection. **61:** via Jon Lake, Anatoliy Artemyev, Peter Batuev Collection (two). **62:** Peter Batuev Collection (two), Anatoliy Artemyev (two). **64:** via Sergey Skrynnikov, Anatoliy Artemyev (two). **65:** Anatoliy Artemyev, US Navy (three). **66:** US Navy (two), Aerospace, Anatoliy Artemyev. **67:** MoD, Anatoliy Artemyev, Swedish Air Force (two). **68:** Sergey Skrynnikov via Jon Lake, US Navy (two), Peter Batuev Collection. **70:** Swedish Air Force (two). **71:** US Navy via Jon Lake, via Jon Lake, Swedish Air Force. **72:** via Jon Lake, Hugo Mambour, Anatoliy Artemyev. **73:** LII via Sergey Skrynnikov, Sergey Skrynnikov via Jon Lake, NFA Press Agency (two). **74:** via Jon Lake (two), NFA Press Agency. **75:** via Jon Lake (three), Aerospace. **76:** USAF, Aerospace (two). **77:** Kondratenkov/Petrochenko, Sergey Skrynnikov, Alexey Mikheyev. **78:** Aerospace (two), Kondratenkov/Petrochenko, Sergey Skrynnikov. **79:** Swedish Air Force, Aerospace (three), Kondratenkov/Petrochenko (two), Alexey Mikheyev. **81:** Alexey Mikheyev. **82-83:** Hugo Mambour, Swedish Air Force, Eric Bannwarth. **84:** Aerospace. **85:** Hugo Mambour, Yefim Gordon Archive. **86:** Yefim Gordon Archive (five). **87:** Nigel Eastaway/RART, Yefim Gordon, Steven Zaloga. **88:** Yefim Gordon, Steven Zaloga (three), Yefim Gordon Archive (four). **89:** Yefim Gordon (two), Steven Zaloga. **90:** Yefim Gordon (three). **91:** Yefim Gordon Archive (three), Steven Zaloga (three), Nigel Eastaway/RART. **92:** Yefim Gordon (two), Frank Rozendaal. **93:** Frank Rozendaal, Yefim Gordon. **94:** Steven Zaloga, Aerospace. **95:** Frank Rozendaal, Yefim Gordon Archive (three), Steven Zaloga (two). **98:** Frank Rozendaal, Yefim Gordon. **99:** Frank Rozendaal, Yefim Gordon (two). **100:** Yefim Gordon Archive (four), Steven Zaloga. **101:** Yefim Gordon (five), Yefim Gordon Archive (two). **102:** Yefim Gordon (six), Steven Zaloga, Yefim Gordon Archive. **103:** Yefim Gordon, Frank Rozendaal (two), US Navy. **104:** Yefim Gordon, Eric Bannwarth. **105:** G. Lewis. **106:** Yefim Gordon Archive (five), Yefim Gordon, Robert Meerding, US DoD, Nigel Eastaway/RART. **107:** US Navy, Yefim Gordon Archive (four), Nigel Eastaway/RART (three). **108:** Steven Zaloga (two), Yefim Gordon. **109:** Swedish Air Force (four). **110:** Yefim Gordon Archive (six), Yefim Gordon (two). **111:** Swedish Air Force (two), Yefim Gordon. **112:** Steven Zaloga (four), Nigel Eastaway/RART (four), Hugo Mambour. **113:** Gordon Upton, via Yefim Gordon. **114:** Sergey Skrynnikov via Yefim Gordon, M.J. Gerards. **115:** Yefim Gordon (two), William Turner. **116:** Sergey Skrynnikov via Yefim Gordon, Yefim Gordon Archive (three), Dennis Thomsen. **117:** Dennis Thomsen, Yefim Gordon. **118:** Yefim Gordon (three). **120:** Yefim Gordon (two). **121:** Martin Baumann, Robert Hewson. **122:** Yefim Gordon (five), Nigel Eastaway/RART. **123:** Yefim Gordon (three). **126-127:** Piotr Butowski, Sergey Skrynnikov. **128:** Sergey Skrynnikov, Piotr Butowski (two). **129-132:** Piotr Butowski. **133:** Hugo Mambour, Piotr Butowski. **134:** Piotr Butowski (three). **135:** Griniuk via Piotr Butowski, Piotr Butowski (two). **136:** Piotr Butowski (two). **137:** Sergey Skrynnikov (two), Piotr Butowski (two). **138-139:** Piotr Butowski. **140:** Piotr Butowski, Sergey Popsuevich via Piotr Butowski. **141:** Piotr Butowski (two). **142:** Piotr Butowski (two), Andreyev via Piotr Butowski. **143:** Sergey Skrynnikov, Piotr Butowski (two). **144:** Piotr Butowski (five). **145:** Sergey Skrynnikov, Piotr Butowski. **146:** Piotr Butowski (two), David Donald (two). **147:** Piotr Butowski (three). **149:** Piotr Butowski, Sergey Skrynnikov. **150:** Sergey Skrynnikov. **151:** Piotr Butowski (three). **152:** Piotr Butowski (nine), David Donald. **153:** Piotr Butowski (six), David Donald. **154:** Piotr Butowski (five), Hugo Mambour. **Back cover:** Sergey Skrynnikov (seven), Alexey Mikheyev (four), Piotr Butowski, Eugène Gadet, Hugo Mambour, Anatoliy Andreyev, Sebastian Zacharias, USAF.